West Town

DISCARD

the illustrated
bead bible

terms, tips & techniques

Theresa Flores Geary, Ph.D.

Photographs by Debra Whalen

STERLING

New York / London
www.sterlingpublishing.com

STERLING and the distinctive Sterling logo are registered trademarks of Sterling Publishing Co., Inc.

Library of Congress Cataloging-in-Publication Data

Geary, Theresa Flores.
    The illustrated bead bible : terms, tips & techniques / Theresa Flores Geary ; photographs by Debra Whalen.
        p. cm.
    Includes index.
    ISBN-13: 978-1-4027-2353-7
    ISBN-10: 1-4027-2353-9
    1. Beadwork. I. Title.

TT860.G4298 2008
745.594'2—dc22   2007026120

10 9 8 7 6 5 4 3 2 1

Published by Sterling Publishing Co., Inc.
387 Park Avenue South, New York, NY 10016
© 2008 by Theresa Flores Geary
Distributed in Canada by Sterling Publishing
c/o Canadian Manda Group, 165 Dufferin Street
Toronto, Ontario, Canada M6K 3H6
Distributed in the United Kingdom by GMC Distribution Services
Castle Place, 166 High Street, Lewes, East Sussex, England BN7 1XU
Distributed in Australia by Capricorn Link (Australia) Pty. Ltd.
P.O. Box 704, Windsor, NSW 2756, Australia

Book design and layout: Nick Anderson

Printed in China
All rights reserved

Sterling ISBN-13: 978-1-4027-2353-7
        ISBN-10: 1-4027-2353-9

For information about custom editions, special sales, premium and
corporate purchases, please contact Sterling Special Sales
Department at 800-805-5489 or specialsales@sterlingpublishing.com.

We gratefully acknowledge Photographic Works of Tucson, Arizona, and photographer Debra Whalen for the photos used in this book.
All photos are by Debra Whalen unless otherwise noted.

Drawings of tools, bead shapes, stitches, finishing techniques, knots, and miscellaneous bead types are by Carin Cronacher. Kim Coxey of
Chappelle. Ltd., created selected stitch diagrams that were previously published in Theresa Flores Geary's *Creative Native American Beading*
(Sterling, 2005). We thank Jim Widess and Ginger Summit for use of beaded gourd dolls from *Making Gourd Dolls & Spirit Figures* (Sterling,
2007); photos by Jim Widess (www.caningshop.com). We thank MonkeyBiz, bead cooperative of South Africa (www.MonkeyBiz.co.za),
for selected photos of members' beadworks; Peg Alston of Peg Alston Fine Arts, Inc., Manhattan, for use of photos of the Fali fertility doll,
beaded Yoruba panels, and Kirdi apron; and bead artist Karin Houben (www.karinalisahouben.com) for photos of her anatomically correct
moths, butterflies, and fish. Photos of selected beading tools and the Fali, Yoruba, and Kirdi beaded creations are by the editor, Jeanette Green.

Contents

Part **I**

Introduction   1

Part **II**

Beads and Beading Terms   17
From A to Z

Part **III**

Beading Tips and Techniques   317

Part **IV**

Beading Tables and Charts   349

Beading Stitches, Finishing, and Graphs 369

Giving Thanks

A Native American Message

To be a human being is an honor, and
we offer thanksgiving for all the gifts of life.
Mother Earth, we thank you for giving us everything we need.
Thank you deep blue waters around Mother Earth,
for you are the force that takes thirst away from all living things.
We give thanks to green grasses that feel so good against our bare feet,
for the cool beauty you bring to Mother Earth's floor.
Thank you, good foods from Mother Earth, our life sustainers,
for making us happy when we are hungry.
Fruits and berries, we thank you for your color and sweetness.
We are thankful to good medicine herbs,
For healing us when we are sick.
Thank you, all the animals in the world,
for keeping our forests clean.
All the trees in the world,
we are thankful for the shade and warmth you give us.
Thank you, all the birds in the world,
for singing your beautiful songs for all to enjoy.
We give thanks to you, Gentle Four Winds,
for bringing clean air for us to breathe from the four directions.
Thank you, Grandfather Thunder Beings,
for bringing rains to help all living things grow.
Elder Brother Sun,
we send thanks for shining your light and warming Mother Earth.
Thank you, Grandmother Moon,
for growing full every month to light the darkness for children and sparkling waters.
We give you thanks, twinkling stars,
for making the night sky so beautiful
and for sprinkling morning dew drops on the plants.
Spirit Protectors of our past and present,
we thank you for showing us ways to live in peace and harmony with one another.
And most of all, thank you, Great Spirit,
for giving us all these wonderful gifts,
so we will be happy and healthy every day and every night.

—Chief Jake Swamp

Acknowledgments

A heartfelt thanks to my husband, Robert, and my children, Jonny and Anna, who all offered invaluable technical assistance with information technology and computer hardware and software.

A special thanks for my dear friend, Sylvia Elam, who contributed so much in the way of encouragement, friendship, technical assistance, marketing, beadwork, and beads. I would also like to acknowledge Linda Pennington of Jay's of Tucson and her family of traders. Over the years, they have provided me and many others with a wealth of information, resources, supplies, and beads.

A warm thanks to Mike and Mimi Haggerty and their daughter Shannon, from Piney Hollow, a historic bead museum and source in Tucson, Arizona. They personally encouraged my budding bead career by buying, selling, and trading my beads and beadwork. Their museum and commitment to beads and beaders has provided a wonderful resource to the entire community.

To my friend, Deb Whalen, thank you kindly for putting out so much effort to photograph the tiny beads and seeing them as objects of beauty. Few photographers are able to capture not only the spirit of the beads but the personality of the beadwork.

For his contribution, I would like to acknowledge bead consultant David Bingell for his technical expertise and assistance in identifying various beadwork techniques. Drawing from his museum experience, he also shared valuable information on the preservation and care of beadwork.

I would also like to acknowledge all of my bead helpers, who made samples for this book to demonstrate bead types, beadwork techniques, or color and design combinations. Those bead artists and contributors are Thurman Bear, Jr.; David Bingell; Rena Charles; Sylvia Elam; Joaquin Flores; Melba Flores; Bonnie Gibson; Tricia Gibson; Donna Haig; Jackie Haines; Barbara Henthorn; Cornelia Hoffman; Karin Houben; Jean Jones; Shawn Koons; Aurora Mathews; Lula Monroe; Laura Moreno; Dana Muller; Linda Pedersen; Linda Pennington; Laura Perez; Jonny Pulley; Janet Schmucker; Karen Sheals-Terranova; Ginger Summit; Drew Sutton; Verona Thom; Shelia Vinson; Gabie Warmuth; and Peggy Wilson. Unless otherwise noted, the beadwork sample items were created by the author, or the artist's identity is unknown.

A special acknowledgment goes to Nancy Ferguson. She originally did business as the Bead Connection, which was instrumental in promoting beadwork knowledge to the beading community. Her thriving business and artistic talents have assured a welcome supply of wonderful beads and findings as well as classes and creative ideas.

Also thank you to Ginger Summit and Jim Widess, who graciously agreed to loan photographs of beaded gourd dolls from their book *Making Gourd Dolls & Spirit Figures* so that they could appear in mine. Those lovely dolls will inspire many artists to expand their medium of expression. And thank you to Andrew H. Bullock for lending me the precious wampum beads.

Thank you also to Peg Alston of Peg Alston Fine Arts, Inc., Manhattan, who graciously shared some of her priceless pieces for photos, including the Kirdi cache-sexe apron, Fali fertility doll, and Yoruba beaded panels.

Barbara Jackson, Mathapelo Ngaka, and Joan Krupp from the beading cooperative MonkeyBiz provided photos of members' beaded animals and dolls. I acknowledge all the kind women and men working with the MonkeyBiz beading cooperative, which provides beading materials, financial opportunities, and medical assistance to the wonderful bead artists from South Africa, notably the Xhosa, Zulu, Ndebele, and Sotho communities.

My thanks to my editor Jeanette Green, who went way beyond the call of duty in producing this incredible book. And thanks to Lisa Smith for her excellent proofreading.

Thank you to all the unnamed people in the bead industry and anonymous beaders who have made a tremendous contribution to the art and technique of beadwork. Especially thanks to our ancestors from cultures and nations across the world.

To my Grandma Leo and my Grandma Flores,
on whose prayers I walk today.

Introduction

The fascinating history of beads begins with the earliest human cultures and continues through the centuries into modern times. Virtually all cultures and nations on earth have fashioned or adopted uses of beads. Beads remain one of the few universal artifacts. Without exploring their historical context in each particular culture, the symbols, messages, and spiritual significance found in certain bead designs may not be readily apparent. Although the art of beadwork offers great aesthetic appeal, further study reveals much more. Beads have been used to declare social status, express feelings, and document important historical events. Beads have served as a medium of exchange for goods and services and have helped express spiritual beliefs through prayer. They have been used as counting tokens in early counting boards and the abacus.

Beads have been cleverly put to use in numerous other ways as well. People tie and weave them into their own hair and that of their pets. They wear beads singly or in strands on the neck, ears, arms, wrists, fingers, waist, and ankles. Beads embellish items from mats to basketry to pottery and utensils made of bark, wood, gourds, animal parts, and textiles. They are woven into fabrics and wire. Beads are used on everyday clothing: shoes, hats, gloves, and bags. They are embroidered on every part of ceremonial and performance costumes throughout the world, from head-dresses, hats, and shoes, to masks, aprons, and fans, and for a range of performers from strippers to belly dancers to Native North American competition dancers. Beads have been used as symbols in storytelling and at events like tribal councils of war and peace. To this very day, they are buried with the dead, often in large quantities.

So exactly what is a bead? Although most people have a general understanding of what a bead is, experienced beaders, along with historians, anthropologists, and museum curators, use highly specialized terminology. Horace C. Beck's (1873–1941) definitive book, *The Classification and Nomenclature of Beads and Pendants* (1928), presented language for talking about beads. In order to describe a bead, Beck wrote, "It is necessary to state its form, perforation, color, material, and decoration." That's a tall order for so small an object of so vast a number and variety around the globe. This book attempts to define that terminology and put together a great deal of other related information in a simple, friendly format.

For the moment, let's just say that a bead's form can be described simply. For instance, it could be said that a bead is circular in shape, with about a 3-mm diameter. The perforation is the hole or channel used for stringing and can be round or square, which we would describe as a round- or square-holed bead. Holes can occur in the middle of the bead or in the top or bottom. Some holes occur naturally; some are drilled or molded by various methods. They can be drilled from top to bottom or side to side.

Describing color may seem easy, but it can be incredibly challenging in this age of computer technology. Most new computers and printing processes display fewer colors than the eye can easily differentiate, and high-tech finishes that multiply the light and color intensities on bead surfaces further complicate description.

Discussing the treatments of bead materials is even trickier: Facets are cut into the surface of glass beads, adding to their beauty by reflecting light. Space-age technology helps create dichroic (visible light split into distinct beams of different wavelengths, or colors) glass beads with layers of multicolored depth; their color appears altered by the angle at which the light is viewed. Intricate decorative designs are carved, etched, or burned into bone and wooden beads. Some wooden beads are hand-carved and boiled in grease to give them a rich dark color and to preserve the wood. And the race is on to make beads more beautiful than nature itself. Interestingly enough, it is nature that produces the loveliest gemstones, and the terminology used to describe them has been adopted by the glass-bead industry.

Many beaders may not fully understand, acknowledge, or admit their obsession with beads. If you think you're immune, we suspect that you'll soon succumb to the joy of beads and beadwork when viewing beads firsthand, if not through these pages.

Beads come in virtually every conceivable material, including organic substances like wood, bones, horn, seeds, and shells. Nuts and seeds are bead materials used universally. Beads are also made from rocks, metals, and synthetic materials, such as rubber, plastic, glass, and silica fibers, and even so unlikely a material as the recently developed "precious-metal clay" (PMC).

Natural resources in the local environment often provide the bead maker attractive materials. Among Native North Americans, called First Peoples or First Nations in Canada, the cuspid (pointed) teeth of the elk were highly valued, as were the teeth of rodents, bears, and carnivores; indigenous artisans also made beads from the horns of goats, sheep, and buffalo. In the Arctic, the Inuit, among others, used walrus ivory and mammal teeth for personal adornment and to embellish vessels made of wood and stone.

With new developments in glass technology, more colorful and interesting glass beads have only compounded the possibilities. Global trade now allows traders on all continents to share resources that were once exclusive to certain regions. Also thanks to this global economy, beading materials are readily available at reasonable prices, enabling modern beaders around the world to maximize their creative expression.

Today, lasers precision-cut long cylinders or tubes of glass into beads. Sophisticated machines, some computerized, drill holes in beads and tumble and polish stones. This means that modern beaders invest less time securing materials and can spend more time on their creations.

Works of art have always been luxuries; most of the beadwork seen in museums today appears on either functional or ceremonial items. Very few museum pieces were created purely for personal adornment, unlike the way jewelry is commonly worn today. A number of cultures developed the use of beads as a medium of exchange, to document historical events, as status symbols, and for healing and prayer. Such diverse uses go far beyond personal adornment.

Although beads have been known to exist since ancient times, the modern word *bead* comes from the Anglo-Saxon term *biddan,* meaning "to pray" or "meditate." For centuries, diverse cultures and religions, notably Catholicism, Hinduism, and Buddhism, have used prayer beads. The practice continues among many pious peoples around the globe.

Hong Kong jacket
from the collection of
David Bingell

Different cultural groups developed and tended to use particular styles, techniques, and colors for beading. Historically, any given region produced beads in a relatively limited color palette. In some cultures, specific bead patterns have a generally accepted cultural meaning; they may even be affiliated with a particular family, similar to a stamp of ownership or a trademark.

Here, it's not so much a matter of who originated a given stitch or technique, but what using it can help create. In such an ancient tradition, the origin of a technique is generally credited to the country or affiliated clan, rather than to any individual.

Today, as in the past, the frequent use of a design or pattern may be strictly a consequence of its popular consumer appeal. Modern laws have precluded holding copyrights on traditional techniques, designs found in nature, and certain shapes (like diamonds and circles) that are common in all varieties of art. Patterns involving angular or straight lines often occur in loomed beadwork because the stitch lends itself to geometric designs.

The earliest beads were probably made from organic or natural materials. It is likely that people discovered by accident that such things as animal vertebrae and other bones, wood, shells, and stones could be strung, since items from nature sometimes have natural holes or perforations. Other natural materials, like bear claws and porcupine quills, became attractive to collect, although obtaining them required skill and involved danger.

Rocks and gemstones are naturally occurring throughout the world, and much work goes into locating and mining or collecting them. Countless methods of drilling, carving, shaping, cutting, and polishing have been developed to make them still more attractive.

Another essential aspect of beading is the preferred threading material, whether from woven plant fibers, like cotton and yucca; animal-based products, like sinew and leather; or nylon-coated wire cable. Even telephone cable, nylon fishing wire, and dental floss have been put to the creative purpose. Inmates in penal institutions recycle materials like unraveled thread from socks to string or weave their beads. The strands all serve the same purpose: to thread or string a bead.

Beads, the Story of Civilizations

Archaeologists and bead historians have affirmed that the earliest use of beads was some 20,000 to 40,000 years ago, with more recent discoveries suggesting a much earlier date, 100,000 years ago. Beads are one of the primary archaeological artifacts, documenting much of what is known about the history of humankind. They are among the oldest forms of art. Bead types and materials also provide insight into the resources of the particular culture in question. In the Stone Age, they most likely involved bodily adornment with natural materials, such as fossilized ostrich or dinosaur eggshells, carved stones, bones, amber, ivory, horn, tusks, wood, shells, nuts, seeds, and other plant and animal matter. While some "found objects" make natural beads, others require tools for shaping them.

Ancient burial sites from a broad range of cultures contain beads, hinting at their importance, whether to particular individuals or to the society as a whole. Plant seeds, shells, small freshwater pearls, coral, wood, and various types of local clays or faience have been found in graves or burial tombs or temples of ancient Egyptians, Syrians, Bedouins, Vikings, Celts, peoples of the Indus Valley, Incas, Andenas from the Ohio Valley, and Mississippians, among others.

While the use of beads in religious ceremonies and fabric embellishment is presumed, it is difficult to prove because natural materials are biodegradable. Beadwork on leather or silk, for example, will last only as long as the fabric.

The shells of *Achatina monetaria*, also called land-snail shells, were cut into circular disks with open centers and used as coins in Benguela in Portuguese West Africa, in what is today western Angola. Other types of shells used as money by various cultures are the dentalium (*Dentalium pretiosum*), money cowrie (*Cypraea moneta*), wampum (*Busycon carica*), Atlantic knobbed whelk, and North Atlantic quahog hard-shelled clam (*Venus mercenaria*).

———————•———————

Northern Africa, from Morocco east to the Arabian Peninsula and the Middle East, has been home to many large beadmaking industries, ancient and modern. Egyptian burial sites and tombs in particular have contained enormous quantities of a wide variety of beads. So-called mummy beads have been found in burial sites of not only the Egyptians, but the Romans, Saxons, central Africans, and Native North Americans. They consist of a variety of glass, gemstone, and brass beads.

The ancient Mesopotamian city of Tell Hamoukar (in northern Syria), circa 4500 B.C., had an obsidian-carving industry that made not just arrowheads, blades, and sharp tools, but beads. The earliest beads made of meteoric iron were found in Jirzah in Egypt dating from 3500 B.C., and a little later iron was smelted in Egypt and Mesopotamia. And by at least 600 B.C., Egyptians fashioned beads from clays and faience, found in a variety of earth tones ranging from light green to blue and soft red. These small ceramic beads were common in the lands surrounding the Mediterranean. Sumerians made their ceramic beads from steatite, which produces black, white, or gray beads.

Beaded netting, sometimes covering the body and face of the deceased, has been found in tombs. Egyptian pharaohs, like King Tutankhamen (who ruled 1334–1324 B.C.), were buried with beadwork and ornaments as well as objects thought to be useful in the afterlife.

For centuries, Muslim merchants crossed the Sahara Desert to cities in West African kingdoms to trade. During the 12th century, blue tubular glass beads were the medium of exchange. On the North African coast, blue coral is found in local waters, but it not easily made into beads. The term for *bead* in several languages means "coral." In the 16th century, the local term was *cori,* and in the 17th century it became *accori.* In the 18th century, Europeans began to call it *aggrey.*

Sand-cast, powder-glass, or sugar beads, made from recycled glass, originated in sub-Saharan Africa. Other glass beads were made from silica or quartz. Beadwork has remained popular throughout the continent, and beading traditions continue in Botswana, Cameroon, Ethiopia, the Republic of the Congo, Nguni, Nigeria, Sudan, Zimbabwe, and South Africa, among other places. Remarkable artisans are found among the Maasai, Kuba, Kirdi, Ndebele, Swazi, Xhosa, Yoruba, and Zulu. In Cameroon, for instance, Bamileke chiefs and notables don lavishly beaded elephant masks that signify royalty, kinship, and wealth. The masks, made of a long cloth trunk panel with two large ears attached, like those of the awesome animal they emulate, are lavishly beaded with glass beads and cowrie shells.

Many people have been uprooted and relocated due to warfare, government actions, or through slavery. However, there has been a resurgence of cultural identity and reclaimed heritage. Among the many tongues, clans, locales, and traditions found in Africa, beadwork remains a significant aspect of cultural history. Beadwork traditions were established long before tourism played a role.

Today, MonkeyBiz, a nonprofit bead cooperative in South Africa, provides materials and support to a broad local community of beaders, whose beaded mother-and-child dolls and animals, like fantasy horses or antelopes with zigzag stripes, are sold on the world market.

———————•———————

The Indian subcontinent, with its abundant supply of precious and semiprecious stones, claims one of the world's oldest beadmaking traditions. Disk beads made of ostrich eggshell have been found dating as early as 23,000 B.C. Beadmakers were already using a fairly sophisticated technology by 7000 B.C., as evidenced by the excavation of Mehrgarh, from which beads of turquoise, lapis lazuli, and alabaster were retrieved. Still more remarkable, beadmaking in this region has continued until today.

In the Gulf of Cambay (Khambat) in the Gujarat state of India, archaeologists have found shipwrecks, submerged cities, ports, and channels. Among the artifacts are beadmaking tools and gemstone beads as well as low-fired and grass-embedded pottery, dating at least to 5000 B.C. The modern town of Cambay today remains a major center for stonecutting and beadmaking. In nearby hills, agate is mined. The stones are heated and dried until they fracture, cut and reheated with iron oxide, and then chipped and flaked into beads that are ground, drilled, and polished. Other gemstones, like carnelians, garnets, emeralds, and diamonds, are cut and polished in the region as well.

In India, beads are closely tied to religion; a Hindu written code mandates the wearing of certain jewelry for specific occasions, regardless of one's ability to buy it. The poor simply wear beads of metal, clay, or seeds, while the wealthy adorn themselves with gold and semiprecious stones. Aside from their religious significance, the wearing of beads conveys status and wealth, and the beads are believed to have protective powers.

A great civilization that flourished in the Indus Valley between 2600 and 1600 B.C. produced beads made from stones and metals of almost every type. Bead shapes unearthed include barrel, biconical, cylindrical, tubular, spherical, and discoid.

Glass beads first appear in India between 1000 and 800 B.C., and the production of glass beads was fairly widespread by about 200 B.C. Conquest by Alexander the Great (356–323 B.C.) introduced Greek designs and techniques, such as granulation, to India.

As Christianity spread through the West, demand for beads was in decline since their principal use was in rosaries. Stone and glass bead production continued in India, however, and Indian merchants sought, and found, new markets. Between A.D. 500 and 1500, a vigorous bead trade was established between India and Africa, the Middle East, and Southeast Asia.

During the Mogul rule of northern India in the 16th to 18th centuries, India enjoyed intense creativity. Persian jewelers set up workshops, infusing a new Indo-Persian aesthetic. As the bead industry in Venice and elsewhere in Europe began to compete, beadmaking in other parts of India began to decline. Today, India has major glass beadmaking centers as well as centers dedicated to making beads from precious stones.

Millefiore beads

The Bondo of Orissa, sometimes called the "naked people," live in mountain villages of eastern India. The women wear mostly beads and a short cloth skirt, covering the body more modestly than any swimsuit. Their breastplates are made of multiple long strands of Indian and European glass seed beads, often with coins and brass pendants. Their headpieces consist of seed beads wound around the head. Wrists are covered with many plain aluminum bangles, and their ears have long dangling earrings. Bondo men are plainly dressed with no ornament.

Today a well-established silver industry, noted for its silver beads, reaches from India into today's Pakistan, Bangladesh, Nepal, and Sri Lanka. These regions also produce exceptional lampworked fancy glass beads and foil beads. Their quality has made them competitive with the well-reputed Venetian and Czech beads.

———————•———————

Eye beads are thought to have originated in Asia during the Stone Age; today they are found in many countries outside that continent. The Bronze Age was heralded in Thailand around 3600 B.C., when tin was added to copper. (The bronze formulated in Mesopotamia a little later was copper alloyed with the toxic substance arsenic.) A comma-shaped bead, magatama, originated in Korea and was later commonly featured among Japanese beads.

Ancient China has been credited for the development of cloisonné, porcelain, and enamel beads. The Far East, dominated by China, has been known for its use of jade and ceramics. However, the region also produced fine glass beads as well as at an earlier stage, more crude ones. The Manchu or Qing dynasty (1644–1911) required government and military officials and their families to wear court chains, modeled after Tibetan rosaries.

The long history of beads in what is today Japan commences in 10,000 B.C., much of it strongly influenced by Chinese and Korean traditions; it has even drawn inspiration from some Western and Middle Eastern designs. The Japanese practiced the custom of entombing the dead with great quantities of beads for protection, the beads being of bone, stone, and shell, and later, jade (jadeite or nephrite). Glass beads first appeared in Japan after A.D. 250.

By the 19th century, Japan had developed a thriving independent bead industry. Today most high-quality cylinder seed beads are made in Japan and the Czech Republic. Those produced in Japan have greater uniformity of size, shape, and finish, with larger holes than their Czech counterparts.

———————•———————

In Europe, small glass beads were first made around 1000 B.C., although they had been produced as early as 3000 B.C. in Egypt, Syria, and later in the Roman Empire. Before the Venetians, the Romans produced and traded glass beads on a global scale, between 100 B.C. and A.D. 400. In the first centuries A.D., Alexandrian and Syrian glassmakers set up shop in Italy; production of so-called Roman glass beads continued there until the 11th century. The Vikings also had sophisticated glassmaking operations in Scandinavia, where they produced millefiori beads, like those found in excavations of burial sites dating from A.D. 800 to 1000. After that time, the production of glass beads in Europe dropped off considerably.

Among the earliest glass beads were drawn-glass, made by two people pulling molten glass, using metal rods, in two different directions. The resulting glass tube, nearly 100 feet (over 30 m) long, was chopped and the pieces (beads) rolled in hot sand to smooth the edges. Such beads today are extruded by machine. A second method of making glass beads is by pressing molten glass into a mold. And a third technique, called lampwork, involves heating a glass rod with a torch and spinning the molten glass thread around a metal rod that has been treated to release the glass easily. Once formed, the wound-glass bead can take a number of treatments to add color and texture, including firing it in a kiln to increase its durability.

It was not until the Middle Ages that glass seed beads, so-called because of their relative smallness, became readily available in the global market. Venice took the lead in the world production and export of glass beads beginning about 1500. Mass production and established worldwide trading routes made it possible. Today Italy, Japan, the Czech Republic, and France produce the bulk of high-quality glass seed beads.

Although evidence of glassmaking in Venice is as early as A.D. 600 or 650, it was not until the 1400s that the craft advanced. In 1292, all glassmaking activity was actually moved from Venice to Murano, a tiny island across the lagoon, as much to keep trade secrets as to protect the city from the constant fires of glass furnaces. Murano glass beads are famous for their quality and uniqueness. Among the designs that distinguish this glass beadmaking center are millefiori, chevron, seed, and trail (wedding-cake) beads. Murano has continued into the 21st century to have a corner on every aspect of the world market in glass beads. Furnace, blown-glass, and handmade lampwork beads are all produced there.

Since the 1500s, European glass-bead centers have included not just Italy (notably Venice and Murano) but Bohemia (today's Czech Republic, Moravia, and Austria), Germany, Poland, France, Portugal, Spain, the Netherlands, and Austria. The area called Novy Bor, north of Prague, is considered the heart of the Czech glass industry. Numerous cottage industries throughout the region produce the fine-quality glass beads. In Lauscha, near the Thuringian Forest region of eastern Germany, the ancient art of glass-blowing and glass beadmaking has survived for centuries. In addition to producing lampwork glass beads, this region originated blown-glass Christmas tree ornaments. In the 16th century, artists in the Netherlands, particularly in Delft, began to imitate the blue and white porcelain beads that originated in China and were refined in Japan.

In Russia, where birch bark is commonly plaited into baskets, the tree bark has been fashioned into beads.

In the New World, the Incas of Peru and Colombia were sophisticated silversmiths and goldsmiths. The Aztecs and Maya of Central America also excelled in metallurgy.

However, when the Spanish visited Cuba in the 15th and 16th centuries, the Taino favored the brass the Spanish introduced from Europe over their native gold brought from Colombia that was typically alloyed with copper and silver. The elite wore and were buried with brass pendants to declare wealth and status as well as to suggest their connection to the supernatural realm. Brass, considered a sacred material, was called *turey,* a word associated with the most luminous part of the sky. Little tubes called aglets, made of brass in Germany, have been found threaded into necklaces in archaeological sites where artifacts of the Taino have been recovered.

The Aztecs and Maya were known, not only for their exotic gold and silver jewelry, but also for exquisite rock-crystal and jade jewelry as well as shells used in regal attire. Green quetzal feathers, jade (jadeite and nephrite), and emeralds were also worn. Mayan stone statues display rulers wearing enormous jadeite beads encircling the head, attesting to its valued status.

In modern Mexico, beads are made of clay, glass, and gemstones like banded alabaster, coral, amber, and shells. The charms called *milagros,* fashioned from cheap or recycled materials, in the shape of body parts in need of healing or wished-for objects are left by visitors in holy places.

The Huichol continue to make intricate beaded designs, inspired by sacred visions, inside small gourd bowls. The beads are adhered in beeswax and resin or another hardening agent. The lovely items created for the tourist market, however, are not necessarily copies of those sacred or traditional designs.

As Spanish conquistadores searched the Americas and parts of the Pacific and Southeast Asia for gold, easy riches, and plunder, ancient civilizations fell. Indigenous populations were terrorized, disease was widespread, and native populations were decimated. The European invaders, however, were not met without resistance. The Jivaro people, called "the unconquered ones," who live in the Amazon Basin of Ecuador, were reportedly so angry at a Spanish governor who was greedy for gold that they poured molten gold down his throat. This incident, in addition to their practice of taking and shrinking heads, has kept outsiders from disturbing them.

The earliest Native North American peoples had ready tools for beadmaking in the Clovis point, fashioned from chert, chalcedony, and red jasper. However, in what are today northern Mexico, the United States, and Canada, the most valued beads were wampum, made from the quahog shell, a variety of hard-shell clam. Wampum was considered a valid medium of exchange not simply among indigenous populations but also by the Europeans from the original Thirteen Colonies.

From 1700 to 1900, the North American bead trade has been influenced by European traders who peddled glass beads from Europe and metal beads from South America. In the 21st century, the United States and Canada continue to produce many varieties of gemstone beads. In addition to bead manufacture, individual beadmakers have established reputations for producing exquisite handmade lampwork, chevron, furnace-glass, precious-metal-clay, polymer-clay, and dichroic-glass beads.

Today, as in centuries past, in Chiapas, Oaxaca, Tabasco, and Michoacan, Mexico, for instance, foreign powers have been guilty of bio-piracy, extracting gold from local mines. Concerns about pollution, scarred landscapes, and disturbed local ecologies as well as local exploitation of native peoples and wars over natural resources have become issues just as relevant today as they have been in the past. The disturbing results have been seen in the so-called conflict or blood diamonds of western Africa sold to arm guerillas. In the marketplace, the law of relative supply and demand will continue to determine the value of global goods and resources. Unfortunately, these so-called laws also help explain centuries of warfare, aggression, and imperialism, as well as more practical matters as productive international trade and sharing valued resources.

Contemporary bead designers and artists throughout the world have not felt restricted in using materials, designs, or colors dictated by cultural tradition. Some often look to nature for examples of beauty, and others are challenged to create their own patterns by using sophisticated software, with breathtaking results.

Anatomy of a Bead

It's helpful to have a vocabulary for talking about beads as three-dimensional objects with width, length, and depth. So here is a simple anatomy lesson.

Horace C. Beck's 1928 publication is credited as being the first to classify and name beads and pendants, primarily for museum curators and academics. Peter Francis, Jr., (1945–2002) another famous bead researcher, did a wonderful job of dissecting a bead to describe its essential characteristics. This scientific approach to bead anatomy owes a nod to anthropologists, archaeologists, and historians.

Francis's first step in classification begins with the *perforation* or drilled-through hole, which makes a bead functional for stringing or threading. The shape of the perforation can be round, square, triangular, etc. He calls the opening of the perforation the *aperture.*

BEAD CROSS-SECTION (DIAMETER VIEW)

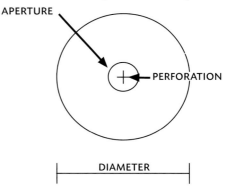

A bead can appear to change when viewed from different angles. Francis helps to orient us by locating the bead's cross-section as the view we see looking through the perforation. The widest part of the cross-section is the bead's *diameter.*

The *axis*, which begins at one aperture and ends at the aperture at the bead's opposite end, defines the thread path along (parallel with) the perforation. The length of the axis is generally considered the bead's length, also called the bead's *profile*.

BEAD PROFILE (LENGTHWISE VIEW)

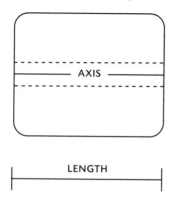

LENGTH

Beads can be described by referring to their cross-section as well as their profile. The orientation of the perforation can determine the profile view. For example, a long tube bead is generally drilled along the length of the bead, but occasionally you will see such beads drilled across the top of the bead, from side to side, determining the way the bead sits when strung. Occasionally a bead will have more than one perforation.

As a general rule, geometric terms like round or spherical, oval, biconal, rectangular, hexagonal, or oblate, used to describe bead shapes, provide measurable or objective dimensions and some consistency among users. Unusual bead shapes draw on a different collection of adjectives to best portray the bead's appearance, surface colors, and textures.

From a bead researcher or anthropologist's viewpoint, it is best to avoid terminology or bead names that reveal little about the bead's appearance or anatomy. For example, historically speaking, the term *African trade beads* offers virtually no information regarding bead anatomy. These beads were, in fact, of many different shapes, colors, and sizes and were traded to the African peoples rather than originating in Africa.

Recognizing Bead Shapes

While you'll find definitions for various bead types in Part II, here are a few hints to help you recognize bead shapes. You'll find drawings of 32 common bead shapes in Part IV (pp. 350–352) that we have compiled, based on those found in the contemporary market. Knowing these common shapes will help you describe, locate, and buy desired beads.

In refining our list, we were concerned only with shapes that are common across various categories of beads but that may sometimes be peculiar to a particular bead type. A seed bead, for instance, may be oval, round, square, and cylindrical. Seed beads are defined in part by their small size, although some originated from actual seeds, like those from the plant Job's tears. Whereas the predominant feature of glass seed beads is their small size, the actual shape is important to experienced beaders. While a cylinder seed bead may look like any other glass seed bead at first glance, its tendency to have thinner walls allows for easier threading and a neater appearance in beadwork.

Scholars and museum curators look to Horace C. Beck's *Classification and Nomenclature of Beads and Pendants* (1928) or to Lois Sherr Dubin's version in *The History* of *Beads* (1987, 2004) for bead shapes found in the ancient world. However, beaders, dealers, and collectors usually rely on more modern terminology to describe what's available in today's marketplace.

Bead shapes may include the abacus (elliptical), angel wing, animal, beehive, bell, bird, bottle, butterfly, button, cabochon (with flat back to fit in a bezel), capsule, crescent, cross, cutout, dagger, daisy, diamond, dice, dime, drum, egg, elbow, fan, flower, free-form, heishi (or heishe), lantern, leaf, lentil, lozenge, oval, half-moon, pear, pillow, pottery, rice, rondelle, Saturn, star, vase, V-shape (like chevron), and walnut. Designer beads have myriad shapes impossible to catalog. They are often handmade and may have unique shapes, such as that of a hummingbird. Naturally, such beads are difficult if not impossible to mass produce. Many new and interesting shapes are introduced into the market, such as duck feet, manufactured in the Czech Republic. Other uncommon beads may be carved and shaped like a bilobal gourd, usually made of glass or stone.

There are many standard names for how many sides a bead has, such as pentagonal (five-sided), hexagonal (six-sided), and octagonal (eight-sided).

The terms *potato, rice*, and *stick* are commonly used to describe pearls but rarely other beads. The term *baroque* may refer to pearls but can also be used to describe other irregularly shaped beads made of glass or stone. Natural vertebrae, shells, seeds, stones, and other shapes from nature are also common in beadwork. Almost any bead can also be made into a pendant. Many beads designed specifically for pendants tend to have a hole drilled near the top. *Faceted, paneled* (Bali has many examples), *segmented, grooved, spiral, puffy, rayed, fluted, wavy, twisted,* and *flat* are terms used to describe characteristics and other markings of bicone, cylinder, barrel, and many other bead shapes. Table-cut describes thick slabs of beads with a tablelike surface.

Cathedral beads

Other terms that appear to describe shapes may refer to a particular bead type. For instance, the term *bottle bead* refers not to the bottle shape but to African beads made from recycled Coca-Cola bottles. There is also an uncommon bottle-shaped bead. Descriptive terms like *rhombus, trapezoid, truncated, lenticular* (double convex), or even *concave* and *convex,* are more commonly used by scholars or museum curators than by beaders, dealers, and collectors. Donut shapes are circular and can often hold one or more beads strung through the center of the large donut hole. Another use of the term *donut* is for a ring or annular-shaped bead. A *sequin* is a very thin, often cup-shaped, type of bead that may appear in various shapes and that tends to be used in a variety of crafts for bright metallic effect and sewn onto fabric. A *spangle* is a generic term for a small shiny object that's also frequently used to decorate fabric. Other beads or findings, like spacers, toggles, and cap beads, may be defined by function. Find gemstone cuts in Part IV.

Beads may be described by appearance and type as well as function. A *spacer bead,* for example, is usually small and not as flamboyant as a *focal* bead because its function is to provide space between beads to accent another expensive, rare, or valuable bead. Spacer beads are made out of a variety of materials and may assume a number of shapes. A cap bead can serve the function of embellishing the top and bottom (or sides) of another bead, but it can also be used alone or in multiples for a different appearance. Certain beads, because of their shape, can function as a clasp or closure or even be used to finish a beading project by discretely hiding the threading.

Here are a few distinctions among the common shapes. The *cylinder* is generally shorter than a *tube* and may have thinner walls. The *disk* may be round, square, or a number of shapes, but its hole is smaller than that of a donut. The *ring* or *annular* has a donut shape, but the hole is larger and the walls relatively thin, like those of a finger ring. The *first type of donut* has a generous hole and may include not just round, but oval beads and the hole may appear off-center. The *second type of donut* is drilled for stringing in addition to the large hole in the center of the bead that allows a smaller bead or beads to be featured. *Nuggets* are generally irregular shapes and may be rough, smooth, or faceted. The *pear-shaped* bead may appear like a drop or teardrop in side view and like a lightbulb in the front view. *Tabular* beads are flat with the hole running parallel to the flat faces; tabular beads may be round, square, or a number of shapes. A *coin* bead resembles a round tabular bead. *Semicircular* beads may be moon-shaped. Note that the *lozenge* has two holes, which allows it to be strung with a flat, broad or a narrow face. A *pear-shaped* bead can be strung vertically or horizontally. A *square* is generally flatter than a *cube.* Almost any bead can be made into a pendant, depending on the location of the hole.

Here in alphabetical order are common bead shapes: *barrel, bicone, briolette, cone, cube, cylinder, disk, dog bone* or *dumb bell, donut* (two types), *drop* or *teardrop, drum, elbow, fluted, lozenge, melon, nugget, oval* or *ellipsoid, pear-shaped, pyramid, rectangle, rondelle, round* or *sphere, saucer* or *lenticular, segmented, semicircular, spool, square, tabular, triangular,* and *tube.*

What's Inside

My motivation for writing this book began at the tender age of 14, when my mother introduced me to beads. I was immediately intrigued, and my fascination grew as I got older and saw more examples of the art form, especially while living in Arizona, with exposure to Native North American beadwork. The more

I learned about the myriad techniques, the more I was exposed to the history and culture of beadwork around the world. The international gem and mineral and related shows in Tucson annually brought wholesale dealers and beads from faraway places like China, sub-Saharan Africa, India, and the Czech Republic.

As an adult, I sought out teachers and bead dealers who could help me learn more. I was also self-taught through magazines, books, and the Internet. Eventually, when teaching beadwork to others, I was further challenged to add to my knowledge. So my personal history demonstrates curiosity about all aspects of beads, beading, and beadwork, especially from the viewpoint of novices. This reference guide is designed to cover all aspects of beading from the beaders' point of view.

While many techniques are unique to beadwork, several have been borrowed from the sewing arts—weaving, embroidery, crochet, and knitting. They have been elaborated on or altered so often that a single technique or stitch may have a staggering variety of names. The photos in Part II will help you identify the technique while the stitch diagrams in Part V will help you learn how to do it. Found throughout the book are examples of beadwork from artists worldwide that showcase the variety of styles, techniques, and art forms involving beads. Here's what you'll find in this book.

Part II, "Beads and Beading Terms from A to Z"

(pp. 17–316), has definitions of selected beading and bead types, tools, and techniques as well as information on selected gemstones and metals. Beads have had myriad uses around the world. We include basic beadmaking processes for creating beads of glass, ceramic, metal, wood, or other materials without making them overly complicated. Remember that the art and manufacture of beads can vary from culture to culture, epoch to epoch, and manufacturer to manufacturer, or indeed craftsperson. After all, beadmaking is an art form. Where possible, we include technical information, a bit of history, cultural value, and photos of individual beads, gemstones, findings, and beadwork. Jewelry components, called *findings,* such as fasteners, clasps, and closures, will help novices recognize them and their practical function. Ear wires, for instance, make ear adornment functional.

Some beaders learn a particular stitch without having any notion of its history, origin, or practical uses. Peyote stitch, for instance, useful for beading around a three-dimensional object, remains culturally important to Native North American artisans of the Southwest United States.

Represented here are samples sufficient to reveal the incredible range of materials used to make beads and the myriad ways they are worn, woven, strung, painted, and otherwise decorated. Every effort has been made to verify the information in this book. Whenever possible, the artisan, bead maker, manufacturer, or trader was the direct source of the beads or beadwork shown. Individual beads were chosen for photos not because they were the most exotic, expensive, or unique, but because of their representative qualities or features. Through the centuries, manufacturing methods have evolved side by side with human creativity in the making and use of beads and beadwork.

While we include a sampling of beads and their uses found around the world, we cannot hope to be comprehensive. Beading is a universal art with many expressions, personal and cultural. We expect this photo reference guide to grow over time and may have inadvertently left out your favorite bead type or technique. Also, when searching for a term, keep in mind that beading techniques may have different names, not just in a different part of the country, but in different languages and cultures.

Part III, "Beading Tips and Techniques"

(pp. 317–348), uses a question-and-answer format to aid beginners when buying beads and learning beading techniques. Sections include beading basics, potential problem areas, mastering techniques, finishing tips, hints on using bead patterns, and care and preventive maintenance of beadwork. Troubleshooting tips may help more advanced beaders, and everyone can enjoy the small collection of bead anecdotes.

Part IV, "Beading Tables and Charts"

(pp. 349–368), offers helpful information, such as comparative bead, needle, crimper, thread, wire, and stringing-material types and sizes; gemstones and gemstone treatments; glass-bead types and finishes; metal and "metallized" beads and metal finishes for findings and beads; the Mohs scale of hardness; gold karats (purity) and millesimal fineness; birthstones; recognized bead shapes; and weights and measures. It also helps provide a clear understanding of the logistics involved in creative beadwork.

Part V, "Beading Stitches, Finishing, and Graphs"

(pp. 369–383), has diagrams of 21 common beading stitches (weaves) as well as knotting, finishing, and embellishing techniques. The three blank beading graphs for brick, peyote, and square (loom) stitches give you a chance to try your hand at creative design; just photocopy the desired blank graph at a reasonable size.

For more in-depth study, you'll find a wealth of information through art exhibitions, museums, books, the Internet, beading stores, and social events that offer arts and crafts to view or buy. However, hands-on knowledge and experience is the most enjoyable way to learn about beads. For readers interested in the history of beads or specialized subjects, such as healing gemstones, we've included a Selected Bibliography of books, periodicals, and Web sites on pp. 385–392. The Index begins on p. 393.

PART II

Beads and Beading Terms

from A to Z

A

AB The *aurora borealis* (or *northern lights*) is a phenomenon of streamers or arcs of light in Earth's northern hemisphere caused by the planet's magnetic field acting on atoms in the upper atmosphere. In beading, the abbreviation for the term refers to a rainbow finish that can be applied to any color or type of bead. An AB finish can be scratched, but should not rub off under normal wear. *See also* aurora borealis.

abacus A mechanical device that uses beads to perform basic arithmetical operations, such as addition, subtraction, division, and multiplication, and to extract square and cube roots. *Abacus* is a Latin word with origins in the Greek *abax* or *abakon,* meaning "slab" or "tablet," and possibly even earlier in the Semitic word *abq,* meaning "sand" or "dust." Before written numbers, it is presumed that outdoor merchants in public markets calculated using a finger or stylus to mark lines in the sand or on the ground. Some vendors began to use a small frame with sand inside.

The *counting board,* an early form of abacus, had a portable flat surface made of wood or stone. Soon it came to have carved grooves or painted lines that held beads, small stones, or tokens in place. It was sometimes seen as a small table. The user placed the beads on the counting board to do a count or perform rudimentary arithmetic. The oldest known counting board discovered was used in Babylonia circa 300 B.C. This simple device minimized the number of pebbles required by having lines that represented, for instance, multiples of ten. One line could represent one item being counted, the next line 10 items, and the line after that 100 items. This way, pebbles or beads could be used to move back and forth, for doing basic adding, subtracting, multiplication, and division.

Another form of the counting board, used by traveling merchants, was made of cloth with embroidered lines. Counting boards in various forms were used throughout Europe, Asia, and the Arab world during the Middle Ages. *See also* counting board.

The abacus as we know it appeared in China in about A.D. 1200. The Aztecs had an abacus called a *nepohualtzitzin,* which appeared around A.D. 900 to 1000. The counters were made from kernels of maize strung and mounted on a wooden frame. Archaeologists have debated about whether the Incan *khipu* was a three-dimensional binary calculator or a form of writing.

The modern abacus, usually constructed with a wood or plastic frame, has vertical (wooden, metal, or plastic) rods that hold beads. Early versions were constructed out of stone or metal. The beads slide easily on the rods and their position(s) are used to perform arithmetical operations, such as addition, subtraction, division, and multiplication. The device can also be used to extract square roots and cubic roots. Prior to the advent of adding machines, cash registers, calculators, and computers, merchants throughout the world commonly used the abacus. The modern abacus is still used in parts of the Middle East, China, and Japan. Teachers throughout the world today have recommended their use for teaching young children concepts of arithmetic.

The concept of zero grew out of the Hindu culture. Combined with the Arabic development of place value to become the Hindu-Arabic numeral system we use today, its spread gradually outmoded the abacus.

abalone The shell of a mollusk from the Haliotidae family (genus *Haliotis* with 100 to 130 species). The nacre inside the shell is iridescent and richly colored. Colors vary with the species. Abalone is also called *ear-shell, ormer* (Guernsey), *perlemoen* (South Africa), *paua* (New Zealand), and *loco* (Chile), depending on native preference. It is found along coastal waters of every continent with the exception of the Atlantic coasts of North and South America. The shells, made of calcium carbonate, are quite strong. Dust created when cutting the shell can cause respiratory distress.

Abalone shell is cut into jewelry components of various shapes, the most popular being a flat disk; it is threaded or strung by one or two holes drilled into it. Among Native Americans, abalone represents the harmonious meeting of water and sky; it is often used in prayer, worn on the body, or carried in a medicine bag. The piece below on the right is used as a centerpiece for a bone hairpipe necklace, popular in Native American culture

and dance regalia. Also shown is a rough piece of abalone, polished for later use in jewelry design.

Abija beads Created by the lost-wax process, these brass beads from Ghana, West Africa, are circular in design. They closely resemble beads produced by the Baule tribe in the nearby Ivory Coast, another nation on Africa's west coast. The resemblance may stem from the fact that the Baule are descendants of a group who separated from the Ashanti tribes of Ghana in the mid-18th century. The most recognizable feature of these beads is their regular, parallel grooves, a design common to both Abija and Baule beads. Such beads are understood to have been used by both tribes as weights for measuring gold. *See also* Baule beads and lost wax.

abrasives Materials, such as hematite powder and diamond powder, used to cut, polish, and drill gemstone beads.

acid wash A chemical process in which glass beads are etched with acid to remove the surface shine. The result is similar to a matte finish.

acrylic beads Often referred to simply as plastic, beads made from this synthetic material have many attractive qualities, including affordability. They resemble more costly gemstone beads and are easily dyed. Their light weight compared with metal, gemstone, and glass beads is also a significant advantage. Available in many of the same shapes as glass and gemstone beads, they are used for making jewelry, garment accessories like handbags, and Christmas decorations. Acrylic products can become brittle and dull over time, and they do not polish as nicely as glass or gemstone, but they are economical for beginners and children to use.

adhesive Any substance used to attach or glue things together. In beadwork, an adhesive is occasionally required to glue a fabric backing onto a beaded piece. Rarely is an adhesive used to stick beads together; they are usually connected by thread, cord, or wire. Jewelry cement and bonding agents are types of adhesive. Virtually all adhesives will fail over time. *See also* jewelry cement.

adularescence An interference phenomenon that occurs when light glides over the surface of a moonstone; when in a cabochon, displaying a bluish white light or an opalescence. Adularia is a common moonstone.

African Christmas beads Strands of multicolored glass beads created by the Venetians for trade with the Africans. The origin of the term is unclear; the beads feature bright colors— red, green, yellow, blue, white, and orange. Available worldwide, they are often worn in multiple strands around the neck and wrists to suggest wealth. Also called *love beads,* they are reportedly worn by some African women to signal their sexual intentions.

African emerald A false or misleading name for green fluorite.

African helix Originating on the African continent, this beading technique produces a rope that is useful for bracelets, belts, and chokers. Other bead ropes are associated with names of individual techniques, such as crochet rope, peyote, netting, and Russian spiral. The bracelet shown was beaded by Shelia Vinson.

African trade beads This general term refers to old beads of glass or stone made in Europe and India and transported to West Africa by Arab traders. Trade beads were used by European traders in exchange for gold, ivory, and palm oil on the trading routes from Europe to West Africa and into the West Indies. Among the many common types of beads are

the chevron, millefiori, feather, skunk, and sand-cast. See individual listings for more information and photos. *See also* African Christmas beads and trade beads.

African turquoise   The gemstone turquoise, composed of hydrated copper aluminum phosphate; found in Africa, it tends to be more green than blue, with characteristic black markings, or *matrix*. The stone's value is based on its availability, color, and aesthetic

appeal. The gemstone has a Mohs scale hardness of 5 to 8. Shown here are beads from a necklace of large round African turquoise beads with chunky silver accent beads; the stone beads have a high luster and identical shape and size, both features of quality.

agate   One of the many types of chalcedony, a cryptocrystalline quartz, with a chemical composition of silicon dioxide, agate is characterized by its bands of concentric, shell-like, irregular rings. Widely distributed throughout the world, agate is found inside spherical nodules (loosely called *geodes*) in areas associated with volcanic lavas. Bands may be in a single color or multiple colors—white, bluish gray, yellow, orange, brown, and black. Agate has a hardness of 6.5 to 7 on the Mohs scale. The great variability of the stone's banding patterns has led to a number of descriptive names for it: blue lace, Botswana, crazy-lace, fire, moss, tree, and Russian agate. Agates from the now-exhausted German mines are pink, red, or brownish with bright gray bands. South American agates are dull gray without special markings; they are sometimes dyed. They vary from nearly transparent to opaque. When cut into thin slabs, even opaque agates can appear translucent. The cabochon shown demonstrates the stone's striations or bands. Agates were used in ancient Egypt over 3,000 years ago for rings, cameos, and drinking vessels. *Cryptocrystalline* means that the crystalline structure is so fine that individual particles cannot be distinguished under a microscope. *See also* quartz.

agate glass This term refers to a type of glass made to look like the gemstone agate with white swirls or bands.

aggrey beads These ancient beads have inspired intense research and debate. These tube-shaped beads are made from translucent blue or dichroic (visible light split into distinct beams of different wavelengths or colors; here blue and often green or yellow appear) glass, strung on a cord. They have been said to be a medium of exchange used by 12th century merchants. Beginning in the 16th century, the beads were known as *kori* among the West African natives who traded them with Moslem merchants. To the natives, they were worth their weight in gold. Some bead historians have suggested that they were made of blue coral found on the African coast. The name *kori* or *cori* became *accori* in the 17th century. By the 18th century, the Europeans began to call it *aggrey*. Of Middle Eastern origin, these glass beads had an unrivaled place in the trans-Saharan gold and slave trade.

Aiko The trademarked name, produced by Toho, for very small glass cylinder beads used in weaving, they are notable for their consistency in size and shape. *See also* Delica beads, cylinder beads, and antiques.

Akosu beads (or Akoso beads) A variety of dry-core powder-glass bead produced in Ghana, West Africa, these are one of three distinct styles of Krobo bead; the oldest variety, Akosu beads prevailed some 50 years ago. Yellow being the most common base color, the beads also exist in green, and rarely, blue or black. They commonly have a double U crisscross pattern or may feature fairly crude decorations incorporating circles, loops, and stripes. Glass from crushed Venetian beads was reportedly used for making the glass powder. These were also generally referred to as *trade beads*. *See also* Krobo beads and king beads.

alabaster This fine-grained variety of gypsum (calcium sulfate) is often used for vases and other ornamental articles like chess pieces. Oriental alabaster is a translucent marble (calcium carbonate) obtained from stalagmite deposits; because of its usually banded structure, which gives it some resemblance to onyx, it is also called *onyx marble* or *onyx*. Its hardness ranges from 1.5 to 3, which is relatively soft and suitable for carving. The finer quality of alabaster is used as an ornamental stone, for staircase rails and ecclesiastical decoration.

alexandrite The gemstone chrysoberyl, beryllium aluminum oxide, that appears green in daylight but light red in artificial incandescent light. The color change is best seen in thick stones, and the stone may also be subject to change under high heat. It has a Mohs scale hardness rating of 8.5. It has a vitreous luster and demonstrates strong pleochroism. Named after Czar Alexander II, alexandrite was discovered in 1830 in the Ural Mountains.

alexandrite imitations Synthetic alexandrite, made in the laboratory, is corundum with trace elements, such as vanadium. Color-change spinel also simulates alexandrite.

alexandritic An adjective applied to transparent gem varieties, such as sapphire, garnet, and spinel, that demonstrate a color change when viewed in artificial light as compared to natural light.

alligator stitch A three-dimensional stitch also called *log cabin* and *chili stitch*, this stitch is often seen in tourist goods from South America. Its exact origin is not clear. The blue alligator shown was made out of pony beads, the small green one using seed beads. Find stitch diagrams in Part V.

alloy A substance of two or more combined or fused elements, at least one of which is metal. The resulting material performs like a metal, and its properties may significantly differ from those of its components, or it may combine the metallic properties of its parents. For instance, steel (iron + carbon alloys) is stronger than iron. Common alloys are brass (copper + zinc), bronze (copper + tin), and sterling silver (pure silver + copper).

almandite A member of the garnet group of gemstones; it has a chemical composition of iron aluminum silicate. The stone is red with a hint of violet. It is sometimes confused with pyrope, ruby, spinel, and tourmaline. *See* garnet.

alpaca silver An alloy of copper, nickel, zinc, and iron; this metal does not rust or tarnish. Alpaca silver has no silver content. Alpaca-silver jewelry and other decorative objects often originate in Peru, are the work of artisans, and may be commonly sold in Argentina and Chile, as well as in other countries. In North America, a similar base metal is usually known as *nickel silver*, an alloy that may also include antimony, tin, lead, or cadmium.

alphabet beads These beads each feature a letter of the alphabet; they are used to spell names or brief messages. Some hospitals use bracelets made of them to identify newborns. The beads pictured are made of plastic, but they are also available in glass and metal.

altered beads This term describes beads that have been changed in some way by someone other than the original manufacturer. For example, the beads can be faceted, etched, carved, dyed, or heated to change the color.

aluminum A metal used to make interesting lightweight beads and findings in an assortment of colors.

aluminum bronze A metal alloy of copper with 4% to 15% aluminum and small amounts of other metals, with a golden color and a high tarnish resistance.

amazonite This stone, also called *amazon stone,* is a variety of microcline feldspar with a hardness rating of 6. It is thought that Spanish explorers who named the stone confused it with a form of nephrite jade found in the Amazon basin, hence its name. The stone is not found near the Amazon but has been mined in the Minas Gerais state of Brazil. The presence of lead and water in the stone is thought to bestow its opaque apple-green to blue-green color. Easily confused with turquoise and jade, the stone is found mainly in Australia, Madagascar, Namibia, Russia, Zimbabwe, and the United States. Shown below are amazonite beads.

ambassador beads *See* French ambassador beads.

amber Technically known as *fossil resin,* amber is the petrified resin of ancient conifer-

ous (pine) trees, and is estimated to be 30 to 90 million years old. Amber is also called *succinite.* Composed of carbon, hydrogen, oxygen, and a mixture of various resins, amber exhibits a bluish white to yellowish green fluorescence. Semifossilized resin, not as old, is called *copal,* which is sometimes misidentified and sold as amber. The Baltic region, along the coasts of Poland, Germany, Latvia, Lithuania, Estonia, and Russia, was the original source for amber, though it occurs elsewhere in the world, including the United States; the Dominican Republic is also a significant producer of amber. Amber is transparent to opaque, ranging in color from yellow to maple-syrup gold, but occurs as well in red, black, and green. Sometimes called *petrified sunlight,* it is a relatively soft material that scratches easily. Baltic amber was once called the "gold of the North." *Blue amber,* found only in the Dominican Republic and extremely rare, is thought to have been caused when hot lava or volcanic ash flowed over an existing bed of natural amber to produce the bluish color. Amber's Mohs scale hardness rating is 2 to 2.5, and its crystal system is amorphous. Shown is a bracelet made of amber chips and a turtle bead of carved amber. *See also* resin, copal, and lac.

ambroid Pressed amber made from smaller pieces of genuine amber, welded under heat and pressure to appear like natural amber. Or an amber-colored liquid plastic adhesive or glue for mending and repairing porous materials. It replaced spruce gum, once used for canoe repairs. *See also* resin and lac.

American ruby A false or misleading name for pyrope, almandite (garnet), or rose quartz.

amethyst This popular gemstone has been found throughout the world in shades of lavender, mauve, or purple. A member of the quartz family, it has a Mohs scale hardness of 7. It is sometimes heat-treated to form citrine, a transparent yellow stone. From prebiblical times in ancient Mesopotamia through the European Middle Ages, amethyst was highly valued; its "purple" color (expensive, rare, or difficult to achieve in clothing dyes) was associated with pharaohs, emperors, kings, and cardinals. Amethyst was once classified as one of the *cardinal* or *precious gems*. Today, because of its wider availability due to the discovery of large deposits in Brazil, it has been demoted to a semiprecious stone. However, such designations are becoming a thing of the past. *Amethyst quartz,* the rough, more compact formation of amethyst that is layered and striped with milky quartz, is used for beads, cabochons, and other ornaments. Amethyst was once fashioned into vessels or worn by ancient Greeks and Romans as an amulet against drunkenness. Shown below is amethyst in its natural crystalline form.

ametrine A gemstone that has color zones that are part amethyst and part citrine. A member of the quartz family, ametrine has a Mohs scale hardness factor of 7. Ametrine occurs naturally and is not the result of heat treatment or other enhancements. Bicolored quartz is similar but consists of a combination of citrine and smoky quartz or amethyst and colorless quartz. It is also called trystine. Ametrine occurs naturally in Bolivia, Brazil, and India. Artificial ametrine may be produced with differential heat treatment of amethyst.

amulet From the Latin word *amuletum*, an amulet is a treasured object that offers some form of protection when worn. It may be in the form of a charm, fetish, or mascot that features gems or stones, coins, pendants, rings, plants, or animals. Coral, onyx, agate, and carnelian are strongly associated with protective qualities. Many amulets have symbolic associations, often linked with the occult. They may also include religious remembrances and relics or medicinal ingredients. They are usually worn or carried on the person.

Gemstones, carvings, figurines, coins, drawings, animal parts, or spoken words or oaths, are thought to repel evil and avoid ill fortune. Homes may be protected by statuary, gargoyles, or live animals. A few talismanic beads thought to protect the wearer are hand, eye, fish, crescent, star, phallic, or chili pepper–shaped beads. In the British Isles, a sheep's bone worn by Whelby fishermen was thought to protect them from drowning, while Thor's hammer was thought to offer protection to those from the Isle of Man. *See also* amulet bag, eye beads, and talisman.

amulet bag A small bag for carrying amulets, sometimes called an *amulet pouch*. Shown is a beaded amulet bag, handmade by Laura Moreno, done in cylinder beads using round peyote stitch, with a flat peyote stitch strap and flap, and fringe accented with crystal beads.

andradite A member of the garnet group of gemstones, its chemical composition is of calcium iron silicate. It ranges from yellow (topazolite) to yellowish brown and green

(demantoid) to brown and black (melanite). *See also* garnet.

Anglican rosary Since ancient times, people have counted off prayers using pebbles, strings of knots, or strung beads, which we know as rosaries. The Anglican rosary has a circular shape (symbolizing the wheel of time) that combines the Roman Catholic rosary and the Orthodox prayer rope; a cross hangs from the rosary. The Anglican rosary comprises 33 beads: four groups of seven beads, called *weeks*, with a single *cruciform bead* separating each week. The bead closest to the cross is called the *invitatory bead*.

animal beads A huge category of beads in the likeness of animals, made from almost any material. The wooden frog shown has

a painted design, as does the ceramic panda. Also shown are a handmade ceramic fly by Tricia Gibson, a cloisonné butterfly and turtle, a fish and ladybug of glass, and a gemstone bear. Animal beads of all kinds are popular on the world market.

anklet A type of jewelry worn in one or more strands encircling the ankle, similar to a bracelet worn on the wrist. The standard size is 9 to 9½ inches (23 to 24 cm) long.

anneal In the manufacture of glass beads, the slow, controlled cooling of the material to relieve stress fractures and minimize breakage. This is part of the process in making glass beads.

annealing kiln A kiln in which the internal temperature, usually ranging from room tem-

perature to over 2,000° F (1,093° C), can be controlled for the purpose of annealing (slowly cooling) glass beads. *See also* annealing temperature.

annealing temperature The temperature at which the molecules inside a glass bead vibrate enough to relieve internal stress and prevent cracks or breaks.

anniversary stones and metals Stones traditionally associated with, or symbols of, wedding anniversaries include crystal for the 15th, turquoise the 17th, pearl the 30th, coral or jade the 35th, ruby the 40th, sapphire the 45th, emerald the 55th, diamond the 60th and 75th, and blue sapphire the 65th. Metals associated with wedding anniversaries are iron for the 6th, bronze the 8th, copper the 9th, tin or aluminum the 10th, steel the 11th, silver the 25th, gold the 50th, and platinum the 70th. Some of these designations were suggested by Emily Post in her book of etiquette published in 1922. Find a chart for birthstones for zodiac signs and months in Part IV.

annular An old-fashioned term to describe wound glass beads. Also the name of a bead shape with a larger hole and thinner band than a donut-shaped bead. *Ring,* a term often used interchangeably with annular to describe shape, tends to have still larger holes and thin walls and to resemble a finger ring. *See* Dogon donuts and wound beads.

anodized A metal that has been subject to electrolytic action, which has coated it with a protective or decorative film. Anodized films are generally stronger and less likely to crack or peel than most paints or conventional metal plates. Aluminum, zinc, magnesium, titanium, and niobium are more likely than other metals to be anodized. When aluminum has an anodized surface, it resists corrosion and can be dyed.

antique beads The word *antique* generally refers to an item more than 100 years old. It also refers to beads that are no longer being produced. Older beads tend to be smaller and more irregularly shaped than newly manufactured ones, as earlier sizing standards were less consistent than today's. Antique beads are still in demand, however, especially to repair old beadwork.

Beads of the brand names Antiques and Treasures (*see* cylinder beads) are not old. They are very small precision-cut glass cylinder beads manufactured by a Japanese company named Toho.

antique beadwork Usually, a beaded item that is at least 75 years old, making it generally collectible and valuable; such items are handmade, predating the mass production era. The headband shown was inherited from a Native American woman, the mother of my mother's best friend. The floral loomwork was in need

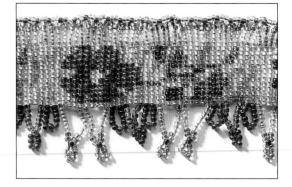

of repair, and was mended and mounted on leather to help preserve it. Originally a belt, it was missing too many beads to restore its entire length, but the beautiful pattern is certainly worthy of preservation.

antique metal buttons Although old buttons are often made of glass, there are also a good many metal antique buttons. Buttons old and new are popular as closures for necklaces and bracelets. Shown is a bracelet made by Jackie Haines that was woven with even-count flat peyote stitch, using size-13 Czech charlotte beads and freshwater pearls. The unique closure makes this a special piece.

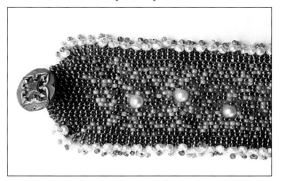

antiqued bronze A metal finish of a yellowish- to greenish-brown color applied to jewelry findings and beads.

antiqued copper A metal finish of a reddish-brown color applied to jewelry findings and beads.

antiqued gold A metal finish of a golden yellow color applied to jewelry findings and beads.

antiqued silver A metal finish of a dark- to medium-gray color applied to jewelry findings and beads.

antler Beads and buttons are made from the antlers of deer, elk, moose, and caribou (reindeer), wherever these herds live. With leatherwork, antler buttons are commonly used as fasteners on bags and jewelry, as well as for adornment. Antler beads and buttons are popularly incorporated into mountain-man, frontier, and other period clothing and into Native North American crafts. Moose antler beads are comparable to ivory in their coloring and texture. Antlers, made of bone and shed annually, differ from horn, which has a keratin covering.

Apache tears Obsidian forms when hot volcanic lava rich in silica, a basic component of glass, runs into a stream or lake that cools it quickly to create a type of natural glass. Obsidian has a Mohs scale hardness of 5 to 5.5, and its chemical composition varies, but the amount of silica present is over 70%. Apache tears are airborne droplets or broken nuggets of this material that have been worn and polished smooth by wind and water. Several Native American stories about the healing power of grief describe this transformation of the tears shed by Apache women for the loss of their husbands, sons, and brothers. *See also* obsidian and Pele's tears.

Apache weave Decreasing each successive row by one bead, a beading technique frequently used to make earrings with a triangular top. It is also called *brick stitch, Cheyenne stitch, Comanche weave,* and *stacking stitch.* Note the white teepee design at the top of the earring, a signature design for some beaders. Find stitch diagrams in Part V.

apatite Apatite is one of the few minerals produced and used in the human body, being a major component of tooth enamel and bones; it has a hardness factor of 5. Mined in Brazil, Russia, Myanmar (Burma), Sri Lanka (Ceylon), Canada, East Africa, Sweden, Spain, and Mexico, apatite can be transparent or opaque, and ranges from colorless to yellow, green, blue, and violet.

Its name comes from a Greek word meaning "to deceive," as apatite very much resembles more valuable gemstones. Shown is a necklace made with fancy faceted apatite ovals, strung by Laura Perez. It is accented with textured gold beads, 8-millimeter (mm) black fire-polish glass beads, gold spacers, and black glass disk spacers.

appliqué A common term used in both the needle arts and beading, this is a method of attaching beadwork to fabric or leather. It is sometimes used synonymously with *couching* and *backstitching*, two different techniques that achieve a similar appearance. Shown is an appliqué brooch sewn onto felt and backed with Ultrasuede, done with the single-needle method of couching appliqué. It features turquoise (blue), carnelian (orange), and black onyx cabochons that are framed with seed beads, using the appliqué stitch. The piece is accented with faceted black onyx rondelle-shaped beads and a single 8-mm round bead in the center.

appliqué earrings The earring designs shown were beaded onto fabric with an appliqué embroidery technique, and are the work of Jackie Haines. The purple pair is stitched onto stiffened felt and backed with leather. The stones are tourmaline, and the beads include Czech charlottes, freshwater pearls, and amethyst dangles. The brown pair is made the same way, with carnelian as the centerpiece, embellished with aventurine, jasper, and unakite.

apron The Ndebele beaded wedding apron symbolizes that a young woman has entered adulthood as a married woman. The Native North American style of beaded apron is seen in fancy dance costumes covered with appliquéd beadwork or solid lane stitch beadwork. In Tibet, during ceremonies to drive away evil spirits, tantric priests wear aprons constructed with beads of skeletal heads sculpted from human bones to symbolize the transient nature of life on earth.

The Kirdi of Cameroon create for women and girls beaded aprons called *cache-sexes,* that function something like a loincloth and that both covers and draws attention to the wearer's sexuality. The style of the individual cache-sexe signals puberty, marriage, or widowhood. Cowrie shells attached to the bottom of the apron symbolize fertility. The practice of cutting the apron on the wedding night symbolizes that the marriage has been consummated. Shown below is a Kirdi cache-sexe beaded with a checkerboard pattern and embellished with cowrie shells. Courtesy of Peg Alston of Peg Alston Fine Arts, Inc.; photo by JG.

aquamarine A transparent to opaque light blue to dark blue or blue-green species of beryl, the gemstone composed of aluminum beryllium silicate. Aquamarine demonstrates pleochroism that's nearly colorless, light blue, blue, or light green. Its name derives from the Latin *aqua marina*, meaning "seawater." It has a Mohs scale hardness of 7.5 to 8, and its crystal system consists of hexagonal prisms. It is mined in Russia, the United States, Brazil, Sri Lanka, and parts of Africa. *Santa Maria* (Brazil) and *Santa-Maria-Africana* (Mozambique) are general trade terms for

locations where the gemstone is mined. *Maxixe* is a deep blue beryl found in the Minas Gerais in Brazil; the color fades in daylight. The stone is brittle and sensitive to pressure. The pale blue gemstone is often confused with blue topaz, tourmaline, zircon, and kyanite. Shown are some delicate saucer-shaped beads.

aquamarine imitations *Brazilian aquamarine* is a false or misleading name for blue-green topaz. There are many glass imitations, and synthetic aquamarine is usually really a blue-colored synthetic spinel.

aragonite Also called *honey onyx* for its creamy golden translucency, aragonite was

first discovered in the Aragon province of Spain. Its chemical composition is calcium carbonate, and its Mohs scale hardness is 3.5 to 4.

Argentium Sterling Silver A high-grade sterling silver that contains germanium, developed by Peter Johns beginning in 1990 at Middlesex University in England. Argentium is a trademark. The usual formula for sterling silver is 92.5% sterling with about 7.5% copper, but this patented formula uses about 92.5% sterling with the rarer metal germanium. The metal alloy is hard, durable, and ductile, with high tensile strength and high tarnish resistance. Argentium Sterling Silver maintains its shine and can be dusted off with a clean soft cloth. To avoid cross-contamination, do not use the cloth on other metals. Or if any film develops, it can be easily washed off with tap water.

Of benefit to silversmiths, it can be annealed or hardened through heat treatment. The final product does not require plating. When heated it does not develop firescale, a disfiguring purple stain that conventional sterling silver does, due to the formation of copper oxide. It can be welded with a laser. The silver can be identified by the "AS" silver mark on products.

Arizona ruby A false or misleading name for pyrope (garnet).

Arizona spinel A false or misleading name for red or green garnet.

armband The armband with decorative beadwork is usually worn for special occasions, like weddings, feasts, or ceremonies. The armband may be beaded or woven and may show, depending on the culture and individual artist, intricate workmanship, an aesthetically appealing design, and balance, symmetry, or asymmetry.

arrowhead A piece of rock chiseled to a sharp point and having a cutting edge, used as a cutting tool and weapon. In modern times it often hangs from the neck as a pendant, wrapped with jewelry wire to prevent injury.

art glass beads A category of fancy glass lampwork beads that are individually handmade. *See also* lampwork beads.

artificial Another word for synthetic (man-made), imitation, or not genuine.

artificial pearls These are also known as *imitation, simulated,* or *faux pearls.* In the past, artificial pearls were in demand because of the rarity and expense of real pearls. With the introduction of cultured pearls to the world market in the early 1900s, it has become easier and less expensive to acquire authentic pearls instead of one of the myriad varieties of artificial ones. Simulated pearls come in numerous varieties. In India, early versions were clay spheres coated with mica powder and baked to an iridescent glow, and in ancient Rome, silver-plated glass spheres were coated with a second film of glass to appear lustrous.

Mineral salts, mother-of-pearl, glass, or carbonate (even lead carbonate, found in Japan) as well as coatings of bismuth and mica powder mimicked the iridescence we associate with real pearls. Some date to prehistoric times.

Artificial pearls come in many varieties and reflect different processes. Here are a few of their names or types: bathed (covered with iridescent nylon film), Bohemian, coconut, coral, elephant, glass-based, hematite, hinge, "I" (imitation or *Ai* for "love" in Japanese), indestructible or Majorcan, mother-of-pearl (mollusks or crushed nacreous shells), Parisian (Paris or French), plastic, Richelieu, Roman, shell, Tecla (brand name), and wax. *See also* glass pearls, pearl, cultured pearls, freshwater pearls, and pearl sticks.

artificial sinew Stringing material, similar to dental floss, made of polypropylene or nylon; the material is often waxed to thread more easily and to resist water. It looks very much like real sinew, which is an organic fibrous material from animal tendons and ligaments, very sturdy and durable, used for making cord, stringing material, and stitching.

asbestos Any extremely fibrous mineral or material. Fibrous serpentine and tremolite contain microscopically fibrous crystals that can be toxic. Do not handle them or bring these stones close to mouth, nose, or eyes. The fibrous varieties are not recommended for jewelry.

asparagus stone Yellow-green apatite.

assembled A term in the gemstone trade for items made of multiple layers or combinations of manufactured and/or natural materials. An example is inlaid cabochons.

asterism Including a starlike phenomenon, pattern, or inclusion in a stone.

ateyun beads Red powder-glass beads made by the Yoruba from Nigeria to imitate coral. The beads are handmade and shaped from finely crushed glass and a little water. A pointed tool creates the perforation before firing.

aught Also spelled *ought*, this word is used for "zero." In beading it is an obscure unit of measurement for seed bead sizes that is listed after another number and written 5/0, for example. Although size numbers were originally thought to indicate the number of beads per inch, the inconsistency of sizing among manufacturers does not allow for accurate measurement in either inches or millimeters. When used as a relative scale, the numbers reflect the relationship between bead sizes— the larger the bead, the smaller the size number. In other words, a size 5/0 bead is larger than a size 14/0 bead.

One source suggests that the term *aught* refers to the approximate number of beads in a 20 mm ($^3/_4$ inch) length of string.

auric Made of gold.

aurora borealis Often abbreviated *AB*, a rainbow finish applied to any color or type of bead. Named after the celestial phenomenon of bands, curtains, or streamers of colored lights that appears predominantly in the Arctic night sky, this rainbow effect is produced by adding a very thin coating of metal, which interrupts the transmission of light to give a rainbow finish. (The aurora borealis is the aurora appearing in the northern hemisphere, also called the northern lights. In the southern hemisphere, the aurora is called the *aurora australis.*) Shown are versatile 6-mm fire-polish beads whose facets cast a multitude of colors. *See also* AB.

ave beads Named for the first two words, "*Ave Maria*" of the "Hail Mary" prayer, ten small *ave* beads are separated by a *pater* or *paternoster* bead (for the Lord's prayer, often called the "Our Father" prayer) to make up a *decade,* or set of ten beads. A standard rosary consists of five decades, plus a few additional prayer or meditation beads. *See also* rosary and prayer beads.

aventurine A semitranslucent, soft green variety of quartz, silicon dioxide, found in Brazil, India, Russia, the United States, Japan, and Tanzania. It has a Mohs scale hardness factor of 6.5 to 7 and is sometimes mistaken for jade because of its color. Minute traces of other minerals can give this stone a slight metallic iridescence. Fuchsite (green mica) makes it greenish, and hematite makes it reddish brown or golden brown. Sunlight can

fade translucent specimens of this stone. The Italian words *a ventura* mean "by chance." It may be confused with aventurine feldspar (sodium calcium aluminum silicate), which is called sunstone. Goldstone, called *aventurine glass,* is a synthetic material made in imitation of the natural stone aventurine.

aventurine effect Obtained by suspending copper crystals or metallic particles (such as gold flake) in glass or by pressing the particles onto the surface of materials other than glass, this effect simulates the iridescence of aventurine quartz. It is also referred to as *aventuresence* when describing gemstones. It creates sparkle or flashes of light. Man-made goldstone exhibits the aventurine effect; it occurs naturally in moonstone and sunstone.

aventurine feldspar Another name for *sunstone,* a natural gemstone. *See* sunstone.

aventurine glass Another name for the synthetic material *goldstone.*

awl A sharply pointed tool, usually with a wooden handle and long pointed rod, designed to poke holes into leather, that's also used in basketmaking and beadmaking. The awl is used to make bead holes larger. An awl differs from a bead reamer in that the awl resembles an ice pick, but is shorter, and the awl's surface is smooth while the bead reamer's is abrasive. Stone Age awls found in archeological sites in the Americas and Europe were small pointed stone hand tools with one or more sharp edges used to slice plant fibers for thread and fishing nets, punch holes in wood and leather, and slice animal hides to make clothing. *See also* bead reamer.

axe stone Nephrite. *See* jade and nephrite.

azurite A fairly soft, brilliant blue, transparent to opaque gemstone, it is virtually impossible to find azurite free of other trace minerals, because it is a by-product of copper mining. The chemical composition of azurite is copper carbonate hydroxide, and its Mohs scale hardness is 3.5 to 4. It is also called *chessylite*. The crystal system is monoclinic with short, columnar, dense aggregates. If it often found along with malachite, turquoise, and lapis lazuli. *See also* malachite.

Shown right is a beautiful cabochon brooch by Sylvia Elam, made with a beaded edging. The azurite cabochon is flecked with turquoise, malachite, quartz, and silver, and bead appliqué embellishes the piece.

azuro A rich bluish gold bead finish used on Czech beads.

B

baby beads Alphabet or baby beads are given to infants as bracelets or anklets to record the name and date of birth, often pink beads to girls and blue ones to boys. In many cultures throughout the world, such beads are designed especially for babies. It is the custom in two small isolated mountain villages in Oaxaca, Mexico, to give a string of beads for a first birthday, which the child keeps for life. In Iran, children's beads are often made from jet, to prevent harm from bad spirits or people. Also in Iran, a square chunk of salt—a symbol of good luck—is pinned into baby clothes, usually with coins or beads of glass, plastic, or shell, so that no one will steal the baby.

In Ghana, West Africa, on the eighth day following birth, a new mother puts small white beads on herself and her baby intended to protect themselves both from getting sick or going crazy; babies also wear special beads to indicate birth order.

Throughout Africa, beads are used to monitor a baby's growth and health. If beads tied snugly around a baby's waist become loose, they indicate weight loss and possible sickness. Mothers also tie beads around the baby's wrists, legs, and neck.

In Germany, families traditionally tied a string of coral beads around a baby's neck to bring good health.

backing material Generally, a fabric used to provide reinforcement and strength to a beaded project. For example, a beaded hatband may be too flimsy to withstand the weight of the glass beads when worn on a hat, so the hatband is reinforced with leather. Found in many sewing and craft stores, backing materials include heavy fabric of all kinds—felt, interfacing, Ultrasuede (a faux suede)—as well as leather. On items such as belt buckles and brooches, everyday recyclable materials like plastic margarine tubs, card-stock paper, and cardboard egg cartons are also used.

backstitch A useful stitch in bead embroidery, the backstitch can create both straight and curved outlines, and can fill in large areas. Several beads are strung together on a thread and tacked down to the fabric. Then the thread is brought back through the last bead strung. Find the backstitch diagram in Part V.

badge-holder clip A piece of hardware, or finding, used to attach an identification badge to a necklace or neck strap. ID badges are often required by employers. Shown are two of many types of findings used to attach badges to a necklace or neck strap.

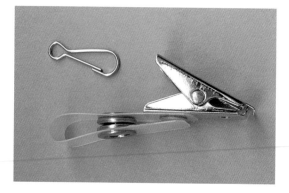

badge-holder necklace A necklace that allows one to comply with an employer's badge requirements and also to wear some attractive jewelry. Shown is a popular color theme of red, white, and blue, accented with cobalt-blue hearts.

baguette Shaped like the long loaf of French bread.

Bahá'í prayer beads The Bahá'í religion uses prayer beads in a string of 95 beads, or five sets of 19 beads.

bail A loop of metal, glass beads, or other material used to join a pendant to a necklace. The silver bail shown is on a buffalo pendant made of black onyx inlaid with a turquoise arrow.

Bakelite A trademarked name for a type of plastic developed by a chemist in the United States. Beads can be made from this material. *See also* plastic.

bala A bangle bracelet worn in India by both men and women. The word *bala* means "power" or "strength." *See* bangle.

Bali beads Beads made by the Balinese people of Indonesia, individually handcrafted from sterling silver. Artisans from Bali have been producing beautiful handmade beads for centuries. Because imitations are made of base metal, pewter, and even metallized plastic, be sure to inquire about the source of the beads. A reputable dealer will tell you exactly where the beads were made and be able to certify whether they are sterling silver. The standard for sterling silver is 925 (92.5%) purity. The photo shows an assortment of small Bali beads. *See also* sterling silver.

ball-and-loop bracelet Balls and loops themselves made of beads sometimes serve as clasps for bracelets and necklaces, and make attractive substitutes for metal clasps when the hardware is not available. Shown top right is a representative ball-and-loop piece, created by a Zulu woman for the tourist trade.

ball closure ring Also called BCR, used as body jewelry, often with various dangling ornaments.

ball post *See* earring stud.

baluster beads Also called *balustrade* or *vase beads,* these beads are often found with Chinese mandarin prayer beads. They are made into a vase, pear, or lace-bobbin shape. The term borrows language from woodworking and architecture for an elaborate turned and tapered shape, like many wooden chair legs. They can be made of wood, glass, gemstones, or nearly any bead material.

bamboo Beads made from thin slices of bamboo are somewhat fragile and usually inexpensive, but they dye well. Bamboo is a grass that is also called *reed.*

bandeau From the Old French word *bandel,* which means a narrow band for the head or an undergarment to support the breasts. Beaded bandeaus usually refer to headbands embellished with intricate beadwork, but the term can be used to describe undergarments, swimming attire, and evening gowns with a torso-hugging fit, similar to tube tops. Such garments are usually made sleeveless and without shoulders.

banded A feature of certain kinds of stone that appears as parallel lines or striations.

banded agate Agate, a member of the chalcedony family of cryptocrystalline quartz, occurs throughout the world in areas associated with volcanic lava flows. Banded agate appears in many different colors with characteristic bands of white, yellow, orange, brown, and black. This gemstone has a hardness factor of 6.5 to 7. Frequently made into beads, this stone is often dyed. Types of agate include blue lace, Botswana, crazy lace, fire, moss, tree, and Russian. Shown is a banded agate cabochon displaying characteristic striations or bands. *See also* agate.

bandolier In Native American tradition, bandoliers for carrying ammunition, slung across one shoulder and worn across the chest to the opposite hip, were often made from leather or cloth. They were decorated with beads such as bone hairpipe, brass, horn, and assorted fancy glass beads. Today bandolier bags are designed more for show than function; these elaborately decorated shoulder bags usually have a strap and are worn across the chest much like the traditional bandolier. The strap and bag may have appliquéd beadwork.

Originally bandoliers were issued to soldiers from the 16th to 18th centuries because they were convenient for carrying and reloading a musket. The design allowed for keeping the ammunition weight off a soldier's hips, which can restrict movement and cause difficulties with efficient retrieval. In later centuries, they were adapted for use with modern weapons to carry magazines, cartridges, and grenades. Frontiersmen, mountain men, hunters, and soldiers from various cultures have worn them for packing bullets or gun powder and other necessities, such as tools, food, and other supplies. These bandoliers are not necessarily beaded or elaborately decorated.

The term *bandolier* may also refer to long strings of beads worn on the body from the shoulder across the chest to the opposite hip, such as that seen on the Fali fertility doll from Cameroon. *See* fertility bead dolls.

bangle An article of jewelry worn on the upper or lower arm or on the wrist; usually circular (or semicircular and called a *cuff* if worn near the wrist) in shape and stiff, unlike bracelets, which are more commonly flexible. Many bangles do not have a clasp but can be slipped over the wrist up to the desired position on the arm. The word *bangle* originates from the Hindi word *bungri,* which means "glass." However, bangles today are typically made not only of glass but of metal, plastic, bone, and wood. The more expensive bangles may be made of silver or gold and encrusted with gems. Sometimes they are worn in pairs, one on each arm. The term *bangle* may also refer to an ornament or disk hung loosely from a bracelet. It may also suggest cheap or gaudy jewelry, clothing, or body ornaments.

barleycorn beads Originating in Venice in the 1700s, these are one of the earliest and most popular wound-glass beads. They come in white, black, and occasionally blue. However, the ancient Romans were among the first to make similar wound-glass beads. A necklace made with these wound-glass beads from Iran on exhibit in the Corning Museum of Glass in New York dates from A.D. 900 to 1300.

baroque pearl An irregularly shaped pearl, usually natural. *See also* pearl.

barrel Beads having a barrel shape. Shown are barrel-glass lampwork beads with gold swirls on the surface. Although they are made of glass, these beads are sometimes called *goldstone*.

barrel clasp A clasp comprising two pieces that form a barrel shape when screwed together. Others have a square wire that fits into a barrel-shaped tube and locks into place. Some barrel clasps have an additional figure-eight safety clasp on the side.

barrette back A metal hardware piece designed to hold hair in place, sometimes embellished with loomed beadwork strips or wire-wrapped beads. Appliquéd beadwork is also attached to a barrette back to create an attractive hair ornament.

basalt This fine-grained form of volcanic rock is usually gray to black, and its mineral components (olivine, pyroxene, and plagioclase) have a tendency to acquire magnetic properties. Its Mohs scale hardness ranges from 6 to 9, and its variable chemical composition primarily includes silica, alumina, calcium oxide, magnesium oxide, and iron oxide. It resists abrasion and can be heat-treated to improve its hardness. Basalt is the most common rock type in the Earth's crust, and it makes up most of the ocean floor. It is sometimes used to make beads.

base metals Strictly, a metal, such as iron, nickel, copper, lead, or zinc, that oxidizes or corrodes relatively easily. Loosely, any non-precious metal, such as aluminum, copper, zinc, nickel, or alloys, like brass. In contrast, so-called *noble metals* resist corrosion and oxidation.

basket beads Any type of bead that resembles a basket in shape or texture. The term *basket beads* also refers to large-hole beads used to embellish baskets woven from various materials.

basket-weave needlepoint A bead embroidery technique in which beads are sewn individually to the intersection of two canvas threads. The stitch is worked in diagonal rows, beginning in the northeast corner and progressing to the southwest corner. The canvas does not need to be turned.

basketry Interweaving flexible natural fibers, like grasses, twigs, inner bark, and bamboo, to form containers like bowl-shaped, bucket-shaped, bottle-shaped, elongated, square, or rectangular baskets for various purposes. The four common types of basket weaving are coiled (grasses and rushes); plaiting (wide ribbonlike plants like palms); twining (root and bark materials, thicker through stiff radial poles); and splint or wicker (reeds, willows, ash, oak, cane). Originally functional, today baskets have developed into a decorative art. Usually the type of basketry characteristic of a particular geographic region is dependent on the types of vegetation found locally. Synthetic materials, like metal wire (often to stabilize or strengthen the basket) and plastic fibers, have also been introduced into basketry. Cultures throughout the world, notably those in sub-Saharan Africa (particularly in Ghana and Botswana), Oceania, China, and Southeast Asia, and native populations of North and South America (Peru) have gained a reputation for excellent basketry. In both the traditional and modern art form, beads have embellished baskets or been used as part of the woven structure.

bauble A small, showy ornament, trinket, or pendant of little value. In British English, the term *bauble* may also refer to a glass, metal, ceramic, or wood Christmas ball-shaped ornament, typically hung from a tree.

Baule beads Prolific producers of brass ornaments and charms, the Baule tribe of the Ivory Coast are descendants of Ashanti tribesmen who emigrated from Ghana in the mid-18th century. Like the Ashanti, they fashioned their beads using the lost-wax method, and artists in both cultures impressed the entire surfaces of the beads with patterns of parallel lines. The forms of their beads are basically simple and abstract—disks, rectangles, tubes, and bicones. Other shapes are uncommon, but they include tusks, horns, and claws. Baule bead makers also modeled and fired clay to make similar beads in terra-cotta. The earrings

shown feature Abija beads, examples of Ashanti beadwork, accented with brass charms and Czech glass beads. *See also* Abija beads and beads made by the lost-wax process.

bauxite A kind of aluminum ore, rich in iron oxides (often found mixed with clay minerals and small amounts of anatase) that is dark rusty chestnut in color, used in making beads. In Ghana, Africa, bauxite beads are traditionally handmade. Villagers in Akyem Abompe today sustain themselves by cutting, carving, polishing, and drilling these beads by hand for the world market. The bauxite attains a warm earthy patina said to be acquired from contact with the human body and absorption of sweat.

beach glass Broken bottle glass tumbled by the action of ocean waves and its salts and minerals on sand smoothes the broken edges and polishes or frosts the glass. When the glass washes up on shore, it can be collected and fashioned into jewelry. A chief area of collection is the Outer Banks of North Carolina.

bead The modern word *bead* comes from the Anglo-Saxon term *biddan*, which means "to pray" or "to meditate." Used as a verb, it describes the numerous activities involved in creative beadwork: stringing, threading, weaving, and otherwise decorating with beads. As a noun, it describes the object itself. Although there are highly technical descriptions of beads, it is generally understood that a bead is an object with a perforation, suitable for stringing or weaving. Horace C. Beck, in *The Classification and Nomenclature of Beads and Pendants*, said that, to describe a bead prop-

erly, one should state its "form, perforation, color, material, and decoration."

bead blanks Bead blanks may be uniform shapes cut from rough gemstone slabs early in the beadmaking process. The term also refers to bead shapes made of low-fire earthenware or bisque that are pressed and extruded, not cast. These are designed for use with precious metal clay, to be embossed, stamped, painted, and enameled. The third usage of the term *bead blanks* is in reference to jewelry forms like rings, bracelets, and barrettes intended for covering with beadwork, charms, appliqué, or weaving.

bead board A lightweight board, often made of plastic, used to lay out and design necklaces and bracelets. It comes with grooves and measurement markers, making it possible to

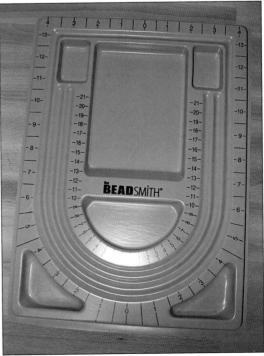

determine the finished length of a piece and to see what it will look like before it is strung. Photo by JG.

bead box Any container, usually a plastic box with a lid and compartments, for holding and separating beads. Recycled freezer containers, plastic margarine tubs, baby food jars, and shoe boxes all serve the purpose.

bead caps Also called *end caps* and *bell caps*, bead caps sit on top of other beads, primarily for aesthetic purposes. During stringing, metal caps can be placed on the tops and bottoms of plain beads to give them a touch of metallic sheen. Caps come in different sizes and are usually concave to fit the curvature of the bead. The photo shows a bracelet of sterling silver Bali beads capping carnelian beads, surrounded by faceted strawberry quartz and turquoise chunks.

bead cement A product designed expressly for beadwork projects, e.g., those that require sealing a knot or fixing the beadwork to something else, such as a picture frame or fabric backing. *See also* adhesive.

bead chain Hollow, round or elliptical metal beads joined by dumbbell-shaped connectors, typically short and functional rather than decorative, used as lamp pulls (to turn on the light) or for securing keys and small objects hung from it. Also may more loosely refer to a necklace or bracelet.

bead cloth A fabric with a soft texture that prevents beads from sliding or rolling off the worktable. Leather, or any cloth with a tight weave, will work.

bead cooperatives Throughout the world, women sometimes pool their resources for the common cause of improving their social and economic status. One such group in Kenya is Beads for Education, which produces beadwork to raise funds to help develop women-owned businesses and support their children's education. Among the handcrafted items they produce and sell are traditional Masai beaded ornaments.

A nonprofit organization in South Africa called MonkeyBiz aims to empower disadvantaged women and create employment opportunities for them; MonkeyBiz provides beads and other materials to some 450 women in Cape Town, who make exquisite and unique hand-beaded artworks. Participants are paid for each piece they produce, and they enjoy the benefit of working out of their homes. The program also runs a wellness clinic and soup kitchen, and offers beadwork training, HIV/AIDS counseling, yoga therapy, and homeopathic treatment, as well as social support.

Several indigenous artists' cooperatives have been formed by the Saraguro people in

Ecuador; these artists are known for producing colorful, intricate beaded collars and necklaces.

Global Marketplace, an online nonprofit organization, has a mission to help craft producers in developing nations better their standard of living by selling their crafts to consumers around the world. *Artisans Campesinas* Women's Cooperative of Tecalpulco, Mexico; *Mahaguthi* Craft with a Conscience in Nepal; and *Comparte* in Chile are among the groups engaged worldwide in similar cooperative efforts.

Shown above are animals beaded by women from the MonkeyBiz bead cooperative. Courtesy of MonkeyBiz.

bead cord *See* cord, cotton cord, elastic cord, linen cord, and leather cord. Find the stringing materials chart in Part IV.

bead-crochet snake ropes Although beaded ropes can be made with a variety of stitches and techniques, this particular item is significant for its history. Such bead ropes in the shape of a snake were made by Turkish prisoners of war during World War II with the words "Turkish prisoner" crocheted into the snake's underside. The beadwork was stuffed with horsehair, cotton, or cloth. The prisoners producing this type of beadwork were detained in Egypt, Mesopotamia, Greece, and Britain, and reportedly had detailed knowledge of the wildlife in their native country; their beaded snakes were remarkably lifelike. They were also known to produce a variety of other beaded items, including handbags, purses, necklaces, and bracelets.

bead curtains Bead curtains originated in Asia but are now popular across many cultures. Made from strands of wood, acrylic, bamboo, plastic, or glass beads strung onto cords or filaments of various lengths, these are generally used as room dividers or in interior doorways to make a space more private. Occasionally they are made from crystal or gemstone beads, and some are of acrylic beads that are molded onto the stringing material (see Mardi Gras beads). Chinese feng shui philosophy (the practice of configuring a room or placing items within it to complement the resident spiritual forces) recommends breaking up a long, narrow space (such as a hallway) by hanging a bead curtain to interrupt the airflow and capture more positive energy within the space.

bead doll *See* beaded doll, bride bead doll, fertility bead dolls, gourd doll, initiation bead dolls, Sangoma bead doll.

bead embellishment This term may apply to a variety of embellishment techniques used to enhance beadwork or other objects, like gourds, fabric, or leather. After a basic piece of beadwork fabric is constructed, other fancy beads, like crystals, butterflies, teardrops, and flower beads are added to the original beadwork surface. The photo shows a small glass vial that was beaded on its surface by David Bingell and then embellished with glass leaves and flowers. *See also* embellishment.

bead embroidery Any number of objects can be surface-embroidered with beads, using many different techniques, sometimes together with silk, cotton, or wool thread embroidery. Shown is a pair of white bead-embroidered high-heeled shoes with matching cigarette case from Hong Kong, from the collection of David Bingell.

bead embroidery techniques Most embroidery techniques can be adapted to beadwork by simply adding beading to the thread. A few techniques include appliqué, blanket stitch, couching, backstitch, basket weave needlepoint, continental needlepoint, seeding, slipstitch, running stitch, lane stitch, and satin stitch.

bead finishes Colors or coatings applied to bead surfaces to enhance their color or appearance. Common surface treatments used on glass beads are shiny, matte, aurora borealis (AB) or rainbow, metallic, frosted, satin, pearl, and vitrail. Many combinations of finishes, such as transparent frosted aurora borealis, or silver-lined matte, are available. Bead finishes may be affected by contact with the human body as well as with certain chemicals, such as hair sprays and perfumes. The beads pictured are transparent red glass beads that have an AB finish applied to one side only, which adds interesting character, play-of-color, and light reflection to a beaded design. Find the bead finishes chart in Part IV.

bead glue *See* adhesive.

bead history Find discussion in Part I. *See* individual entries for bead types.

bead holder A pair of usually wooden pincers, shaped something like ice tongs, used to hold an individual bead while performing some operation, like using a bead reamer to enlarge or smooth out the hole on the bead.

bead-hole cleaner This fireproof tool used in glass beadmaking does what its name suggests.

bead knitting A knitting technique that adds beads on the stitches rather than between the stitches. The beads must be strung prior to knitting. The resulting product is much tighter and stiffer than in beaded knitting, which feels softer and more flexible. *See* beaded knitting.

bead knotting The practice of tying knots between each bead when stringing a necklace

or bracelet. The technique is often used to prevent pearls from abrading each other, and with other types of beads, to create very fluid pieces of jewelry. In the case of precious or semiprecious gemstone beads, it prevents their loss should the strand break.

bead loom The structure on which beadwork fabric is created, using the basic concept of warp and weft weaving. Looms are sold commercially but can be easily constructed at home. They can be made of wood, metal, or plastic. Bead looms are useful for making large pieces, such as belts, hatbands, wall hangings, and bead strips for embellishing fabric or leather. Less common bead looms are the back or body, foot, finger, and bow loom. Shown is a small loom suitable for beginner projects like bracelets and barrettes. *See also* bead weaving.

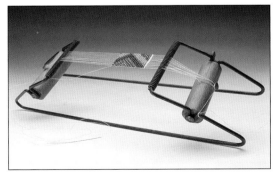

bead loops   Short strands of beads, like fringe, often used for embellishment. The loops can hang from a piece, like earring fringe, or trim a piece of beadwork as edging.

bead needles   *See* beading needles.

bead netting   *See* netting.

bead pimp   Used humorously; a bead artisan who had originally made beaded objects for friends and family for fun who later turns to profit from buying beads in large quantities from wholesalers to resell at craft shows and other public venues.

bead rake   A hooked fireproof metal instrument resembling a dental probe, used for manipulating hot glass on the bead's surface, this is one of many tools that come in handy to pinch, pull, poke, snip, or otherwise manipulate the hot glass in beadmaking. With the rake, the bead maker can drag, feather, swirl, or rake the bead surface to create desired textures or patterns. The bead rake can also poke holes or create air bubbles in the glass bead. It is also used to shape metal, ceramic, and graphite objects. *See also* marver and other tools.

bead reamer   A tool with a wooden or plastic handle and a metal shaft, rod, or file used to widen a bead hole. It is similar to the awl, but the bead reamer usually has an abrasive tip.

bead release   Also called *bead separator*. It is available as a sludge, mud, or powder to be mixed with water to achieve a consistency resembling that of pancake batter. The fireproof thick liquid, usually a mixture of alumina and high-fire clay, is used to coat the mandrel or other surface, such as a kiln shelf, that the glass contacts in glass beadmaking, preventing the glass from sticking and making removal easy after the finished beads cool. *See* glass beadmaking.

bead ropes   Many beadwork techniques can produce a circular shape, or rope, for bracelets, necklaces, and chokers. Examples of rope technique include round and flat peyote stitch, square stitch, Ndebele or herringbone stitch, brick stitch, spiral stitch, and wrap stitch. In general, bead ropes are quite sturdy and do not break easily. They may have a hollow center or be beaded around a cord, a metal hoop, or soft leather, which determines the flexibility of the rope. Photos here illustrate African helix, crochet rope, herringbone stitch, Russian spiral, Dutch spiral, and circular netting.

bead roughouts   This term generally refers to unfinished beads made of wood, stone, glass, or other materials, like antlers. Roughouts are finished using such techniques as surface carving, polishing, sanding, or tumbling.

bead scoop   Any number of tools useful for picking up loose beads and placing them back into the tube, box, or other container. Scoops that look like little shovels, specifically designed for picking up beads, are on the market. One beader recommends going to

Russian spiral

African helix

Dutch spiral

Crochet rope

Herringbone stitch

Circular netting

your favorite ice cream store, asking for a sample of ice cream, and reusing the little plastic spoon as a small, free bead scoop.

bead sculpture Generally any three-dimensional beaded object, which may combine the use of several different beading techniques, whether stitching, netting, wire wrapping, coiling, or free-form stringing. Bead sculptures range from the utilitarian—bowls and vases—to the purely ornamental, and may feature animals, flowers, food items, buildings, or even scenery and abstract images.

bead separator *See* bead release.

bead shapes Bead shapes may seem virtually infinite in number, but a good many of them are standard, among them barrel, bicone, chips, coin, disk, donut, oval, pyramid, rondelle, round, square, teardrop, triangular, tubular, and tabular. Specialty or novelty shapes (such as flowers, stars, animals, coins, and insects) are too numerous to mention. Find discussion in Part I and the chart for common bead shapes in Part IV. *See also* individual bead name or shape.

bead sizes In seed beads, the size generally indicates the number of beads per inch (25.4 mm or 2.54 cm), meaning that a size 10 seed bead strings approximately 10 beads per inch. This is often not the case, however, as the standard has not been firmly established across manufacturers or among artisans. Larger types of beads are measured in millimeters, e.g., a 2-mm bead. Find the bead sizes chart in Part IV.

bead therapy Working with beads in a therapeutic context as treatment for certain physical, emotional, spiritual, or psychological conditions. Specific exercises using beads can be helpful for many physical injuries affecting fine motor coordination, such as those resulting from stroke, brain trauma, and arthritis. A variety of rehabilitation programs for addictions use bead projects to help people focus on treatment goals, improve concentration, foster communication skills, and understand the meaning of symbolism. Children with behavior disorders and learning disabilities can also improve academically by using beads as a concrete form of positive reinforcement to change their behavior.

bead thread Typically, for durability, bead thread is made of a synthetic material like nylon or polyester, but it also comes in natural fibers like linen and cotton. Its packaging depends on the manufacturer. It may be wrapped around a bobbin (as shown), a larger

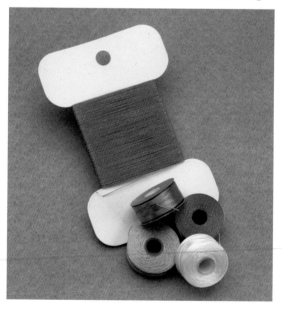

spool, or around cardboard for individual projects. Although white and black are the most commonly used colors, there are many different thread colors available to match a particular project. *See also* stringing thread. Find charts for needles and threads in Part IV.

bead tip A bead tip is a finding or a specially designed metal bead, either cup-shaped or clamshell-shaped, that encloses and conceals the knot at both ends of strung beads. It also has a small loop which can attach to a clasp or ear wire.

bead tray A container with sides and sometimes a lid to contain beads, as well as projects and tools. *See also* bead box and bead board.

bead types Beads both natural and manufactured come in a nearly boundless variety, and new types are always in the making with different finishes, shapes, and facets. A few common types are charlottes, bugles, two-cuts, three-cuts, cylinder, hex beads, seed beads, and white hearts. General categories are bone, ceramic or clay, glass, horn, metal, seed, shell, plastic, stone, and wood. Beads are also classified by shape, size, ethnic origin, rarity, manufacturer, and cost. The major glass bead producers are Africa, the Czech Republic, India, France, Italy, Japan, China, and the U.S. Find charts with notes about specific bead types, such as glass or "metallized" beads as well as for selected finishes or treatments, in Part IV.

bead wasters Artifact by-products of bead production which reveal to archaeologists, historians, scholars, and bead researchers the types of bead manufacturing techniques used at the archaeological site under study.

bead weaving To weave is to create a material by interlacing strands of thread called the *warp* with filling threads, or *weft*. When weaving on a bead loom, it is strung first with warp threads, and beads are then strung on the weft. The weft with strung beads passes under the warp, placing the beads between the warp threads, and then passing the needle and weft thread through the beads over the warp, being careful not to pierce the warp threads with the beading needle. There is also a different technique for placing beads on the warp threads.

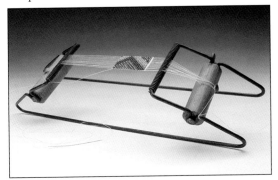

bead whore A recently coined term that describes the male or female practice of flashing one's chest or breasts in public in exchange for Mardi Gras beads. The practice of flashing is generally tolerated during the festivities, but only if it does not spark blatant public disruption, violence, or sexual assault. Some people call themselves bead whores because they enjoy collecting Mardi Gras beads, even though they are not willing to expose themselves for the strands of cheap plastic beads. There is also a system of trading for specialty beads, favors, and trinkets. *See also* Mardi Gras beads.

bead wire Many different wires are designed specifically for beading. The wire can be a stiff metal that is loaded with beads and bent or wrapped to form a shape or it may be a nylon-coated wire cable more appropriate for jewelry projects requiring flexibility, such as necklaces. *See also* stringing wire.

beaded beads These are smaller beads strung, stitched, or knotted together to form larger individual beads, as for earrings or buttons. Alternatively, they may be beads to which others are attached by means of brick, peyote, or netting stitches. Shown are several different types of beaded beads.

beaded beards A German explorer in the late 1800s claimed that beaded beards were fashionable at the time in West Africa. Captain Jack Sparrow, the movie character in *Pirates of the Caribbean,* sports beads in his beard and hair.

Not necessarily a custom among pirates, weaving beads into hair is a fairly common practice throughout the world, especially in the Caribbean and Africa. Former Minnesota Governor Jesse Ventura has reportedly worn a dyed, beaded beard that was braided and split into a devil's fork.

beaded braids Large-hole beads like crow beads used to decorate both human and horsehair braids. A big-eye needle helps to pull the strand of hair through the bead. Plaited beadwork, on the other hand, is a braid made out of beads. *See also* plaited beadwork.

beaded clothing A wide variety of garments are embellished or covered completely with beads. Shown is a black silk jacket from Hong Kong, beaded with a phoenix and dragon motif, showing bead embroidery; the beads range in size and texture. From the collection of David Bingell, the piece dates from about the 1960s. *See also* bead embroidery.

beaded collars Married Maasai women wear an elaborate beaded collar, with multiple stiffened and flattened circular strands. One beaded-collar necklace can be worn on top of another in steps with multiple necklaces, which also serve as a sign of wealth.

beaded crowns In Africa, beads are strongly associated with royalty; among the Yoruba of Nigeria and Benin, the largest ethnic group in sub-Saharan Africa, strands of beads are considered emblems of the gods. Accordingly, Yoruba crowns feature beaded figures attached to a cone-shaped basketry frame, the entire surface of which is decorated with beads. An attached veil of beaded strands shrouds the ruler's face. These crowns usually display faces that represent ancestors and images of birds gathering, which suggests the king's ability to mediate between the spirit and human realms. Headdresses from other cultures that may be loosely called crowns also may feature elaborate beadwork.

beaded dolls In certain cultural contexts, beaded dolls are objects rich in ritual and religious symbolism, and they have accepted places in initiations and other ceremonies, especially during the periods of courtship, marriage, and childbirth. The Ndebele people of southern Africa are known for beautiful beaded artifacts, including dolls. An important export item and valuable income source for Ndebele women, beaded dolls also strengthen the tribe's cultural identity. The beaded dolls shown were made by women in the MonkeyBiz bead cooperative in South Africa. Courtesy of MonkeyBiz. *See* bride bead doll, fertility bead dolls, gourd doll,

initiation bead doll, Sangoma bead doll, wrapped stitch, and Zulu beadwork.

beaded gourd A gourd that has been embellished with beads. The gourd vessel shown is the work of Bonnie Gibson, featuring a buffalo carving on the front and a buffalo robe design

on the back. It has two inlaid beaded circles, or rosettes. A channel cut around the gourd is inlaid with a mixture of shell, stone heishi, and copper seed beads.

beaded hair While certain cultures more commonly weave beads into the hair, beaded hair has been worn through the centuries in nearly every culture. Women, girls, and some men and boys generally use large-hole beads, such as crow beads, of glass, plastic, bone, or wood. Beads incorporated into braids, corn rows, hair extensions, and more elaborate hairdos appear throughout the world and may have particular cultural expressions. Beaded bangs (called *fringe* in Britain) and beards are seen at some celebrations and cultural events. Around the world, everyday hairdos embellished with beads have never gone out of style. Beads, feathers, and leather traditionally adorned Native American braids. In mainland China, bead-hair crowns serve as virtual wigs for special occasions. In European tradition, a bead may be attached to a sweetheart keepsake lock of hair. African-American braids and corn rows, artfully executed, may be adorned or held in place with beads, beaded bands,

and barrettes. Beads are used to decorate even the hair or manes of such animals as horses in Latvia, donkeys in Mexico, or llamas in Peru. Beaded hair pins and barrettes also support selected hairstyles worldwide. *See also* beaded beards.

beaded hatband A piece of beadwork embellishment worn around the crown of a hat. Often a loomed piece of beadwork attached to fabric or leather, it may also be a bead rope, further decorated with conchos, leather fringe, or braids.

beaded knife sheaths Functional artifacts of early American history often collected as art, beaded knife sheathes were the traditional Native American fashion. Replicas are still being made for dance regalia and ceremonial use. Usually the length of the knife blade, plus an extra inch or two for the handle, lane stitch typically covers both sides of the sheath, most often using size 10 or size 12 glass seed beads. There is abundant documentation of the diverse colors and patterns associated with different tribes, such information being crucial to collectors and art enthusiasts. Some bead manufacturers exploit the market by continuing to produce beads in the traditional colors.

beaded knitting A technique of knitting in which the beads are added between the stitches, not on the stitches, giving a softer and more flexible product than bead knitting. For this method, the beads must be prestrung. Shown opposite page, top left, is an angel brooch made by Sylvia Elam. *See also* bead knitting.

beaded purses Intricate beaded bags, often vintage or antique, that are both functional and works of art. Considered collector's items, their limited availability often makes them quite expensive. In a world of throwaways, collectors appreciate these beaded purses for their fine workmanship, as well as their age. A few modern beaders are reproducing vintage designs, and manufacturers are even reproducing some of the colors seen in antique beads.

beaded rosette A three-dimensional bead structure that simulates tiny flowers. The project shown (top right) is the unique design of Aurora Mathews. The beaded roses or rosettes can be used to embellish bracelets, necklaces, amulet bags, and clothing.

beaded wirework Also called *wired bead-work*, this term refers to seed beads strung onto fine-gauge craft wire that is bent or molded into jewelry of various shapes, such as flowers or insects. In countries where craft materials may be more difficult to acquire, copper telephone wire or plastic-coated colored electrical wire sometimes substitutes for craft wire. Verona Thom, author of *Bead N' Bugs,* designed the delightfully detailed ladybug and dragonfly shown here, crafted from thin craft wire and seed beads.

beading Any work that uses beads. Besides the strung variety, beading can refer to decoration that resembles rows of beads (without string) carved, molded, or otherwise shaped on metalwork, woodwork, glassware, ceramics, clay, stone, or other materials. It may be commonly found on picture frames, furniture, ceramics, glassware, and woodwork or used as architectural details, like molding, openwork, or trimming, for house and building interiors or exteriors, such as on banisters, door frames, light fixtures, garden pots, or various ornaments.

beading needles Specially designed needles thin enough to accommodate small seed beads. Different from sewing needles, the needle eye has to accommodate both the bead hole and the thread. Beading needle sizes usually correspond to bead sizes: a size 10 needle works with a size 10 bead. However, beading needles are versatile in that the hole size is more important than the bead size. A size 10 needle is a good general size for size 10, 11, and 12 beads. When working with a size 12 or 13 bead, try a size 12 needle. There are many types, sizes, lengths, and manufacturers of needles, a few of the types being long, short, fine, twisted wire, big eye, and glover's needles.

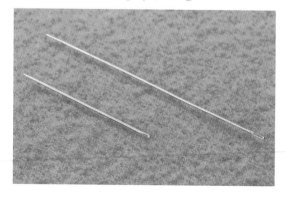

beading party A gathering for the purpose of making beaded objects. These parties, often hosted by retail bead stores as well as home-based bead businesses, are customized for special occasions, like wedding showers and birthdays. They are usually project-oriented and may last 2 to 4 hours. Most contain all the necessary tools and materials for a set fee per person. It's a great way to make matching necklaces for bridesmaids, for instance.

beading stitches Beading stitches and their variations are numerous, and their use depends on the surface or shape to which they are applied. Among the most common bead stitches are brick stitch, peyote stitch, lane stitch, loomwork, spiral stitch, square stitch, stacking stitch, edging stitch, appliqué stitch, right-angle weave, wrapped stitch, side stitch, raised stitch, running stitch, backstitch, and netting. Even a common stitch such as peyote may encompass a great number of variations, including flat, round, flat round, gourd stitch, two-drop peyote stitch, three-drop peyote stitch, and free-form peyote stitch. *See also* individual bead stitches by name. Find stitch diagrams in Part V.

beadmaking *See* glass beadmaking.

beadstone Also called *hornblende*, beadstone is a major rock-forming mineral in the class of silicates. The term *hornblende* derives from the Old German words *blenden*, which means "to deceive," and *horn*, which may suggest the color of horn. Venetians used this raw material late into the 1400s to make wound-glass rosary beads.

beadwork This term encompasses the many uses of beads as decoration and functional objects. Simple stringing is an obvious use, but the term usually refers to something more elaborate, involving skills, techniques, cultural traditions, and beliefs. Other beadwork involves fiber or fabric, such as bead weaving (this may call for a loom, on which threads are intermeshed to create material), netting, and embroidery. Another category requires no loom and is called *off-loom bead weaving*. In bead embroidery, the beads are sewn onto a fabric surface, such as leather, cloth, or synthetic materials such as faux suede, polyester, or cardboard. Other techniques borrowed from the sewing arts include bead knitting, crochet, and cross-stitch. One unique category of beadwork is the Huichol, which uses beeswax and resin to embed beads in elaborate designs carved into ironwood or gourds. In wire wrapping beads, manufactured metal wire is used to embellish and shape beads and gemstones. Beadwork is used in everything from clothing and jewelry to wall hangings and sculpture.

beeswax A natural product of bees, usually harvested along with honey. A wonderful thread conditioner, it helps waterproof the thread and minimizes tangling. A valuable aid to beaders, a small cake of beeswax lasts a long time. Other waxes and resins can also serve as thread conditioners. Beeswax is used in combination with other products to press glass beads into the surface of gourds and ironwood carvings. Shown is a turtle made from ironwood with beads pressed into the beeswax in the Huichol style. *See also* Huichol.

beggar beads Large tumbled stone beads, usually of agate. This is also another term for prayer beads.

bell caps Beads that sit on top of another bead, primarily for aesthetic purposes. For instance, metal caps can be placed on the top and bottom of a glass bead during stringing, to add a touch of metallic sheen to plain beads. They are usually concave to match the curvature of the bead and come in different sizes. Also called *bead caps* and *end caps*.

bells Beads with a clapper or ringer. Sometimes called *clapper beads*, they can be used as charms on belts, earrings, necklaces, and bracelets. Technically, if they have no ringer, they are not bells. Ring-bells or fingerbells of the ancient Tellem culture in Mali or jingle bells are variations that can be made into beads. Shown are brass bells that produce a pleasant sound with movement. *See also* clapper beads.

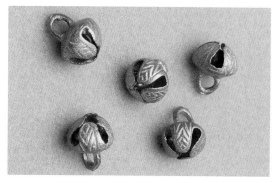

belly beads Flattened disk-shaped beads with a center hole. *See also* rondelle.

bent-nose pliers A tool similar to chain-nose pliers, except that the nose is bent for easier access to hard-to-reach places.

berry beads These beads, made of glass and a variety of other materials, feature a bumpy surface that simulates real berries, especially raspberries. *See also* rudraksha.

beryl Transparent to opaque gemstones, composed of aluminum beryllium silicate, that come in many varieties. The deep green gemstones are called *emerald*, the blue ones are called *aquamarine*, and all other colors are called *precious beryl*. Precious beryl, depending on the color of the stone, may also be known as *bixbite* (raspberry), golden beryl (lemon to golden yellow), *goshenite* (clear or colorless), *heliodor* (light yellowish green), or *morganite* (pink to violet or salmon). All varieties have a Mohs scale hardness factor

of 7.5 to 8. Beryl is colorless but impurities impart color in the various stones.

The ancient Druids used beryl stones for scrying (crystal gazing), and the Scots called them "stones of power." The earliest crystal balls were made from beryl; rock crystal was preferred in later centuries.

bezel In jewelry, usually a thin strip of metal that surrounds and secures a cabochon or gemstone. Beads can also form a bezel, as shown here in the beaded bezel around a piece of pottery, or shard. The pendant is strung on bead wire (nylon-coated wire cable) with abalone pieces, copper pearls, amber chips, and carnelian beads, and finished with a copper clasp.

bicone A bead shaped like a cone at both ends. The widest part of each cone is in the middle of the bead and the pointed part is at

the ends. Beads in a wide variety of materials and finishes have this shape. Those shown are made of glass.

bida beads Wound-glass beads from Nigeria made from recycled glass.

big-eye needle A very useful invention for people who have imperfect vision, this variety of needle has an extra-large eye, which makes threading easy. The eye is constructed from two very thin pieces of metal welded together at the ends, which open in the center.

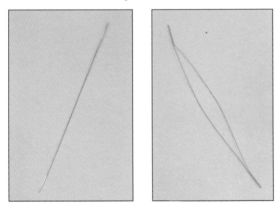

big-holed beads Beads with larger than usual holes are needed with heavier cord or jute that may be used for weaving, macramé, stringing, and knotting projects. They are also favored in craft projects for small children, people

with disabilities, and patients in rehabilitation settings. The wooden bead shown here measures approximately 12 mm in diameter.

birthstones These are gemstones traditionally assigned to personal birth months or to sun signs of the zodiac. Birthstones may also be part of and differ according to mystical (Tibetan), ayurvedic, talismanic, healing, and other distinct cultural traditions or disciplines. Some believe that they originated from the breast-plate of Aaron (Exodus 28:15–30) that refers to the twelve stones for the Twelve Tribes of Israel and were later assigned to the twelve months or zodiac signs. In 1912, the American National Association of Jewelers, Jewelers of America, adopted a list of birthstones. In October 2002, the American Gem Trade Association added tanzanite as a December birthstone. Find birthstone charts in Part IV.

bismuth A heavy, brittle metal with a lustrous pink tinge. It is used as an oil paint pigment and is sometimes used in glazes that produce an iridescent luster finish. It is classified as a poor metal.

Biwa pearl This cultured pearl is grown in the freshwater mussel from Lake Biwa in

Japan. Biwa pearls are also called freshwater cultured pearls.

black lace or web A decoration on the surface of a bead, using black glass.

black onyx Typically an opaque black, this gemstone is a chalcedony (silicon dioxide), cryptocrystalline quartz, sometimes bearing bands of black and white in a layer stone. Some of the gemstone is naturally black, but much of the onyx on the market is stained. Its Mohs scale hardness is 7.

blackstone A common name for black jasper. *See* jasper.

bleaching A common treatment in which chemical agents are used to lighten or remove color from a gemstone.

bloodstone A variety of opaque, dark green chalcedony, cryptocrystalline quartz made of silicon dioxide. Pieces of chlorite or hornblende needles cause the green color while the red spots are made by iron oxide. It rates a 6.5 to 7 on the Mohs scale of hardness. In ancient times, the stone was known as *heliotrope* because it resembled the setting sun on the ocean. In medieval times, it was called *martyr's*

stone and associated with stones at the foot of the cross stained by Christ's blood. Christians carved crucifixes and images of martyrs out of the stone. The stone has been called *blood jasper,* but it is not a jasper. The stone is commonly found in India, where it is used medicinally and as an aphrodisiac. It is also mined in Australia, Brazil, China, and the United States.

blown glass In this glassmaking method, the craftsperson blows air into a glass tube to give form to a small piece of molten glass placed at the end of the tube. He turns the tube slowly over heat until the material achieves the appropriate size and shape. The blown-glass beads created by this method are often slightly irregular; one hole in the bead is small and another (closest to the glass blower) is larger. Blown glass also tends to result in teardrop shapes rather than round beads. In the 17th century, *Roman pearls* were created from blown-glass beads in which fish scales (the protein guanine) and wax were inserted to simulate natural pearls. Blown-glass beads have been popularly made in the Czech Republic, Germany, France, Japan, Mexico, Peru, and India.

Since blown-glass beads are made one at a time, like wound beads, the technique is

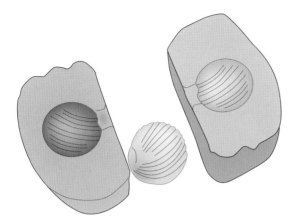

generally reserved for unique and expensive beads. More efficient methods are used for mass production. Traditionally the air came from the lungs of the glassblower, but in the 20th century, machines began to do the work. Shown is a drawing of a mold for blown-glass beads; note the two halves of the mold and the space for blowing air into the glass inside the mold. *See* drawn beads, glass beadmaking, and Roman pearls.

blue goldstone A synthetic stone, very dark navy blue to purple, with finely dispersed metallic particles of copper or other metals in

a glass base. It is also called *purple goldstone*. In the 17th century, the Miotti family in Venice developed goldstone, a type of glass made with copper or copper salts with a reducing flame applied. *See also* goldstone. Shown are blue-goldstone rondelles.

blue topaz Often indistinguishable to the naked eye from aquamarine, this is a transparent light blue gemstone with a Mohs scale hardness of 7.5 to 8. Today nearly all blue topaz is produced by the irradiation and heating of natural colorless topaz, a neosilicate of aluminum and fluorine. A blue synthetic topaz has been made since 1976. *See also* topaz.

blueberry beads Round beaded beads in shades of blue. It also refers to rudraksha beads that are covered by an outer shell that is blue when fully ripe. The term can more loosely refer to an assortment of lampwork, glass, porcelain, and ceramic beads, or a cluster of round blue glass beads. *See* beaded bead and rudraksha.

bodhi seed A seed from the bodhi tree (*Ficus religiosa,* or sacred fig tree), often used to make malas, or prayer beads. According to the Buddhist canon of scriptures, Buddha was sitting under the bodhi tree when he attained spiritual enlightenment. The mala typically has 108 bodhi beads on unknotted thread, about 24 inches (60 cm) long. The 109th bead, known as the *guru bead,* is thought to be that of the master.

bodom beads Originating in Africa in the ancient overlapping kingdoms of Ghana and Mali, bodom beads are made by the wet-core powder-glass technique, which dates back over 1,000 years. Bead mold fragments have been found dating from the 9th to 12th centuries. Rather than using saliva to hold the core together, as in kiffa beads, these large beads have cores that have been wet by other organic materials, such as gum Arabic or date juice. Firing turns the core dark.

body jewelry Screws, studs, rings, or chains worn on the nostril or nose septum, belly-button or navel, nipple, eyebrow, tongue, cheek, or other body part, that usually has been pierced for the purpose, as distinct from more conventional jewelry like necklaces, bracelets, anklets, and toe rings that can be easily removed and do not require body piercing. Many of these ornaments have names associated with where they are worn, such as the labret worn on the lip. Industrials or constructs and other types of ear ornaments worn on pierced ear cartilage, not just the fleshy earlobe, may also loosely fall into this category or be classed as earrings. Beads may be part of these various body ornaments. *See* body piercing.

body piercing The earlobes and fleshy parts of the outer ear as well as the lip, nose, tongue, eyebrow, navel, cheek, nipple, and other body parts have been pierced in diverse cultures in both ancient and modern times. Body piercing allows one to wear studs, rings, gemstones, screws, or chains, some of which may have dangling or beaded additions. For a new piercing, commonly recommended metals are surgical stainless steel, surgical implant titanium, niobium, or yellow or white 14 kt or 18 kt gold. For people allergic to metals (body piercing could result in a new-found allergy to nickel, for instance), a special plastic called Tygon is favored. With any piercing, one must watch closely for danger of infection, which if untreated can lead to more serious diseases.

bog oak *See* bog wood.

bog wood The most common kind of bog wood is bog oak, partially decomposed wood of the oak tree that has rested in low-oxygen Irish or Scottish peat bogs for thousands of years; the process blackens, hardens, and preserves the material. The acidity and tannins of the bog water help preserve the wood from decay. After millions of years, the wood fossilizes, forms lignite, and then finally coal. Bog wood is carved into beads, buttons, bracelets, and brooches. Other common bog woods are bald cypress and kauri.

bolo tie A cord, often of leather, worn as a necktie, with an ornament of beads, silver, or gemstones. The ornament slides up and down the cord, and the leather laces dangle. The photo shows a beaded bolo tie of dark-brown braided leather with a chrysocolla cabochon, made by Sylvia Elam. Jewelry adhesive attaches the beadwork to the metal bolo slide. The braided ends are beaded with peyote stitch, using the same beads and colors as in the bolo. Using a right-angle weave, the artist attached her own design of beaded copper rose beads, which hang freely from the bottom row of peyote stitch. The tips were attached with a size 12 beading needle and Fireline, a four-pound test-weight fishing line. *See also* chrysocolla.

bone beads Since earliest times, beads have been made from animal bones, frequently those of the bovine family, such as cows and water buffalo; snake vertebrae, bear claws, and other animal materials have also been used. Some, such as vertebrae, have natural "holes," making them easier to string. After they are bleached, cattle bone beads are sometimes treated with a batiklike process in which patterns are painted on the surface with wax. They are called *mud beads*. When the beads are subsequently dyed, the pigment adheres to the bare surface, while the waxed areas remain uncolored. While rare, human bone beads have been used as prayer beads in Tibet and Nepal. The bone beads shown have intricate carving; the small round beads are vertebrae. Bone beads are on either side of the mud bead shown lower right.

bone hairpipe Tubular beads carved from animal bone, frequently used in Native American chokers, breastplates, and bracelets. These items, once considered battle armor and displayed as such in museums, are now more commonly seen as jewelry in dance regalia. The beads shown immediately below are carved from bone and horn.

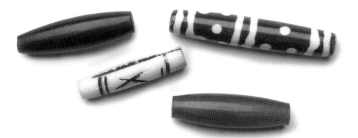

borosilicate glass Also called *hard glass*, this material uses borax as a flux, making it stronger. It also has a greater tolerance for temperature changes, called a *coefficient of expansion* (COE), so it is less likely to pop, which can cause injury. Originally formulated for scientific use, it was intended for containers that would not break easily or interact chemically with their contents.

botanical beads Beads made from parts of plants, like seeds, pods, pits, pinecones, rose hips, petals, beans, berries, nuts, herbs, hemp, bamboo, or palms. Typically, the plant material is used whole and dried, or it is pulverized into a powder, wetted and shaped with a sort of adhesive, and dried. Although wood comes from trees and shrubs, the term *botanical* is rarely used to describe wood products shaped into beads.

boxwood (Chinese boxwood) The boxwood is a small tree or shrub. Because of its small size, the wood is used more often for small carved objects and decorative inlays than for furniture. The wood itself is very dense and durable; excellent for carving, it polishes to a silky smooth finish. Bonnie Gibson assembled the two necklaces below, using gourd-shaped boxwood beads hand-carved in China.

bracelet A type of jewelry typically worn around the wrist and occasionally used as a necklace extender. The standard length for a bracelet is 7 to 8 inches (18 to 20 cm), including the clasp. *See also* bangle.

braid A beaded braid consists of three or more strands of beaded thread interwoven or twined in a diagonally overlapping pattern.

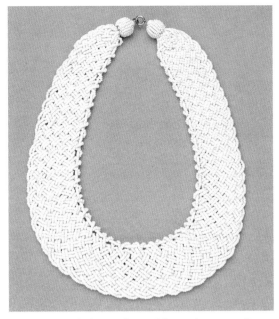

The braided Czech necklace shown is from the collection of David Bingell.

branch coral Also called *branched coral,* the natural form of coral before it is harvested, cut, dyed, polished, and drilled for use as beads. Shown is a necklace of red branch coral accented with sterling silver Bali spacers.

branch fringe Also called *branched fringe* or *corralling,* which simulates the branches of coral. A short strand of beads is strung and then other short strands of beads are added to the main strand to create short branches. This is a way to add interesting texture to beaded objects. The brooch shown features dichroic glass cabochons handmade by Bonnie Gibson, embellished with seed beads and fire-polish beads. The hair is branched fringe.

brass An alloy of the metals copper and zinc. The different proportions of copper and zinc produce different colors and other characteristics in the resultant metal. Brass is copper most commonly alloyed with about 30% zinc, while *red brass* is copper with about 15%

zinc. The term *brass* is also used in jewelry-making to designate raw metal that has not been plated or lacquered. Brass (made from copper and zinc) first came to the Americas with the arrival of the Europeans. Nuremburg, Germany, was a center for brass production in the Middle Ages.

The Taíno in the late 15th and early 16th centuries on the island of Cuba eagerly exchanged gold with the Spanish for the coveted brass, not seen before in the Caribbean. According to one report, they exchanged 200 pieces of gold for a single piece of brass. Brass was called *turey,* meaning the most luminous part of sky, and *guanín,* one of the sacred materials. Brass tubes that originated in Europe were woven into textiles as pendants. Local chieftains wore it in pendants and medallions to display their wealth, influence, and connection with the supernatural realm. The elite were buried with it.

brazing A process of joining two metals or alloys with use of a third melted filler metal or alloy that does not contain iron and a flux. The original two pieces are fused when they melt at the joint with the third metal in sandwich layers. The capillary action of the metals helps them fuse at the joint. The flux, often borax-based, helps prevent oxides from forming and the metals from spreading. Filler-metal alloys may include copper, zinc, silver, and other metals. A few brazing processes are torch, flow, furnace, infrared, resistance, block, induction, and dip brazing.

breastplate In Native American regalia, breastplates are made from leather and bone hairpipe or horn beads. Breastplates were traditionally worn by Plains Indian warriors as armor, but today they are worn for ceremonial occasions as a type of spiritual armor. In Judaic tradition, a breastplate is a square cloth that has been set with the twelve precious stones that represent the twelve tribes of Israel. Ancient high priests wore it over the breast. It may also be made of silver or gold and set with stones and placed over the mantle. In Medieval Europe, the breastplate served as a plate of armor, usually metal, designed to protect the chest or torso. While it may have had a painted coat of arms or been attached to protective chain mail, beads were not included. According to some theologians, biblical references to the *breastplate* suggest that it was designed to protect the wearer from "unrighteousness."

brick stitch A beading technique also called *stacking stitch, Apache weave, Comanche weave,* and *Cheyenne stitch.* It is frequently used to make earrings with a triangular top, since the stitch automatically decreases every row by one bead. Although the flat, two-dimensional form of the stitch is most common, it can also be done in a circular, three-dimensional form. Shown below is a pair of earrings done in

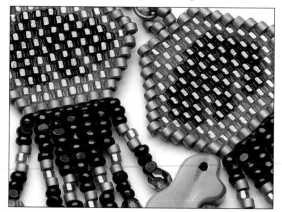

brick stitch in a shape different from the common triangle. Above is circular brick stitch.

bride bead doll Found among the Ndebele people of southern Africa, this doll wears a dress like that of a Ndebele bride. The panels of the doll's apron have symbols of the deposit of five head of cattle as the down payment toward the bride price. The doll, like the bride she represents, wears a beaded train called a *nyoga*, which hangs from her shoulders. The face is covered by a beaded veil.

briolette A faceted bead, generally in the shape of an oval or teardrop. Shown are briolettes of Turkish purple jade strung on purple thread, separated by transparent plastic spacers.

brittle The quality of being easily broken or crushed into a powder, usually in reference to certain minerals or metals.

bronze A strong, tough metal; an alloy of copper and tin, usually containing from 2% to 13% tin. Copper alloys for bronze (symbol Bz) may also include phosphorus, manganese, aluminum, silicon, or other elements. Many may be called phosphor bronzes because an alloy of phosphorus (0.01 to 0.05%) is added as a deoxidizing agent for casting. While *brass* is copper alloyed with zinc, some brasses have been loosely called *bronzes*. The introduction of bronze, harder and more durable than iron (which rusts), more easily fashioned than stone, and stronger than copper alone, heralded the Bronze Age (3200–1200 B.C.). The term *bronze* may also simply refer to the reddish yellow color of a given metal or other material.

bronze beads Metal beads made from the alloy of copper and tin. Also called bronze beads are glass beads coated with gold mixed with other materials that are baked on to create a finish resembling bronze. Beads the color of bronze but made from other metals may loosely be called bronze beads. *See* bronze.

brooch Also spelled broach; generally, a relatively large decorative pin or clasp. The brooch shown features a cabochon of amazonite beaded around the edge and across the face.

browband A headband that's worn across the forehead.

brushed metal A textured finish on metal, such as gold, silver, or platinum, that was created by brushing the metal with a material something like sandpaper. Little brushstrokes sometimes appear.

bugle beads These tubular glass beads are cut lengths of glass cane, popular in jewelry design and available in a wide range of colors and finishes. They are most commonly found in bead lengths of 1 mm, 2 mm, 3 mm, and 5 mm. Shown are 3-mm silver-lined gold bugle beads. *See also* twisted bugle beads.

bugtail Satin cord that is 1 mm in diameter.

bull necklace A rather interesting necklace designed to be worn by sacred bulls in southern India. One version is made with cowrie shells sewn onto leather and embellished with silver beads and a prayer-wheel bead.

bullion Ingots, lumps, or bars of gold, silver, platinum, or palladium are used by some central banks for international transactions. The value of the precious mineral depends on the metal content rather than its form. Coins and other forms of raw metals sometimes fall in this category. This definition is distinct from bullion wire used in beading.

bullion (wire) Also known as *French wire* or *gimp*, bullion is wire wound over thread or other core material, or tightly coiled into springs. It is used to attach findings to closures.

bumpy beads Raised dots or other embellishments adorn these beads that come in various shapes.

buri nuggets Hand-carved beads from the nut of the buri tree, a palm native to the Philippines, often sold dyed in a variety of appealing colors. Shown is a strand of blue buri nuggets, somewhat translucent in appearance.

burin An ancient stone tool used for carving or engraving bone, antler, or wood, found in Europe and the Americas over 50,000 years ago. This Stone Age implement has a sharp, angled point, called a burin spall, and may or may not have a wooden handle. The stone flake produced by the burin's blow has an edge like a chisel.

butterfly backs Another name for the backing used to secure post or stud earrings.

butterfly beads Also known as double-axe beads, these beads are shaped to look like a butterfly with two open wings or like two axe heads, with the hole down the middle between the two halves. Such beads represent Neolithic stonework technology and were often made from serpentine or steatite. They may have been regarded as symbols of power between 8000 and 6000 B.C. The term also applies to any bead shaped like a butterfly.

button Although a button is primarily a fastener, it generally has holes (or a shank) for attaching and can be strung, so it can also function as a bead. Used most often in jewelry design as a clasp or closure, the button is also sometimes seen as a centerpiece or pendant. Native American bone hairpipe chokers frequently feature a round abalone-shell button. Shown is a fancy Czech glass button of recent manufacture.

they easily transform the appearance of a garment.

C

cable A wire rope or metal chain of great tensile strength or one that contains multiple strands of wire or fiber. Find stringing materials chart in Part IV.

cabochon A polished stone that is cut with a rounded dome (convex curves) on the top and sides, and frequently a flat bottom. Often cut from opaque gemstones, "cabs" may be bordered with a beaded or precious-metal bezel.

button cover A finding that slides over an existing garment button, used in making beaded buttons. The beadwork or beaded cabochon is glued onto the metal finding. Button covers are very clever and versatile;

Cabochons are used for pendants, brooches, and colliers, or as ring stones. In the French expression, these stones are "*en cabochon.*" The photo shows a variety of cabochons.

cache-sexe A beaded apron or loincloth worn by the Kirdi girls and women of Cameroon for identifying marital status and group affiliations. *See* apron.

caged beads These are beads of any material, set within a wire wrapping, or cage.

calipers A precision instrument used to measure diameter or thickness in millimeters or inches, especially for areas or small objects difficult to access. Many different types of calipers exist. *Vernier calipers* are geared for precise measurements of fine objects and include a fixed and a sliding jaw, internal or external jaws, scales, a detail scale, and a clamping screw. Shown is an inexpensive simple type; photo by JG.

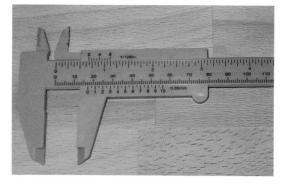

cameo A relief cut, usually from a gemstone, so that the sculpted image is raised. This engraving style is popularly done with *layer stones* and is used for pendants, brooches, and focal beads. Typically, agates and other chalcedony stones are used with the lighter

layer carved into the relief and the darker layer serving as its base. Sometimes the lower layer is dyed.

cane beads These handmade beads have a clear glass shell with a core made from a number of colored glass rods combined at the torch in the molten state and then cut. Cane beads appear to be striped with the colors of the various rods within. Also called *furnace beads* or *art beads*, they come in shapes ranging from cylinders to squares to rectangles to triangles. Those with multicolored stripes on the surface are called *latticino.* Shown are some very bright and colorful cane beads, manufactured by hand in the United States. *See also* furnace beads and glass cane.

cane mass The volume of glass that contains the design of the cane before the glass is pulled out to the smaller diameter suitable for making beads.

capstans Ear spools or ear "plugs" used to adorn the earlobe. They may be perforated and strung to suspend from the earlobe.

captive-bead ring Also called a ball-closure ring or a captive-ball ring. The bead or ball fits into the opening of a circular ring. The bead may be drilled or have dimples so that it stays snugly in place. It is often used for body jewelry.

carat (mass or weight) The unit of weight for gemstones, it is equivalent to 200 mg (0.2 grams) or 3,086 grains (avoirdupois). The name originated in the diminutive of *keration, kerat,* a Greek word for "carob seed." The measure is equal to the weight of four grains of rice or that of the carob seed. Carob seeds are uniform in weight. Gem carat weight is not the same as the term *karat* used regarding gold. A diamond weighing 100 carats would be 20 grams; a carat can be divided into 100 *points* of 2 mg each. Carat refers not only to a unit of mass (noted here), but to a unit of purity. *See* carat (purity) or karat and points.

carat (purity) Usually spelled *karat,* this unit of purity is used for precious metals, usually gold and platinum alloys. In the United States and Canada, the spelling and standard usage is *karat.* Pure gold is expressed as 24 kt; 18 parts gold and 6 parts other metals, such as silver or copper, is 18 kt gold; and 14 parts gold to 10 parts of other metals is 14 kt gold. The minimum that can be legally sold as gold in the United States is 10 kt. Here is the formula: $X = 24 [M_g/M_m]$

Abbreviations of the term may be *k, kt,* or *ct.* The centuries-old karat system has been more recently complemented with the *millesimal fineness system.* In this system, the purity of precious metals is denoted by parts per thousand of pure precious metal in the alloy. *See also* carat (mass or weight), relating to gemstone weight, not purity. For more on the karat and gold, *see* karat. Find chart in Part IV.

carbonado A natural polycrystalline diamond that is impure, dark-colored, very porous or spongy, and luminous. The aggregate of finely grained diamond particles makes it especially tough and therefore valuable. It is found in Brazil and Central Africa in alluvial deposits. A similar material found in Siberia is called *yakutite.* Theories on its origin are uncertain, and some scientists have even suggested that the mineral arrived from outer space, the result of an explosion of a supernova. It may have inclusions, and unlike the diamond, it is rarely used as a gemstone.

cardinal red A vivid red cloth worn by Catholic cardinals. It also refers to the rare flash of red, which can appear in amethyst.

cardinal gemstones Worn by the clergy of the Roman Catholic Church, usually by cardinals and archbishops, in rings and amulets as signs of pious virtue. The five cardinal or precious gemstones were the diamond, sapphire, ruby, emerald, and amethyst. Amethyst, often associated with the emblematic colors of the Church, later lost its precious status when large deposits of the stone were found in Brazil. *See* precious gemstones and gemstones.

carnelian A natural gemstone, member of the chalcedony family, a cryptocrystalline quartz made of silicon dioxide, found worldwide in a range of colors from lemony orange to a rich caramel orange. It is translucent to opaque and may have a cloudy distribution of color, owing primarily to its iron content. Note that carnelian is thought to have been named after the kornel cherry because of its color. It rates a 6.5 to 7 on the Mohs scale of hardness. It is also known as cornelian, sadoine, Mecca stone, and pigeon's blood agate. Notable deposits are found in India, Brazil, and Uruguay. Archaeologists have found carnelian beads that date at least as early as 1800 B.C. The color may be enhanced by heating. Many gemstones sold as carnelians are really agates that have been dyed and heat-treated. The 10-mm round carnelian beads shown are from China.

cased-glass beads When core beads are covered with a casing or layer of clear or transparent glass to give the design added depth, the product is cased-glass beads. They are also called *cased, overlay,* or *layered beads.*

casing Forming an outer covering on a core material. *See* cased-glass beads.

cast To give form to a substance—like plastic, glass, or metal—by injecting it into a mold while in a liquid state and allowing it to cool and harden. To make beads by the casting process, some type of core is required to form the hole or perforation in the bead. A mold is also sometimes called a cast.

cast iron A gray or white iron with many possible alloys, most commonly with carbon (2.5 to 4%) and silicon (1 to 3%). It tends to be brittle but can easily be cast in molds and machined. It is wear-resistant. It can be made by remelting pig iron, scrap iron, and scrap steel. Contaminants such as phosphorus and sulfur are removed. Gray cast iron contains silicon; white cast iron has a lower silicon content.

casting A process, such as lost-wax, for molding beads, sculptures, and other finished forms into desired shapes by using a wax, clay, wooden, or other mold, and pouring in molten metal, glass, or another material, which when cooled, assumes the shape of the mold.

castor-bean beads Seeds (also called beans) from the castor plant *Ricinus communis* are drilled for use as beads. In India, castor beads are often used as prayer beads. The seeds are poisonous; moles die when eating roots of the plant. The plant has been used in ancient Egypt, China, and India, principally for its oil, which is used in lamps and as a purgative.

cathedral beads Sometimes called *window* or *windowpane beads*, these popular beads come in a variety of sizes and shapes and have many styles of facet. They are finished

on the edges or tips with different colors, often bronze, gold, or silver, and in the example shown opposite left, blue.

cat's-eye The transparent or translucent yellowish gemstone chrysoberyl (cymophane) or chalcedony that has reflections within. These come in a variety of colors, with the most common being gold or brown. The gemstone properly called cat's-eye or *chrysoberyl cat's-eye* is always made of chrysoberyl, beryllium aluminum oxide, and has a Mohs scale hardness factor of 8.5. It is strongly pleochroic (trichroic). The term *cat's-eye* has been loosely applied to marble with concentric circles that appear eyelike. Genuine chrysoberyl cat's-eye should not be confused with quartz cat's-eye or prehnite cat's-eye; the latter two gems are referred to with a qualifying term before *cat's-eye*.

cat's-eye beads These beads, also called *fiber-optic beads*, change hue and simulate the opalescent reflective quality of some natural gemstones, like tiger's-eye and cat's-eye. In the particular gemstone, tube- or needlelike crystals running the length of the stone create a band of light; the same effect, called *chatoyancy*, is achieved in beads by fusing quartz

fibers—the same material used in fiber-optic telephone cables—and by machine-cutting them into various shapes. *See* cat's-eye. Shown are a fiber-optic dove bead and a mala bracelet of cat's-eye beads strung on elastic cord.

Cebu-lily shell beads Cut and drilled to make heishi, this small purple and white seashell is native to Cebu, an island in the Philippines. The shells are also sometimes called Mactan-lily shells, if from Mactan Island.

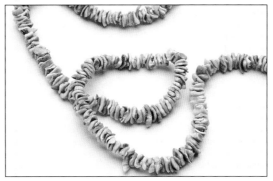

cedar-seed beads The so-called cedar seeds are really juniper berries (cones) from what is commonly called a cedar tree but what's really one of many juniper varieties (usually the desert juniper) hand-picked and hand-drilled

for use as beads in necklaces and other jewelry. They are also called *ghost beads* because of their association with the Ghost Dance, once forbidden by the United States government. The essential oils from cedar and juniper trees have a distinctive odor, and antibacterial as well as other medicinal properties. Native North Americans referred to the tree as Grandfather Cedar; the leaves are used in cleansing ceremonies. *See also* ghost beads.

century beads Century beads, also called *antique*, *Bohemian,* or *vintage* beads, are reproductions of beads made in Czechoslovakia during the late 19th and early 20th centuries. Beadmaking at that time was very labor intensive. Beads were made in molds, often only one or two at a time; they were next cut and shaped with lathes and other tools, and then glued. In the Communist era, different economic priorities prevailed, and producing such beads became an unaffordable luxury. Fortunately, the molds were safely stored in people's homes, and in time Czech glass bead makers were able to start a cottage industry producing the vintage bead shapes and colors.

ceramic beads Beads made of clay and fired in a kiln. Any of three kinds of bisque or clay

(earthenware, stoneware, or porcelain) may be combined with a variety of chemicals to produce differing degrees of hardness, color, and texture. Surface effects and color are the result of slips or glazes applied before firing. The beads may also be hand-painted or set with a decal. The nature of ceramic-bead manufacture instills a good deal of individual variation among the beads in size, shape, and effects. Handmade clay beads may be somewhat asymmetrical and perforated with a toothpick before firing.

ceremonial beadwork Much Native North American beadwork relates to specific ceremonies or dances, such as that on the beaded leather armband shown. It bears the image of a deer's head, typically associated with deer dancers, who honor their animal brother and express gratitude that he offers his life to support them. Holding the animal sacred, the dancers mimic the deer's movements. An elderly dancer gave me this armband, which he had beaded and worn, to give to my son when he came of age. He expressly forbade my wearing it or allowing anyone else to do so, because of its significance. Adorned with leather ties accented with crow beads and tin cones, the armband features symbolic patterns reflecting the four sacred directions.

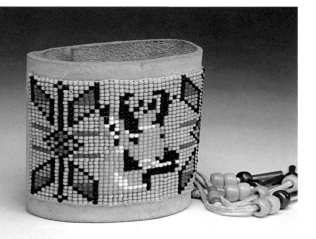

among manufacturers. Besides beading, decorative chains are used for hanging lamps, plants, draperies, and other interior-design effects. *See also* jewelry chain.

chain mail A metallic meshwork created from multiple interlinking chains once used to supplement protective body armor in the Middle Ages and earlier. Today some jewelry makers create chain-mail bracelets and necklaces with interlinking open circles or other shapes of metal to form a sort of pliable metallic meshwork. It is also sometimes referred to by the French term *chaîne maille.*

Ceylon pearl beads Also called simply *Ceylon* or *pearl,* glass beads with an opaque to translucent satin luster or pearlescent finish, often produced in pastel colors, manufactured in Japan, France, Taiwan, and the Czech Republic. Ceylon, the island in the Indian Ocean known as Sri Lanka, is not the primary source.

chain-nose pliers A tool, available in different designs, for opening and closing links on a chain or for handling metal wire. Some chain-nose pliers have a serrated edge for gripping. Others have smooth nylon jaws that minimize scratching of precious metals like silver and gold. Still others have a cutting edge that cannot only bend wire but cut it, which makes the tool more versatile. Chain-nose pliers are great for closing bead tips, crimping beads in tight places, and wrapping wire. They are also called *rosary pliers.* Photo by JG. *See* pliers for various jaw types.

chain A series of beads, rings, or metal components linked together or fitted into one another to create a strand. Among the many different types are those made of linked ovals or loops. A few popular chain types are the *box* or *Venetian, bead, Byzantine, rope, rolo, snake,* and *wheat* chain. Other types are the *Figaro, curb, fancy,* and *mariner*; names and styles may vary from jeweler to jeweler or

chain stitch   Any technique for making a chain of beads to be used as a bracelet, necklace strap, or clothing embellishment, etc. *See also* daisy chain, right-angle weave, crochet, and tambour.

chain types   Here are some common jewelry chain types. The *box chain* link is wide, square, and interconnected with the next link. In the *Byzantine chain,* two pairs of oval links are linked and then separated by a larger, thicker third link attached to each pair. In the *cable chain,* round rings of the same size are linked together. The *curb chain* uses oval links that are twisted and may be diamond-cut so that they lie flat. The *Figaro chain* alternates use of circular and rectangular links, usually three small circular links followed by a single long link. The *herringbone chain* consists of a series of short, flat, slanted, and parallel links in two or more rows with the direction of the slant alternating row by row. The *mariner chain* has oval links with a bar dividing the middle of each link. The *omega chain* is flat and has rectangular, smooth, rounded metal plates side by side that are crimped along the ends onto a metal mesh strip. The rope chain has two thick strands that are woven together, creating a spiral appearance. The *serpentine chain* has a series of small and flat S-shaped links that are close together and held in place by a twin set of links below them. The *Singapore chain* has a series of flat, diamond-cut, interwoven loops and resembles a twisted herringbone. The *snake chain* has a series of round and wavy metal rings joined side by side to form a smooth, flexible tube.

chalcedony   Microcrystalline or cryptocrystalline (having a microscopic crystal structure) quartz group, composed of silicon dioxide, that includes many varieties of gemstones that have a waxy luster, including carnelian, sard, agate, flint, jasper, chrysoprase, onyx, bloodstone, moss agate, chert, thundereggs (geodes), and petrified wood. The stones are often semitransparent or translucent but sometimes opaque or dull and display radiating stalactitic or grapelike shapes. The crystal system has trigonal fibrous aggregates. On the Mohs scale of hardness it rates 6.5 to 7. The word *chalcedony* originates from the name of an ancient Greek town, Chalkedon (Chalcedon), located in Asia Minor. Chalcedony is porous and can be dyed. It is often used as a species name by gemologists for all cryptocrystalline quartzes as well as for the bluish-white-gray variety, actual chalcedony in the narrow sense. To confuse things more, this group is sometimes called the agate group. *See also* quartz.

chandelier   An elaborate light fixture hung from the ceiling with two or more branches bearing lightbulbs (or candles in earlier centuries). Chandeliers are decorated with faceted glass, lead crystal, and other reflective materials designed to reflect, catch, and scatter light that are often strung like beads or suspended like pendants with wire or another sturdy material. A fancy pendant or elaborate earrings with suspended fancy dangling beads that resemble a chandelier in design are also sometimes called chandeliers. Actual crystals and beads from old chandeliers can be recycled for jewelry making.

channel-set Jewels that are channel-set sit in a metal channel held in place by a rim which runs along the edge. Most are round or baguette-shaped.

chaplet A string of beads that can be worn as a rosary bracelet or carried in the pocket, convenient for counting prayers at whatever time of day; or a set of prayer beads called a *decade*, meaning ten beads, part of a rosary with five decades. Also called a *single-decade rosary*, the beads can be repeated to count all the prayers in the rosary. An interesting example is the trademarked Virtues or Vices Chaplet, designed to promote personal spiritual growth by helping overcome vices and practicing virtues. Each time you exercise a virtue, like avoiding gossip, you move a bead on the string, the goal being to move ten beads throughout the day. Chaplets are sometimes sold as souvenirs at sacred places. The photo shows a delicate child's bracelet, made with pressed-glass rose beads accented with Bali

silver beads and a sterling silver cross and clasp. *See also* chotki, mala, paternoster, and rosary beads.

charlotte beads Usually made in Europe, these glass beads have a single, flat facet, often cut by hand. Charlotte beads have usually been size 13/0 or smaller, but newer beads are also sold in size 8. The facet, or cut, provides a wonderful sparkle when it reflects light. These beads are extremely popular and are usually sold in small hanks, approximately 6 inches (15 cm) long. The same type of bead in sizes other than 13/0 is known as a *one-cut* or a *true-cut* (referring to the single facet). However, some dealers have considered charlottes to be the French antique metallic-cut beads made of gold, silver, and bronze.

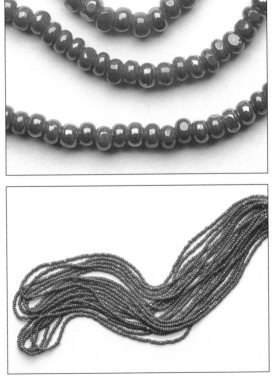

charms These jewelry components or findings represent a worldwide multicultural trait: that of wearing certain small objects assigned a special significance. They may include amulets, spiritually protective pendants, religious medals, and talismans supposedly having magical, protective, or lucky qualities. Charms may represent symbolic animals, plants, or totems; some, like flowers, are merely attractive ornaments. Shown is a human figure stamped out of brass and then gold-plated.

charoite Named after the Chara River in Russia near where it is found, an opaque to translucent mineral in colors ranging from lavender to lilac to violet to dark purple, with swirls of white, gray, and black fibrous material. Charoite is composed of silicon, calcium, potassium, hydrogen, and oxygen; it can be mixed with manganese and quartz. It may have inclusions of the mineral tenaksite that may appear as golden spires. Its Mohs scale hardness factor is 4.5 to 5. The mineral was not discovered until the 1940s.

chasing In metalwork, typically in silver, embossing or adding ornamental flourishes, such as gadroons, to a piece, particularly notable in the baroque style.

chatoyancy An effect that resembles the narrow band of white light in a cat's eye, caused by the reflection of light by parallel fibers, needles, or channels. Various gemstones, as well as glass beads made to simulate them, exhibit chatoyancy. The adjective is *chatoyant,* from the French *chat* for "cat."

check valve Also called a *flashback arrestor,* a piece of safety equipment on a gas tank, like that used to supply gas to a torch used in glass beadmaking. The valve allows the gas to flow in one direction only.

cherry quartz A type of dyed quartz; also, a glass imitation. *See also* strawberry quartz.

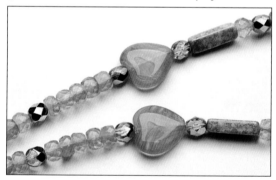

chert Cryptocrystalline sedimentary rock made of finely grained silicon dioxide (silica). Chert varies in color from white to black and many colors in between, dependent on the trace elements present. Small fossils may be included in the rocks, since it resists weathering, recrystallization, and metamorphism. Jasper, for instance, is a kind of chert that is red due to iron inclusions. Chert is found in spherical and irregular nodules and in thin or thick beds. *See also* flint.

chevron beads A type of multilayered bead made from glass cane, sometimes called *star* or *rosetta beads*. Thought to have its origins in Venice with hot-shop techniques for making the original tubing, the bead can have as many as seven layers of different colors of glass with facets cut into the ends. Common colors are blue, red, white, green, and yellow. Chevrons are commonly associated with African and Native North American beadwork. Shown are a variety of colors and sizes, some more collectible than others.

chevron chain Also called *zigzag stitch*, a good basic stitch for beading bracelets, anklets, and necklace straps.

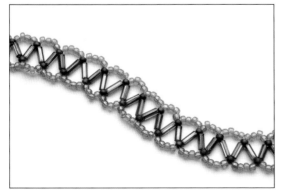

chicklettes Flat, rectangular beads about 5 mm long, 4 mm wide, and 3 mm thick; also spelled *chiclets*, like the gum (Chiclets).

chili beads Popular beads made in the colors and shape of chili peppers, often of glass or clay. The beads here were handmade from clay by Karen Sheals-Terranova.

chili stitch A three-dimensional bead stitch also called *log cabin*, *alligator*, and *gecko*. The alternate spelling is *chile stitch*. The origin of the stitch is uncertain, but many South American trinkets sold to tourists use this stitch. The chili stitch refers to the chili pepper, as pictured in the photo. *See also* gecko and alligator stitch.

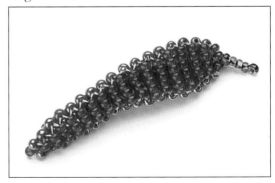

Chinese boxwood beads The hand-carved and usually large and gourd-shaped beads are from the dense, durable wood of the boxwood tree

commonly tie garments closed, rather than buttons, favored in the Western world. Knotting, created with bone needles and rope or threads, was originally merely functional; however, the use of knots in clothing and jewelry has developed through the centuries into a decorative art form.

choker A necklace that fits snugly around the neck, generally around 14 to 16 inches (35 to 40 cm) in length. Shown is a choker of abalone pukalets, garnets, and silver beads strung on 18-gauge bead-stringing wire, and finished with a barrel clasp, created by Joaquin Flores.

or shrub (genus *Buxus*), with varieties found on five continents. Boxwood can be polished to a silky smooth finish. Bonnie Gibson assembled this necklace by adding the cord and beads. *See also* boxwood (Chinese boxwood).

Chinese knotting An ancient decorative craft in which knots symbolize longevity, prosperity, happiness, and the like. Knots made in a rope were once used to record time. Among other purely decorative uses, Chinese knots

chotki This is the Russian term for a set of prayer beads used by Eastern Orthodox Christians (Greek and Russian). The Greek term is *komboschoinia*. These particular prayer beads consist of a set of 25, 33, 50, 100, or 103 beads, not including spacer beads. The original chotki was a prayer rope made out of knotted wool (sometimes with beads as well as knots at intervals), which had a knotted cross at the end. The various knots were said to have been made in the shape of a cross so that the devil could not untie them. Many monks traditionally wore them as wristlets on the left wrist as a constant

reminder to pray. Today many chotki are made of beads rather than rope and have either a tassel used to wipe one's tears or a cross at the end. Typical bead materials are olivewood, rosewood, bodhi seeds, rudraksha seeds, rattan, yak bone, glass, or metal. *See also* prayer beads and komboschoinia.

Christmas beads Beads that feature symbols, shapes, or colors commonly associated with Christmas. The beads in the bracelets shown have colored-glass images of Santa Claus, trees,

snowflakes, snowmen, candy canes, reindeer, and stars. These beads were made in China. *See also* African Christmas beads.

chromium A lustrous, malleable, silvery or steel-gray metal, often alloyed with other metals to achieve hardness. Chromium can take a high polish and has a high melting point. As a surface metal coating it prevents the base metal from tarnishing or oxidizing. It is commonly used for chrome plating or alloyed with stainless steel for tableware because of its ability to achieve an attractive metallic sheen. Chromium is the coloring agent for the gemstone ruby (corundum), and its salts are used to tan leather. It is found in the mineral crocoite, a source for various pigments in paints. The term *chromium* includes the root word *chroma,* from the Greek for "color." It is found in Africa, Turkey, Kazakhstan, and India.

chrysoberyl The transparent to opaque gemstone beryllium aluminum oxide. It has an orthorhombic crystal system of thick-tabled or ingrown triplets and a Mohs scale hardness factor of 8.5. Colors range from golden yellow to greenish yellow, green, brown, and red. In Greek the word *chrysoberyl* means "gold." Alexandrite and chrysoberyl cat's-eye are the most valued varieties. The mineral is found in deposits in Brazil, Russia, Zimbabwe, Madagascar, Sri Lanka, and the United States.

chrysoberyl cat's-eye Chrysoberyl with inclusions produce a fine, silvery-white line that appears as a light ray that seems to move, much like the cat's pupil. It is also simply called *cat's-eye.*

chrysocolla This mineral is hydrated copper silicate that's green or blue, opaque or translucent, with a greasy vitreous luster. Its Mohs scale hardness factor is 2 to 4. It is found near copper deposits in Australia, France, Chile, Zaire, Republic of the Congo, Israel, and Cornwall in England, and in New Mexico, Arizona, Utah, and Pennsylvania in the United States. It is found with trace elements of quartz, turquoise, copper, and silver. Chrysocolla is sometimes mistaken for malachite or turquoise. This brooch designed by Sylvia Elam uses a chrysocolla cabochon.

chrysocolla quartz Chrysocolla with a quartz intergrowth.

chrysolite *See* olivine and peridot.

chrysoprase A translucent to opaque green or apple green variety of chalcedony, composed of silicon dioxide. Its Mohs scale hardness is 6.5 to 7 and its crystal system is trigonal microcrystalline aggregates. Chrysoprase is considered the most valuable gemstone in the chalcedony group. The coloring agent is nickel and may fade in sunlight or when heated but recover when stored in a moist area. The stone may be confused with chrome chalcedony (which gets its color from chromium rather than nickel), jade, prehnite, smithsonite, and variscite. Some chalcedony on the market may be dyed green. *Chrysoprase matrix* has brown or white matrix in the rock. Chrysoprase, commonly used in cabochons, was once favored for interior decoration in Prague and Berlin.

cinder beads Beads characterized by black specks or "cinders" embedded in the surface.

cinnabar This dye or pigment, made from mercury sulfide, is cinnamon to scarlet or brick red in color. The Mohs scale hardness of the mineral ore is 2 to 2.5. It was mined during the Roman Empire for its mercury content and has been the main ore of mercury throughout the centuries. Since cinnabar is toxic, in more recent times, substitutes for this warm red pigment have been developed. A type of Chinese lacquerware with a distinctive red was originally derived from the mineral ore.

cinnebar Wood from the cinnebar tree that grows in Southeast Asia; not to be confused with the mineral cinnabar (mercury sulfide, a common but toxic dye). Patterns are often pressed or carved into the soft wood.

cinnebar beads These wooden beads are made from the wood of the cinnebar tree that grows in Southeast Asia. The beads are carved by hand or pressed by machine and treated with multiple layers of lacquer or resin and usually dyed.

circlet This headpiece or crown without arches or an internal cap can be described as a tiara or a metal band crafted in a circular form and worn on the crown of the head. Circlets can be made from bands of metal, metal braid, wire, or ribbon, with dangles of beads or fabric draping.

circular Comanche weave A beading stitch that produces round flat designs, such as those for pendants. It is a variant of brick stitch or Apache weave. The pendant shown uses this stitch with bugle beads, tile beads, seed beads, and 3-mm fire-polish beads, around a center fire-polish bead 10 mm in diameter. Such rounds are used in hair ties, necklaces, and other pieces of jewelry.

circular gourd stitch This interesting technique is the foundation for baskets and vessels. Shown is a miniature basket made by David Bingell.

See also three-dimensional gourd stitch and circular peyote stitch.

circular netting rope One of several categories of bead netting. The rope shown here has a hollow core, although some ropes are beaded around a cord or rope. This rope, finished with sterling silver cones and a toggle clasp, has a four-color pattern that seems to spiral.

circular netting stitch This stitch can be used for either a round flat object or a three-dimensional one. It also makes an attractive bead rope. Shown are a netted basket (below) and a bag (next page) made with a netting stitch.

example of a horsehair hatband, popular in the southwestern United States and Indian country. It is beaded around a fabric cord for durability. The rope actually uses five different patterns with a rainbow color scheme. *See also* round peyote stitch.

citrine A transparent light yellow to orange variety of quartz, silicon dioxide, with a Mohs scale hardness rating of 7. The name suggests its lemon yellow color; the coloring agent is iron. Natural citrines are rare. Commercial "citrines" are often heat-treated amethysts ("burnt amethysts") or smoky quartzes. Nearly all heat-treated citrines have a reddish tone; natural citrines are usually pale yellow. Citrine is commonly mistaken for the more valuable gemstone topaz. (It has sometimes been falsely called gold topaz or Madeira topaz.) Citrine deposits are found in Argentina, Brazil, Namibia, Myanmar, Russia, Spain, Scotland, and the United States. Shown are some delicate saucer-shaped beads for use in jewelry designs.

circular peyote stitch Also called *gourd stitch*, this stitch is most useful for making three-dimensional objects. Shown is a colorful

clapper beads Shown are clapper beads made of copper. When such beads have a small piece of metal inside to make a ringing sound, they are called *bells*. Clapper beads come with and without ringers. When strung

together, they strike against each other to make a nice sound, especially when worn on the ankle. This type of bead, popularly used to accent bracelets and necklaces, functions as a sort of charm.

clarity The amount and quality of light transmitted through a gemstone relative to the type of stone. Clarity depends on the internal quality of a gem and whether it has inclusions, cracks, spots, clouds, blemishes, or imperfections. Some gemstones may undergo *clarity enhancements* that disguise the gem's flaws and may improve its appearance but not its inherent quality or value. The Gemological Institute of America has eight grading levels for clarity; the lower the clarity, the less valuable the stone.

clasp A closure for bead or jewelry strings, such as necklaces or bracelets. A functional finding that connects two ends for a comfortable fit, clasps can be made of metal, bone, glass, gemstone, or even woven fibers. Some common clasp types are the lobster claw, barrel, spring ring, S-hook, hook and eye, and toggle. There are various types of safety clasps, sometimes with an added safety chain.

Many unusual designer clasps, too numerous to mention, are also on the market.

claws Animal claws, usually bear claws, have been drilled to use as beads or pendants. The thread hole is typically at the top of the claw, allowing the pointed end to dangle from a necklace or other item. In some cultural traditions, the wearer may be thought to assume something of the spirit of the animal. The wearer of a bear claw, for instance, may emulate or hope to realize the bear's strength.

clay A natural material made from earth that can be molded when moist and fired or heated to produce beads, pottery, and other objects. The term also applies to polymer clay and a number of other similar materials that may include tissue paper, newspaper, and water-based glue. Commercial clays contain diverse ingredients that act as hardening and coloring agents. To make a homemade clay for molding and shaping beads, combine cornstarch, flour, salt, and water. In the Andes Mountains, artisans often fashion intricate pottery pendants for necklaces from local clay.

cleavage Used to define how a rock, mineral, or crystal fractures or breaks along certain planes within it.

clip-on earring finding A piece of hardware that allows earrings to be attached to an ear without the benefit of a hole or piercing.

clip-on earrings An alternative to having ears pierced in order to attach jewelry, clip-ons have a hinge or screw design that grips the earlobe.

cloisonné A technique for applying enamel to metal surfaces. Designs are outlined first with fine-gauge bronze or copper wire that is bent or hammered into the desired shape, and soldered or pasted onto the surface, creating *cloisons* (French for "partitions") that separate colors. Glass paste or powder colored with metallic oxides is applied by hand to the enclosed spaces, and the piece is fired, melting the glass. There is no limit to the objects that

can be worked in cloisonné. Shown are a turtle, a cross, an oval, a butterfly, and a heart.

C-LON *See* stringing thread.

clutch A finding used to fasten a post earring. The clutch, also called an ear nut or an earring nut, attaches to the post behind the ear.

coating A treatment in which some type of finish is applied to enhance a gemstone's natural appearance by altering its color or adding special effects.

cobalt beads Also called *Russian blues*, these fine Bohemian glass beads are prized for their color. A collector or dealer probably coined the name, since they are not made in Russia. Paradoxically, they also do not contain the metallic element cobalt. The five-sided or six-sided cane beads are faceted on each corner. Although cobalt blue is a favorite color, the so-called Russian blues are produced in other hues as well.

coco beads Beads made from coconut shells.

COE This stands for *coefficient of expansion*, a scientific term denoting the degree to which a material expands and contracts in a fixed temperature range. *See also* borosilicate glass.

coiling A beading technique in which the strung beads are wrapped or coiled around an object. Shown here are a wooden spoon and fork, and a doll with coiled beadwork. The origins are unknown, but the technique is often seen in African beadwork. *See also* wrapped stitch.

center. Chinese coins are very popular for this purpose. As portable wealth for nomads, coins have been used in lands as diverse as India by the Sherpa and the American Southwest by the Navajos. The coins, originally valued for their precious metal content, were often worn or carried on the body for trade purposes. The Native American concho belt uses stamped silver components that can be removed when necessary. Coins may be an important part of dowry necklaces used by diverse cultures.

collar The raised lip around the edge of the bead hole or near the end of the bead seen in profile.

collared bead A bead shape with extra material resembling a collar at the lip or neck of the bead hole.

collier A choker, from the French for "necklace" or "collar."

color-lined A bead that is usually clear glass on the outside with a separate opaque color inside the bead's hole. If the color is only a surface dye, not inherent in the glass, it tends to fade with time and light exposure.

coin beads A bead shape that is round and flat like a coin. Coin beads are thinner than tabular beads, which may also be flat but can assume various shapes, such as round, square, diamond, and more. Coin beads are sometimes referred to as *dime beads*.

coin silver A product that is at least 900 thousandth of pure silver.

coins Where the law permits, real currency or imitations of coins are used as beads, especially when the desired coin has a hole in the

color-shot Dyed.

color wheel A tool (showing the color spectrum in a circle) used for color matching and coordinating that helps discover new or better color combinations. Visit your library or community college, or consult the Internet for more information on how to use this tool for beadwork projects to discover primary, secondary, tertiary, complementary, and other color schemes. The three colors found in the small circle in the center of the color wheel are the primaries yellow, blue, and red, here shown as yellow, cyan, and magenta (printer's colors). Secondary colors are created by mixing two of the primaries, so yellow + red = orange or blue + yellow = green.

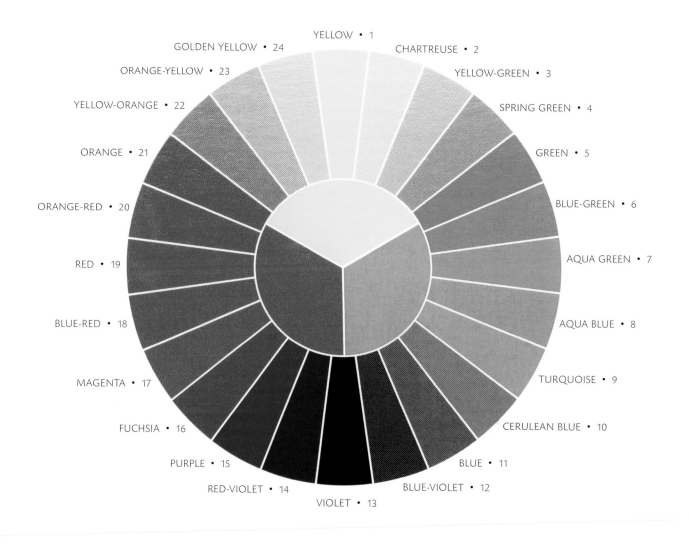

colored stone Generally, all gemstones, even those that are colorless, except diamonds.

Comanche weave A particular bead stitch also known as *Apache weave, brick stitch,* or *stacking stitch*, popular for making earrings. It is equally good for relatively three-dimensional objects like amulet bags, since it produces a sturdy beaded fabric. *See* circular Comanche stitch, Apache weave, and brick stitch. Find stitch diagrams in Part V.

combing Dragging a metal tool through soft glass in the process of making wound-glass beads to achieve various decorative effects (other glass colors may drain into the cuts, for instance) or to create permanent grooves, ribs, or ridges, such as those found in melon beads.

compatibility In glass beadmaking, a term denoting the degree to which different types of glass can be used together. Some glass varieties cannot be combined in the molten state, because the mixture will fracture in the cooling process. *See* hard glass.

concho From the Spanish *concha*, meaning "shell," a finding, usually of stamped metal,

used for decorating clothing or jewelry. It is often strung with leather and beads to make earrings, pendants, and segmented belts. Conchos were originally made in sterling silver and worn as signs of wealth, but today they are more often made in German silver or nickel silver, which is an alloy of nickel, copper, and other metals, containing no elemental silver. The concho belt popular in the southwestern United States is strung on leather or silver rings so that the individual conchos can be removed. Shown below left is a concho of silver-plated base metal. *See also* nickel silver.

cone A finding used to end bead strings in necklaces and earrings. Shown is a half-inch (12.5-mm) sterling-silver cone. The photos under *circular netting rope* and *rosette necklace* show how cones are used.

confetti beads Tortoise beads with multi-colored stripes and swirls, typically pink, blue, and green. Sometimes the stripes are uniform, and sometimes they are poorly formed.

connector Anything used to attach components together, such as a jump ring, clasp, head pin, or chain.

Conso *See* stringing thread.

construct Also called an industrial, a long bar usually worn on the upper part of the outer ear through two holes pierced through the cartilage.

continental needlepoint An embroidery technique in which beads are sewn individually onto the intersection of two canvas threads. This traditional technique is worked in horizontal rows from right to left. At the end of the row, the work is turned and the stitching proceeds again from right to left.

conus shell A cone-shaped shell of mollusks usually cut into disk-shaped beads or strung whole. Conus shells may come from any of about 700 species of marine snails of the *Conus* genus. Their first use dates at least to 3000 B.C.

copal A semifossilized form of amber, this mature tree resin has been used as an incense, notably during the sweat lodge ceremony and for energy cleansings and aura healings by indigenous cultures in Mexico. The word *copal* is derived from the Nahuatl word *copalli,* which means "incense." While its softness limits its uses, copal sometimes substitutes for amber. One way of distinguishing amber from copal is that the former can build up a static electrical charge. Heat and pressure are thought to support the process of polymerization and turpene evaporation that occurs in the creation of amber. Copal might be thought of as what's created in the transition phase between tree resin and amber. This tree resin is also sometimes called *pom. See* amber and resin.

copper A pinkish red or golden colored metal that has been a popular component of jewelry from ancient to modern times. Copper does not easily tarnish or corrode and is hygienic (it has even been found to slow the growth of *E. coli* bacteria). It is lightweight, tough, ductile (drawn out or extended with ease), malleable (easily shaped), and nonmagnetic.

Among common alloys of copper are zinc (brass), tin (phosphor bronzes), aluminum (aluminum bronzes), silicon (silicon bronzes), and nickel (nickel silvers and copper nickel, sometimes called cupro nickel). Over 2,200 alloys of copper are said to exist, with varying compositions, densities, hardness, tensile strength, elasticity, and electrical resistance or conductivity. Copper alloys tend to be harder and stronger than pure copper.

Copper can be easily joined by soldering and brazing. Copper has been found in Bronze Age arrowheads and coins. Through the ages, copper has been used for statues, ornaments, cookware, building components, piping, and myriad industrial uses.

copper drill This coring tool was used in ancient Egypt for making holes in beads in soft stones. In more recent centuries, most beads are machined and molded around metal tubing, which avoids the need for drilling holes. Handmade lampwork beads are also molded around tubing. Harder metal drills that use diamond or steel drill bits are used to drill gemstones. Other common hand tools used specifically for beaded jewelry-making include tweezers, awls, bead reamers, crimper or cutting tools, and various types of pliers, such as round-nose or flat-nose.

copper-lined Beads that have a reflective copper lining, giving them additional sparkle. Other similar beads may have linings of silver, gold, or other metals.

coral This popular gemstone with naturally occurring branch shapes, found in shades of red, pink, gold, blue, and black, derives from living sea creatures from the class Anthozoa that are harvested from reefs in tropical waters and polished. The marine animal's hardened exterior (exoskeleton) is made of calcium carbonate and protein. Coral animals (many individual polyps a few millimeters in diameter act together as a single organism) live in colonies that grow undersea in clear or shallow tropical waters where sunlight can reach them. A colony begins with one polyp that replicates to create others. A coral reef is made of countless coral colonies that grow on and among the exoskeletons of those that lived before them, plus other organisms that deposit limestone. In tropical waters, reefs can grow to be hundreds of miles long. Some worry that harvesting coral from reefs around the world has disturbed the natural underwater ecology. Among other places, coral is found in the Mediterranean and Caribbean Seas and off the Pacific coast of Japan and Taiwan, around the Malaysian Archipelago, the northern coast of Australia, and Hawaii.

Coral is translucent or opaque, and unworked coral is dull. When polished, usually with sandstone and emery and then with felt wheels, it achieves a vitreous luster. Coral can be sensitive to heat, hot solutions, and acids. When worn, the color may fade.

Coral is popularly made into prayer beads and good-luck charms against the "evil eye." In use worldwide since ancient times, the organic material has been harvested and cut into cabochons and beads that are carved, faceted, and sometimes dyed to enhance their color. Many beaders prefer coral's natural branches. With a Mohs scale hardness factor of 3 to 4, it is somewhat porous and fragile. The crystal system is trigonal and micro-crystalline. Noble coral (*Corallium rubrum*) is the most desirable type. Black coral, an organic horn substance, is the least desirable. The peach-veined tiger moth, designed by Karin Houben, has wings of glass Delica beads, a body of large antique glass pearl,

tiger's-eye for eyes, and branch-coral antennae. *See also* pink coral, branch coral, and prayer beads.

coral imitations *Sherpa coral* is red or orange glass, typically made into beads for Tibetans who could not afford genuine coral. Most such beads are 200 to 400 years old.

coral seed The glossy red seed with a black spot is also called *crab's eye* or *mescal seed.* This brightly colored seed, which originates in tropical jungles, is poisonous to humans and animals if ingested. Its botanical name, *Arbus precatorius,* means "prayerful" or "praying." Possibly different seeds, such as the *Ormosia monosperma,* imported from India and used in Europe for rosaries, appear quite similar to these toxic seeds.

cord In general terms, cord is a flexible length of fibers or thread twisted into a long strand. Anything used to string beads, such as elastic, hemp, cotton, or leather. A bead cord can also consist of beads sewn onto a cotton, polyester, nylon, leather, or fabric cord. *See also* individual cord types and bead ropes.

cord caps Also called *tips, coils,* and *end caps,* these metal findings, generally used on leather, cotton, or satin cord, give a neat, professional finish to a necklace or bracelet.

core-formed The process of making a glass bead in which material other than that from the bead's exterior is used to form the base or perforation of the bead and is later removed or disposed of. The core material is usually heat-resistant and unlikely to burn. When a metal rod is used in the same process, the bead is "rod-formed."

corn beads Real corn kernels can be dyed and strung as beads in colorful jewelry, as shown in these necklaces. The corn must be treated for microscopic mites by freezing and drying before it is used. Though somewhat fragile, biodegradable jewelry will provide years of enjoyment if protected from harsh conditions like extreme heat or moisture. The item on the right with the turquoise-blue beads is called a *cornflower necklace.*

corn stitch This versatile technique, also called *square stitch* and *round stitch*, produces what looks like rows of corn. The beadwork is done in a rectangular shape and then seamed into a three-dimensional bead tube. Shown is a beaded corn earring stuffed with bits of real leather to create the corn husks.

cornaline d'Aleppo This bead type is made with two layers of wound or drawn glass, usually with white glass in the center, but other colors are sometimes used. They date from the 1500s or earlier. The Italian name *cornaline d'Aleppo* ("carnelians of milk") may refer to the appearance of this antique bead or to Aleppo, Syria, which was located on major trading routes. (Some sources attribute

this name to a type of agate stone commonly found in Aleppo thought to ward off a red boil with a center of pus.) Notable manufacturing centers are in Italy, France, Czech Republic, and northern Africa. These beads are also known as white-heart beads for their white core. They are also called Hudson Bay beads because early settlers and fur traders around the Great Lakes and Hudson Bay once traded them to Native North Americans (*First Nations* in Canadian parlance) for fur pelts.

Today they are commonly seen with a dark red outside color, but they are also available in green, blue, pink, yellow and lighter shades of red. Sometimes the center is off-white or yellow. They range in size from small seed beads to larger pony or crow beads. They have also been considered African trade beads because they were once traded to Africa. They are also found in antique and contemporary Native American jewelry designs. *See also* white-heart beads and Hudson Bay beads.

corundum Transparent to opaque precious gemstones, composed of aluminum oxide, have a Mohs scale hardness of 9, second only to that of the diamond. Corundum is more popularly known as the *ruby* (red) and *sapphire* (usually blue but may include other colors) species. Corundums of all colors except red are classified as sapphires; colors may include various blues, colorless, pinks, oranges, yellows, greens, purples, and black. The crystal system for rubies is trigonal with hexagonal prisms, tables, or rhombohedrons, and that for sapphires is trigonal, double points, barrel and tabloid shapes, and hexagonal pyramids. Both species exhibit pleochroism. *Emery,* used as a polishing material, is composed of fine-grained corundum, magnetite, hematite, and quartz. The term *corundum* is thought to have originated in India in reference to the ruby.

costume jewelry Designates inexpensive jewelry typically using synthetic or artificial stones, glass, plastic, and base metals rather than more precious ones. Faux gems are commonly used in creations worn by both rich and poor. The term derives from its use to supplement costumes worn onstage by actors. Today screen actors may wear fabulous fakes. Some older pieces, however, may be collectible and expensive.

cotton cord Shown are examples of woven and waxed cord, useful for stringing and leatherwork projects. Cotton cord comes in different thicknesses or diameters.

couching In this method of sewing beads onto fabric, the strung beads are tacked down with thread. Often called *appliqué*, this technique is one of several methods of attaching beads to fabric. There are both single-needle and two-needle methods of couching. *See also* appliqué, backstitch, and bead embroidery.

counting board An early form of abacus that used pebbles, tabular beads, or tokens to rep-

resent numbers assembled in columns along a line. Original counting "boards" were probably lines drawn in the sand in the marketplace on which pebbles or other tokens were placed to indicate specific sums. The Babylonians, Romans, Egyptians, Chinese, and probably the Incas (who used the *yupana*) and other groups had counting boards. *See also* abacus.

court beads Deriving from Buddhist prayer beads or Tibetan rosaries, these bead strands, also called *court chains,* were at one time required as official dress for Chinese court attendants during the Qing (Manchu) dynasty (1644–1912). Military officers as well as their wives and children were also required to wear them. Although they made glass beads and exported them, the beads preferred were the very finest, often made with special designs, colors, or shapes, or fashioned from gemstones.

cowrie shell Also spelled *cowry shell*. A type of glossy or highly polished and sometimes brightly marked seashell from any of the tropical marine gastropods, various snails of the *Cypraea* genus, used to embellish clothing and beadwork. Cowrie shells were once used as a medium of exchange for goods imported or traded among tribes, especially in Africa and the South Pacific. When used as beads or in decoration, cowrie shells are drilled at both ends to attach to fabric, or they are drilled at the top so that they can dangle from jewelry or clothing. Some cultures consider the shell a symbol of female sexuality. Called *eye crackers* in Iran, cowrie shells are thought to be effective against the evil eye because of their general eye shape. Associated in folklore with envy, a glance from the evil eye is thought to impose a curse. The Ojibway have used them in the Midewiwin (Grand Medicine Society) ceremonies in Canada and the United States. The Dahomey have used them in divination. They have also functioned as ornaments, symbols, and dice in board games. *See also* amulet.

crab's eye *See* coral seed and jequirity bean.

crackle beads Beads with a surface resembling that of cracked ice. The process for making crackle beads was invented by Venetian glass bead makers in the 16th century. It involves heating, cooling, and reheating the glass. Crackle beads are usually sold as round beads and as polished chips.

cradle board The Kiowa, Yakama, Nez Perce, Okanogan, and Navajo, among other nomadic Native North American peoples, used the cradle board for swaddling, securing, and carrying infants on the mother's back or for resting the cradle and baby upright against a tree. Straps were secured from the board around the mother's shoulders or head. This practical carrying device freed the mother's hands. Cradle boards are constructed of various materials, woven fibers, cloth fabric, wood, leather, feathers, fur, horsehair, straw, canvas, ribbons, fringe, leather laces, thread, sinew, and nearly always beads, according to local availability, tradition, and preference. Kiowa and Yakama mothers adorn their cradle boards, sculpted works of art lovingly made, with beadwork. Okanogan mothers may have elaborate beaded appliqués on theirs.

crazing A network of fine cracks that can be produced in the surface of dichroic glass by the application of heat.

crazy-lace agate A kind of chalcedony, member of the quartz family, composed of silicon dioxide, this agate has a Mohs scale hardness factor of 7. Mined only in Mexico, it is also called *Mexican lace agate*. Crazy-lace agate exhibits distinctive bands and swirls of both translucent and opaque color, including white, gray, brown, orange, and sometimes black. *See also* quartz and agate.

created A dealer's term sometimes loosely applied to synthetic or imitation gemstones that have the chemical composition of their counterpart in nature.

crimp-bead cover A metal finding designed to neaten the appearance of a crimp bead by covering it.

crimp beads A small bead of soft metal designed to collapse or crush easily when pinched (squeezed) with flat-nose or chain-nose pliers or a crimping tool, used to attach stringing wire to a clasp. Crimp beads, also called *crimper beads,* generally come in round and tubular shapes, with a smooth or textured finish. Copper, sterling silver, base metal, and silver-, gold-, nickel-plated, and gold-filled varieties are available. Crimp beads range in size from 1 mm to 4 mm. The sizes easiest to find are small and large. The main consideration in selecting a crimp bead is the size of the wire in the project. The wire is usually passed through the crimp bead at least twice; a larger bead can accommodate several strands of a multistrand necklace. Shown are sterling-silver crimp beads. Find the chart of crimp sizes to use with stringing wire in Part IV and drawings in Part V related to finishing techniques. *See also* crimp pliers, also called crimpers.

crimp ends Used the same way as crimp beads, crimp ends are larger findings, good for leather, rubber, satin, or cotton cord. They are too large to use with stringing wire. Apply a dab of strong jewelry adhesive to the cord, push it into the crimp end, and squeeze, or *crimp* it slightly, with flat- or needle-nose pliers.

Crimp ends usually come with a clasp attached, or a ring for attaching a clasp. These designer findings are often handcrafted or custom-ordered, so the style varies.

crimp pliers Also called crimping tool or crimpers, a tool designed for use with crimp beads; its nose has two indentations. One indentation creates a groove in the crimp bead between the cables that run through it; the other rounds out the crimp bead around the cables against the groove. Crimp pliers give jewelry a more finished look and make the crimp bead more discrete. Flat-nose pliers will produce a flat, rather than a curved, crimp bead. However, both tools will work for attaching stringing wire to a clasp. The finished crimp can be hidden in a clamshell-type bead tip or a larger-hole bead. Find finishing techniques in Part V.

crimp tube A crimp bead that has a more elongated shape; it functions the same as a round crimp bead. *See* crimp bead.

crochet Needlework using interlocking stitches; the process of creating fabric from a length of cord, yarn, or thread, using a crochet hook. *See* crochet rope.

crochet rope A technique of bead crocheting in which beads prestrung on heavy-duty polyester thread are slip-stitched onto the exterior of a crocheted tube or rope. The finished product has great flexibility and durability. The crochet rope bracelet shown was beaded by Sylvia Elam. It is made with glass and copper (metal) seed beads in a distinctive pattern. *See* bead-crochet snake ropes.

cross-hole A bead hole or channel drilled vertically or side-to-side through drop beads or pendants.

cross-stitch A bead-embroidery term borrowed from sewing and needlepoint; in this technique, beads and thread are added to the fabric with each stitch, usually done on even-weave fabric specially designed for the purpose. The fabric is woven with the same number of vertical and horizontal threads per inch (or cm) so that each stitch will be the same length.

cross-trail beads Beads first produced in Venice in the mid-19th century, characterized by horizontal and vertical lines that cross paths.

cross-weaving A number of techniques that use beads woven together with thread or cord.

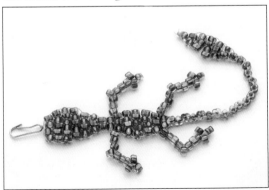

Shown here is a common starter project for children; it's a zipper pull made by Drew Sutton, age 9. Beginners use large-hole beads, especially crow beads, to make animal figures. This piece was made with artificial sinew and two-tone triangle beads, which give it a bumpy texture.

crow beads Sometimes called *roller beads*, crow beads are the large-hole beads often seen on leather fringe and in Native American beadwork. Approximately 7 to 9 mm wide, with a hole of around 2 mm, the beads are made of glass in France, the Czech Republic, Germany, Africa, and India. All such beads are similar in appearance but not totally consistent in size. Smaller beads of this type (5 to 6 mm) are often confused with other small beads, especially pony beads and tile beads

(tile beads have a thinner wall). Glass crow beads are much heavier than plastic and are usually cold to the touch, but crow beads come in plastic as well. Plastic has the advantage over glass of being lighter, more economical, and more readily available. However, plastic is not as durable; it's subject to becoming scratched and may become brittle over time. The first photo shows blue plastic crow beads with a molding seam visible around the perimeter. These are often used in children's craft projects and as clothing embellishments, where their light weight is an asset. The second photo shows glass crow beads of lavender, pink, and turquoise.

cruciform beads A separator bead set between sections of seven beads in an Anglican rosary. The bead is called *cruciform* for its cross shape.

crumb beads Solid-color, often black, wound-glass beads sprinkled with or rolled while hot in crushed glass, glass chips, or glass crumbs. Glass-bead makers call the glass bits *frits*. Crumb beads may have originated in Venice and are seen in the African trade.

cryptocrystalline An extremely fine crystalline rock texture, also called *microcrystalline*. The crystalline structure can be revealed only by high-powered microscopes in very thin sections when transmitted by polarized light. Chert and flint, types of sedimentary rocks, are cryptocrystalline, as are some volcanic rocks and a type of diamond, the carbonado. *See also* cryptocrystalline quartz.

cryptocrystalline quartz Also called *microcrystalline quartz,* this type of quartz has individual crystals only visible under very high magnification in thin slices with polarized light. Cryptocrystalline quartz, generally known as chalcedony, includes agate, petrified wood, chrysoprase, bloodstone, jasper, carnelian, moss agate, and sard. *Macrocrystalline quartz,* in contrast, has individual crystals that are visible to the naked eye. *See also* quartz.

crystal In chemistry and mineralogy, a term that describes a solid in which the atoms, molecules, or ions have been packed in a regularly ordered, repeating pattern that extends in three dimensions. The regularly repeating internal arrangement of the crystal's atoms determines its physical characteristics or properties, such as the number of its external plane faces. Crystals may be classified into seven systems based on their symmetry: *isometric* (or *cubic*), *trigonal, hexagonal, tetragonal, orthorhombic, triclinic,* or *monoclinic.* Crystalline structures can occur in all classes of materials with all types of chemical bonds. Many gems are found in crystal form. Crystals can be identified by their individual optical properties and physical properties, such as hardness, cleavage, heat conductivity, and electrical conductivity. The term *crystal* also refers to quartz that is transparent and colorless, or almost so.

crystal beads Beads of high-quality glass. They have a distinctive sparkle and come in a variety of shapes and sizes. Crystal glass is defined by the manufacturer and contains a specific lead content. At one time, the lead ingredient added weight to the finished product, which was taxed accordingly. That's when producers decided to cut expenses by faceting or cutting the crystal. Shown are Swarovski crystal beads. *See also* Swarovski crystals.

crystal geode A hollow, roughly spherical rock with a core lined with a bed of crystals. *See also* geode slice.

crystal pearls Crystal glass beads with a pearlized coating to give the appearance of pearls. *See also* glass pearls.

crystal system Crystals are categorized according to the way the crystals form. Crystals are homogeneous bodies that have regular lattice atoms, ions, or molecules. They are arranged geometrically so that their outer faces are flat. The arrangement of faces of a mineral is called its *habit*. Most crystals are small. In crystallography, crystals are divided into seven systems, which describe the axes and angles at which these axes intersect. Here are the seven crystal systems: *cubic, tetragonal, hexagonal, trigonal (rhombohedral), orthorhombic, monoclinic,* and *triclinic*. Other crystals may be described as amorphous.

crystalline quartz Crystalline quartz produces the hexagonal crystals seen in amethyst, rose quartz, rock crystal, and citrine. *See also* quartz.

crystallography The scientific study of crystals.

cube beads Beads in the shape of a cube, having six sides. The cube shape is common in other materials, including gemstones, wood, bone, and metal. Shown are two-tone glass beads.

cubic zirconia A simulated diamond of high quality, made in the laboratory. Composed of zirconium dioxide, these stones are popular for their attractive appearance and cost, which is a fraction of that of genuine diamonds.

They are optically flawless and usually color-less. Cubic zirconia have a Mohs scale hard-ness of 8.5 and isometric, single-crystal growth. They can be made in a variety of col-ors. (Do not confuse with zircon, composed of zirconium silicate.)

cubical right-angle weave A three-dimensional form of the flat right-angle-weave stitch, also called *tubular right-angle weave*. Four sides of right-angle-weave stitch create a squared-off cube or tube.

cuff (or cuff bracelet) A type of bangle or bracelet that does not close in a complete circle, often semicircular in shape, that is put on from the side of the wrist or the side of the upper or lower arm instead of being slipped over the hand. It is usually a wide metal band worn as a bracelet. *See* bangle.

cultured pearls Cultured pearls are products of nature induced by a little human engineer-ing. In nature, pearls result from the oyster's protective response to an irritant that the oyster isolates from its body and coats with nacre. To create a cultured pearl, someone introduces a tiny nucleus of shell or metal (mussel shells make the best nuclei) along with a tiny piece of oyster epithelial membrane (the lip of the mantle tissue) into the oyster. This stimulates the tissue to form a little sack that secretes nacre to coat the nucleus and form a pearl. This technique, invented and refined from 1896 to 1916 by Japanese entrepreneurs, revolutionized the pearl industry, making pearls more available and affordable. Pearls can also occur naturally. All pearls are graded based on shape, size, nacre thickness, lack of blemishes, and luster.

Round is the most popular shape. Cultured pearls are also sometimes called *cultivated pearls, saltwater pearls, or marine pearls. See also* freshwater pearls and pearls.

cut beads Beads that have one or more facets. Charlotte beads, also called *true-cuts,* are single-facet Czech glass seed beads, usually hand-cut. Other types of cut beads include two-cuts, three-cuts, and hex beads, which are six-sided. Facets on beads can be created in many ways: the bead may be drawn into tubes to form several-sides, wound with facets formed by a paddle while the beads are hot, molded, or formed by a rotat-ing wheel. Hand-faceting requires skill and precision. The term *tin-cut* describes the metal of the rotating wheel that was used to create the bead's facet(s).

cylinder A bead shape that's generally shorter than a tube and may have a larger hole. Also a type of bead; *See also* cylinder beads.

cylinder beads The barrel or tube shape of a small seed bead. For so small a bead, it tends to have a generous hole, making it easier to use than some other seed beads. There is considerable competition in the market among manufacturers of these beads. Until recently, Japanese manufacturer Miyuki Shoji was the chief producer of fine, precision-cut, glass cylinder beads, under the brand name Delica, and Miyuki set the standard for bead sizing and color numbers. However, a competitor named Toho now manufactures similar beads under the names Treasures and Aiko, and Magnifica is a third brand of cylinder beads, a registered trademark of Mill Hill. There is generally no guaranteed consistency of color numbers and sizes across manufacturers, so the beads cannot be used interchangeably.

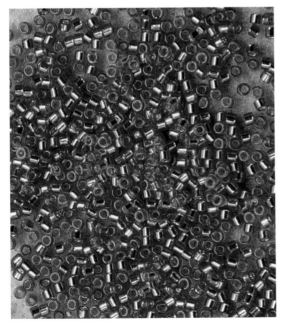

D

D thread Bead thread comes in a variety of thicknesses, or gauges, the most common being A, O, B, D, and F. Size D thread is recommended for loomwork, because its greater thickness can handle the extra weight involved in loomed beadwork. For similar reasons, it is also recommended for stringing larger beads. Nymo is a manufacturer of thread, the thickness of which sets the standard for the beading industry; the sizing of thread among other manufacturers is not always consistent. Most beading thread is slightly waxed and lightly twisted. *See also* nylon thread.

daisy chain A simple stitch linking flower designs together, popular with children and beginners. The photo shows one of the many different types of daisy-chain patterns.

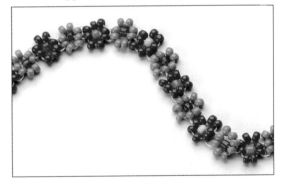

Dana Classification System A classification system for minerals that divides them into these groups: (1) native elements; (2) sulfides; (3) oxides and hydroxides; (4) halides; (5) carbonates, nitrates, and borates; (6) sulfates, chromates, and molybdates; (7) phosphates, arsenates, and vanadates; (8) silicates—neosilicates, sorosilicates, cyclosilicates, inosilicates, phyllosilicates, tektosilicates, and silicates not classified; and (9) organic minerals. This system has been revised to include various classes. See *Dana's New Mineralogy*, edited by Richard V. Gaines, et al. (1997). *See also* Stunz Classification System.

dance cape In New Guinea, dance capes are made of elaborate beads and fabric. The Plains Native North Americans in Canada also fashioned dance capes with elaborate beading designs, cowrie shells, brass, and leather. Exotic dancers from various cultures, ancient and modern, may also use beaded dance capes to reveal and conceal.

dangle Another term for a bead or bead fringe that hangs down from a beaded project. *See also* fringe.

date beads Beads marked with a specific date to commemorate an event, such as an anniversary, graduation, or birthday; or individual beads with names of months or numbers strung together to make up a date. This term also is used for beads that resemble the color and shape of the fruit of the date palm tree.

decreasing Shaping beadwork by reducing or decreasing the number of beads used in a row, achieved by several different techniques. The actual logistics of decreasing varies from one technique to another.

Delica A trademarked product of Miyuki Shoji, a Japanese manufacturer; this bead is known for its laser-cut precision sizing and uniformity

of shape. Until recently, it set the standard of quality for its type, a cylinder bead. Other manufacturers now produce similar beads, all trademarked, and each makes similar claims of quality. The Toho products are named Treasures and Aiko; Mill Hill produces a bead called Magnifica. None of these cylinder bead brands is interchangeable.

dendritic agate A translucent, white, gray, or colorless chalcedony (silicon dioxide) with brownish or black markings that resemble ferns or trees (dendrites). These inclusions are caused by iron or magnesium, not organic substances. Since this gemstone lacks banding, it is not strictly considered agate. It is also called *mocha stone,* and varieties include *scenic agate,* which resembles a landscape with browns and sunset accents, and *mosquito stone,* which resembles swarms of mosquitoes. Still other inclusions resemble ice crystals.

dental floss A synthetic fiber often coated with wax, this oral hygiene product is great for stringing beads and many other craft projects. The material is very sturdy and the wax helps minimize tangling.

dentalium shells The former "house" or shell of small tubular mollusks, shellfish with the appearance of tiny elephant tusks about 2 to 3 inches (5 to 7.5 cm long). The genus *Dentalium* includes over 300 species. This shell's hollow center makes a natural bead that's easy to string. Dentalium shells, *Dentalium (antalis) pretiosum,* were used as currency by Native North Americans of the Pacific Northwest and later by the Dakota and Plains tribes. Like wampum, lengths of shell beads were measured to determine their trade value. It has been said that traders tattooed their arms to mark a standardized length of strung beads against which they could measure. Today Asia supplies most dentalium shells used in beadwork.

devesting Removing the investment from the metal cast in the lost-wax process. After the metal cools, hammers and chisels may be used to knock off the investment to reveal the fresh, solidified metal cast from the mold.

devotional beads *See* prayer beads.

diadem A jeweled ornament, similar to a tiara, worn over the forehead. It is worn like a wreath around the head. *See* circlet.

diamond With a Mohs scale hardness factor of 10, the diamond is the hardest and among the most valuable gemstones. Made naturally over eons in the earth from crystallized carbon, these precious gemstones are graded by carat weight, color, clarity, and cut. Its crystal structure is cubic, or isometric-hexoctahedral. It is transparent to opaque with a strong luster.

Although diamonds are found worldwide, Australia, South Africa, Brazil, and Russia produce most of the diamonds rough-mined today. Natural diamonds range from colorless to slightly yellow or brown; other colors, such as green, blue, reddish, and orange black occur rarely. More often, the latter are induced by irradiation and/or heat treatment. Natural red diamonds are among the rarest of gemstones; only two are known to exist. Flaws in diamonds may be air bubbles, cracks, or embedded nondiamond materials; surface flaws or blemishes may be scratches, pits, or chips. It is not uncommon to remove flaws within diamonds by using a laser drill. Because of their superior hardness, diamonds are used for cutting other materials. Its hardness is 140 times greater than that of the ruby or sapphire. Although they are extremely hard, diamonds are brittle and can crack if subjected to a sharp blow. De Beers is thought to control about 80% of the world's diamond production and rough supply.

diamond imitations Matura or matara diamond is zircon (zirconium silicate), which is sometimes misrepresented as genuine diamond. A colorless diamond may be thought to resemble rock crystal, precious beryl, sapphire, topaz, or even glass. Also some yellowish stones may appear like diamonds. The synthetic stones strontium titanate (fabulite), linobate, and zirconia are among them. Diamond doublets consist of an upper part that is diamond and a lower part that's synthetic. Mexican, German, Bohemian, Maramarosch, Alaska, or Arkansas diamond are misleading names for rock crystal (quartz). Ceylon diamond is a misleading name for colorless zircon. The synthetic gemstone made in the laboratory, cubic zirconia, has a Mohs scale hardness of 8.5 and resembles the diamond.

dice beads These beads resemble the gaming pieces used in gambling, and are popular as worry beads among Moslems, who do not condone gambling. Dice beads are also popular in casinos and areas where gambling is a big business, like Las Vegas, New Orleans, and Atlantic City.

dichroic The property of certain crystals and gemstones of absorbing one of two polarized planes of light more strongly than another, depending on the angle from which the specimen is viewed. Exhibiting different colors by reflected or transmitted light; sometimes termed *dichromatic. See also* pleochroic and trichroic.

dichroic glass Created by a highly technical process developed by the National Aeronautics and Space Administration for use in space technology, dichroic glass results from the

application of several microlayers of metal oxides (among them gold, silver, titanium, chromium, aluminum, zirconium, magnesium, and silicon) to glass, followed by kiln-firing at high temperature. Dichroic glass is characterized by its ability to reflect more than one color; it can be fused with other glass in multiple firings, each time producing a unique result. Although the term *dichroic* means "two-color," this is a bit misleading. Visible light is split into distinct beams of different wavelengths of color (and often multiple colors). Both dichroic cabochons here were handmade by Bonnie Gibson.

dichroism A color-changing stone or a stone that has two colors, with each color being revealed depending on the angle at which the stone is viewed. Alexandrite and iolite display dichroism. *See also* trichroism and pleochroism.

diffusion A chemical process that is used to deepen the color of a gemstone or to produce asterism (starlike inclusions).

dime bead Another name for a coin-shaped bead that's the size of an American or Canadian dime. The crystal bead manufacturer Swarovski produces a round, flat, faceted bead it calls a dime bead.

dinosaur bone and eggshell beads Dinosaur eggshells and bones were made into beads over 20,000 years ago in Africa, India, and China. *See also* ostrich eggshell beads.

diopside This gemstone, a calcium magnesium silicate with a monoclinic or columnar crystal system, is found in diverse areas around the globe. It is transparent to translucent, green, yellow, colorless, brown, or black. *Diopside,* from the Greek, means "double appearance." Star diopside, which has an unusual star pattern, is found mainly in India. Its Mohs scale hardness is 5.5. Other varieties are the black star, cat's-eye, dark emerald-green chrome, and violet-blue violane.

disk A bead shape. These beads are generally round and flat, but they sometimes appear as

ovals or custom shapes. They can be made of wood, glass, shell, bone, horn, or clay. For distinctions, see also *donut*. Shown are glass disk beads, also called dot beads because of their surface ornamentation.

divining stone This stone may be made of various natural stones, according to the local folklore of the given culture. The Cherokee used quartz as a divining stone.

Djenne beads Ancient glass beads from Djenne, Mali, West Africa, dating from between 2,500 and 1,500 years ago. Many of these are eye beads excavated from an area in Africa that has little control or oversight of archaeological digs, making dating difficult. For the most part, the beads' surface designs are worn off, but the colors are commonly blue, green, and more rarely, gray.

Dogon donuts Colorful wound beads best known for their unique donutlike (annular) shape, these African trade beads generally have a distressed surface and fairly large holes. Originating in Germany in the mid-1800s, they were traded extensively by the Dogon people living in Mali, West Africa. They are also known as *wound annulars* or *Dutch beads*.

dolphin teeth *See* porpoise teeth.

donut A bead shape characterized by a large hole in the center and often used for making pendants, donut beads are made from a multitude of materials, including true gemstones. The term *donut* can describe many sizes and shapes of beads, such as the octagonal or rondelle, but with a generous hole in the center

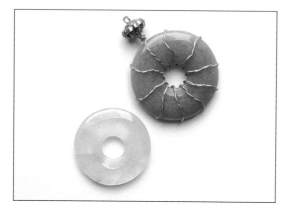

or even offset. The disk shape tends to be flatter with a smaller hole, and the annular or ring shape has a still more generous hole and thinner walls. A second type of donut bead has four holes, which allow one or more beads to be strung and to appear in its open center. The green donut pendant shown here is carved from aventurine, and the pink gemstone is rose quartz.

donut gemstone Similar to rondelles and also called *donut beads*, donut gemstones appear to be puffed-up versions of the shape seen in the photo above for donut beads. Faceted and made of glass, these beads were named gemstones by the manufacturer. Donut beads are also made from real gemstones.

dot beads Also called *bumpy beads*, these are usually made of glass, with colored dots, either raised or level, on the surface. The dots can be made using frit or glass stringer (also called *glass spaghetti cane*), a very thin rod of glass, often only about 1.5 mm thick.

double beads Two beads stuck together or strung together as a deliberate manufacturing or design element. Occasionally, double beads occur accidentally when two beads are not properly cut or when they are stuck together when the finish is applied.

dozen A common unit of measure; 12 of something.

drawn beads Beads made by the drawn-glass process (which, *see below*), including seed, pony, crow, and bugle beads.

drawn glass Glass made by any one of many techniques of drawing, or pulling, a tube of molten glass until it is long and thin. The glass tubes may be over 325 feet (100 m) long for making seed and bugle beads. To make beads, the molten glass must have a bubble in the center to serve as a hole in the finished product. Once pulled, or drawn, the glass is cut into small pieces that are heated and tumbled or polished to create beads. Japanese bead makers today cut the beads with lasers to achieve precision sizing consistency.

The basic principles of drawing glass have been refined for industrial mass production of beads, especially seed beads. Edward Danner of the Libby Glass Company of Toledo, Ohio, patented an automatic drawing machine in 1917, and such machines remain the backbone of European seed-bead production. Certain techniques remain highly guarded trade secrets in the industry. *See also* glass beadmaking and white-heart beads.

dream catcher A popular craft item made from a variety of materials, the dream catcher has been credited to Ojibwe (Chippewa) and other peoples living in the Great Lakes region, Minnesota, and North Dakota, but its exact origin is not clear. Dream catchers have been adopted by the Cree, Lakota, Navaho, and people from many other cultures. Traditionally, it contained only natural materials, including a ring or hoop made from the branch of a willow tree, plant fibers, a crystal gemstone, leather, and feathers. Crystal or glass of some type woven into the center allows positive energy and good dreams to enter, while the web is purported to entangle negative energy and bad dreams, so that the dreamer sleeps protected. Traditional objects woven into the design represent sea life (coral), rock life (turquoise), four-legged creatures (bone), and winged creatures (feathers). The first rays of sunlight at dawn are said to make bad dreams evaporate as they pass through the web. Other symbolism in the dream catcher resides in the sacred hoop, which represents the circle of life—the cycles evident in nature from birth

through death. The hoop also symbolizes the balance of nature and humankind's relationship with the earth and all that dwell in it. The traditional dream catcher earrings shown have nontraditional components; they are of sterling silver, and the center bead is malachite.

dream-catcher hoop The ring in a dream catcher, made of willow or less often, metal, wrapped with leather or beads. The hoop may encircle a web woven from sinew or thread that is decorated with beads and feathers.

dream-catcher webbing The webbing or network inside a dream catcher, traditionally woven with sinew but today usually artificial stringing material. *See* dream catcher.

drop beads Beads that hang from a design like a dangle or as part of the fringe. They may be in the shape of a teardrop, or pressed-glass beads shaped in any number of forms, such as flowers or leaves. Drop beads are often drilled from side to side near the top, but may also be drilled vertically, depending on the bead's shape.

drop down A step in the process of peyote stitching: If you are working a round peyote-stitch pattern from the top down, at the end of each row you will have to pass the needle through the first bead added in the previous row in order to move down to begin the next row. If you are working from the bottom up, the same maneuver is called *step up*.

druk A smooth, round glass bead, available in a wide variety of finishes and colors, popularly used as spacers. Druk beads are Czech. While the word *druk* is also associated with Bhutan, the Thunder Dragon and sovereign, and peoples of that nation, most suppliers

sell the Czech variety of round glass bead. The bracelet shown here features bone mud-beads and swirl-glass druk beads in shades of brown, orange, black, gray, white, and blue, flanking the amber turtle bead in the center. The turtle bead has dark brown swirls, sometimes referred to as tiger stripes.

druse In geology, a nodule filled with crystals inside the central cavity; sometimes also simply called a *geode*. Filled or unfilled nodules may be called geodes. Until the geode or nodule is sliced open, it would be difficult to tell if the interior contained a cavity with crystals. Also called *drusy*.

duck feet Beads shaped like a shell, fan, or duck's webbed foot. The hole is at the top of the bead, which influences how it will sit when strung.

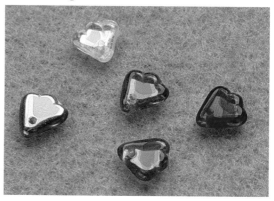

ductile Capable of being drawn out or extended with ease, usually applying to certain metals.

dulling Brushing a metal bead surface, sometimes with a matting powder, to achieve a dull or matte finish. Chemicals can be applied to glass beads to create a matte finish.

dumortierite A dull violet to bright blue transparent to opaque mineral, aluminum borate silicate, used in the manufacture of high-grade porcelain, this aluminum borosilicate is also called *blue-denim stone*. It is also sometimes red-brown or colorless. It has a Mohs scale hardness of 7 to 8.5. It may be mistaken for sodalite and sometimes substitutes for lapis lazuli. Dumortierite quartz is quartz intergrown with dumortierite.

dung beads Reportedly made from recycled waste products of animals, like moose, horse, buffalo, or cows. The dung is sterilized and deodorized, and then processed in a way similar to that of paper production. The sanitized dung is then formed into beads and other jewelry components, which are shellacked. Some "pellets" straight from the animal are already bead-shaped. Sweden and the states of Alaska and Maine reportedly market these naturally available moose droppings and sell them to tourists, which is a rather novel way to recycle a natural material for profit. (Most so-called moose droppings are really chocolate, not dung.) The material is often processed with some type of hardening agents and finishes like acrylic, varnish, or shellac to stiffen and shape the dung or droppings into beads. The Center for Bead Research offers other interesting bits of information on this somewhat rare and unusual bead.

duralumin A tough, ductile, and malleable metal alloy of over 90% aluminum with copper, magnesium, and manganese. Its lightness, hardness, and tensile strength have led to its use in the aerospace industry, but it also has been used by eclectic jewelers.

Dutch donuts (Dogon donuts) Wound beads in the shape of a ring or donut, originating in Germany in the late 19th century and traded in Asia and Africa. *See* Dogon donuts. The Dogon people, after which these beads are named, live in Mali in West Africa.

Dutch spiral A technique for making a beaded rope with a hollow center, featuring a spiral design along its length. Shown is a black and pink bracelet made by Shelia Vinson, finished with a magnetic clasp.

dyed beads Glass beads that are dyed to impart surface color often have questionable permanence, since such a finish is prone to fading and rubbing off. A reputable bead dealer will tell you if a bead's finish is vulnerable. Acrylic color fixatives can prolong the life of dyed beads, but manufacturers rarely apply them. Ask at your local bead store how to fix the color of dyed beads, or buy beads that are not dyed. If an irresistible color tempts you, however, it may be worth the extra effort of treating your beads. In any case, do not allow exposure of dyed beads to strong natural or fluorescent light or solvents like water, hairspray, perfume, and alcohol. *See also* glass bead colors, painted beads.

dyeing A process in which gemstones are treated with color additives or dyes to alter their natural color or improve uniformity.

Thin glass appears clear, but thick glass tends to be green. In small amounts, manganese, selenium, and cobalt can help decolorize glass. Nickel and cobalt used together in small amounts decolorize lead glass. In larger amounts, these metals produce certain colors.

For *colored glass,* metals and metal oxides are added during manufacture. Iron oxide creates a blue-green glass, which when mixed with chromium creates a green color. Sulfur, carbon, and iron salts with iron produce amber. Borosilicate glass, which contains boron and sulfur, makes blue; adding calcium makes a deep yellow. Manganese can produce an amethyst or purple color. Selenium in high concentrations creates pink, red, or ruby glass. Cobalt makes blue glass, especially when mixed with glass containing potash. Tin oxide with antimony and arsenic oxides produces an opaque white glass, once made in Venice as an imitation porcelain. Copper oxides produce turquoise, while pure copper produces an opaque, very dark red glass. Nickel can create blue, violet, or black. Chromium results in dark green to black. Cadmium and sulfur make yellow, but cadmium is toxic. Titanium makes yellow-brown glass. In tiny concentrations, metallic gold produces a cranberry to ruby-colored glass. Uranium dust creates a fluorescent yellow or green. While not highly radioactive, uranium dust is considered a carcinogen. Silver nitrate and other silver compounds make yellow to orange-red.

dZi beads Pronounced "zee," meaning brightness, shine, or splendor, these tubular beads are an important part of Tibetan culture and thought to have originated in Tibet, Nepal, or India. They are also called "jewels from heaven." Tibetan religious law prohibits archaeological excavation, making it difficult to verify or add to what is known about such artifacts. Esteemed throughout the world, the beads are thought to protect from the evil eye. Typically made of etched agate or chalcedony, these black-and-white or brown beads have characteristic patterns of eyes and stripes or bands, marked indelibly with alkali or acid. The technique of etching agate is over 5,000 years old and pure dZi beads are thought to be at least 1,500 years old. Many stories suggest their divine origin, while others describe them as petrified insects, and still others as coming from meteorites. According to lore, their magnetic field is thought to be greater than that of crystals. They serve as talismans. The bead shown is most likely a glass replica.

E

E beads Synonymous with pony beads, these are also called *size 5-aught* or *6-aught beads*.

ear plugs Ear ornaments, made of clay, shell, stone, feldspar, copper, or covered wood, consisting of a narrow column or shaft that fits into the outer ear's entrance to the ear canal, often having a terminal disk. These were once worn by the native Caddo people of the Mississippi.

ear spools Following a form of body piercing in which the large round ear plugs, also called capstans, adorn and enlarge the hole in the earlobe. The ear spools are sometimes perforated and strung to suspend from the earlobe. To wear the ear spool, the wearer's ear was sliced open and the ornament inserted. As the wound healed, the spool—typically as large as 2 inches (5 cm) in diameter—was sealed into place. Open and closed disks were worn; some ear spools also contained a shaft. They are found in myriad cultures, but notable examples are those once worn by the ancient Caddo and Spiro people of the Mississippi, the Chimu and Incas of Peru, and the Aztecs and Mayans of Mexico.

earring A piece of jewelry, sometimes called an *earbob,* usually worn from the earlobe for adornment. A variety of wire designs attach by running through a hole or piercing in the earlobe or other part of the ear. For ears that are not pierced, there are a variety of clasps that screw or clip onto the lobe. Ear cuffs wrap around the edge of the ear, and a specially designed ear wire wraps around the back of the ear. Earrings may also be worn around the ear's rook, the tragus, or across the helix. Piercings on other parts of the outer ear (pinna), such as the targus, daith, conch, or rook, are often called cartilage piercings. An industrial piercing involves two piercings of the upper outer ear linked by a single straight bar ornament. A few earring types are the stud, hoop, dangle, huggy, cuff, thread, needle, and so-called slave (a stud connected to an ear cuff via a chain) popularized on the television series *Star Trek*.

Shown above are earrings made by Jackie Haines, using size 13/0 charlotte cuts, cylinder beads, freshwater pearls, semiprecious stones, silver findings, and beaded beads, sometimes called *bumpy beads*. The beads were made with flat peyote stitch and formed into a tube with a zipper stitch. Then they were surface embellished with other beads.

earring clip An earring component for securing an earring to the ear when the ear is not pierced.

earring hoop A circular-shaped earring component, usually of metal. Beads can be hung from both the small metal ring at the top of the hoop and from the hoop itself. The hoops shown have a number of flat spots, which are useful as space markers in making dreamcatchers.

earring nut The finding that secures the ear stud or post behind the ear. The nut slides onto the post. Nuts come in many shapes and sizes; the two most common are bullet-shaped or with broad flat disks.

earring post *See* earring stud.

earring stud Also called an *earring post* or *ball post,* this earring attachment goes through the hole of a pierced ear and is held in place with a finding behind the ear called an *ear nut.* The photo shows a type of ear stud with ear nuts; rings are attached from which to hang beads or other findings. *See also* clutch.

earlobe stretching The people of Borneo today stretch their earlobes, which may extend to their shoulders, by wearing very heavy ear adornments. This was once more common throughout Asia.

earth rosary Not associated with any particular religious tradition, the earth rosary generally consists of 52 beads representing the weeks of the year, divided into four sets of 13 beads for the number of weeks in each season. Its origin being unclear, there are many variants of these prayer beads, and their characteristics are often highly individual. Some earth rosaries have ecological and ecumenical themes. Others are simple variations of the standard Catholic rosary.

ear wire Any of several types of finding used to attach an earring. A great number of such findings are referred to as ear wires, among them kidney, French wires, posts, lever backs, and a multitude of designer creations. Shown is a commonly used French wire.

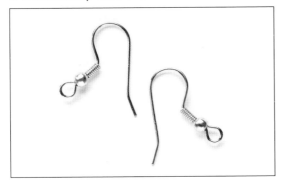

earth beads Indian reds or *mutisalah* given to brides, usually from the lower class, at weddings in India.

ebony Wood from the *Diospyros ebenum,* an evergreen tree, known as India ebony or Ceylon ebony, depending on where it is found, and characterized by a deep black color, hardness, very high density, fine grain, heaviness, and ability to take a high polish. Ornamental, sculpted, and beaded objects are made from ebony as well as furniture and architectural elements.

edging stitch Stitches used to attach beads to the edges of beadwork, clothing, fabric, and leather. Fretting is a common edging

stitch. Others are wrap stitch, whipstitch, scalloped stitch, picot, and lace stitch.

eggshell beads Beads made from ostrich and dinosaur eggshells and less commonly from the emu eggshell. *See* ostrich eggshell beads and dinosaur eggshell beads.

elastic Capable of being bent but resuming its shape after pressure is released. The term may apply to the quality of certain metals, minerals, plastics, and fabrics.

elastic cord As a material for stringing beads, elastic or stretchy cord provides a number of advantages. It is comfortable and easy to wear, the size is adjustable, and it requires no clasp. Available in many fashion colors, as well as clear, it may be all elastic or covered with fabric or thread. *See* floss.

elbow beads A curving tube bead shape. The term *elbow beads* also describes a pasta product, macaroni, used in children's stringing projects. *See also* flour beads.

embedded beadwork Decorative beadwork is sometimes embedded in utilitarian and aesthetic objects. In some cases, the beadwork's

embedded appearance may result over time from the accumulation of dust and other environmental debris; in other cases, the embedding is intentional, using wax, pitch, resin, tar, or some other adhesive. This technique is practiced in India and Africa, and by the Huichol of Mexico. The spider pendant shown on previous page exemplifies embedded Huichol beadwork.

embellishment Any decorative technique that dresses up an object. In beadwork, this may be the adding of beaded fringe or embroidery to clothing or jewelry. The small glass bottle shown was first covered with gourd stitch, and then, surface embellished with seed-bead vines, and leaf and flower beads. David Bingell created this beadwork embellishment.

emerald Composed of beryllium aluminum silicate with chromium, this gemstone is a variety of the mineral beryl, colored green by traces of chromium and sometimes iron. Most emeralds have inclusions. It rates 7.5 to 8 on the Mohs scale of hardness. Emeralds are the rarest of gemstones and by weight considered the most precious. Still more rare is the *trapiche emerald* found in Columbia with a sort of dark carbon star pattern. Synthetic or "created" emeralds, with a chemical composition the same as natural emeralds, are also available on the market. Shown is the stone found in nature in rough form. To create a desirable gemstone for jewelry, it must be cut and polished.

emery Used as a polishing material, emery is composed of fine-grained corundum, magnetite, hematite, and quartz.

enamel The result of a process called *enameling,* in which colored glass is fused to metal or glass. A highly pigmented form of glass paint or powder is meticulously applied to the

surface a layer at a time, and then melted and shaped, using a small propane torch. *See also* enamel paint and enamel powder.

enamel beads Beads that have undergone the process of enameling, described in the entry above.

enamel paint A paint made of finely ground glass powder, mixed with water, oil, or an acrylic base. It is applied with a delicate brush to paint details on the surface of a cold, annealed glass bead, using the mandrel as a handle. The bead is then reheated to fuse the paint to the bead surface. *See also* enamel powder.

enamel powder Finely pulverized glass that is highly pigmented by the addition of certain metal oxides. Enamel powder has more intense color than glass frit. The substance is used to apply a durable and colorful decorative finish to metal, glass, and ceramic objects.

encasing The process of coating a bead or decorative element with transparent glass.

end caps Also called *bead caps* or *bell caps,* these are findings that sit atop a bead or at the end of a rope or cord, primarily for aesthetic purposes. Metal end caps can be strung on the top and bottom of a glass bead, for example, to add a touch of metallic sheen. They are also handy for concealing knots. End caps are usually convex to fit against a bead's curvature. *See also* cones.

end cutter A tool used for making a flush cut on wire or bead cord.

end-of-the-day beads Glass beads, assumed to have been leftovers from the day's glasswork or lampwork activities because of the use of different colors in the glass or frit, such as that found in crumb beads. Although scrap materials from glassmaking can be used in this way, such beads were probably intentionally made.

engraving The process of etching a design, writing, or otherwise drawing on the surface of a metal, whether done by hand, machine, or sophisticated computerized techniques. Gemstones may also be engraved.

enhanced This adjective refers to a gemstone improved or made more attractive by some treatment, such as heating, oiling, or filling. Many gemstone enhancements are routine.

enhancement Used as a noun, an *enhancement* typically refers to a stone or other appendage hung on a necklace. Beads or gemstones used to embellish other types of jewelry, like bracelets, may also be considered enhancements.

epidote Also called *pistacite,* transparent to opaque pistachio-green stone, composed of calcium aluminum iron silicate. Its crystal structure is made up of monoclinic prisms, and its Mohs scale hardness is 6 to 7. It has a bright, vitreous luster.

etched carnelian Carnelian gemstone beads that have a design etched or drawn chemically with an alkali (or an acid) to create decorations. The resulting smooth lines are indelible. These beads were commonly created in India and Persia as early as 2000 B.C. *See* dZi beads.

E

etching A process in which designs are cut into the surface of a bead. The area to be left unmarked is covered with a masking material called a *resist*; a chemical solvent is then applied. The etching solution may be a cream or a liquid, and the means by which it is applied depend on such factors as the complexity of the design. The solvent may be poured over the bead, applied to the bead's surface with anything from a brush to a fine metal point, or the bead may be gently immersed in it. Both alkali and acid can etch beads, and the design is permanent.

etching solution A chemical solution used for giving glass beads a matte finish.

ethnic beads Also called *tribal, ethnographic,* and—if old enough—*ancient,* this is a generic term for beads relating to groups of people having common racial, national, tribal, spiritual, or cultural origins or backgrounds. Such beads often hold specific cultural significance, such as social status, power, or protection from evil. Generally handmade and therefore somewhat crude, ethnic beads may be made of natural materials, like seeds, bones, shells, and gemstones, and of metal and glass. The earliest beads were made from animal bones. With the rapid spread of modern bead technology, more nations have acquired the ability to make competitive products. The name of a bead, by itself, provides virtually no clue to a bead's origin. For instance, what are known as *African trade beads* were historically made in Venice to be traded on the African continent and elsewhere. Although the term *Venetian* once referred to a particular Italian method of glass beadmaking, beads with this name are now produced around the world. *Heishi,* or rolled shell beads, once traditionally handmade by Native North Americans, are now mass-produced in the Philippines.

Shown is a triple-strand necklace from India that includes a variety of unusual beads and charms. The beads are most likely of base metal rather than sterling silver, but their darkened or tarnished appearance has wonderful appeal.

even-count peyote stitch A peyote stitch that uses an even number of beads in a row. The major difference between even-count and odd-count peyote stitch is the technique by which a row of beads ends and a new one begins, owing to the varying number of beads in consecutive rows. *See also* odd-count peyote stitch.

everlasting shell A light pink or red to dark chocolate brown shell cut into slices, drilled,

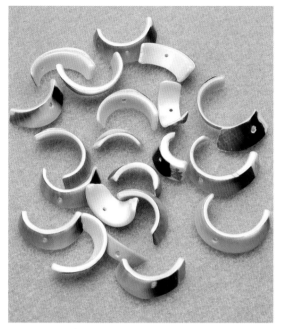

a circle, dot, or natural shape like a cowrie shell—that is carved, molded, painted, or embedded into its surface. Still popular in the Middle East, Turkey, India, and Italy, eye beads were first and most plentifully recovered in western Asia, India, and Egypt. They appeared later in Europe, and still later, in Africa. Mirror beads may serve the same function. *Dot beads* are sometimes also called eye beads.

The zipper pull shown has blue eye beads, disk spacers, and light-blue faceted fire-polish beads, strung on a flat-head pin and attached to a lobster-claw clasp. The bracelet has fire-polish and painted Egyptian eye beads, and green glass rondelles with gold swirls. *See also* shisha.

and strung for use as beads, as shown. Other types may be white, black, or green.

eye A round marking, such as with a dot for a pupil and a circle, on the surface of a bead that resembles the human or animal eye. These are commonly found on dZi beads, for instance. *See also* eye beads and zone patterns.

eye beads Made from ceramic, glass, bone, wood, and a variety of other materials, eye beads have been used since the Stone Age as amulets of sorts to protect against harm from the "evil eye" and to bring good fortune to the wearer. Some cultures still acknowledge the so-called evil eye as a malevolent force; eye contact with it purportedly causes one to suffer misfortunes (like death or illness) or bad feelings (like jealousy or rage). The protective strategy is to distract the evil eye by making it look first at something other than your eye. The bead features a symbolic eye—

eye pin A finding used in earrings, bracelets, and necklaces, this pin or wire slips through the hole in a bead or pearl. It has a loop at one end against which the bead rests, and the other end is bent with pliers to hold the bead

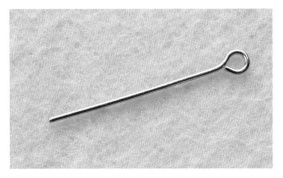

in place. The typical eye pin is base metal with a 20 to 21 gauge (a measurement of the pin's thickness). Gemstone beads often have smaller holes than glass beads and require eye pins ranging from 22 to 24 gauge. Pin length ranges from a half inch to 3 inches (1.3 to 7.6 cm); eye pins are trimmed easily with a jewelry-cutting tool.

eye screw A finding used to attach a half-drilled bead, commonly used for earrings or pendants.

eyeglass holder A functional piece of jewelry, shaped like a rope with findings for holding eyeglasses, that keeps the glasses from getting lost. When not being worn, the glasses hang safely from the bead strap, like a sort of necklace. The eyeglass holder shown is a string of black pony beads, 4- and 6-mm fire-polish

beads, and peacock-blue puffy rondelles. The average eyeglass holder strap is 26 inches (66 cm) long.

eyeglass holder finding The hardware that attaches eyeglasses to an eyeglass holder.

F

face beads A bead bearing facial features, i.e., eyes, a nose, a mouth, and sometimes hair. The features may be of any color glass or other material, painted or carved into the bead. Shown are some face beads made in China.

faceted beads Beads that are shaped with cuts that reflect light to make the beads sparkle. Typically such beads are of glass or gemstone, and the facets are smoothed by tumbling, or exposing them to high temperatures. Generally, the value of a bead increases with the number of facets.

faceted gemstone beads These gemstone beads are shaped by angular cuts that reflect light. Those shown here are briolettes (a faceted teardrop shape) of blue topaz.

fagoting A technique in which short bead strands are sewn between two finished edges of fabric, ribbon, or cord, in effect, joining them over an open area. It generally serves as a decorative trim or seam.

faience This well-known, traditional hand-decorated pottery derives its name from the Italian town Faenza, where it was first produced during the Renaissance. The term *faience* has come to include a similar pottery produced in Egypt as early as 4000 B.C. The core of the beads consists of quartz particles that are fused together; over this core a surface glaze is applied. Today only Iran continues to make traditional faience; in Egypt, soapstone or clay is often substituted. The beads shown are of the kind sold to tourists in modern-day Egypt and elsewhere. The beads are sometimes called *mummy beads*.

fakes See main entry for the desired gemstone or the gemstone name with the word *imitations* following. The buyer must beware and be sure to buy from reputable dealers who can give details about materials, treatments, and origins of the particular gemstone. *See* various precious metals, such as gold and sterling silver, for hints about determining their value. *See also* specific gemstone imitations.

false beads *See* false pearls.

false pearls Indian reds or *mutisalah* are sometimes called false beads or false pearls. In some cultures, the word *pearl* is used interchangeably with the word *bead*.

fan A necklace or decoration of graduated, carved gemstones, as in the cut goldstone here.

fancy glass Any number of assorted bead shapes, colors, and finishes that are outside the ordinary. The term particularly denotes a large decorative accent bead in a beadwork project.

fancy jasper An opaque variety of jasper with subtle patterning in a wide array of shades, ranging through gold, yellow, blue, green, red, pink, and lavender, often in a single piece. Like jasper, it is a type of chalcedony with a grainy structure. The beads shown demonstrate the range of colors. *See* jasper and chalcedony.

fancy sapphire A sapphire, corundum, a crystal form of aluminum oxide, found in any color except blue or red. *See* sapphire and ruby.

fantasy jasper Fantasy jasper, a species of chalcedony, has a distinctive pattern that suggests wood grain. A relatively new find from Mexico, the colors red, cream, and brown predominate, but the stone also exhibits shades of yellow, rust, blue, green, and wine. The neckpiece shown, made by Jackie Haines, is appliquéd with beads on stiffened felt around a cabochon of fantasy jasper, and backed with leather. *See also* jasper and chalcedony.

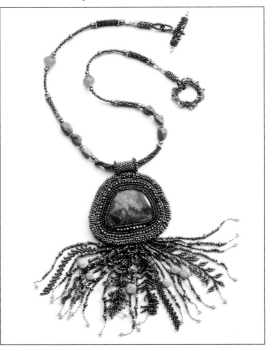

faux A French word meaning "fake," commonly used in English to designate something that is not genuine, like faux gemstones. *Fabulous fakes* is the term applied to jewelry, usually elaborate, which is typically worn by movie and television actors, whether at public events or when playing roles, that imitates real jewelry that few could possibly afford. Many feature numerous faux gemstones, pearls, rich gold, and the like. Of course, nonactors wear them, too, on special occasions like fancy-dress balls.

The words *synthetic* and *imitation,* which have different meanings when describing gemstones, can easily confuse laypeople. These stones, when made in the laboratory, can create beautiful beads and jewelry. Strictly speaking, man-made products can have physical, optical, and chemical characteristics in common with natural gemstones. The term *imitation* is used in the gemstone trade to designate those stones which do not have counterparts in nature. Unlike imitation gemstones, *synthetic gemstones* share chemical and physical properties with natural gemstones. The diamond simulant *cubic zirconia* (zirconium oxide), for instance, is a synthetic gemstone that rates 8.5 on the Mohs scale for hardness and is optically flawless and usually colorless.

Another example of an imitation gemstone is the turquoise block, which is a mixture of plastic resin and dyes that contain no rock of any sort. Turquoise rock is used for inlays and heishi beads. *Reconstituted turquoise* is a mixture of turquoise stone, chips, and powder mixed with blue-green dye and a plastic binder. Imitation and simulated turquoise can be made from other stones, such as howlite and dolomite, that are dyed to appear like turquoise. Other materials, like polymer clay, faience, plastic, and glass, can also be made to look like turquoise.

Rhinestones made of high-quality glass were deliberately fashioned to look like gemstones, and the colors given (emerald, ruby, sapphire) were of the same name as real gemstones. Although real gemstones have been popular for centuries, only the rich could afford to use them for adornment, ornamentation, and prestige. Rhinestones were developed so that more people could appreciate sparkling gem-like stones at affordable prices.

Reputable dealers will be honest and informative.

feather beads These glass lampwork beads originated in Venice, but are made in India and Africa as well. They have a characteristic swirl design within the glass through which a thread has been dragged, making it look like the veins of a feather or leaf. The term also refers to a bead of any material carved or molded into the shape of a feather.

feather stitch Another name for the *Ndebele stitch* or *herringbone stitch,* practiced by the Zulu. *See* Ndebele stitch.

feathering The process in glass beadmaking of raking or combing a trail with a thread on the bead's surface to make a feather design. The term also applies to the characteristic marks made in this manner. *See* bead rake.

Federal Trade Commission The United States Federal Trade Commission (FTC), a government organization, publishes guidelines to protect consumers from dishonest or unfair trade tactics. It provides facts about marketing, selling, and advertising jewelry, precious metals, gemstones, and pearls. Find the FTC Web site in the Selected Bibliography in Part V.

feldspar A group of crystalline minerals, aluminum silicates that may have potassium, sodium, calcium, or rarely, barium. (These are essential constituents of almost all crystalline rocks.) Two main subgroups are suitable for gems: the potassium feldspars and the plagioclases. The latter includes a series from calcium to sodium feldspars, with many gemstone varieties. The term *feldspar* comes from the German *Feld* for "field" and *Spath* or *splaten* for "to split." Among feldspars are amazonite, moonstone, orthoclase (potassium aluminum silicate), and labradorite and sunstone (sodium calcium aluminum silicate). Feldspars are rock-forming minerals that make up as much as 60% of the earth's crust. Feldspar is also a common raw material in ceramics.

fertility bead dolls Fertility dolls are found among many of the peoples of sub-Saharan Africa. Betrothal dolls related indirectly to fertility are given to prospective brides by men of the Fali tribe of the Republic of Cameroon in western Africa; adorned with beads, these small wooden figures symbolize a future child and a commitment to marriage. In South Africa, a similar custom exists among the Ndebele and the Ntwane, and intricate beadwork is essential to the Ndebele dolls' construction.

In northern Nigeria and Cameroon, men make for their brides these dolls of corn cobs or wood and hang multiple strands of beads around the doll's neck, suggesting wealth. The man gives the doll the gender he would like his firstborn child to have. The woman cares for the doll as she would for a human baby, carrying it with her, feeding it, and more. The doll symbolizes the marriage commitment and

represents their future child. After the first child is born, the fertility doll is stored in a safe place.

The Fali fertility doll shown has an arrangement of beads across the chest called a *bandolier*. Courtesy of Peg Alston of Peg Alston Fine Arts, Inc.; photo by JG.

fertility beads Married women of the Samburu tribe in Kenya wear elaborate collars of giraffe hair and glass beads that can stretch from shoulder to earlobe; thought to enhance the wearer's fertility, these ornaments are reserved for ceremonial occasions.

Given their resemblance to the female sexual anatomy, cowrie shells are in many cultures a symbol of fertility, and they are easily strung as beads. Fertility icons such as corn, frogs, rabbits, elephants, squash blossoms, and goddess amulets—even blatant sexual objects shaped as male or female organs—are carved into beads, which may be regarded as fertility beads.

Beads and amulets of stones like rose quartz, chrysoprase, turquoise, and fluorite are purported to have special powers over fertility. However, without any particular cultural or traditional significance to the belief, it seems this is merely a marketing device.

Another distinct type of fertility beads, commercially produced as CycleBeads, are sold as an adjunct to family planning. The color-coded beads represent a typical monthly cycle, each bead being a day. A small ring moves daily from bead to bead, the bead's color indicating how likely a woman is to be fertile on that day.

fetish An object believed to be the embodiment or habitation of some magical spirit or power, often in the form of a carved stone animal. Having the supposed power to aid and protect, fetish animals' traits are admired and imitated. Technically not a bead, a fetish can be adapted for use as a jewelry component. Since it has no hole for stringing, it is tied with sinew to some other part of the piece.

The carved gemstone turtle fetish here, handmade by Jose Garcia, features a feather accent and small pieces of turquoise and coral attached with artificial sinew.

fetish beads Beads carved in the shapes of animals, often from gemstone, bone, metal, wood, clay, or horn. They are drilled for stringing, which technically makes them beads. Fetish animals are associated with particular characteristics or traits that people wish to emulate, or from which they hope to benefit.

fetish necklace Typically, a fetish necklace is strung with heishi beads and a variety of carved animal fetishes, as is the one shown below. It

features a hummingbird, a dolphin, a whale, an elephant, a bear, a bird, and a rhinoceros, strung with heishi beads and finished with a barrel clasp.

fiber blanket In the process of making beads, glass is heated to melting, and while the beads cool, they are very vulnerable to cracking. Placing them between layers of an insulating blanket of nonasbestos ceramic permits them to cool more slowly and makes them less prone to breakage. Another insulating option is to place beads in vermiculite heated in a slow cooker or electric skillet.

fiber-optic beads These synthetic beads are made of fused quartz fibers, which have the quality of chatoyancy—the unique shimmery quality of cat's-eye gemstone. Shown are a bird pendant (below) and a mala bracelet (above right) of this material. *See also* chatoyancy.

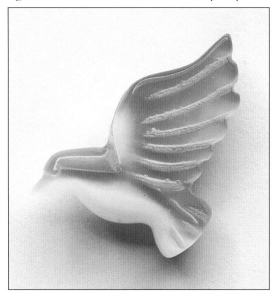

filigrana Glass rods with cores of opaque glass cores encased in clear glass.

filigree As an adjective, *filigree* describes fine, elaborate designs in any medium. It can apply to glass, metalwork, beads carved from gemstone, and more. The name derives from the Latin *filum* and *granum*, meaning "thread" and "grain," respectively.

Delicate metalwork made by a technique using fine twisted wire, generally of precious metal, is called filigree. It was in evidence in Mesopotamia by 2500 B.C., where filigree was created for members of the royal family. Beads of this type were worn as status symbols, and royal figures were entombed draped in cloaks made of them. Ancient Greeks and Romans practiced the technique of filigree. Until the Edwardian era (1901–1910), when the art form reached its peak, all filigree was done by hand; today, only the best examples are handmade, primarily by the Chinese and the Italians.

The process of filigree employs fine metal threads that are twisted or woven together in intricate designs (such as scrolls, vines, spirals, and rosettes); the threads may be solid precious metals or merely electroplated. Filigree may be openwork—a network of assembled metal threads held together by strategically soldered "joints"—or it may be applied to a foundation material that holds it in place.

When the spaces between the metal threads on the underlying material (generally gold, brass, or copper) are filled in with enamel, the work is called *cloisonné*. The beads shown are of gold-plated brass.

filigree glass Also sometimes called *latticino,* glass decorated with fine lines. The glass is often twisted to achieve this effect.

filling A gemstone treatment difficult to detect, in which surface fractures or flaws are filled with glass, oil, clear epoxy resin, or other substances, to improve the stone's appearance or weight. The process, also called *infilling,* involves heating the rough stone to an extreme temperature, and packing a powdered filling material around it. The intense heat melts the filling, which penetrates and fills cracks in the stone.

Fimo clay beads Beads made of a polymer clay manufactured by the firm Fimo. Although the name Fimo is often used synonymously with polymer, several manufacturers, each with its own trade name, produce these beads. Fimo is especially popular for its firm consistency; owing to this, it holds fine detail very well. Once fired, it can be buffed to a high polish.

findings A generic term for the many small hardware components used in jewelry construction, such as clasps, ear wires, pin backs, and jump rings.

finish A broad term that may be used to describe: (1) The surface treatment of beads, such as the additive applied at the end of production to alter or enhance its appearance; the surface treatment of metals. Common finishes of glass beads, for instance, are matte, satin, frosted, aurora borealis or rainbow, pearl, metallic, and vitrail. (2) The ends of the bead when describing bead anatomy. (3) Finishing a necklace or other stringing project, particularly the use of specially designed hardware, materials, and techniques that neaten the appearance and ensure the stability of the necklace or other strung jewelry or beadwork. *See also* bead finishes and metal finishes.

FireLine *See* stringing thread.

fire-polish beads Created as an inexpensive alternative to crystal beads, fire-polish beads are made by hand in the Czech Republic. The beads are first pressed in a mold, and then the facets are cut. The fire polish follows, as the beads are run through a furnace at a high temperature; the surface just barely melts, imparting gloss and scratch-resistance. The beads are available in a variety of sizes, surface coatings, and color linings for a wide array of finished appearances. Find the bead finishes chart in Part IV.

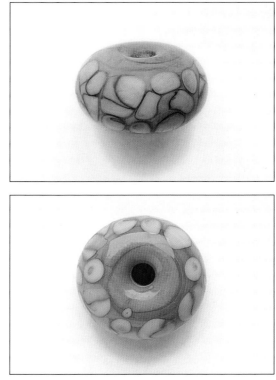

fishing-net weights For centuries, large terra-cotta beads, each about 4 inches (10 cm) long, roped together in strands, were used in the ancient lands of Sudan, Mali, and by other seafaring cultures as weights for fishing nets.

flake *See* gold flake.

flame annealing The process of slowly cooling a fired glass bead to relieve internal stress. This method uses the flame from a torch as opposed to annealing in a kiln.

flame cutting The use of a torch flame to cut or separate glass into sections.

flameworked beads Also called *lampwork beads,* from the traditional technique of glass beadmaking. The process calls for heating glass rods to a molten state, and then winding

the glass around a metal rod (called a *mandrel*) that has been treated to release the glass easily. This is only one of several methods that use heat from an open flame to manipulate glass. The flameworked beads shown above were handmade by Shawn Koons.

flameworking *See* lampworking.

flameworking tools Fireproof tools used for making glass beads by various techniques, such as lampworking. They include bead rakes, various kinds of marvers and marvering plates, pin vases, pendant plates, leaf mashers, parallel bead press, torches or burners, tweezers, mandrels, bead-hole cleaners, graphite paddles, tongs, heat-resistant work surfaces, hot-glass shears, Mapp gas-bottle holders, twin hoses, and more. Sludge bead-release is a compound made to ease the release of beads from a mandrel or other surface or bed.

flash glass A type of mouth-blown glass that is not colored throughout, but only on its surface. The flash technique uses one or more colored glasses applied to a clear or colored glass called the carrier. Multicolored glass can be produced with a variety of shading, clouding, or torn effects.

flash technique A technique for achieving coloration when blowing glass. One or more colored glasses applied to a clear or colored base or *carrier glass* can produce a wide variety of multicolored glasses as well as shaded, milky, translucent opal appearances.

flashback A hazardous event that occurs when the torch flame burns back into the torch, the hoses, and possibly the fuel tank.

flashing Refers to concentration of color in the glass.

flat-head pin A metal pin with a flat base, used in making jewelry, especially earrings. The flat head keeps the beads from falling off. Such pins are also used to make drops, dangles, and charms.

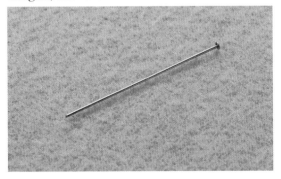

flat netting An off-loom beading technique that results in a flat, two-dimensional piece of beadwork. Due to the fluid nature of the beadwork fabric produced, the resulting jewelry can be considered three-dimensional, since it can wrap around a collar or wrist. One flat-netting technique can be woven on a horizontal plane, and another flat-netting technique can be done on a vertical plane.

Both bracelet photos below show examples of vertical netting.

flat-nose pliers This tool is typically used for holding, flattening, or bending wire and open jump rings as well as for bending wire or sheet metal at angles and closing jump rings. The flat, smooth jaws (nose) hold the components without marring the surface of the jewelry. Flat-nose pliers are designed for making sharp bends and right angles in soft wire. They can also grip flat objects and work well for straightening bent wire. Flat-nose pliers that have a flat jaw inside that's curved on the outside cannot be used to make a round loop or ring. Flat-nose pliers are also sometimes called *chain-nose pliers*. Other types are needle-nose and round-nose pliers. Photo by JG. *See* pliers for jaw close-ups.

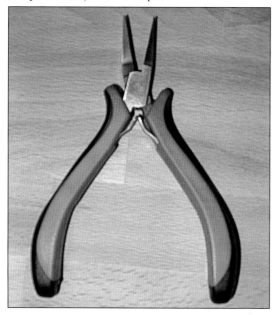

flat ovals This term describes the shape of a bead. Shown are two different types of flat ovals, one with rounded edges and one with sharp edges. The yellow beads are top-drilled,

and the shell beads are drilled from top to bottom. The position of the drill hole determines how the bead will sit when strung.

flat-pad ear studs This finding is used to attach a beaded cabochon to an earring. It is used with a comfortable clutch earring back, usually made of plastic, with a larger surface area helpful in making a heavy earring lie flat against the earlobe.

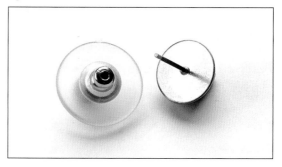

flat peyote stitch A useful stitch for a variety of jewelry projects, flat peyote stitch is versatile and creates a nice fluid piece of bead fabric.

It can produce two- or three-dimensional beadwork. Shown above is a necklace made with flat peyote stitch and embellished with an edging stitch.

flat, round peyote stitch A variation of peyote stitch, also called gourd stitch, that creates a circular pattern. It is used for the flat bottoms of beaded bottles or round vessels and for three-dimensional baskets and other jewelry components. Shown below is a three-dimensional basket beaded with this stitch by the author. The second miniature basket was beaded by David Bingell.

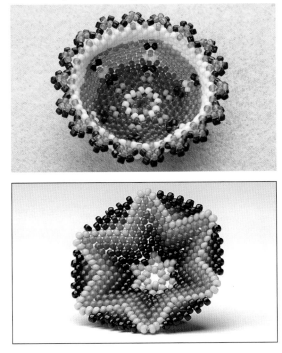

flattener A shaping tool also called a *bead press,* this implement features two stainless steel (or other metal) pads mounted on a spring-loaded steel frame. It is used in the process of glass beadmaking to press the beads and flatten the surface. *See* tabular beads.

flexible Easily bent without breaking; a quality of some metals and metal wire.

flint Also called *flintstone* or *silex,* a crypto-crystalline quartz that commonly occurs in hard sedimentary form in spherical nodules and masses. This silicate (silicon dioxide) is a variety of chalcedony. It is typically glassy dark gray, smoky brown, blue, or black as distinct from chert, which tends to be a pale gray. In Europe it has been used for making stone tools since the Stone Age since it can split into sharp splinters called flakes or blades when struck by another hard object. Flint is more readily shaped than other stones. When struck with steel, flint produces sparks that may be used to start a fire. It was later used to create a spark to ignite powder or the charge of a bullet from a flintlock firearm. It has been used as a building material for stone walls, especially in England, since the 13th century. Flint pebbles have been used to grind glazes for ceramics.

flintstone *See* flint.

floss A special type of elastic cord made with fibrous materials that retain their memory, or shape, very well. It is not the same as the stringing material commonly known as *dental floss,* which is not elastic.

flour beads A generic term for homemade beads made with any of a variety of recipes using flour or farina and some glue or other adhesive material. Recipes variously call for ingredients like cornstarch, rice or wheat flour, gelatin, baking soda, salt, peanut butter, white glue, dryer lint, sugar, corn flour, sand, sawdust, newspaper, and dried fruits and vegetables. Making these beads is a simple project that's great for children.

flower beads Generally any bead in the shape of a flower or having the image of a flower in or on it. It can also refer to a bead made from a real flower. The flower beads shown are drilled from top to bottom.

fluorescence Response to ultraviolet light.

fluorite A somewhat brittle translucent or transparent gemstone, composed of calcium fluoride, with a Mohs scale hardness factor of 4. Fluorite has a vitreous luster and characteristic bands or streaks of purple, pink, red, yellow, green, blue, brown, and sometimes black. It is found in Brazil, Canada, China, England, Germany, Mexico, Norway, Switzerland, Russia, and the United States.

This stone is fluorescent under ultraviolet light. It is also called *fluorspar*. Blue John is a variety of fluorite.

Accented by gray pearls and Bali sterling-silver star-shaped spacers, the necklace shown below features one of the stone's many guises, with round and chunky fluorite beads strung on nylon-coated wire.

flush-eye beads Originating in Venice in the late 1500s, this bead is characterized by an eye motif that is embedded flush with the bead surface.

flute A musical wind instrument used throughout the world; it is chiefly the wood varieties created by Native Americans that are decorated with beads. The beads may serve as an accent on the flute.

flux Melting agents used in lampworking of beads that can soften glass at lower temperatures. The more sodium oxide present in glass, the slower it solidifies. Lampworkers appreciate flux because it allows them more time to shape heated glass into the desired shapes. Flux is also used in metalworking for soldering, brazing, or welding. Flux helps remove oxides from the surface of a metal, seals to prevent further oxidation, and helps "wet" metals to be fused together. Flux is also used for soldering stained glass, lead came, or copper-foil glasswork.

focal bead The main or central component in the design of a piece of jewelry. The focal bead is also called a *station*.

foil beads Glass beads with an inner lining of metal foil of some kind. The lining may be of several different layers and colors. Shown are beads lined with silver foil and gold foil, respectively.

foiling The process in which a gemstone is mounted on a solid background that is layered with foil to enhance the stone's reflectivity and brilliance.

folded beads Beads formed by folding a warm pad of glass around a mandrel, which results in a longitudinal seam. This is an out-dated method for shaping beads.

forging Shaping metals by plastic deformation done by a smith, such as a silversmith. Cold forging is done at relatively low temperatures and hot forging at higher temperatures. The *forge,* or *smithy,* is the workplace for silver-smiths and other smiths, used for heating materials. The forge is sometimes called the hearth. Typical tools include furnace, bellows, hammers, anvil, tongs, slack tub. Some metal-working processes that are essentially forging but require special tooling are rolling, swaging, drawing, raising, and sinking. Forged metals are usually stronger than machined metal parts.

fossil The term *fossil* comes from the Latin *fossu,* meaning "having dug up," and refers to the preserved remains or evidence of ancient animals, plants, and other organisms, which may include leaf impressions, footprints, shells, bones, eggs, feces, and mineral sediments. To qualify as a fossil by paleontologists, the specimen must be over 10,000 years old.

fossil beads Beads whose basic makeup is the fossilized remains of ancient sea creatures. These are relatively inexpensive beads avail-able in natural and off-white, but usually dyed vibrant colors.

fossilized wood *See* petrified wood and quartz.

foxtail A delicate-looking but sturdy metal chain used for stringing glass, metal, and certain gemstone beads, especially those that have rough or sharp holes that might cut through ordinary beading thread. Foxtail is usually sold by the foot or spool in various gauges, as needed for various bead weights and hole sizes.

fracture How a mineral breaks when broken contrary to its natural cleavage planes. Fractures include *chonchoidal, hackley, fibrous,* and *irregular.* The chonchoidal is a smooth, curved fracture with concentric ridges. Hackley is jagged with sharp edges.

frankincense One of the most evocative scents from the ancient world, frankincense has been used to awaken higher consciousness and spirituality. Its biblical references indicate that it was highly valued. Frankincense has been used with prayer beads. It has medicinal properties as an anti-inflammatory. This natural insecticide has been used in fumigating wheat silos and repelling moths. It has been said to improve the acoustics of the room in which it is burned as an incense.

Similar to myrrh, this dried amber-colored resin from a tree (genus *Boswellia*) common to the Arabian Peninsula and the Horn of Africa is collected by cutting the tree back, which causes the sap to ooze. Both frankincense and myrrh are used as incense and mixed with spices, seeds, and roots to create various aromas added to some beads.

free-form peyote stitch This variation of flat peyote stitch uses beads of different sizes together with embellishment techniques that create a more three-dimensional object. The bracelet shown top right incorporates seed, bone, and glass fire-polish beads with abalone, turquoise, and pearl accents.

French ambassador beads These usually elongated, black matte beads with a delicate floral design applied to the surface are said to have originated in Venice in the late 19th century. In truth, no evidence substantiates that they are old or were made in Venice, and the origin of the name is likewise without basis in fact. French ambassador beads are also simply called *ambassador beads.*

French beaded flowers Seed beads strung onto fine-gauge craft wire and molded into flowers.

French hook A very common S-curve ear wire finding for pierced ears, popular for its functionality, comfort, and reasonable cost. Also known as *French wire,* it comes in base metals that are sometimes plated as well as in gold, silver, pewter, and other precious metals or alloys.

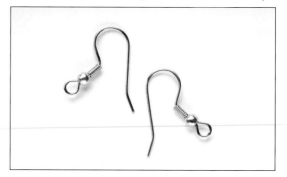

French ivory Also called Celluloid, Ivoride, and Pyralin, a plastic that simulates ivory, introduced in 1866.

French jet Neither French nor jet, this faceted black glass was created to compete with items made using genuine jet, a velvet-black fossilized coal. Aside from price, the chief difference between the two is that glass is cold to the touch and a good deal heavier than jet. French jet enjoyed its greatest popularity following the death of Prince Albert, when Queen Victoria wore it as a symbol of mourning, although the custom may have originated much earlier. Although French jet originated in France, most of it was subsequently produced in Bohemia, the Czech Republic. Today, true jet is somewhat difficult to find and therefore costly. Consequently, the name *jet* is often applied to anything solid black, whether it is French jet, onyx, black rhinestone, black glass, or true jet. *See also* jet.

French wire Also known as *bullion* or *gimp,* wire of an extremely fine gauge that is coiled into a tube or cylinder through which the stringing material can be threaded. The coil disguises and protects the bead cord from friction and wear, near crimps and closures, and provides an attractive finish to a string of beads. It handily attaches findings to the ends of beaded closures.

freshwater pearls Mussels produce freshwater pearls in much the same way that oysters produce saltwater pearls. An irritant—some type of foreign matter—gets into a mussel, causing the mollusk to wall off and isolate it by secreting a shell-building substance around it. This substance, called *nacre,* is the essence of pearls—the lustrous, satiny material that gives pearls their characteristic beauty and value.

To culture pearls, or artificially stimulate their production, the mussel's shell is pried open just enough to cut a small slit in the animal's "skin" and insert what is basically a bit of skin (or a tiny pearl) from another mussel. This process is called *nucleating.* The first Chinese cultured freshwater pearls had the irregular, elongated shape of a popular breakfast cereal, for which reason they earned the name *rice pearls,* or *rice crispies.* The larger, fatter versions are called *potato pearls.* The shape of a cultured freshwater pearl derives from the shape of its nucleus. Mussels are increasingly being nucleated with round beads, and the resulting quality of freshwater pearls has begun to rival that of natural salt-water pearls.

Natural freshwater pearls are rarely perfectly, or even nearly, round. They are noted for their wide range of colors: silvery shades of white, cream, yellow, pink, salmon, red, copper, bronze, brown, purple, lavender, blue, and green. Generally, pearls have the color of the shell in which they form. Freshwater pearls are often dyed, as were those on the strand shown.

Other common types of freshwater pearls are called *coin, nugget, button, blister, cross,* and *stick,* terms that generally describe their shape. Like cultured or natural pearls, they are sometimes identified by geographic location, parent (type of mollusk or oyster), color, shape, and more. The *Biwa* and *Keishi* are common types. *Dancing pearls,* also known as *top-drilled, end-drilled,* or *teardrop pearls,* are pearls in which the hole is drilled through the narrowest rather than the widest part. *See also* cultured pearls and pearls.

fretting Any one of a number of beading techniques used to edge leather or fabric. It is also referred to as *picot edging.*

fringe Multiple strands of leather, fabric, thick threads, or beads that hang from the edge of an object. The red bag shown here has a few beads attached to the leather fringe. The green beaded bag by David Bingell has fringe made with glass beads, pearls, and branch coral.

fringe beads Also referred to as *drop beads,* these beads hang from the ends of fringe strands. Fringe beads are shown on the opposite page, top right.

fringe earrings Typically, earrings that are made with beaded fringe, composed of multiple strands of beads. Shown are three pairs of earrings created by Jackie Haines, using Swarovski crystals, Bali silver beads, size 13 charlottes, size 15/0 Japanese seed beads, turquoise, and peridot.

frit Fused or partially fused materials used in making glass; also, a vitreous substance for making porcelain, enamels, or glazes. In glass beadmaking, frit is colored glass that has been crushed or ground into a grit of various degrees of fineness. One method of producing it is to plunge a ball of molten glass into water, which shatters it. Applying frit to the hot surface of a bead can create interesting patterns. Frit, glass crushed to a powder, is used in a water-based paste and painted onto cloisonné. When it is dried and fired, it melts onto the metal. Several coatings may be built up for the finished cloisonné.

frosted glass A dull or matte finish given to a bead by an acid wash that strips the sheen from the bead's surface. Shown below are frosted red beads reportedly from Italy.

F

fuel In making lampwork beads, oil lamps or spirit lamps were once used to heat the bead's glass core and the bits of colored glass applied to it. More common today is a flameworking torch. Depending on the type of torch, it may use propane, brazing fuel (modified propane that burns hotter and cleaner than regular propane), or natural gas. In the most versatile type, which uses a "surface mix," the oxygen and fuel gas are kept separate until both gases exit the torch; the two gases mix just beyond the surface of the torch's face. This makes for a quieter, cleaner flame that is more easily adjusted. For the purpose of glass beadmaking, acetylene is never used.

fuming A method of transferring a thin coat of silver or gold with a high-karat content to a glass bead surface by heating the precious metal. The process gives luster to the bead's surface. The gold or silver sources include casting grain, wire, leaf, or foil.

funk beads Unusual beads made from recycled rubber that come in a variety of shapes and colors.

furnace-glass beads These beads, also known as *cane* or *art beads,* have a clear glass shell

around a core of different colors. They are handmade with an Italian lampworking technique that uses a large furnace. Beads with multicolored stripes on the surface are called *latticino*. The simple bracelet shown has peacock blue furnace beads, star-shaped Bali silver spacers, and 6-mm fire-polish beads with a glassy finish, strung on elastic cord. *See also* cane beads.

fuse To blend or join glass by melting it together. Glass can also be fused to metal, as in enameling.

fused glass *See* dichroic glass. The square example shown here is a handmade creation of Bonnie Gibson.

fused rod *See* fustat beads.

fustat beads Often called fused rods, this bead type has been found in Egypt from about A.D. 800–1000. The name comes from the place of origin. The beads are formed by fusing sections of mosaic glass to create interesting visual and color effects. The beads are made by manipulating a pad of mosaic glass around an iron mandrel.

G

gadroon Found in silver and other metalwork, an ornamental band embossed or embellished, typically on the edge, with fluting, reeding, beading, cable, or another continuous pattern. Gadroons (godroons or gadrooning) is a common feature of architectural ornaments as well as work in porcelain and may consist of notching and carving done in wood or another medium.

gadrooned beads These beads may be similar in appearance to melon beads. *See* gadroon.

gahu In Tibet, a prayer box, suspended from a necklace and secured to clothing, contains a written prayer intended to appease evil spirits. The prayer box and necklace are often made with pearls and precious gems. It may be worn with an embellished shoulder ornament that, because of its weight, is also attached to clothing.

Gallé beads A style of lampwork bead named after Emile Gallé, an Art Nouveau glassmaker from the late 1800s who invented the technique. Produced in China today, these beads begin with a glass core of one color that is layered with glass of a contrasting color. The artist hand-carves small birds, flowers, or other images through the outer color to reveal the base. Each bead is unique.

galvanized Plated with zinc in a shiny or a matte finish. The zinc coating tends not to be durable and can rub off during beading. An acrylic spray may help stabilize the finish.

gangidana A zigzag bead, such as the glass court bead of the Edo period in China.

garnet A group of transparent to opaque minerals or gemstones with related chemical composition and a vitreous luster. The color is most commonly deep red, but garnet also occurs in a variety of colors. What is more popularly known as garnet is the red carbuncle stones *almandite* or *pyrope*. Garnet has a Mohs scale hardness factor of 6.5 to 7.5, and the crystal structure is cubic, rhombic dodecahedron, or icositetrahedron. The garnet group includes six different mineral species: *almandite* (or almandine); *pyrope*; *spessartite* (or spessartine); *grossularite*; *andradite*; and *uvarovite*. The red varieties of the stone are usually called garnets. Pyrope (magnesium aluminum silicate) may be red with a brown hint; almandine (iron aluminum silicate) is red with a violet hint; spessartite (magnesium aluminum silicate) orange to reddish brown; grossular (calcium aluminum silicate) is colorless, green, yellow, and brown; andradite (calcium iron silicate) is black, brown, and yellow-brown; and uvarovite (calcium chromium silicate) is emerald green. Garnets are found in Argentina, Brazil, Australia, Burma, Scotland, Switzerland, Tanzania, and the United States.

Shown is a double-strand choker with 3-mm garnets and blue goldstone rondelles, accented with Bali sterling-silver beads, strung by Melba Flores.

gaspeite Also spelled *gaspetite*, a gemstone distinguished by its apple-green color, gaspeite has a Mohs scale hardness factor of 4.5 to 5. It is a nickel, magnesium, iron carbonate. Found only in Canada and Australia, it is somewhat rare, but has grown increasingly popular among jewelers. In the strand of beads shown, the apple-green specimens are gaspeite. The name comes from the location, the Gaspé Peninsula in Canada, where it was discovered.

gauge A standard unit of measure for metal thickness, whether of wire or sheet metal. The measurement 20-gauge wire is thicker in diameter than, say, 34-gauge wire. Here the lower the gauge, the stronger and thicker the metal wire or sheet.

In jewelry-making, gauge also may refer to a standard of measure, such as the millimeter, inch, microinch, or microns. A microinch is equal to one-millionth (1,000,000th) of an inch. A micron is one-thousandth (1,000th) of a millimeter; a micrometer is one-millionth (1,000,000th) of a meter.

A gauge can also refer to a tool for measuring, such as calipers. Usually stated in metric measurements, a *micrometer caliper tool* can be used to measure very small lengths, diameters, or thicknesses.

gauging Stretching earring holes in earlobes.

gecko stitch Also called *alligator, chili,* and *stacking stitch,* this fairly unusual three-dimensional stitch may be seen in South American goods, although the exact origin of the stitch is unknown. Shown is an adorable creature beaded by Dana Muller in dainty glass seed beads. Notice the interesting effect of the striped beads used for the eyes.

gem chips This term applies to small gemstone bits that are polished and drilled. The bracelet shown below, finished with sterling cones and a magnetic clasp, has a base of spiral stitch with seed beads and gem chips that give it added dimension.

gem-setting pliers A tool designed for professional precision work in setting faceted gemstones. The pliers are used to bend the metal prongs that hold a gemstone in place.

gemology The scientific study of gemstones, concerning such properties as their chemical composition, physical characteristics, optical qualities, and industrial uses.

gemstone Gemstones, commonly referred to as *gems* or *stones,* include a wide range of natural materials that have specifically defined characteristics. Most gemstones are minerals, mineral aggregates, rocks, or petrified matter, and many, like amber, coral, and pearls, are of organic origin (products of once-living plants or animals).

To describe gems, gemologists use many technical specifications, such as the stone's chemical composition and its *habit,* the form in which the stone is usually found. Gems are also classified into different groups, species, and varieties. They are noted for their *refractive index, specific gravity, hardness, dispersion, cleavage, fracture*, and *luster.* Gems absorb a distinctive spectrum. Flaws or other material found within a stone are called *inclusions* (which could increase or decrease the gem's value), and where the gem is found is called an *occurrence*. Not all minerals or mineral aggregates are discovered in the quality appropriate to a desirable gemstone. Gemstones are typically cut, faceted, polished, and then used in jewelry or collected. Gems that are crystals are also classified by a *crystal system,* such as *cubic, trigonal,* or *monoclinic.*

Precious gemstones (cardinal gems) include the diamond, ruby, emerald, sapphire, and amethyst. Since amethyst is now more widely available, it has dropped from this original list devised by clerics centuries ago. Pearls were also sometimes loosely included in the "precious" group. The designation *semiprecious gemstones* usually applies to all other gemstones. The term *semiprecious* must be used with caution because it implies that the stone has less value than other (more precious) gemstones. What most influences a gemstone's value is supply and demand. Color, cut, clarity, and size are also main factors, along with hardness, enhancing treatments, and popular appeal.

Gemstones are noted for their beauty, durability, and rarity. Other materials, like bone, glass, metal, and wood, also used for personal adornment, are not technically considered gemstones. Metals (like gold and silver) and fossils are commonly used along with gemstones to make jewelry and other precious objects. A particular gemstone's popularity depends on local availability and the whims of fashion. New gemstones have been discovered in recent times.

The multigemstone bracelet shown here offers a sampling of five popular stones used in Native American designs. From left to right, the gemstones alternating in this bracelet are

turquoise, gaspeite, turquoise, coral, turquoise, malachite, denim lapis, coral, gaspeite, and turquoise.

gemstone cuts Common gemstone cuts and shapes include: American, antique, baguette, ball, barrel-shaped, briolette, bud, Ceylon, coat of arms, double brilliant, double rose, drop, emerald, French, free-form, half-brilliant, heart, hexagon, highlight brilliant, jubilee, king, magna, marquise, navette, needle brilliant, net, octagon, olive, oval, pear-shaped, pentagon, petal, recoup-rose, rhomb, round, shield, simple rose, square, star, star brilliant, Swiss, trapezoid, triangle, and whirl. Find common gemstone cuts drawings in Part IV.

gemstone holder A spring-loaded device with a long handle and prongs at the end; used to hold a single gemstone to avoid losing the stone on carpeting while showing it to customers. Used by jewelers and jewelry-makers but not essential for beaders.

gemstone points A gemstone cut with a point at one or both ends; gemstones with points do not occur naturally. Such stones are usually top-drilled from side to side.

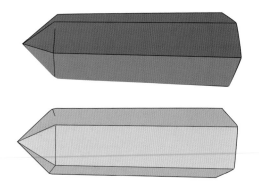

gemstone treatments As products of nature, gemstones are noted and named for their distinctive mineral composition, color, and hardness. After they are mined, many gemstones undergo accepted treatments to improve their color, appearance, clarity, luster, durability, brilliance, and, hence, their value. The treatments may involve bleaching, coating, filling, foiling, heating, irradiating, oiling, reconstituting, or waxing. Even gemstones identified and sold as pure may have been subjected to one or more of these treatments. Only a *natural* gemstone can be guaranteed not to have been treated in any way. Most reputable dealers will disclose what, if any, treatments to which the gemstone may have been subjected. Most treatments are done to stabilize color, because natural gemstones will fade over time. Find the gemstone treatments chart in Part IV.

geode Geodes, also called *thundereggs,* are spherical rocks that form in buried cavities; they may develop in trapped air bubbles or vacant pockets in tree roots underground. These geological rock formations occur in sedimentary and certain volcanic rocks. The wall of the cavity hardens over time, and the interior fills with crystals. A geode's outer shell is often composed of limestone or related rock, and the crystals inside, quartz or chalcedony; however, the crystals may be of any kind. Geodes commonly have hollow centers; when they are completely solid, they are called *nodules.* An open cavity in a geode is called a *druse.* There is no telling in advance what kind of crystals a geode may enclose, but geodes are uniquely magnificent. The term comes from the Greek *geoides,* which means "earthlike"; people once imagined that geodes resembled the internal structure of the Earth. Geodes are common in certain formations in Brazil, Namibia, Mexico, and the United States.

geode slice Slices of geodes can be used in jewelry. Geodes are often halved or otherwise sliced and polished to use for display or jewelry. They are also sometimes dyed. Shown here are dainty geode slices suitable for use as pendants or earrings.

German silver Also referred to as *nickel silver*, this silver-colored alloy made of copper, nickel, and often zinc is sometimes used as imitation silver. Contrary to its name, it contains no genuine silver.

germanium A silvery gray or white metalloid similar to tin that can be alloyed with silver to make the patented *Argentium Sterling Silver*, which is highly tarnish resistant. It is ductile, lustrous, brittle, and hard with the same face-centered cubic crystal structure as the diamond and has some of the same properties as silicon. It is classified as a semimetallic element. It acts against certain bacteria. The name comes from the Latin word *Germania*,

for "Germany." When added to glass, it increases its refraction index. It is stable in air and water and unaffected by alkalis and most acids, with the exception of nitric acid.

ghost beads Seeds of the cedar tree (really berries or cones from the juniper tree) that have been drilled through are called *ghost beads*. The tree, called Grandfather Cedar or more recently Grandfather Juniper, is considered sacred by Native North Americans who use its leaves in ceremonies. (Various juniper trees have the common name of cedar, although that is a different genus in more recent scientific classifications. The beads have traditionally been made from trees of the genus *Juniperus*.) The tree produces an essential oil with a potent fragrance that repels insects. Cedar-tree beads are associated with the Ghost Dance ceremony, once prohibited by the United States government. The ceremony played a key role in the Wounded Knee Massacre of 1890 when government officials misunderstood the Ghost Dance to be a war dance and feared that rioting and aggression would erupt. However, the dancers were, in fact, defending their right to perform their sacred ceremonies. Shown is a strand of cedar beads.

ghost finish A glass-bead finish achieved by applying an aurora borealis or rainbow finish to a matte surface. Beads with a ghost finish are sometimes sold as *frosted beads*. Shown are beads with aurora borealis and frosted finishes.

gilt A very thin finish of gold or the color of gold and therefore not necessarily real gold. *See also* gold-plated.

gimp Also known as *bullion* or *French wire,* a fine wire that is wound over thread or other core material, or tightly coiled into tubes. Stringing cord can be threaded through it to finish a beading project, and it is used to attach findings, such as clasps.

givre beads The French word *givre* means "frosty." These clear or translucent glass beads, originally made by Swarovski, have a colored core or swirls of color in part of the bead.

glass Myriad types of clear and colored glass, such as enameled, screen-printed, and sand-blasted, are made into beads. *See* glass types, lampworking, and *specific glass or bead types.*

glass-bead colors The colors in glass come from various metals and oxides that go into its making. Glass without color is actually a translucent (or bottle) green, deriving from a minute quantity of iron oxides naturally present in sand, the major constituent of glass. The sand, or quartz sand, used for this purpose is a very pure form of crystalline quartz. Small amounts of manganese are sometimes added to neutralize the effect of the iron oxides and to produce a more colorless glass. A wide variety of colors are possible with the addition

of copper, cobalt, arsenic, gold, selenium, coal, sulfur, tin, and even uranium. Colored-glass recipes are guarded trade secrets in the glassmaking industry.

glass-bead disease Conservationists and museum curators use this term when concerned with ancient beads and the potentially harmful chemical interactions in the glass that may occur over time. Stable glass is composed of silica, flux, and stabilizers, as well as other components. In older beads, these ingredients may have been mixed in less than ideal proportions, which may lead to unstable glass. Symptoms of glass-bead disease are broken beads, sweating beads, crusty deposits on the beads or stringing material, *crizzling* (a fine network of cracks), and bleaching or darkening of the wool, silk, leather, or other fabric in direct contact with the deteriorating glass beads. Preventive conservation techniques may slow deterioration.

glass bead game The glass bead game is central to a novel titled *Magister Ludi* (*The Glass Bead Game: A Novel*) by German author Hermann Hesse, for which he won the 1943 Nobel Prize for literature. The futuristic novel is set in a fictional province of Castalia, an isolated community of intellectuals in Central Europe. Castalia members devote themselves to exploring associations of ideas, keeping universal knowledge alive in a world that has deteriorated spiritually, socially, philosophically, and politically. While the actual mechanics of the game at the core of the novel are somewhat elusive and the rules are never disclosed, the story brings together the entire spectrum of letters, arts, and science.

Why glass beads? The game central to the novel is thought to have been originally played with beads or tokens, like those found on an abacus or used in the Chinese game of Go. In the story, the glass beads served as tokens representing music, art, mathematics, science, religion, and other intellectual pursuits. In later centuries, such props became obsolete as abstract spoken formulas replaced them.

The glass bead game serves as a metaphor for the game of life and has been compared to shamanistic spiritual revelation, psychedelic experience, and the universal knowledge base found on the Internet. Players have to incorporate many symbols of knowledge into a cohesive understanding of their place in the universe. The novel's chief question is whether or not intellectuals have the right to withdraw from participation in the floundering, teeming world at large.

Hesse grew up in a part of Germany that excelled in glass beadmaking. The glass bead game has inspired other bead games, many bearing no relation to Hesse's original idea.

glass beadmaking   The process of making glass beads; heating, sculpting, and embellishing glass with a torch and a few other tools or basic supplies. The craft has been developed into a highly sophisticated process that builds on more advanced techniques and creativity. Learning the craft requires hands-on experience under a skilled glass-bead maker. Glass beads date from at least 2500 B.C. Terms related to glass beadmaking: *kiln, anneal, frit, mandrel, cane, trailing, torch, marvel, enamel paint, enamel powder, aventurine,* and *thermal shock. See* lampwork and seed beads.

glass cane   Also called *glass rods*, glass cane is the basic building material used in glass beadmaking. Glass is basically a mixture of silica (quartz sand) and oxides (chemical compounds of oxygen), to which potash (potassium carbonate, especially that from wood ashes) or soda (sodium carbonate) and lime (calcium oxide) are added and heated. These ingredients are mixed and melted together, shaped into long, slender rods, and then cooled. The finished glass canes come in various sizes, but are generally 7 to 8 mm in diameter, although they may come in thicker sizes.

To make beads, the glass canes or rods are manipulated by heating them into a liquid state, after which they are shaped and cooled into a different shape. The proportion of silica to oxides affects the melting point of the glass. Many glass beads are made out of soft glass, which has a lower melting temperature than hard glass. *See also* furnace-glass beads.

glass pearls   Also called *pearlized glass*, these glass beads have a pearl coating. Less expensive than cultured pearls, they are nevertheless attractive and come in a variety of colors. In the past, artificial pearls were in demand because of the rarity and expense of real pearls. However, with the introduction of cultured pearls in the world market, it has been easier and cheaper to acquire authentic pearls. The chief advantage of artificial pearls is their uniform size and appearance.

An early form of artificial pearl, called *Roman pearls,* was produced by coating the interior of a blown glass bead with guanine, the pearlescent element found in fish scales (sometimes called *alabaster glass*) and then coating it with wax. Artificial pearls have been defined as blown beads with fish-silver or a solution of fish scales. The term (glass) *pearl beads* is also applied to drawn or blown beads with colored or metallic lining; these are similar to seed pearls or seed beads.

glass rod *See* glass cane.

glass types Glass for beadmaking is sold in *rods* or *canes* (from 6 to 15 mm in diameter) available in a wide array of opaque, translucent, and transparent colors. *Sheet glass,* cut into strips, is also used. *Dichroic glass,* sold in narrow strips of sheet glass as well as in rods, is made with a thin film of metal fused to the glass surface. For beadmaking, the glass can be *pressed* or made with *lampworking* techniques. Beads made from dichroic glass have a metallic sheen, and the colors visible vary depending on the angle of viewing. Mosaic cane slices were used to make millefiori beads. *Furnace glass* beads with liner or twisted stripe patterns are made from decorated canes built up from smaller canes that have been encased in clear glass and then exuded. Furnace glass, as the name implies, is worked in a large glass furnace and an annealing kiln.

The amount of heat and time required for melting and working the various glass types varies. Hard glass or *borosilicate glass,* such as Pyrex, requires more time to heat than soft glass made from soda lime, such as Effetre (also known as Moretti or Vetrofond), Bullseye, and Oroboros. Soft glass is usually recommended for making beads because it melts at relatively low temperatures.

Lead crystal, because of its lead content, tends to sparkle and is more fragile than other glass. Lead crystal beads are machine-cut and polished. The finest may be cut with a diamond saw.

Molded beads are made from very thick glass rods heated into molten glass, stamped, and the hole pierced with a needle. To soften seam lines and remove any "flashing," the molded beads are rolled in hot sand. Molded-glass beads may also be called *pressed-glass* beads.

Frit or *powder glass* is used for surface decorations in lampwork beads.

The *wound-glass* beadmaking technique, in which beads are made by twisting or wrapping hot glass around a rod or mandrel, is one of the oldest ways to create glass beads. It is also called *lampworking.* Fine rods or stringers of colored glass are typically used.

Drawn-glass beads, made by drawing or pulling a tube of molten glass until it is long and thin, is the method for making seed beads and bugle beads. Seed beads may be mechanically drawn.

The major centers for producing these beads each made their own glass, with a few exceptions. *See also* borosilicate, soft glass, hard glass, dichroic glass, and lampworking.

glover's needle A sturdy needle with a very sharp triangular tip used for piercing and sewing leather as well as for beading. Tapestry needles sometimes substitute for use on leather, but the leather may first require punching a small hole with an awl or glover's needle.

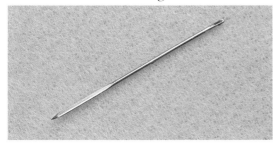

glow beads A type of bead that glows underwater, used in fishing with live bait to attract fish. Such beads may have the nonmetallic element phosphorus in them, or be painted with glow paint containing phosphorus, which is found in the soil and most living things. The English word *phosphorus* comes from the Greek *phosphoros,* which means "light-bearing." Other glow beads are basically party favors, associated with events such as Mardi Gras. They are plastic or glass beads that glow in the dark and under black and ultraviolet light. This glow is called *phosphorescence.*

glow finish A sheer golden finish on a transparent bead that imparts a radiant luster.

glyptic The art or process of carving or engraving. *See also* glyptography.

glyptography The art of carving and engraving gemstones. In *niccolo,* popular for engraving coats of arms and monograms, a thin upper layer and translucent color tones reveal some of the color of the base. In *intaglio,* used principally for creating seals, a negative image is engraved. And in *cameo,* a relief is raised or cut. *See also* layer stones.

gneiss A common type of metamorphosed igneous rock resembling granite, except with minerals in bands, that may include feldspar and quartz, with a coarse texture.

gold A shiny precious yellow metal, gold is resistant to corrosion and damage from moisture, air, heat, and most solvents (such as nitric acid). Its malleability, ductility, density, and relatively low melting point (for a metal) allows gold to be easily manipulated, shaped, pressed, or molded into components for jewelry. It was one of the earliest metals, following iron and bronze (copper and tin), to be worked and valued by humans. Gold, which is easily scratched or dented, is often made into an alloy with other metals to increase its strength. It also forms a rich plate or coating over base metals. Egyptian hieroglyphs dating from as early as 2600 B.C. describe gold. The word *gold* is from the Anglo-Saxon, which was in turn, taken from the Latin word *aurum,* which means "shining dawn."

Jewelers describe gold in karats, which designate its purity. The purest gold is 24 karat; that means it has a millesimal fineness of 999. Other common karat measures in decreasing order of millesimal fineness are 22 karat (millesimal fineness 916), 20 karat (833 millesimal fineness), 18 karat (millesimal fineness 750), 16 karat (millesimal fineness 625), 14 karat (millesimal fineness 585), 10 karat (millesimal fineness 417), and 9 karat (millesimal fineness 375). Naturally distributed throughout the world, found in nuggets or grains in rocks or alluvial deposits, gold is valued as one of earth's rare substances. In alloys, gold can vary from yellow to white (platinum), red (copper), blue (iron), black

G

(bismuth and silver), and even purple (aluminum), with yellow being the most common. Native gold may contain 8% to 10% silver. Gold can be made into a thread for embroidery. Gold is weighted in troy ounces. The terms *white gold* (gold + nickel, zinc, palladium, or platinum), *rose gold* (gold + copper), and *green gold* (gold + silver) describe the color effects of alloys with gold.

For centuries, gold has been used as currency of exchange (often in coins) and as a store of value. In modern times, it has been adopted as an international monetary standard. A good thermal and electrical conductor, gold has been used in electronics and mechanics. It was also once commonly used in dentistry and has found many modern uses in science and industry.

gold-filled Base metal, such as brass, to which a thin gold layer has been applied, used in jewelry findings such as chains, ear wires, and beads. The fill is generally 14-carat gold. Such a finish is less likely to cause an allergic reaction than other metals, but the gold may wear off (how quickly depends on its thickness) with use. This is an obvious substitute for solid gold, given its lower cost.

According to the Federal Trade Commission in the United States, when an object, such as silver, is first covered with a base metal like nickel and then covered with a certain thickness of gold, it may be described as gold-filled, and cannot qualify as vermeil. *See also* vermeil.

gold finish Base metal electroplated with a nonstandardized thickness of gold, also called *gold color*.

gold flake Similar to gold leaf, this product consists of small particles of gold used in glass beadmaking. In one process, the hot glass on the mandrel is rolled in the gold frit and then encased with clear glass. The metallic particles, often really made of copper or silver rather than gold (although considered "gold" by color), may create an *aventurine effect* (or sometimes *aventurine* or *aventurina*), not to be confused with the natural gemstone called aventurine. Gold, silver, or copper flake adds sparkle or glitter to the colored glass and may be mixed with glass in the form of rods, frit, or even powder. What many people call "gold flake" is really the less expensive copper because the perceived color of the metal is influenced by the color of the glass. Gold flake, or aventurine, is also sold in chunks and preformed rods. An edible variety of gold flake, leaf, or dust was first used as decoration in sweets and other confections in medieval Europe.

gold-foil beads Also called *gold-lined*; these glass beads have a thin layer of genuine gold metal called *gold foil* embedded within the layers of glass, or applied to the inside of the hole to reflect a golden light. As a bead type, the term may loosely refer to beads with silver or copper linings, not simply gold. The second photo here shows silver-foil beads.

gold-lined *See* gold-foil beads.

gold luster A transparent glass bead to which a gold-luster finish is added, creating subtle gold highlights.

gold-plated Having a thin coating of gold electroplated to the surface of another metal, often silver or copper. Thin gold foils may also be applied to the surface of an object by chemical or mechanical means, called *gilding.* Gold-plated silver may be a sandwich of silver with layers of copper, nickel, and gold on top. The barrier copper or nickel layers prevent atoms of silver diffusing into the gold top layer and tarnishing the surface. The industry standard for plating, whether of gold, silver, or nickel, is for a thickness of 15 to 25 microns. According to the U.S. Federal Trade Commission, "the term *gold plate* is acceptable as long as the product contains a coating with a minimum thickness of half a micron, or 20 millionths of an inch, of 24-karat gold or the equivalent." *See also* vermeil.

gold swirl A glass lampwork bead embellished with swirls of gold sparkly glass painted on or applied to the bead surface. Shown top right is a bracelet strung with rondelles or disk-shaped green beads with gold swirls.

gold thread One of many metallic threads used for textiles, embroidery, cross-stitch, beading, and any number of art and jewelry projects. The products range from single-filament gold thread to gold-colored cotton or other threads wrapped around a core.

gold topaz A false or misleading name for citrine (quartz).

gold wash Also known as *vermeil,* the ancient technique of applying a coating of gold to the surface of metals, typically bronze or silver. The object is then burnished to bring out the richness of the gold.

goldstone An imitation of the natural gemstone called *sunstone* or *aventurine,* this synthetic stone has a base of glass fused with flecks of copper or other metallic shavings to make it sparkle like glitter. Goldstone, a type of glass made with copper or copper salts (with a reducing flame applied) was developed by the Miotti family in 17th century Venice. It is sold in the form of beads, chips, cabochons, figurines, and other shapes. It comes in reddish brown as well as dark blue or purple, and sometimes green with silvery accents. Goldstone can be carved. The glass itself is colorless. The various colors of

goldstone may be based on metals besides copper, such as cobalt, manganese, or chromium, suspended in the glass. Goldstone is sometimes called *aventurine glass* since it resembles that natural stone. It has also been called *monkstone* or *monk's stone* since in folklore its discovery had been attributed to an Italian monastic order.

Goldstone is opaque and usually a dark coppery brown or dark blue, almost black. Natural aventurine is light green, natural sunstone is orange and transparent, and natural moonstone is white and translucent.

Shown above are pieces of goldstone and below are blue goldstone rondelles.

gooseberry beads Named for their resemblance to the fruit; translucent pale or clear beads with faint white stripes. They are thought to have originated in Venice around the 16th century. Their shape is somewhat oval. Bead researcher Peter Francis describes them as "white stripes on a clear base." The glass may have a gray or yellow tinge.

gossamer A lightweight, sheer, delicate, or gauzy finish that produces a golden glow over transparent beads.

Goulimine beads Colorful Venetian glass millefiore beads sometimes generically called African trade beads. Also spelled Guelmim and Guelmin, the beads were named after a sub-Saharan town in Morocco, noted as a trade center and camel market.

gourd doll A doll created from a gourd. Several different types are made by various peoples around the world; many use beading. The first doll shown here has beads for hair and clothing, and no fabric foundation for attaching the beads; the beads are attached with needle and thread to each other, without any adhesive. A similar technique is called *knotless netting*. The skirt was made using a netting stitch, and the hair is beaded fringe.

The Mijkenda people in Kenya use small bottle gourds to create dolls completely covered with beads. The bilobal gourd shape suggests the human figure. First the gourd is covered with a loosely woven fabric before the gourd is beaded. Cowrie shells are commonly used as symbolic adornment.

Another gourd doll type uses a technique found throughout sub-Saharan Africa that is similar to the Huichol technique of embedding beads into beeswax. Africans use a thin layer of pitch or tar to cover the gourd and then press strung beads onto the surface. *See also*

Huichol. Ginger Summit created the tar-beaded gourd doll and Dawn Schiller created the Huichol-style beaded gourd resembling an owl. Courtesy of Ginger Summit and Jim Widess, *Making Gourd Dolls & Spirit Figures*; photos by Jim Widess. *See also* fertility bead dolls, initiation bead dolls, and Sangoma bead doll.

gourd embellishment A general term for the use of beads to decorate gourd art. Gourds are cut, carved, painted, etched, and pyroengraved (surface burned; the technique is called pyrography) in a variety of ways to produce creative and functional objects, like birdhouses, ladles, vases, and jewelry. The doll shown, assembled from cut and painted gourd pieces by Jean Jones, has beaded jewelry and carries a beaded basket. The shawl is made of corn husks. *See also* wrapped stitch and gourd doll.

gourd necklace A piece of jewelry made with gourd pieces or a whole gourd. The necklace shown was created by Bonnie Gibson from a small gourd that was embellished with assorted beads and knotless netting made of waxed linen.

gourd shekere Pronounced "she-KE'-ray," a percussion instrument from Africa made from a natural gourd. Shekeres come in a variety of sizes and shapes, limited only by the supply

of gourds available. They can be small enough to be played with one hand, using the neck as a natural handle, or large enough to require both hands. The shekere shown, made by Bonnie Gibson, uses a bottle gourd approximately 12 inches (30 cm) tall. The mesh is woven with waxed linen and glass crow beads.

gourd stitch Similar to peyote stitch and often called by that name. The blue doll necklace here demonstrates gourd stitch and its usefulness for making three-dimensional beaded objects. It was made by Cornelia Hoffman of the White Mountain Apache tribe. Find discussion of distinctions between peyote and gourd stitches in Part III.

graduated beads A string of beads, whether glass, gemstone, or metal, that increase (or graduate) in size, generally with the largest beads in the middle and the smaller ones on the ends.

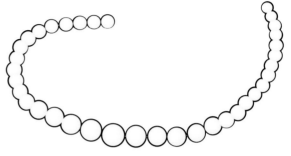

grain Also called a *pearl grain;* a unit of weight formerly used for pearls, diamonds, and other precious stones. It corresponds to about 50 milligrams or one quarter of a carat. Pearl weight is often expressed in both carats and grains.

gram The metric unit of weight used in the trade for gemstones. It is nearly equal to the mass of 1 cubic centimeter of water at its maximum density.

granite A natural stone material sometimes used to create beads in Mali, Africa, and other places. Granite, a type of common intrusive, felsic, igneous rock, may be found in white, black, buff, gray, or pink, sometimes coarsely grained. Because it is massive, hard, and tough, it has often been used for construction of buildings and roads. *See also* soft stones and hard stones.

granny knot This knot, sometimes called a *slip knot*, is insecure and not advised for beadwork. Find knotting diagrams in Part V.

graphite paddle Graphite is lightweight and will not stick to hot glass, making it a good shaping tool. For the paddle, a flat piece of graphite attaches to a long handle. *See* bead rake.

greasy glass A glass bead made with greasy glass is shallowly translucent and uniformly murky, as if coated with petroleum jelly. The glass has richness and depth and resembles dense opal glass. Greasy colors recede against opaque colors but come forward against transparent colors. The term may also be applied to beads said to have glass bead disease.

green gold An alloy of gold and silver that's greenish yellow. The term is also applied to the practice of attempting to minimize or eliminate human-rights abuses and environmental damage when mining, selling, or transporting gold, diamonds, and other valuable products.

green hearts These glass beads originated in Venice, probably in the 17th century; they have dark green centers and an opaque brick-red exterior that simulates jasper. A variety distinct from white hearts, the two bead types share their place of origin, and drawn and layered means of manufacture. Green hearts went out of production in the early 1800s. *See also* white hearts.

gris-gris A small cloth or leather pouch often decorated with cowrie shell or other beads. Found throughout West Africa, the gris-gris can contain an incantation or a variety of personal objects, such as stones, bones, or hair, used as talismans and worn for luck and protection.

gross A common unit of measure defined as twelve dozen, or 144 pieces. This measurement is frequently used in wholesale lots of beads and findings, such as ear wires, bead strands, and clasps.

grossularite Also called *grossular.* From the garnet group of gemstones, grossularite, composed of calcium aluminum silicate, is colorless, green, yellow, or brown. A subgroup is hessonite (brownish red), also called cinnamon stone or Kaneel stone; leuco garnet (colorless); hydrogrossular (greenish); tsavorite (green).

gunmetal The color of steel or gunmetal gray, resembling the color of hematite or shiny gray glass beads. Also called *red brass,* gunmetal can refer to a kind of bronze that is an alloy containing copper, tin, and zinc. Although the alloy was originally used to make guns, today guns are generally made of steel.

guru bead Also called a *meru, sumeru,* or *stupa* bead; the terminal bead in a mala, a set of Buddhist or Hindu prayer beads. Sandalwood beads and bodhi seed beads are commonly used in malas, but the terminal bead, usually larger than the rest, may be made of metal, bone, or a gemstone, like coral, turquoise, carnelian, lapis lazuli, or amber. This is also characteristic of Islamic amulets.

H

hairpipe *See* bone hairpipe.

half-drilled bead A bead with a hole that is drilled only halfway through the length of the bead so that it may be attached to the proper finding, such as an eye screw, with jewelry cement.

half-hitch knot Also called an *in-line knot,* this is a simple knot tied by looping a line around an object and across the main part of the line, and then through the resulting loop. It is very useful for securing tension in bead-work. Find knotting diagrams in Part V.

Hamilton gold A high-quality form of gold plating used in costume jewelry. The propri-etary formula (from a protected and patented process) yields a warm yellow color, and it provides a durable finish. However, various dealers have defined it differently. One describes Hamilton gold as ion-plated titanium nitride and zirconium nitride used as fundamental gold-plating material while another calls it a brass-toned metal with a small amount of real gold. Check the United States Federal Trade Commission for standards on gold.

hammered metal A metal finish created by pounding a metal with a soft mallet to give it an uneven or wavy surface design.

handmade The entire shaping and forming of the product, from raw materials to its finishing, is done by hand. According to Federal Trade Commission guidelines in the United States, to qualify as handmade or handwrought, these conditions must be met.

handwrought *See* handmade.

hank Several strands of beads bundled or looped together and sold as a unit. For instance, seed beads of common sizes are usually sold in hanks of ten to twelve strands, each 10 inches (25 cm) long. Hanks of size 13 charlotte-cut beads are usually only 6 inches (15 cm) long. Twelve hanks bundled together are called a *rope* or *bunch.*

hard glass Hard glass, also known as *labora-tory glass,* such as Pyrex, has a borosilicate base and is stiffer than so-called *soft glass* (made of soda, lime, and lead). The propor-tion of silica to oxides affects the melting temperature of glass. Hard glass has a higher melting temperature than soft glass and does not hold heat very long, giving it a shorter time during which it can be worked or shaped. *See also* borosilicate glass.

hard stones Granite, basalt, marble, and precious gemstones, like diamonds, are more difficult to cut, carve, facet, or inscribe (the work done by a lapidary or stone artisan) than softer stones like limestone, soapstone, and sandstone. The Mohs scale of hardness (ratings are from 1 to 10, with 10 indicating the hardest) is the standard, used by geolo-gists and gemologists worldwide for rating the relative hardness of stones and other minerals. The harder stone can scratch one of less hardness. In general, the marketplace value of a stone increases with its hardness factor.

Inlay techniques in marble using hard stones, known as *pietra dura,* may involve onyx, jasper, and carnelian. *See also* soft stones. Certain stones are more desirable for carving and faceting, but even soft stones are suitable for beads. Semiprecious stones rate about 5 to 7 on the Mohs scale of hardness, while precious stones, such as diamonds and sapphires, are among the hardest. Relatively soft soapstone, rating 1 to 3 on the Mohs scale, can easily be fashioned into beads.

hardness scale *See* Mohs scale of hardness and find Mohs scale in Part IV.

hatband A band that encircles the brim of a hat, embellishing the crown. Beadwork hatbands can be of any kind—loomed, stitched, or a rope design, or even embroidery. Beaded hatbands may be backed with fabric or leather to be more durable.

hawk's-eye A type of quartz, silicon dioxide, with iridescent planes and a silky luster. The crystal system is trigonal and the Mohs scale hardness factor is 7. Fine, fibrous blue-gray to blue-green opaque aggregates are formed when the translucent quartz replaces the mineral crocidolite. Cabochons display chatoyancy. *See also* quartz cat's-eye and tiger's-eye.

head pin *See* flat-head pin.

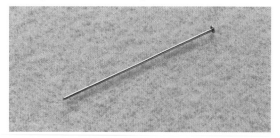

headband Similar to a hatband, this band is worn on or around the head itself, whether for decoration or keeping hair in place. It is tied in the back and, for comfort, often backed with fabric or leather and beadwork. When worn across the forehead, it is sometimes called a browband. While some headbands also serve as sweatbands, the beaded variety does not.

healing Gemstones, crystals, and certain minerals and metals have been used in traditional healing. Gemstone healing treatments have appeared in medical manuscripts dating from ancient Turkey, 6th century China, Medieval Germany, and Renaissance Judeo-Spain. Modern New Age or alternative-health practitioners claim that certain gemstones, when worn, may be used to purify and heal the physical body, support the hormonal and immune systems, resolve negative emotional patterns, clear the mind, increase the ability to focus, and much more. Homeopathic remedies have also included certain minerals in tinctures or highly diluted solutions. In the United States, the Food and Drug Administration regulates certain homeopathic products, so that we cannot attest to the safety of any given remedy; some may even be toxic. *Lithotherapy* (use of stones in healing) is a branch of homeopathy. People who wear copper bracelets have reported that the copper helps relieve symptoms of arthritis, for instance. For any concerns about health, consult a physician. Biochemistry and pharmacology are complex studies.

heat treatment Heat may enhance a gemstone's color or clarity; it is often used in combination with irradiation. In most cases, the results of heat treatment are permanent. Heat treatment can, for instance, turn a light-blue aquamarine into a more desirable, permanent deeper blue. However, heat that's too high could cause discoloration. Neutron and gamma irradiation may also improve color, but the results are not permanent.

Hebron beads A variety of coarse, opaque, wound-glass beads produced in Hebron, near Jerusalem, from as early as the 12th century until about 1878. Glassmaking may have drawn on alkaline Dead Sea mineral salts. Hebron was a major glass and glass-beadmaking center between the sixteenth and nineteenth centuries. In the Middle Ages, the glass beads were traded far and wide, and were especially in demand in Egypt and West Africa. In Nigeria, they picked up the name *Kano beads,* after the country's capital. Yellow and green are the most common colors for Hebron beads, which are also sometimes blue, black, or white.

heishi An ancient Pueblo style of tiny disk-shaped or tube-shaped bead cut from shell. Heishi (pronounced "HEE'-shee"), also spelled *heishe*, means "shell bead." The shell is first cut into strips that are then cut into small, irregular squarish bits. The squarish bits are snipped again to remove sharp angles. Then the individual bits are hand-drilled and strung on wire to prepare them for grinding. The strung bits, originally ground on fine-grained sandstone, are today machine-ground into fairly smooth rounds. Although originally made from shells, today heishi are made from a great many materials, including gemstones. The Philippines produces a large amount of

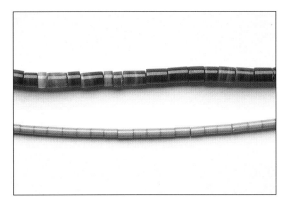

finished heishi beads. Pictured are heishi of pen shell and turquoise.

heliolite Another name for *sunstone.*

hemalike (hemalyke) *See* hematine.

hematine A synthetic form of hematite that, like its namesake, is a shiny gun-metal gray. Like most simulated gemstones, hematine has the advantage of lower cost than the genuine substance and can be manufactured in any shape. Also known as *hemalyke* or *hemalike,* it is made from ground hematite or artificial iron oxide powder, mixed with resin and molded into beads or findings. Owing to its iron ore content, it has electromagnetic properties and considerable weight. Hematine and

hematite can be difficult to distinguish; hence, hematine is often sold as hematite. Shown are hematine beads in various shapes.

hematite Its name derives from the Greek *haimatites,* meaning "bloodlike." This opaque stone, composed of iron oxide, occurs in variations of gray, from silvery to very dark, as well as in reddish brown. The bloodlike allusion refers to the red-rust streaks or spots that characterize the stone. A very common mineral and rather heavy, hematite is the principal ore of iron. It is also spelled *haematite.* Varieties include bloodstone, kidney ore, iron rose, specularite, rainbow hematite, titanohematite, and paint ore. Hematite is harder but more brittle than raw iron and sometimes called *black diamond.* It rates 5.5 to 6.5 on the Mohs scale of hardness. Well-crystallized hematite varieties are called *iron luster,* while finely crystallized hematite is called red iron ore or *red ironstone.* The polished stone is metallic and shiny. When cut into very thin plates, it appears red and transparent. Beads of *hematine,* an imitation material, are often sold as the real thing.

hemostat A stainless-steel tool used in jewelry-making for holding parts temporarily in place. It is also a medical instrument used in surgery.

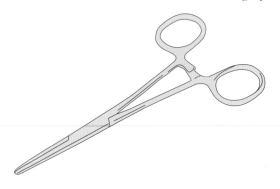

hemp A stringing or weaving material, made from a tough plant fiber of the Asian herb of the mulberry family (*Cannabis sativa*). Jute and plants other than true hemp, when put to similar purposes, such as the making of cords, may also be loosely called hemp.

herringbone stitch Also called *Ndebele stitch,* a useful technique for creating flat or three-dimensional beadwork like ropes or chokers. Shown is a flat belt of the stitch. Find stitch diagrams in Part V.

hex beads Beads of a hexagonal, or six-sided, shape. When the beads are very small, the six sides are barely perceptible; they simply give a subtle sparkle as the facets reflect light.

high-polish Shiny or highly reflective, typically describing the surface treatment or finish of a particular metal.

higher metallic Referring to a finish whereby the beads are surface-coated with gold, followed by a spraying of oxidized titanium. Higher metallic beads have a distinctive shimmer and a bright, lasting finish.

Hilltribe silver Handmade silver by the Karen tribe of Thailand that contains 95% to 99% silver. This softer metal can be easily bent and shaped.

hollow bead A glass bead with a large hollow center. Shown here is an unusual two-tone

handmade bead in blue and purple. It can be accented with small beads strung inside it, since the holes are generous.

hook clasp A fairly common jewelry finding that serves as a closure, also called a *hook-and-eye clasp*. It consists of a curved metal piece (the eye) into which the hook can be inserted.

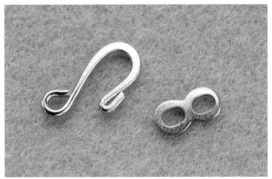

horizontal netting The direction of the thread path along a horizontal plane. Netting can be woven flat or circular, in three dimensions, such as a net of beads around a vase. Shown is a perfume bag necklace made with circular netting on a horizontal plane.

horn beads Carved from animal horn, usually those from cows or water buffalo, in a variety of shapes. Probably the most common bead

shape is the hairpipe bead shown below, composed of horn and bone. Horn beads come in a rich golden brown, black, amber, and sometimes dark red. Synthetic beads made of resin can simulate the rich, deep colors of horn and amber. *See also* keratin.

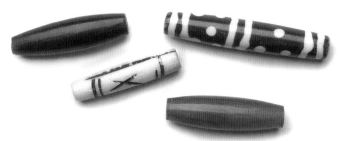

hornblende A common dark green, brown, or black rock-forming mineral found in igneous or metamorphic rocks from the amphibole group that consists of silicates of calcium, sodium, magnesium, aluminum, and iron. Hornblende's composition changes gradually in a highly complex way, depending on temperature, pressure, oxygen activity, and the rock's composition. The color may change accordingly. It is translucent to opaque and has a Mohs scale hardness of 5 to 6. The word *hornblende* comes from the Old German *horn,* perhaps for its resemblance to that bony process, and *blenden,* which means "to deceive." Venetians made wound-glass rosary beads in the late 1400s from hornblende.

hot-pinched beads *See* pinch beads.

howlite An opaque milky white stone with veins of gray, black, or dark brown. It is composed of calcium borosilicate hydroxide and has a Mohs scale hardness rating of 3 to 3.5. Named for Henry How, a geologist from Nova Scotia who first described it in 1868, howlite is found in Nova Scotia, Newfoundland, New Brunswick, and California. It is often dyed to simulate turquoise and lapis lazuli but is otherwise untreated. The howlite shell beads shown were carved in China.

Hubbell beads Turquoise-colored round glass beads, named after the Hubbell Trading Post in Arizona. No written documentation has proven that they were commissioned by the trading post, established in the late 1800s. Hubbell beads are reportedly the last known beads made for trade with Native Americans. The wound-glass beads were made in China and later in Czechoslovakia between 1915 and 1920, where they continue to be manufactured. Any glass bead resembling turquoise in the marketplace today may be informally dubbed Hubbell.

Hudson Bay beads Another term for *white-heart* and *cornaline d'Aleppo* beads. They were once commonly traded by the Hudson Bay Company and other early fur traders in the Great Lakes and Hudson Bay regions in Canada and in northern Michigan territory with Native North Americans (First Nations) for fur pelts. This type of bead, made from wound and drawn glass, originated in Venice in the early 1800s. It was also produced in Czechoslovakia and France. *See also* cornaline d'Aleppo and white hearts.

Huichol The name of a Native tribe in Mexico, pronounced "wee-chol," the term also refers to their famous style of beadwork. Their most widely known technique is that of embedding seed beads in the surfaces of carved gourds or wood. The beads are individually applied, and fixed with beeswax, sometimes mixed with a resin or hardening agent, to create detailed and intricate designs. Huichol work

is characterized by meticulous craftsmanship and depicts themes of nature, especially animals, in deep, brilliant primary colors. Because objects with smaller beads are more labor-intensive to produce, they are usually the more valuable. The pieces shown here indicate the characteristic attention to detail in these designs. The gourd bowl, from the collection of David Bingell, features a scorpion design. *See also* embedded beadwork.

Huichol lace A beadwork technique that resembles delicate lace, most commonly identified with the Huichol tribe of Mexico. Most often made in a circular netting pattern, it is commonly used to make earrings and suncatcher ornaments. It is also called *African flower, Mexican lace,* and *flower mandala.*

hurricane-glass beads Reminiscent of vintage hurricane lamps, these beads have swirls of different colors in the glass. (Hurricane lamps are oil-burning lamps designed to protect the flame from drafts and wind. Glass chimneys come in an assortment of sizes, shapes, frosted finishes, etchings, and colors.)

hypoallergenic This term applies to materials unlikely to cause an allergic reaction, such as a skin rash. Hypoallergenic metal findings, particularly those that come in direct contact with the skin (or body piercings), are made of metals least likely to provoke an allergic reaction. Palladium, platinum, titanium, and surgical steel are the most commonly used metals for this purpose. Niobium, used in medical devices, also has this quality. Gold is alloyed, or mixed, with nickel, silver, copper, and small amounts of zinc to create a variety of colors, chiefly white, rose, and yellow. Similarly, silver is alloyed with nickel and copper. These added metals make gold and silver longer-wearing and more durable as jewelry, but the nickel and copper in them can cause allergic reactions. Those with sensitivities should wear the purest forms of (the highest karat) gold possible, and avoid alloys containing nickel and copper. A few people, however, may be allergic to gold itself.

I

imitation Made to resemble natural or synthetic gemstone materials, typically assuming the appearance, color, and effect of the original substance without possessing its chemical or physical characteristics. Also, synthetic stones without a counterpart in nature can be called imitations. See particular gemstone descriptions or the gemstone name plus the word *imitations* to find less valuable stones that may be misleadingly named and sold as more expensive ones. Note the characteristics of particular precious metals to help

determine their authenticity. Finding a reliable dealer is your best insurance against any misrepresented beads, gemstones, metals, or other beading materials.

imitation gemstones Imitation stones, whether glass or synthesized in a laboratory, can make beautiful beads that are much less expensive than genuine, natural gemstones. Rhinestone "emeralds" are one example. Although they may imitate the color and appearance of natural gemstones, they do not possess their chemical makeup or physical characteristics. An honest dealer will disclose exactly what he is selling. Sometimes natural gemstones are treated to imitate others; for example, howlite when dyed can look like turquoise. *See also* reconstituted and synthetic gemstones.

inclusions In gemstone terminology, foreign matter or other irregularities detectable in gemstones. The industry prefers to avoid the word *flaw* because of its derogatory meaning, implying imperfection. Since gemstones are rarely perfect in the sense of containing no inclusions, the term was developed as a way to define the character of the gemstone deposits. An inclusion is considered negative in a gemstone if it interferes with the light as it passes through, making it less brilliant. Some types of inclusions can make a gemstone more vulnerable to shattering. Other inclusions can be removed by laser drilling. Organic inclusions in amber, like plants or insects, are highly sought after by collectors. Organic inclusions occur only in amber. In glass beads, inclusions may mean a transparent or opaque color or colors within a transparent body of another color. In some cases, the presence of inclusions may help determine whether a gemstone is natural or synthetic, although some laboratories have developed methods to grow inclusions even in simulated gemstones.

Indian reds Also called *mutisalah,* these Indo-Pacific beads made of drawn glass are small, opaque red or orange beads. The red beads are also called earth beads since they are used by the lower classes to give to brides at weddings. The orange beads, called brick beads, serve the same functions but are more expensive. Both types are considered heirlooms among the peoples of the Indonesian archipelago. The king's beads are made from wound glass with significant lead content; these are very expensive and indicate the highest social status. *See also* Indo-Pacific beads.

Indo-Pacific beads Small, monochromatic drawn-glass beads first produced around A.D. 100 to 300 found in excavations in Arikamedu, south of Pondicherry on the southeastern coast of India. Later the beads were made in Vietnam, Thailand, Malaysia, Indonesia, and Sri Lanka. Some researchers claim that Indo-Pacific beads are the precursors of modern glass seed beads, made by a similar technique of drawing the glass into thin tubes that are cut into beads, which are then polished and rounded by tumbling. Extensive excavations have unearthed Indo-Pacific beads some 1,500 years old in sites throughout the Pacific Rim and in parts of Africa. They are sometimes loosely referred to as *trade-wind beads.*

industrial An ear ornament; *see also* construct.

infilling A gemstone treatment in which surface fractures or flaws are filled with glass, clear epoxy resin, or other substances, in order to improve the gemstone's appearance and/or weight. As a result of heat enhancements, other colorless substances may be present. Also called *filling.*

initiation bead dolls In western and southern Africa, dolls are given to girls as part of their initiation ceremony into adulthood. One common style of initiation doll, found in South Africa, is a gourd that has been beaded. Two rounded gourds attached in the middle are wrapped with cloth or leather, plant fibers, and strings of beads. Most of these dolls are faceless, but some include shells for eyes or other suggestive facial features. Similar dolls are shaped as fertility dolls. The initiation doll shown, beaded by Ginger Summit, has a strap so that the doll may be worn around the neck or waist. Courtesy of Ginger Summit and Jim Widess, *Making Gourd Dolls & Spirit Figures;* photo by Jim Widess.

The weighted doll, another doll type, consists of two small gourds first filled with sand or gravel and then glued together and decorated with cloth rope or beads.

Among the Ndebele in Africa, a small doll is used to signify that the young woman has achieved the status of a married woman and mother. This type of doll wears a beaded apron, the traditional dress of a married woman who has borne a child within her marriage.

Yet another type of initiation ceremony for young boys is kept secret. The boy is honored by his mother, who wears strips of beadwork that stretch from her headdress to the ground. The bead strips, called *linga koba,* translated as "long tears," reflected her sadness at losing a boy as well as tears of joy in gaining a man. *See also* fertility dolls and gourd dolls, and Sangoma bead doll.

inlaid beads   Also called *inlay beads*; a design set onto or into a surface, with or without being pressed into a cut or cutout area. Metal, wood, seashells, bits of glass, and precious or semiprecious stones are commonly used for this purpose. Shown here are specimens using two different inlay techniques: first, beads imported from India (possibly produced in Nepal or Tibet) that have small pieces of turquoise and coral, possibly glass, pressed into

the surface, and then framed with silver wire. The second—a heart, a turtle, and a round bead—illustrate a pattern of cut gems or other material that are pieced together in a cut outline, glued in place, and then polished.

inlay beads   *See* inlaid beads.

inlay cabochons   An inlaid bead that is cut and shaped into a cabochon, a convex shape with a flat back, that can be strung and may serve as a pendant. *See also* cabochon.

in-line knot   A common sewing knot made right in the thread itself (not wrapped around another object, like a bead or another thread) to secure the beads and adjust tension. Also called a *half-hitch knot* or an *overhand knot,* in one type the thread simply loops once through itself. Find knotting diagrams in Part V.

inside-color beads Much like color-lined beads, these beads are transparent—either colored or clear—with a different color of glass inside the bead. The better quality beads have the color in the glass itself rather than a coating that may fade or flake off. Shown is a simple pony-bead necklace with lavender inside-color beads that are clear on the outside. The necklace is accented with two-tone purple and blue 8-mm fire-polish beads.

intaglio An engraving technique for incising or creating a negative image on a stone. When made into a seal, for instance, the stone can be pressed into wax or another soft substance and then onto paper, leather, glass, or cloth, to create a lightly sculpted, raised image. This engraving technique is opposite that of the *cameo,* which is a relief, or raised positive image.

interlocking beads When strung, these beads are designed to fit into each other to form a tightly linked or smooth strand. *See also* snake beads.

investment The initial wax, clay, plaster, or sand-and-water mold used in what is generally called the lost-wax process for producing metal beads and other jewelry.

investment casting *See* lost-wax process.

invitatory beads In the Anglican rosary, the bead closest to the cross is called the *invitatory* (to invite or call to prayer) bead.

iolite A blue-violet or brownish, transparent or translucent gemstone, composed of magnesium aluminum silicate, also called *cordierite* or *dichroite*. It was named for the Greek word *ios,* meaning "violet," and rates 7 to 7.5 on the Mohs scale of hardness. The stone has strong pleochroism; its color changes depending on the angle from which light strikes it. This makes iolite useful as a polarizing filter to help determine the sun's direction on cloudy days, for which it earned the nickname *Vikings' compass*. The stone may have inclusions of hematite and goethite that could cause *aventurescence* or a reddish sheen. Mined in Sri Lanka, Burma, India, Madagascar, and Brazil, iolite is sometimes mistaken for tanzanite, which also exhibits pleochroism. *Water sapphire* is a misleading trade name for blue iolite. The bracelet shown features three-facet iolite nuggets, accented with 6-mm lavender opaline, 3-mm iolite, and 6-mm amethyst beads.

iridescence Lustrous rainbowlike waves of color that occur in some gemstones, also called *play-of-color* and *fire,* iridescence results from cracks or structural layers within the stone that change the way it refracts light when viewed from different angles. Fire agate is a natural gemstone that demonstrates this phenomenon.

iridescent finish A rainbow-metallic finish that is applied to a bead. This treatment is also termed *iris* or *AB* finish. *See also* aurora borealis.

iris beads An iridescent or aurora borealis finish applied to glass beads, iris beads come in a wide range of colors. The hank of purple iris beads here are size 12, made in the Czech Republic. The close-up view brings out the teal, bronze, and green colors reflecting off their surfaces.

iron A tough metal which, however, corrodes easily, and is more often used in alloys. Iron alloy phases include austenite (hard), bauxite, martensite, cementite (iron carbide), ledeburite (4.3% carbon), ferrite (soft), pearlite (88% iron + 12% cementite), and spheroidite. Wrought iron has almost no carbon, and cast iron has less than 2.1% carbon. Malleable iron exhibits good ductility and may be preferred for castings.

ironstone A gray heavy sedimentary rock that contains less than 50% iron. Composed of iron carbonate or iron oxide, clay, or sand, and sometimes calcite and quartz, its surface oxidation causes the gray color. Ironstone is sometimes considered a form of siderite (iron carbonate). The stone *hematite* contains more iron. Red or black banded ironstone is sometimes used in jewelry.

irradiation A relatively new process using gamma or electron bombardment to alter the color of a natural gemstone or to induce color generation in artificial gemstones. Irradiation may be followed by heating. The term can also refer to neutron radiation in combination with any other bombardment or heat treatment designed to alter a gemstone's appearance. Unlike most heat treatments, irradiation does not necessarily produce a permanent color change.

ivory The white, creamy, translucent to opaque material, calcium phosphate, composing the teeth and tusks of elephants, walruses, narwhals, orcas, sperm whales, hippopotamuses, warthogs, and other mammals; ivory is similar to bone, but harder and more dense. The teeth and tusks consist of pulp cavity, dentine, cementum, and enamel. Most carved ivory comes from the dentine, a mineralized connective tissue with a matrix of collagen and proteins. Its hardness and creamy color and

smooth texture make ivory valuable for carving and etching, and carved ivory beads are among the oldest known. It rates 2 to 3 on the Mohs scale of hardness. Archaeological evidence confirms that ivory beadmaking existed in ancient Egypt, Assyria, Greece, Cyprus, Crete, Mycenae, Western Europe, India, China, and Japan. Netsuke, scrimshaw, piano keys, small statues, inlays, and jewelry are composed of ivory. The sale of new ivory was banned in 1989 worldwide largely because of the slaughter of elephants by poachers; the United Nations modified the ban in 2002. A hard-nut vegetable "ivory," called tagua, sometimes substitutes for the real thing. Deposits of *odontolite*, fossilized tooth or bone from prehistoric large animals, have been found in Siberia and the south of France. The ivory piece shown here was engraved by a technique known as *scrimshaw*.

J

jaclas A small loop of strung shell or gemstone beads, originally worn as earrings, as noted in the Navaho term *jaclas,* which means "earring."

Today they are worn as looped pendants on necklaces of the same materials.

jade The term *jade* actually applies to two different rocks: *jadeite* (sodium aluminum silicate) and *nephrite* (basic calcium magnesium iron silicate). Shared characteristics and archaeological histories kept the fact that they were different minerals from being recognized until the 1800s. This translucent to opaque stone has a Mohs scale hardness factor of 6 to 7. Nephrite, sometimes called *axe stone* and noted for its toughness, was used in prehistoric times for arms and tools. It was commonly carved in China and pre-Columbian Central America. It occurs throughout the world, in Central Asia, Siberia, Russia, Australia, Brazil, Taiwan, China, Europe, Africa, and Switzerland. Jade's color range is wide, from yellow and brownish red, to white, gray, orange, blue, pink, lilac, and dark purple, though it is best known for its many shades of green. Jade is also dyed fairly often. Still in great demand, jade beads have been esteemed in cultures ranging from China, India, Japan, and Korea, to Mesoamerica, where it adorned people both alive and dead in the Mayan culture of Belize, Mexico, and Guatemala. The traditional Chinese character for "king" depicted a string

of three jade beads. In China, aventurine is often sold as jade since any green stone, such as serpentine, chrysoprase, and green quartz, is held in high esteem. *Russian jade,* the color of spinach, comes from the region near Lake Baikal. *Imperial jade,* emerald green with chromium, from Myanmar, is the most desired variety of jadeite. Jade untreated except by surface waxing is the most desired. Jade may be enhanced with bleaches or acids and polymer resin to improve its transparency or color. It may be artificially stained or dyed. *See also* jadeite, nephrite, apple jade, and lime jade.

jade imitations Many imitations are made from plastic and glass. Indian jade is a misleading trade name for aventurine and aventurine glass. Mexican jade is a misleading name for artificially tinted green marble. Wyoming jade is a trade name for nephrite from that state as well as for a green growth of tremoite with albite. American jade or California jade is a misleading name for green idocrase (vesuvianite). In China and some parts of the world, any green stone, no matter what its composition, may be referred to as jade. Minerals sometimes deceptively sold as jade are serpentine, soapstone, carnelian, grossularite (Transvaal jade), and Australian chrysoprase. Korean, Canadian, Styrian, Suzhou, olive, and new jade are serpentine.

jadeite The translucent or opaque gemstone, sodium aluminum silicate, is one of two stones generally known as jade; the other is nephrite. Of the two, jadeite occurs in a greater range of colors. This tough stone with tiny interlocking grains has a Mohs scale hardness rating of 6.5 to 7. A sodium- and aluminum-rich pyroxene, jadeite is more rare and costly than nephrite, and highly valued in a translucent to nearly transparent emerald green. Found in very few sites worldwide, it is mined principally in Myanmar. Untreated jadeite, with the exception of surface waxing, is even more expensive than the diamond.

japa mala *See* mala.

Japanese seed beads Glass seed beads produced in Japan are notable for their uniformity of size and shape. They come in an immense array of beautiful colors and finishes. These beads are usually sold loose in plastic tubes rather than strung into hanks, as is the common practice with Czech beads. The loose beads shown are Japanese and the strung beads are Czech.

jasper A gemstone of silicon dioxide, considered an opaque variety of chalcedony, has also been grouped with cryptocrystalline quartz. It has a dull luster but can take a high polish. Jasper occurs in colors ranging from yellowish white or gray to brown, yellow, red, and green and is typically striped or spotted. Popular for jewelry, ornamentation, and stone mosaics, it has a Mohs scale hardness factor of 6.5 to 7. The name derived from the Greek means "spotted stone," although ancient references mention a different stone. Jasper varieties include Egyptian or Nile pebble (strong yellow and red), banded (layered with wide bands), basanite or touchstone (finely grained and black), blood (a name also sometimes used for bloodstone), hornstone or chert (finely grained usually gray or brownish red), scenic (brownish landscape appearance with iron oxide), moukaite (Australian pink to light red and cloudy), nunkirchner (sometimes dyed to imitate lapis lazuli), plasma (dark green with white or yellow spots), and silex (yellow and brownish red with spots or stripes). A few jasper varieties are imperial, zebra, leopard, picture, dalmation, Picasso, fancy, poppy, rainbow, and silver-leaf. The cabochon shown is called *Rocky Butte jasper*. *See also* fancy jasper and fantasy jasper.

jequirity bean Sometimes used as a bead, this bean or seed from the *Abrus precatorius* plant is toxic. It is also called *crab's eye* and *rosary pea*. Poison entering the bloodstream even from a pricked finger when stringing the beads can be fatal. The plant is found in India, Egypt, the Caribbean, and the state of Florida.

jet A hard form of bituminous coal (lignite) that is deep black in color, jet is actually fossilized wood; in some specimens, the original wood pattern is distinct. Jet is made from carbon compression; saltwater forms hard jet, and freshwater, soft jet. The word is derived from the French *jaiet* and the material has been used since 10,000 B.C. in what is today Germany. Trade in jet beads dates from the Roman Empire; at that time, the finest jet came from Whitby, England. The properties of true jet suit jewelry design quite well; it is lightweight, inexpensive, and hard enough to keep a cut edge, yet carves easily. It has a velvety, waxy luster and may be worked on a lathe. Its Mohs scale hardness rating is 2.5 to 4, which has made it popular for carving fetishes. Jewelry incorporating jet came into vogue in the late 1820s in England and remained fashionable in Europe throughout most of the 19th century. It is commonly used for mourning jewelry, rosaries, cameos, and ornamental objects. Sometimes called *black amber*, jet can produce an electric charge when rubbed. Pyrite inclusions create a brassy color and metallic luster. It may be confused with black onyx. The term *jet* is also popularly used to describe a deep black color.

jet imitations *Anthracite* (hard coal) and *vulcanite* have been used to imitate fine jet. *Cannel coal*, a wax extracted from rich layers in coal seams formed by plant spores and pollen, achieves a high luster when polished and resembles jet. Jet's popularity led to the creation of so-called *French jet*, an imitation made of black cut glass, distinguished from true jet by being cool to the touch. *See* French jet.

jewel This term refers to both precious and semiprecious natural gemstones; a piece of jewelry containing one or more gems set in precious metal; a cut but loose (unset) gemstone; or any individual ornamental piece. *See also* jewelry.

jeweler's saw Tool used by jewelers for cutting shapes from copper, silver, or other metal sheets and for sawing through wire. Some types, ranging from light-duty to heavy-duty, can also be used for cutting wood, plastic, rubber, and thin metal.

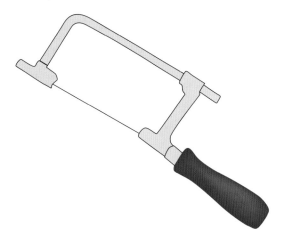

jewelry From the root term *jewel,* this category includes a huge variety of personal adornments, made from many materials besides gemstones, including cheaper, mass-produced, and synthetic materials like glass and plastic.

jewelry cement Many different manufacturers produce different glues or adhesives that can be used on glass, metal, gemstones, and fabric. Consult your local retailer or read the packaging for the best type of adhesive for a specific jewelry project. Epoxy-type cements are not necessarily appropriate for jewelry projects,

because the bond can become brittle over time. Use in well-ventilated areas.

jewelry chain Beads or metal components or both joined together with interlocking links, loops, or rings, such as a silver or gold chain used with a pendant, ornament, or decorative jewelry. *See also* chain and chain types.

jewelry cleaner A category of products designed for cleaning fine jewelry. Read the label carefully to make sure the product is appropriate for the type of jewelry you want to clean. With beadwork, you must consider the thread, backing material, and adhesives, any of which may not be compatible with the cleaning product, and so may be damaged by using it.

jewelry pliers Any number of tools with jaws and handles fashioned like conventional pliers but specifically designed for use in making jewelry. In general, they are easier to handle and are suited for more delicate jobs than similar tools found for standard or heavy-duty household purposes in a hardware store. *See also* pliers.

jewelry wire Also called *craft wire, stringing wire,* or *bead wire;* wire for beading comes in a variety of metals and metal alloys and gauges. Generally jewelry wire appropriate for stringing beads bends easily. On the market, among other types, are silver, gold, gold-plated, gold-filled, and copper-colored wires. Precious metals are used for wire-wrapping of expensive gemstones, but other types of wire are generally used for beads made of other materials.

Gauge is a term that expresses a wire's thickness, using both microinches (U.S. inches) and microns (metric). A microinch is equivalent to 1,000,000th (one millionth) of an inch. A micron is 1,000th (one thousandth) of a millimeter.

Wire is available in sizes determined by its thickness or gauge. Rather than trying to remember all the sizes or gauges of particular jewelry wires, keep in mind that 24-gauge and 28-gauge wire works best with size 11 seed beads; 20-gauge wire is better suited for larger glass beads, like those of 4 mm, 6 mm, and 6 mm. Larger beads from China, the Czech Republic, India, and parts of Africa will fit on 18-gauge wire. Wire selection depends not only on the bead hole size but whether the project requires more than one pass of thread through the hole. Some beaders who do not have access to other materials have used telephone and electrical wire. Find stringing materials in Part IV. *See also* gauge and stringing wire.

Job's tears One of the earliest plants domesticated for food, it is uncertain exactly where Job's tears (*Coix lacryma-jobi*) originated; most likely it was tropical Asia, where the grain was the basis for cereal. It has been naturalized in North and South America. Closely related to corn and maize, this tall annual grass produces a mature grain or seed enclosed in a casing shaped somewhat like a teardrop. This hard, light-colored shell easily makes a tubular bead; a natural hole runs through its center. For this reason, some have speculated that the seed could be the earliest bead ever used. The hole at its tip allows the flower to emerge; when picked, the hole remains and its soft center allows easy stringing. An archaeological site in western India provides evidence that Job's tears were used as beads, as was steatite (soapstone), around 2000 B.C. The plant was named after the long-suffering Job of the Old Testament. These seeds have been dyed and used as beads for rosaries (the seeds are then called Mary's tears), necklaces, belts, bracelets, earrings, and gourd musical instruments in various parts of the world. The Tarahumara of Mexico wear the bead-seeds to protect against illness. The Yagua from the Amazon region of Peru create necklaces with it as well as with other seeds, beetle legs, and anteater claws.

According to Cherokee legend surrounding the Trail of Tears, when the Cherokee were forcefully evacuated from their homeland, the tears shed along the route became Job's tears that later sprouted into the plant.

jug beads Originating in China in the late 19th century, these crudely made wound-glass beads were reportedly used as stoppers on jugs and other containers. What are sold today as jug beads are similar in size and also called crow beads.

jump ring A small ring or circular piece of wire that functions as a connector or fastener when used as a jewelry component. Shown below is a jump ring that is open and ready

to attach to another finding, like a clasp. A good substitute for this finding is a split ring, also shown here. The split ring is designed like a miniature key ring that will not open as easily as a jump ring.

juniper berries *See* cedar-seed beads.

junk jewelry A term sometimes used by vendors and manufacturers among themselves for costume jewelry.

K

kaolinite A soft earthy clay silicate mineral, also known as kaolin and China clay, traditionally used to make porcelain in China. It may have traces of other minerals. Kaolinite beads are treated like other ceramic objects and fired to make them hard.

karat (purity) A unit of measure (abbreviated as *kt* or *ct*) that quantifies the fineness, purity, or quality of gold and platinum; that is, how much pure gold or platinum is found in a given alloy or mixture. It signifies what proportion of an alloy is pure gold or platinum. The preferred spelling when referring to the purity of gold is *karat* (not *carat*), commonly abbreviated *k* or *kt*. The purest gold, 24 karat, has a millesimal fineness of 999. Here are other common karat measures in decreasing order of millesimal fineness: 20 karat (833 millesimal fineness), 18 karat (millesimal fineness 750), 16 karat (millesimal fineness 625), 14 karat (millesimal fineness 585), 10 karat (millesimal fineness 417), and 9 karat (millesimal fineness 375). In this system, 18-karat gold would consist of 18 parts gold and six parts other metals, for a total of 24 parts. Although the words *carat* and *karat* stem from the same root, do not confuse this with the word *carat (mass or weight),* a unit of weight used for gemstones. *See also* carat (mass or weight) and gold. Find the karats chart in Part IV.

keratin This tough, fibrous, insoluble protein is the primary structural component of hair, nails, horns, and hooves. Beads made of these materials (including those from claws, porcupine quills, tortoise shells, and horns) are very durable.

keta awauzi beads Blue cylindrical powder-glass beads, made by the Yoruba and originating from Nigeria or Togo. The beads were reportedly made from the blue glass of cold-cream jars until the 1940s.

Kevlar A very strong yet thin beading thread, originally used in bulletproof vests.

key chain A chain or string, usually formed in a loop for stringing one or more keys so that they are secured. The keys effectively become beads since they can be strung through a hole drilled near the top of them. All kinds of key chains are on the market, from simple to fancy. The term *key chain* is often used interchangeably with *key ring*.

key ring A very useful and functional finding made of metal. As in a split ring, the sturdy wire opens up to accommodate keys, which do not easily come off. The key ring shown is decorated with assorted inlaid and ceramic beads and waxed cotton cord, enhanced with Chinese knots. *See also* split ring.

kidney wire A metal earring finding that is shaped somewhat like a kidney bean; it loops through the ear and usually hooks around itself at the bottom.

kiffa beads These powder-glass beads from Mauritania, West Africa, embody exquisite skill and artistry in beadmaking. The handmade process involves crushing glass to a fine powder and mixing it with human saliva to create the core of the bead. They are then fired in a small oven, tin can, or piece of pottery over hot coals. More crushed glass mixed with a binder is applied in complex patterns in a second firing until the end product reveals intricate designs in a variety of shapes and colors. This West African beadmaking process dates back almost 1,000 years. Today artisans have been reviving the tradition; the original ancient ones are rare and quite expensive.

kiln An insulated, temperature-controlled oven used to process bead materials by heat or to gradually cool them down. The drying or firing of the material hardens it, and can change its color and other properties, depending on additional treatments it may be given prior to firing. The kiln can control temperature ranging from room temperature to those as high as 2,000° F (1,093° C). Following heat treatment is *annealing,* or controlled cooling; this prevents thermal shock from rapid or uneven cooling, which can cause cracks or breakage.

kilt pin A pin resembling a large safety pin designed as a closure or fastener for clothing, especially for a kilt or skirt. The kilt pin may be used with beads as a decorative pin with sweaters, scarves, shawls, ponchos, and even T-shirt sleeves. Beads may hang from small rings attached along its length. The pin shown features turquoise rondelles, fire-polish beads, and fancy lampwork beads with flowers layered inside the glass.

king beads Although members of royalty, chiefs, emperors, aristocrats, and other dignitaries throughout the world have been known for their gem collections, crown jewels, or other precious adornments, in Africa two bead types in particular have been associated with specific tribes and their kings. Asante kings wore *bodom* powder-glass beads as symbols of greatness or wealth. Ewe kings wore *Akosu* powder-glass beads. Both bead types, commonly called king beads, are handmade, rare, and expensive; gold flakes are usually found in the bead's body or core. The traditional Chinese character for "king" depicts a string of three jade beads.

Kingman turquoise Recognizable by its bright blue color flecked with black matrix, Kingman turquoise is increasingly rare these days, and correspondingly valuable. The stone is mined in an area northwest of Kingman, Arizona, that was once the capital of turquoise mining; it has a matrix ranging from white to light brown to black in a stone of variously hued blues, some with hints of green. Nuggets of the characteristic sky blue with black matrix represent the highest quality of this stone in the industry.

knot Using one or more knots allows the beader to connect, attach, or intertwine two strands of thread, cord, rope, or wire. A similar result can be achieved by tying both ends of a single length of thread, cord, rope, or wire. Knots may be used for a variety of purposes, such as to secure an object, serve as a mnemonic or counting device, function as a closure for things like clothing, aid in climbing, and more. A few types of knots favored in beading include the surgeon's, square, in-line (overhand or half-hitch), and Lark's-head knot. Special knotting techniques are used for stringing pearls that prevents individual pearls from abrading each other. Chinese knotting, like that found on clothing, is largely decorative. Because security is desired in beading, slip knots or granny knots are not advised. Find knotting diagrams in Part V.

knotless netting A technique using thread or cord, such as waxed linen, hemp, or rope, to wrap a gemstone or other object, like a vessel or a wood flute. It produces a lacy covering that can be embellished with beads. For examples, *see* gourd shekere and gourd necklace.

knotting *See* Chinese knotting.

knotting tool A tool designed for pearl or bead knotting; knots tied between each bead or pearl prevent the whole strand from slipping off if the stringing cord should break. The knots also protect pearls or beads strung side by side from abrasion. Tweezers, T-pins, and straight pins can also serve as knotting tools.

kodama Round bead made by winding or drawing and cutting a tube. It is like the *marudama* but smaller than 50 mm. They have been found in Old Tomb graves from about A.D. 250 to 550 in China.

kogok *See* magatama.

komboschoinia The Greek term for *chotki,* a set of prayer beads, much like a rosary, used by Eastern Orthodox Christians Also spelled *komvoschonion* and *komboskini. See also* chotki.

Krobo beads Among the Krobo people of Ghana, West Africa, several families produce distinctive dry powder-glass beads. Three types of modern Krobo powder-glass beads are (1) translucent fused-glass fragments shaped and perforated after firing; (2) bicones or spheres joined in a second short firing; and (3) so-called *writing beads* made from finely ground glass that are written on or decorated with glass slurry, fused in a second firing.

According to bead researcher Peter Francis, the Krobo beadmaking method dates from the 1600s. Very finely crushed glass is funneled into a vertical mold fashioned from local clay. The bead's hole is formed by a straw or cassava-leaf stem inserted into the center of the mold that burns away when the mold is fired in a wood-burning kiln.

kukui beads The beige and black oily nuts of the candlenut, a plant found in the Hawaiian Islands, made into beads.

kyanite A transparent to translucent mineral, aluminum silicate, with a vitreous or pearly luster. The stone may have irregular streaks and demonstrate pleochroism. It has a triclinic crystal system with long, flat prisms. The Mohs scale hardness varies from 5 to 7, depending on the axis measured. Colors range from deep blue to blue-green and brown. Kyanite, also called *disthene,* is used as a gemstone as well as in ceramic and porcelain beads and other products. The stone may be confused with aquamarine, iolite, sapphire, and tourmaline. It may be found in Kenya, Zimbabwe, Austria, Switzerland, Myanmar, Brazil, and the United States.

The anatomically correct peacock butterfly pin, designed by Karin Houben, has a long kyanite bead (20 × 7 mm) for the main body. The wings are constructed of Delica beads; strung or linked with the kyanite body bead are faceted Baltic amber, cape amethyst, Austrian crystal, and 22 kt gold vermeil spacers.

L

labradorescence The word comes from the mineral labradorite. Labradorescence is the optical effect of iridescence in metallic hues that change with the angle of light refraction, also called the *schiller effect*. Although shades of blue and green are common, the entire color spectrum can be observed in gemstones having this quality. *See also* labradorite.

labradorite A transparent to opaque variety of feldspar, sodium calcium aluminum silicate, displaying a strong play-of-color known as *labradorescence*. A grayish brown gemstone that displays iridescent flashes of blue, violet, and green, and sometimes shades of yellow-gold. It has a vitreous luster and is sensitive to pressure. Its Mohs scale hardness rating is 6 to 6.5, and the crystal system triclinic, platy, and prismatic. *Spectrolite* is the trade name for labradorite from Finland that shows spectral colors, and *Madagascar moonstone* is the trade name of oglioclase moonstone with a strong blue schiller effect. First found in Labrador, Canada, other deposits are located in Mexico, Australia, Russia, and the United States. Shown are faceted beads of varying shapes.

lac This substance is the byproduct of a scale insect, a parasite known as *Kerria lacca* or *laccifer lacca*. The plant-sucking insect (also known as the lac beetle) secretes a resinous material that accumulates on the bark of its host tree, most often the banyan. Lac is a product of India, used chiefly in the form of shellac as the base for beads, varnishes, and sealing wax. It was used as a dye for textiles and leather goods in ancient China and India. *See also* resin.

lacquer Deriving from the name of the parasite, *laccifer locca,* lacquer consists of a resin dissolved in a fast-drying solvent. This clear or colored coating dries by evaporation to produce a hard, durable finish that can be polished to a high gloss. *See also* lac.

lacquering A gemstone treatment in which some type of lacquer or other substance is applied to the surface to improve its appearance.

ladder stitch A bead stitch or technique that produces a bead strip resembling a ladder when made with bugle beads, although it can be employed with other beads. The simple bracelet shown uses this stitch with a multi-

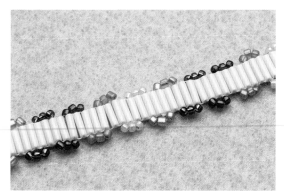

colored edging. Also shown is a ladder-stitch bracelet in which teal three-cut beads give a different look.

ladybug beads These beads are made to mimic real insects. Shown are red ladybugs, but they come in a lively assortment of other colors, including blue, green, orange, and pink. Also shown is a ladybug of beaded wirework by Verona Thom.

Lakota umbilical pouch After the birth of a baby to a Lakota mother, the umbilical cord is cut and placed inside a beaded pouch that the mother, while pregnant, had prepared. The turtle pouch, symbolizing long life and strength, is used for a female child, and the lizard pouch, symbolizing speed and the ability to change, is for a male child. The Lakota keep these pouches for a lifetime and may be buried with them. Other Native North American tribes have followed this ancient tradition.

lalique Originating from the famous Frenchman, René Jules Lalique, a glass designer whose works date from the early 1900s. In beading, the term refers to a frosted or matte finish on a bead.

lampshade In the Victorian age, beaded fringe, swags, tassels, or borders were popularly added to lampshades found in both parlors and boudoirs. The fancy lampshade fashion reemerges periodically.

lampwork beads Handmade wound-glass beads created by the technique of lampworking, also called flameworking or torchworking. Glassblowers are also called lampworkers. The beautiful coral-colored bead pictured was

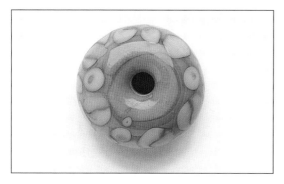

handmade by Shawn Koons. *See* flameworked beads, glass beadmaking, and lampworking.

lampworking A wound-glass beadmaking technique practiced since ancient times, developed into an art in the 1300s in Venice and Murano, Italy. Lampworking, also called *flameworking,* is basically the working of glass canes, or rods, over an open flame. The original glassblowers or lampworkers used oil lamps, stoking the flame with hand-pumped bellows. Later lampworkers, often called *flameworkers* or *torchworkers,* favored a small torch fixed to a worktable to heat the glass rods to over 1,700° F (927° C) and manipulate them in the flame. Threads of molten glass are wound around a metal rod called a *mandrel,* covered in *bead release.* The mandrel serves as a handle, which allows the lampworker to shape the beads with the aid of gravity and special tools and to add designs or to augment the beads with glass bits in other colors as desired. After the beads are shaped, they are *annealed*—cooled slowly in a temperature-controlled kiln to prevent stress points in the glass or cracking.

In the Venetian and Murano lampworking industry, men produced the bead cores in workshops that held large furnaces. Women working out of their homes had the labor-intensive job of applying the elaborate finishes by hand. *See also* bead release, fuel, and wound glass.

land-snail shell beads The shells of *Achatina monetaria* were cut into circular disks with open centers and used as coins in Benguela in what is today western Angola. Other types of shells used as money by various cultures are the dentalium (*Dentalium pretiosum*), money cowrie (*Cypraea moneta*), wampum (*Busycon carica*), Atlantic knobbed whelk, and North Atlantic quahog hard-shelled clam (*Venus mercenaria*).

lane stitch A technique very similar to satin stitch in embroidery, but with the addition of beads, lane stitch can cover a large area with neat little rows of beadwork. It is often the stitch that attaches beads to items made of leather, like vests or moccasins. The West African wedding bracelet shown, from the collection of David Bingell, displays the traditional colors of black, green, red, and yellow.

lantana Also called Nigerian jasper, a dense microcrystalline quartz of deep red or reddish brown used to make beads in Llorin, Nigeria. During the 19th and 20th centuries, red jasper, banded agate, chalcedony, and occasionally carnelian were also used to make these beads. The word *lantana* originates from the Hausa girl's name for "Monday's child." Beads, especially red beads, were very important and considered royal beads owned by kings, the royal family, and the privileged elite.

lanyard hook Also called a *lanyard clasp,* the lanyard hook is used to clip or attach items like a key ring, badge, watch face, or zipper pull. This finding comes in a number of sizes.

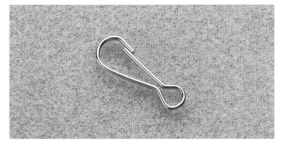

lapidary The work of cutting or polishing precious gemstones. The person who does the cutting is also called a lapidary. Most lapidaries specialize in working on particular stones and are sensitive to such characteristics as depth of color, hardness, and the effects of light when viewed from various angles or axes. Three broad categories of lapidary arts are tumbling, cabochon cutting, and faceting. The term may also refer to inscriptions on stone; a "lapidary style" may be graceful, accurate, formal, or condensed.

lapis lazuli Also known simply as lapis, lapis lazuli is a popular opaque gemstone found in dark to light blue with metallic (pyrite) or white streaks (calcite). Its Mohs scale hardness factor is 5 to 6. *Lapis* is the Latin word for "stone" and *azul* is the Arabic word for "blue," so the term means "blue stone." Considered a rock rather than a mineral, it typically contains about 25% to 40% lazurite, a silicate mineral composed of sodium, aluminum, silicon, oxygen, sulfur, and chlorine. Composition may vary, but it usually contains calcite (white), sodalite (blue), and pyrite (yellow). The blue coloring agent is sulfur. Lapis lazuli may also contain the minerals augite, diopside, enstatite, mica, hauynite, hornblende, nosean, and sodalite. In high-quality lapis lazuli, the color and pyrite are well distributed in the stone, but too much pyrite may create a dull green color. Lapis may occur in crystalline marble and is found in Afghanistan, Angola, Canada,

Pakistan, Russia, Chile, and the United States. Lapis lazuli with a significant amount of white calcite inclusions is called *denim lapis*. Found since about 7000 B.C. in the Indian subcontinent and what is now Pakistan, it has been valued as a gem. Ancient Egyptians made lapis amulets, seals, scarabs, and other ornaments, and ground the mineral into a powder for use as a cosmetic eye shadow. Ancient Sumerian tombs contain sculpted lapis artifacts. The ancients called it *sapphire,* a general term they applied to blue stones but which today is reserved for blue corundum, a variety of sapphire. During the Middle Ages, lapis lazuli was used as a pigment for producing paints or dyes. Shown is a beautiful necklace with matching earrings made of lapis and freshwater pearls, strung by Linda Pennington.

lapis lazuli imitations   Imitation lapis lazuli may be created from pieces and powder pressed or bound with artificial resin. Synthetic grainy spinel colored with cobalt oxide imitates lapis lazuli, as does some glass. Nunkirchner jasper, found in the Rhineland or Palatinate region, when dyed blue may (misleadingly) be called German or Swiss lapis. Dyed sodalite and howlite have also been marketed misleadingly as lapis.

lariat necklace   A long necklace or rope, typically 48 inches (about 120 cm) or longer. Shown is a crochet rope lariat made by the author's mother, Anna Flores. The interesting design in which the blue beads cross the red beads and spiral in opposite directions is the result of following a specific pattern when prestringing the beads before crocheting them.

lark's-head knot A simple knot used commonly in macramé and other crafts. Find knotting diagrams in Part V.

laser drilling Also called *lasering,* a permanent gemstone treatment that improves a stone's clarity through the use of lasers and chemicals to remove inclusions or flaws, especially in diamonds. In the process, a laser beam drills minute holes into a stone to access the flaw. If the laser itself does not eliminate it, the offending particle can be bleached or vaporized. Under magnification and from the correct angle, an experienced jeweler can detect the drilling holes. *Fracture treatment* involves filling in tiny cracks or laser drilling with a clear, glasslike substance that allows the stone to appear relatively unflawed to the human eye.

latticino Glass that has been decorated with fine lines; also called filigree glass or *retorte* ("twisted") glass. It was once used to describe milk-white glass.

lavaliere From the French word *lavalière,* for a type of necktie. This term refers to a pendant, ornament, or adornment that hangs from a piece of jewelry or chain, such as a necklace or earring.

layer stones Multilayered materials used in gem carving and engraving. Among the various types of carving and engraving are niccolo, intaglio, and cameo. In *niccolo,* popular for engraving coats of arms and monograms, a thin upper layer and translucent color tones reveal some of the color of the base. In *intaglio,* used principally for creating seals, a negative image is engraved. And in *cameo,* a raised relief is cut into the stone. Because the color layers of natural stones like chalcedony, onyx, or agate are somewhat rare in nature, these stones are commonly dyed for the proper effect. Both natural and dyed stones are referred to by the same name: *layer stones.*

lazy stitch With this stitch, several beads are added at once, making it rather quick to cover an area. However, it is not as secure as a stitch that tacks down every bead. This stitch is useful with knitted fabrics that stretch, or with leather, which you may have to pierce with an awl. *See also* lane stitch.

lead glass Used for lampworking, lead glass is potassium silicate glass impregnated with lead oxide during its formation. Because it refracts light more efficiently than standard glass, it is used to make prisms and jewelry. Cut lead glass is known as *lead crystal.*

leader bead The first or last (terminal bead) in a string of prayer beads, often larger than all other beads in the necklace or chaplet. In Muslim prayer beads, for instance, the 100th bead serves as the leader bead that ends the cycle of devotion after the 99 beads. A short two-bead cord and a tassel are suspended from the leader bead. In some cultures, dangling objects have been thought to ward off the evil eye.

leaf beads Generally, beads made in the shape of a leaf. In the leaf beads shown (next page), one is drilled top to bottom, the second side to side, and the third has a loop for stringing. The direction of the drilled hole dictates how the bead will sit in a jewelry design.

leather Cleaned and prepared hide or skin from a number of animals, most often cows, sheep, or goats. The small dyed-leather medicine bag shown has a whipstitch bead edging and is embellished with fringe, bone beads, turquoise, an abalone tube bead, a bear fetish, and a piece of abalone shell.

leather crimp A special clasp designed for use with leather lace or cord; it may be a round or flat metal finding whose ends are pinched closed over the leather with flat-nose pliers.

leather lace Real leather, usually cow or goat hide, cut into thin strips and used for stringing or as fringe in many different craft and clothing projects. The leather, cut into different widths and often dyed in an array of colors for commercial sale, is also called *leather cord* or simply *thong*. Leather lace is often used

with pony beads because their large stringing hole can accommodate the leather.

lemon quartz A yellow-colored quartz.

lenticular A double convex or lentil shape. Find bead shapes in Part IV.

lever-back ear wire A metal earring finding with a hinged part that opens and closes.

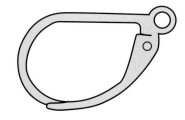

Lewis and Clark beads The famed Lewis and Clark Expedition (1804–1806), headed by Meriwether Lewis and William Clark, used glass beads for trading with native peoples in their exploration of territories en route to the Pacific northwest. Lewis and Clark beads are not a particular bead type but rather an assortment. While historical records are rather vague, they reveal that their Corps of Discovery carried assorted beads, necklaces, and mock garnets in addition to specific colors of beads like red, white, yellow, orange, and blue with quantities indicated in bunches, pounds, cards, and maces. Most beads are thought to have been monochrome glass seed beads from Venice and Bohemia. Some were described as light blue round glass beads, probably the highly prized "chief beads" from China. Although the expedition journals indicate that they carried wampum, the beads were more likely glass rather than the genuine shell wampum Native North Americans valued for trade. The groups encountered also had decided preferences for specific bead types and colors.

lighter case Made to encase a disposable lighter and constructed of metal, wood, or plastic, lighter cases are often covered with fabric and decorated with beads. The fabric cushions the beads from normal wear and tear. A Chippewa woman made the lighter case shown, using brick stitch; it was purchased in Minnesota.

lime jade A lighter shade than that typically seen in jade, with a distinct yellow cast. Nature produces jade in a great variety of colors and shades, and it is sometimes color-treated. Shown are disk- or saucer-shape beads. *See also* jade.

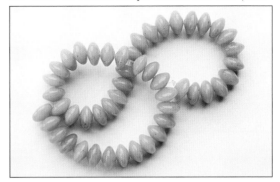

lined beads A bead having a lining of some material, such as silver-lined, gold-lined, copper-lined, and inside-color beads.

linen cord This cord, made from linen and used for stringing beads, is often waxed to make it easier to use. Sometimes sold as waxed linen, it is also available in colors.

link A jewelry component that attaches to another component, as in a chain. Specific components like split rings, jump rings, and beaded rings are used as links in jewelry design. In the Y-necklace below, the triangular link attaches the pendant beads.

lip One of either end of a bead surrounding the hole through which it is threaded.

liquid gold Very small gold tube beads threaded to appear like the molten metal, often worn in multiple strands. *See also* liquid silver.

liquid silver These dainty bugle beads of sterling silver, or gold or silver plate, are often assembled in multiple strands—as many as 50—for a fluid waterfall appearance. Turquoise heishi or gemstone pendants are great accents for them. The beads are thin and tubular, straight or twisted, approximately 1.6 mm in diameter by 6 mm long. *See* bugle beads.

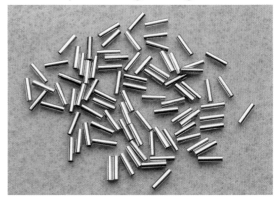

lithotherapy The traditional and modern use of gemstones for healing.

lobe A rounded part or shape; often many lobes are found or fashioned together in a bead or object from nature.

lobster-claw clasp Named for its resemblance to a lobster claw, this metal finding is used to attach bracelets and necklaces. It has a catch on one side that, when pulled back, opens the clasp on the side opposite.

Loctite The brand name for a group of products used as adhesives, including an anaerobic adhesive based on methacrylate used to bind glass and metal.

long-nose pliers Pliers with a long jaw or nose. Needle-nose pliers are a more delicate version with a more slender jaw and better suited to working with jewelry components.

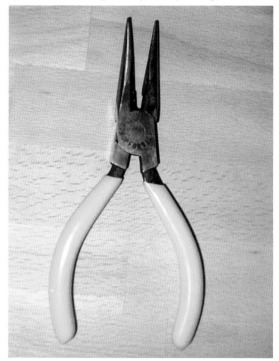

Shown are long-nose pliers. Photo by JG. *See* needle-nose pliers and pliers.

loom *See* bead loom.

loom stitch Also called *loom beading,* beadwork or bead fabric produced on a bead loom. Although the finished work looks the same as square stitch, loomwork is an entirely different technique. With loom stitch, the finished product is more pliable than with the stiffer square stitch. *See also* square stitch.

loomwork Beadwork that is produced on a bead loom. The bead loom is used to make larger pieces of bead fabric, like belts, hatbands, necklaces, purses, and wall hangings. Smaller looms are designed for bracelets and barrettes. Lula Monroe crafted the beautiful barrette shown here. The other beaded pieces are carefully restored antiques.

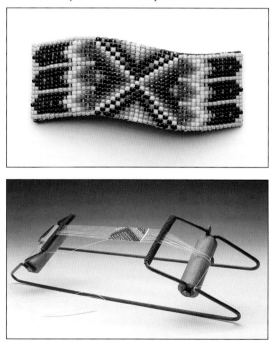

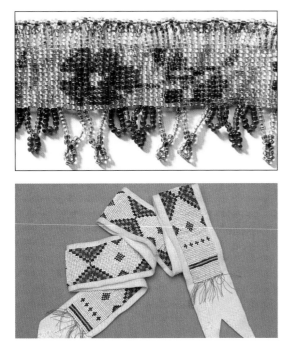

lost-wax process A casting technique, also called the *investment process,* that produces metal jewelry parts (such as metal settings for stones or fancy metal beads). Lost wax involves sculpting a model from wax, coating it with a heat-resistant material to create a mold, heating the piece until the wax melts and runs out, and then pouring the desired metal into the empty mold. The investment may also be made of plaster, sand, and water.

Developed in the fourth millennium B.C. by Chinese bronze workers, the desired form was carved in wax, coated with clay, and baked. The melted wax then ran out through vents in the clay, and molten metal, such as bronze or gold, was poured inside. When the metal cooled, the clay was broken off to reveal the metal casting. Each mold could be used just once. This technique was used for casting gold in ancient Central America and South America as well as for complex forms,

like statues. Other materials, such as beeswax or latex, may replace the lost wax.

loupe A small magnifying glass that jewelers use to examine a gemstone closely for internal flaws or blemishes. The magnification makes it easier to assess the color, cut, clarity, and other aspects of the stone. Consumers find it a useful tool to take on buying trips for examining stones. The Federal Trade Commission set the standard of ten times magnification for all gemstone grading performed in the United States.

love beads One element of classic hippie style was a strand of love beads, necklaces of small assorted beads, worn by so-called flower children. A universal symbol for love and peace, love beads could be big or small, bright or plain. The hippie movement in the 1960s was a social reaction protesting the Vietnam War, racism, and the inequality of women. Nonconformity, Eastern mysticism, pacifism, free love (sex), and the liberal use of hallucinogenic drugs and alcohol characterized some hippie practices. Love beads were given or traded as a gesture of love. *See also* love letters.

love letters In Zulu beadwork, symbols, geometric patterns, and colors form coded communication between prospective or married lovers and are called love beads or love letters (*icwadi*). *See also* Zulu beadwork.

luhanus shell Also called *strawberry shell,* a small chambered seashell, *Strombus luhanus,* with a pinkish or reddish interior. The shell's exterior is cream, with light brown to slightly orange or pink markings. Depending on how

the shell is cut, it may have any number of shapes, which are drilled and strung. *See* heishi.

luminescence From the Latin word *lumen*, meaning "light," this collective term denotes the emission of visible light under the influence of certain rays independent of temperature. Gemstone labs test for this quality using ultraviolet light, which is called fluorescence.

luster The way a mineral surface interacts with light, ranging from dull to glassy (vitreous). Descriptions of types of luster may be applied to various bead and gemstone (cut or uncut) surfaces. A *metallic luster* is highly reflective, like metal. *Submetallic luster* is a little less reflective than a metallic appearance. *Nonmetallic lusters* include *adamantine* or *brilliant* (or *diamond luster*), the luster found in diamonds, cerussite, and anglesite. *Vitreous* is the luster of broken glass or quartz. *Pearly* or *iridescent* resembles pearls, talc, or apophyllite. *Resinous luster* has the luster of resin, like amber, sphalerite, and sulfur. *Silky luster* has a soft light resembling silk, shown by fibrous materials, like gypsum and chrysotile. *Dull* or *earthy lusters* are shown by finely crystallized materials, like kidney ore, a variety of hematite. *Waxy luster* is a dull shine of coarse and uneven stones, like flint. *Greasy luster* is not common

in gemstones and resembles the shine of grease spots on paper or the surface of turbid stones.

luster finish A finish applied to transparent, translucent, or opaque beads that imparts a rich pearlescent quality. Such a coating may be white, colored, or metallic. Shown is a double-sided ornament with the image of a thunderbird; all the beads on its surface have a luster finish.

luvulite *See* sugilite.

M

MOP Abbreviation or acronym for *mother-of-pearl*. *See* mother-of-pearl.

machining Shaping metals or other materials by machine, such as milling, turning, grinding, drilling, casting, or sawing. It contrasts with *forging*.

maco tube beads Similar to bugle beads, these are tiny glass tubes, 1 mm in diameter and 1, 2, or 4 mm in length. Maco tubes of silver and gold metal are called *liquid silver* and *liquid gold*. They can have either flat or rounded ends. *See also* bugle bead.

macramé A textile craft using sequences of simple knots to create both decorative and functional items, macramé works as well with heavy, crude fibers like hemp as it does with more delicate ones, such as cotton, rayon, and silk. Macramé enjoyed immense popularity in the seventies, and it is still used for making jewelry, as well as plant hangers, wall hangings, belts, purses, and the like. The bracelet shown incorporates black bone hairpipe beads; red, white, and blue glass chevrons; and metal beads.

macramé beads These beads have large holes to accommodate the heavier jute or hemp cord often used in macramé knotting projects. Some beads are made of glass, but they are most often of wood, clay, ceramic, and faience in earthy tones.

macrocrystalline quartz This type of quartz has individual crystals visible to the naked eye, while the individual crystals of *microcrystalline* or *cryptocrystalline quartz* are visible only under high magnification. Varieties of macrocrystalline quartz (sometimes called

species) include amethyst, aventurine, rock crystal, blue quartz, citrine, hawk's-eye, prasiolite, quartz cat's-eye, smoky quartz, rose quartz, and tiger's-eye. *See* quartz.

Mactan-lily shell A dainty purple and white shell, also called *Cebu-lily shell,* that can be drilled and used as beads for stringing. These shells, found in Mactan Island near the larger Cebu Island of the Philippines, are also used to make heishi. *See* Cebu-lily shell beads.

magatama An ancient bead, often carved from stone, shaped like a comma or a crescent, often with an off-center hole. This bead, exclusive to Japan and Korea (where it is known as *kogok*), dates from the first millennium B.C. Both nations regard magatama as a sacred symbol and claim to have originated it. Magatama have been unearthed in great numbers from ancient tombs, leading to the notion that these beads held spiritual meaning, and this comma-shaped jewel is revered as one of the Three Imperial Regalia, or Three Sacred Treasures, of Japan. In this context, the jewel represents benevolence; it is used in the ceremony of imperial ascension.Whatever the beads' religious significance, they were associated as well with the ruling elite and were popular

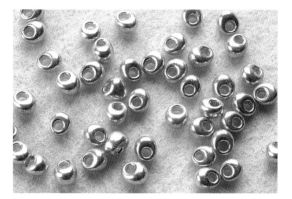

as personal ornamentation. These days, the magatama is variously used to represent the human spirit. The modern manufactured magatama bead is shown here.

magnetic clasp A variety of clasps feature a magnetic closure; this mechanism is very easy to operate. The two parts of the clasp are magnetized, drawing them together to close the strand. Magnetic closures are convenient for those who have difficulty with fine motor dexterity, such as children and adults who have arthritis. The magnetism needs to be strong enough for a heavy bracelet. However, the magnet may adversely affect a pacemaker or a watch worn on the same wrist. In the photos the open clasp is on the left and the closed clasp on the right.

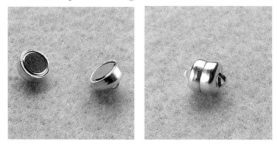

magnetic hematite Beads of strongly magnetized "hematite" are not hematite at all. They are composed of synthetic barium or strontium ferrite that has been magnetized by heating it to a prescribed temperature and then cooling it in a strong magnetic field. Pure hematite cannot be magnetized, but most hematite has enough impurities in it to be able to be very weakly magnetized. Magnetic hematite in jewelry is usually the same attractive dark silver-gray as natural hematite, and its magnetic property is helpful for making strands of beads lie flat against each other. Magnetic beads should not be worn by people who have a pacemaker. *See* hematite.

magnifiers Visual aids that increase the optical view and reduce eyestrain and glare. This is important for many beaders, who spend long hours doing detailed work with small objects.

mala From a Sanskrit word meaning "garden" or "garland of flowers," mala (or *japa mala*) are Hindu prayer beads, possibly the oldest known form of prayer beads. They are most common in Tibet and India, where they are used in meditation. Hinduism has two main deities in addition to Brahma: Shiva and Vishnu. In Shiva rosaries, the counting beads are rudraksha, seeds of a tree that grows exclusively in Myanmar (Burma), Indonesia, Java, Nepal, and Sumatra. Vishnu rosaries use beads of tulsi, a species of basil. Other types may use bone (human, yak, or past Lamas), wood of the bodhi tree, seeds of the lotus, sandalwood, or semiprecious stones like carnelian and amethyst. Colors of the beads may relate to specific practices. Prayer beads are not all alike, but are generally used to count the repetition of prayers, to recite or chant a mantra, or to engage in other forms of *sadhana* (spiritual exercises), generally known as *japa*. Malas are regarded as practical tools for meditation, and the beads themselves often draw on religious symbols.

The Buddhist mala typically has 108 beads, corresponding to the number of earthly desires a disciple must overcome. The Hindu mala adds one more to the 108, the guru bead, while Tibetan malas have 111 for 100 mantras plus 11 to account for errors. Wrist malas have 27 beads connected to a Buddha bead or tassel. In China the 27-bead malas are called *shu-zhu* and in Japan they're called *juzu*. An alternate name for the shorter malas is *prostration rosaries.*

According to legend, a novice collecting bodhi seeds asks, "Teacher, how many beads will make a perfect mala?" The Sensei replies, "Every single one, and not one less or more."

The mala shown is an inexpensive version made of glass beads, but it has the same symbolic value as one of precious metals and gemstones. *See also* prayer beads and rudraksha.

malachite Malachite, basic copper carbonate, is an opaque green mineral with distinctive light-green and dark black-green banding that make it one of the most easily recognizable stones. In thin plates it is translucent. Malachite is often sculpted. It has a Mohs scale hardness factor of 3.5 to 4 and a small, monoclinic, long prismatic and usually aggregate crystal system. The ancient Egyptians, Greeks, and Romans used malachite for jewelry, amulets, powdered eye shadow, and pigment. Associated with copper ore and sometimes found with azurite and calcite, malachite is mined in Chile, Zaire, Namibia, Zimbabwe, Australia, England, the Eurasian Ural mountains, and Arizona. *Azure-malachite* is an intergrowth of azurite and malachite, while *Eliat stone* is an intergrowth of turquoise, chrysocolla, and malachite. When cutting, carving, or breaking malachite, the dust can pose a serious health hazard. In the bracelet shown, the dark green nugget fifth from the right is malachite.

Mali wedding beads In the shape of a light-bulb or a fat teardrop, what most distinguishes these beads is that they are drilled through the top so that they hang "sideways" on the cord and can rotate around it. A gift to the bride on her wedding day in Mali, West Africa, the necklace is composed of many glass beads, often of Czech manufacture.

mallet A soft-face hammer used in jewelry-making with a large cylindrical wooden, rubber, plastic, or rawhide head with a wooden handle. It can be used for bending metal or securing wood or other objects in place without marring the surface. The mallet shown below has a wound rawhide head with a lacquer fixative. Photo by JG.

malleable Capable of being pressed or beaten into shape, a characteristic of certain metals like gold.

mandrel A long stainless-steel rod around which a cane of molten glass is wound in the making of flameworked beads. A tapered mandrel may be used to adjust hoops, coil wire, or measure sizes of rings.

mangal sutra Also spelled *mangalsutra*; beads given by a groom to his bride in northern India that typically include small black beads strung with gold beads and one or more gold pendants. The amount of gold indicates the wealth of the groom. The mangal sutra is worn by the wife until the death of her husband, much as women wear wedding rings in the Western world. In southern India, a string of beads called a *taali*, a gold or silver chain and anthropomorphic pendants, is given as a traditional wedding gift. *See also* taali.

man-made A product that is fabricated, created, or constructed, and not occurring naturally; synthetic.

marble Rock created by the metamorphism of limestone and composed of calcite, a crystalline form of calcium carbonate, capable of achieving a high polish. Marble comes in many color patterns, depending on impurities, such as layers of chert, iron oxide, clay, silt, or sand found within the limestone that recrystallized under intense heat and pressure during its formation. *Marver*, a tool for manipulating glass beads, derives from the French word for marble.

marble beads Made of blown glass fashioned in the mid- to late 1800s by glassmakers from the village of Lauscha in the Thuringian forest of Germany, these beads are somewhat fragile compared with the more solid ones made by other lampworkers. This region of Germany is famous for its glass Christmas tree ornaments, glass marbles, glass marble beads, laboratory glass, and eyeglass prosthetics. Modern marble beads made here look like marbles with stringing holes and are not necessarily hollow. The term *marble beads* also applies to beads made of the stone known as marble. Shown are tiny black marble beads affixed to large metal beads.

Mardi Gras beads Mardi Gras, a term deriving from the French for "Fat Tuesday," falls on the day before Ash Wednesday, the official beginning of the Lenten season in Christian tradition. Beads associated with this celebration are usually bright-colored strands of metallic, opaque, or translucent plastic in a variety of shapes. Until the 1960s such beads were of multicolored glass, and were imported from Czechoslovakia and Japan; they now come from China. Although some are strung beads, most are molded by machine directly onto the stringing material. The Rex Krewe was reportedly the first to toss the inexpensive glass beads among other "throws" from floats during Mardi Gras parades, which can take place between January 6 through Fat Tuesday, associated with Carnival (or *Carnaval* in Brazil), pre-Lenten excess. Elaborate Mardi Grass celebrations take place in Europe, Latin America, the United States, and other parts of the world.

Mardi Gras, or Carnival, was imported to Louisiana from France while that country still held the territory later transferred to the United States in the Louisiana Purchase. A national holiday as celebrated chiefly in Europe, Latin America, and the Caribbean, it has origins in pre-Christian Roman pagan rituals honoring Bacchus. Mardi Gras indulgences, dancing, singing, and revelry precede the sacrifices and strictures in the season of Lent.

Mardi Gras bead-twisting Mardi Gras bead-twisting of the cheap trinkets, strands of Mardi Gras beads, into animal and other shapes, mimics in some ways balloon-twisting. It is said to have originated on riverboat casinos in the Midwest.

marea A sheer coating, similar to an aurora-borealis finish, applied only to a single side of Czech and Bohemian glass beads, marea provides an opalescent metallic cast ranging from golden to pinkish. Shown are 6-mm fire-polish beads with a marea finish.

marriage *See* anniversary stones and metals, apron, armband, beaded collar, beaded dolls, beading party, earth beads, fertility beads, fertility bead dolls, Indian reds, initiation bead doll, lane stitch (photo of African wedding bracelet), love beads, love letters, Mali wedding beads, mangal sutra, mutisalah, social-status beads, taali, trail beads, wampum, wedding beads, wedding-cake beads, wedding dowry, and specific bead types. *See also* philosopher's stone, rhinestone, seed pearls, sequins.

married metal Designs or images formed when deliberately placing various metal alloys, such as bronze, copper, or silver, next to each other.

marudama A round bead made by winding or drawing and cutting a tube. It is 50 mm or larger; the smaller *kodama* resembles it. They have been found in great quantities in Old Tomb graves from about A.D. 250 to 550 in China.

marver The term *marver* can refer to a surface, a kind of paddle, or two plates that work together something like a garlic press. The term originated from the French word *marbre*, meaning "marble." The marver plate is a heatproof ceramic, metal, crystallized limestone, or graphite surface on which molten glass is worked in the making of beads. In small operations, a chunk of marble, smooth piece of aluminum, or the flat underside of a stainless steel bowl are sometimes used. A marver draws heat from molten glass fairly rapidly; thermal shock (cracking or breaking the glass) can result from not handling the glass properly on the marver. The marver paddle can be used like a bead rake to shape or flatten the beads or to make patterns on the bead surface. The marvering press typically uses two plates joined together to make an impression on the beads or otherwise shape them.

marver paddle A heatproof ceramic, metal, or graphite paddle usually fixed to a handle that is used to flatten or otherwise shape a glass bead. It can also make incisions, patterns, or decorations on the bead surface. With the paddle, glass beads can be combed or raked to produce featherlike and other decorations. *See also* marver.

marvering Using a marver in glass beadmaking to shape the glass beads' surface, by raking, feathering, swirling, flattening, or creating other patterns.

mascot An animal image thought to be protective, influential, or inspiring, often worn as an amulet, charm, or talisman. The meaning of the particular animal depends on the cultural iconography. Essentially, the bearer of the image or animal part may be thought to assume of the animal's character, such as strength or speed. The mascot may also indicate clan affiliation, like that of the totems of the First Peoples or Native Americans of the Pacific Northwest of Canada and the United States.

mass A common unit of measurement in the wholesale bead and jewelry industry. A mass is 100 dozen or 1,200 units or pieces. For example, a mass of beads could be sold as 24 strands of beads, each strand holding 50 beads.

matrix The striping, striations, or other patterns visible in certain minerals and gemstones, often created by inclusions of different minerals or elements. In glass beadmaking, core glass into which other colored glasses are fused may be considered the matrix.

matte A bead finish with a satin, sometimes dull, unreflective surface rather than a shiny or reflective surface. Such beads may also be

described as frosted or velvety. The effect is achieved by applying an acid wash to a shiny bead. Metals may also have a matte or satin finish that is less shiny or less polished than that possible. The tile bead shown here has a matte finish.

medallion A jewelry component which functions as a pendant. It is typically made of metal, circular in shape, large, and bears an inscription or impressed image. Sometimes large coins, actual medals, or other large round symbolic objects are used as medallions worn as fashion accessories, hung from a necklace.

medical-alert jewelry Usually an identification tag or charm, bracelet, necklace, or anklet worn daily and used to alert authorities of the wearer's sensitivities or conditions, such as penicillin allergy, asthma, hemophilia, or diabetes, that might demand immediate medical attention or special care.

medicine bag While it has been valued as a Native North American cultural artifact, seen in museums, the medicine bag is still used today to carry special objects or totems, healing herbs or stones, or sentimental remembrances. It may even carry modern pharmaceuticals. Also called an *amulet bag,* it is typically made of leather or beadwork fabric. The dyed red leather medicine bag shown has a beaded edge created by whipstitch, leather fringe, and a braided strap. It is embellished with an abalone shell piece with two strands of beads, including tubular bone, carved bone, turquoise, abalone bear fetish, and abalone tube bead.

melon bead A bead shape characterized by regular ribs or pronounced ridges on the surface of a round, oval, or elongated oval bead that resembles a melon (fruit). The ancient Roman glass beads and the Viking combed-glass beads made into the shape of a melon usually had generous thread holes. The term is sometimes spelled *mellon.*

These beads first appeared around 2500 B.C. in jewelry crafted for Sumerian royalty. Melon beads were popular in the Etruscan period around 800–600 B.C. when gold jewelry was produced in the western Tuscany region of Italy, then called Etruria or Tyrrhenia. Such beads became common in the Mediterranean and western Asia, but made their way along the silk routes into China around 200 B.C. Ancient melon-shaped beads were commonly made of metal, glass, or gemstones like carnelian or lapis lazuli.

melon shell Seashell (*Melo aethiopica* or *Melo tesselkata*), also called baler shell, common to the Philippines and found from Malaysia to the South China Sea. The shell has a wide aperture, a creamy orange interior, and a creamy exterior with brown markings. Colors may vary in intensity and markings according to the location. The shell can be cut or broken into squared-off pieces, drilled, and prepared for heishi or used as is. Shown is a strand of light-orange or peach melon-shell beads from the Philippines.

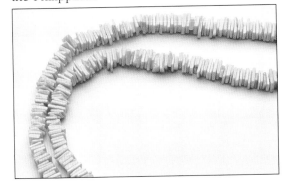

memory wire A coiled jewelry wire made of base metal or tempered stainless steel designed to retain its curved shape. This coarse wire requires heavy-duty shears or memory-wire cutters, not the more delicate jewelry wire cutters. Memory wire is used for stringing rings, bracelets, and chokers that are referred to as *wraparound jewelry* because they are flexible and require no clasp. When ordering memory wire, which usually ranges from 14 to 30 gauge, the larger the number, the smaller the wire's diameter. For example, 20-gauge wire is 0.813 mm in diameter. When determining the proper size for a bead project, be sure that the bead hole is large enough to allow the wire to pass through. Many bead stores stock a single size. Popular finishes are silver-

plate and gold-plate. Shown is a memory-wire bracelet strung with African Christmas beads, pony beads, bone beads, and metal bells.

memory-wire cutters A tool designed for cleanly cutting memory wire. These snips are a special required tool since memory wire is a thick coil of tempered steel. They may also be called heavy-duty wire cutters or shears. Tools designed specifically for the use of cutting memory wire are often easier to use effectively than tools found in a hardware store. Photo by JG.

mescal bean This red bean or seed from the *Sophora secundiflora* plant was used as a bead. In past centuries a small part of the bean was ingested as an oracular, divinatory, or hallucinogenic medium by Native Americans of southwest Texas and Mexico in a vision-seeking Red Bean dance. Contrary to popular notions, the bean does not contain mescaline or any of its chemical derivatives but does actually contain several toxic alkaloids that can cause nausea, seizures, and even death. It is not advisable to ingest any substance without knowing the potential toxic effects. Typically, the beans are drilled and strung into necklaces used for ceremonial purposes, such as in the gourd dance, rather than being ingested. The term *mescal* (also spelled *mezcal*) refers to an alcoholic beverage made from the agave plant as well as the peyote cactus, probably alluding to the mind-altering properties of the bean, the alcoholic beverage, and the cactus. *See also* coral seed.

metal The so-called noble metals, like gold, resist oxidation and corrosion, unlike the so-called base metals, like iron, nickel, zinc, copper, and lead. Precious metals, like gold, silver, platinum, rhodium, and tantalum, are considered precious because they are relatively rare but highly desired in the marketplace. Base metals are relatively inexpensive. Ferrous metals contain iron. Metals tend to be lustrous, ductile, malleable, and good conductors of electricity. Metallic elements readily lose their electrons to positive ions. Painting, applying a coating, or anodizing metals helps prevent corrosion. Mixtures of metals are called *alloys,* which can improve their properties. *See* base metals, precious metals, and specific metals, such as gold.

metal alloy *See* alloy.

metal beads While obviously referring to beads made of metal, the term can also indi-cate beads of other materials, but having a metallic finish. *See also* sterling silver and metallized plastic.

metal earring hoop A metal hoop or ring with an attached ring for adding an ear wire or charm.

metal finishes High-polish (shiny or highly reflective), satin or matte (less shiny), brushed or textured, and hammered are the most common finishes for metals, such as gold, silver, and platinum, used in jewelry. Brushed metal appears to have little brushstrokes or marks created by its having been brushed with a material like sandpaper. Hammered metal takes on a wavy texture from a soft mallet being struck on the surface.

metallic A finish or surface coating that may be applied to beads, giving them the appearance of metal. Noniridescent metallic finishes may be subject to wear. The coating is produced when beads are heated and sprayed with oxidized tin. A thicker coating will create a darker metallic finish. If exposed to skin oils or other chemical agents, metallic coatings are susceptible to being rubbed off or changing color. Metallic finishes used on plastic beads (see *metallized plastic*) are generally reliable.

Of course, beads made entirely of metal are also called "metallic."

metallic thread A filament of metal or a metallic blend of fibers, used in sewing, beading, and other craft projects. Shown is copper-colored thread.

metallized beads *See* metallized plastic.

metallized plastic Plastic beads coated with a type of metal finish like silver, copper, or gold to give the bead the appearance of metal. This bead type may be less expensive and weigh less than its denser all-metal equivalent. Metallized plastic beads are also called simply *metallized beads*. Beads shown are popular rose beads; notice the plastic seam lines on the beads' edges.

metalwork Finished metal pieces, such as scrolls or filigree, often artfully made, created as part of jewelry. Beads, chains, and wires made of metal are also generally called metalwork. Metalwork is commonly featured in architectural or decorative elements.

metalworking Working with metals, using such processes as milling; turning on a lathe or other device; cutting; drilling; threading (for screws); grinding; casting (sand, shell, die, or investment casting or lost-wax); bending, drawing, pressing, spinning, rolling, or flow-turning sheet metal; forging, rolling, extruding, or spinning with plastic deforming; welding; marking out or laying out; and hand fabrication. Other metalwork techniques include hammering, embossing, repoussé, chasing, engraving, inlaying, enameling, and gilding.

metamorphic rock Rocks of various types compacted by intense pressure and heat during their formation deep inside the earth.

meteyi beads Made by the Ashanti people of Ghana until about the 1940s, these powder-glass beads have longitudinal seams that indicate they were made from molds. They are typically opaque yellow with multicolored stripes.

mica powder Also called *pixie dust,* mica compounds in the form of superfine powders give glass beads a soft metallic or pearlescent luster, or a dusting of color. This is done by rolling a hot glass bead in mica powder on a flat surface (a marver), or dipping or swirling a hot bead in a small container of mica. To add depth, a second layer of colored glass can be added to the original bead to encase the mica. For other effects, the mica powder can be brushed on hot glass or rolled up inside molten glass. Shaking or mixing the mica powder may cause particles to float in the air. They could burst into flame when coming into contact with hot glass.

micro-beads Any small bead; typically antique seed beads. The term also refers to tiny glass or metal marbles with no holes that are adhered to various craft projects. Technically, these marbles are not beads since they have no holes for strings, but are commonly called beads in the marketplace. They can be adhered with a tacky tape or a heat-activated adhesive powder to such objects as vases, ink pens, or jewelry.

micro-bugles Very small bugle beads, measuring approximately 2 mm by 1 mm. They come in even smaller sizes than those pictured.

microcrystalline quartz Also called *crypto-crystalline quartz,* this type of quartz has individual crystals visible only under high magnification. *Macrocrystalline quartz,* in contrast, has individual crystals that are visible to the naked eye. *See* cryptocrystalline quartz and quartz.

microinch A unit of length, 1,000,000th of an inch, typically used to measure thickness of metal plating.

micrometer A caliper tool or precision instrument used to measure very small increments, such as the thickness or diameter of a bead or gemstone. One millimeter is a metric unit of length equal to one thousandth of a meter, and a micrometer is equal to one millionth (1,000,000th) of a meter. *See* gauge.

micron Also called a micrometer; a unit of length, 1,000th of a millimeter, typically used to measure the thickness of metal plating.

milagros A Spanish term for charms ("miracles") commonly used in Mexico and other parts of Central and South America. At Catholic shrines and other holy places, visitors or supplicants pray and leave these charms, usually made of recycled or inexpensive base metal(s), as reminders. The charms are shaped to represent afflicted body parts or other wished-for objects, such as a car.

milk glass White, opaque glass developed in 16th century Venice. Tin oxide is added to the glass. Around 1900, milk glass was popularly made into jewelry and decorative pieces, which today attract serious collectors. In the 1930s and 1940s, the milk glass or so-called Depression glass was more workmanlike. It is also sometimes called *latticino.*

milk stone An informal name for an opaque white variety of quartz, silicon dioxide. The cloudiness is caused by liquids or gases trapped inside during the formation of the crystals.

millefiori beads The Italian word *millefiori,* meaning "thousand flowers," is a glassmaking technique with its origins in Alexandria in the third century B.C. and Rome in the first century A.D. Millefiori beads were made by what was then called mosaic glass, created by assembling thin glass canes of various colors to form patterns that often resemble flowers. The bundle is heated to melting, which fuses the canes that are then pulled; when cool, the bundle is cut into cross-sections. The beads are then made individually by hand by working cross-sections of mosaic glass cane into plain molten wound-glass bead cores. The resulting beads display intense colors and assume a three-dimensional appearance. This glassworking technique was given the name *millefiori* when it was revived and modified in 16th century Venice and the nearby island of Murano. This traditional bead design enjoyed its greatest popularity from the late 1800s to the early 1900s. The beads may be impressed with a single mosaic slice or a number of them in combination.

In the necklace shown, the beads are capped and knots are tied between each. In the close-up photos, you can see cane slices embedded in the bead. While not the best quality, because the slices should be flush with the bead surface to best show off the floral design, rather than aligned sideways, these beads are still collectible.

millefiori cane Glass rods or canes are elongated tubes that may be arranged in a small bundle to form floral or mosaic designs. They can be fired and fused, then sliced into beads, pins, or pendants, or embellished with gold leaf and other surface decorations. It may also be called *mosaic cane. See* millefiori beads.

Polymer clays can also be used to create millefiori or mosaic beads. After being fired, fused, and sliced, the finished clay pieces are put inside a low-temperature oven or kiln to cure and harden the clay. The cane-making process may be done by hand, but sometimes a pasta machine can do the work of extruding the clay into canes. The finished clay is strong and lightweight and less fragile than glass. Shown are a variety of Fimo-clay beads.

millefiori chips Pieces of multicolored cane tumbled into smooth chips. These colorful chips are attractive when mixed with other beads.

millesimal One of 1,000 parts or the quotient of a unit that has been divided by 1,000.

millesimal fineness system In this system, the purity of precious metals, such as gold and platinum, are denoted by parts per thousand of pure precious metal in the alloy. Compare definitions for carat (mass or weight), which relates to the weight of gemstones, with carat (purity), which deals with the purity of precious metals gold and silver. Note that the preferred spelling when talking about millesimal fineness is *karat(s)*. Find the karat and millesimal fineness chart in Part IV.

millimeter A common unit of measure, abbreviated *mm*, for measuring the length or diameter of a given bead. One millimeter equals $^1/_{10}$ centimeter or about 0.0394 inch (about 0.04 inch). The measurement 3 mm is about $^1/_8$ inch, and 10 mm is slightly more than $^3/_8$ inch. Beads are usually measured in millimeters.

mineral Identified by specific chemical compositions and crystalline structures, minerals are naturally occurring, solid homogeneous elements or compounds such as coal, salt, sand, stone, sulfur, and water that are produced by inorganic, geological processes. Minerals distinguished by their chemical properties are grouped into the *silicate, carbonate, sulfate, halide, oxide, sulfide, phosphate, element,* and *organic* classes. They range in composition from pure elements and simple salts to complex silicates with thousands of known forms. *True minerals* are solid, naturally occurring, homogeneous substances with a crystalline structure and a defined chemical composition. The *organic class,* however, has more recently been added to the modern classification system. Geologists may refer to mineral classification systems, notably the Dana or the Strunz systems. Terms commonly used to describe minerals are *crystal structure* and *habit, hardness, luster, color, streak, density, cleavage, fracture, specific gravity,* and such properties as *fluorescence* (response to ultraviolet light), *magnetism, radioactivity, tenacity* (response to mechanically induced changes of shape or form), *piezoelectricity,* and *reactivity to dilute acids.*

mineralogy The scientific study of minerals.

miracle beads A process using a Lucite acrylic lining or core that's then given a silver-mirror plate finish and finally adding several layers

of colored lacquer gives miracle beads the appearance of glowing from the inside. The mesmerizing reflection from the mirrored core also lends them the illusion of depth. The miracle or *wonder beads* shown were bought in Germany but manufactured in Japan.

mirror beads Many types of mirror beads exist. They can be glass beads with a silver layer applied to the bead surface as a finish which reflects rather than transmits light; sterling-silver beads with reflective facets that may resemble small disco balls; or shiny glass fire-polish beads with a reflective metallic finish and other beads with a mirrorlike finish. Mirror beads may be faceted or plain. *See also* shisha.

mirrored A surface with a reflective, usually silver, finish.

mnemonic beads Beads used as memory devices for a series of prayers, meditations, mantras, treatment goals, or such mundane things as birthdays and anniversaries. Similarly, wampum beads may document important events and treaties. *See* wampum.

Mohs scale The Mohs scale of hardness is the standard in the field for rating the hardness of gemstones. It was named for Friedrich Mohs, the mineralogist who devised it in 1812. This relative scale uses the numbers 1 to 10 and expresses the ability of one mineral to resist scratching by another. The lowest number is the softest mineral, and Mohs chose the scale's minerals based on their ready availability, except for the hardest, diamond. In order, starting from the softest, the minerals are talc, gypsum, calcite, fluorite, apatite, feldspar, quartz, topaz, corundum, and diamond. Typically, the value of gemstones increases with their hardness. Each mineral higher on the scale scratches the previous one (the one with the lesser hardness) and can be scratched by the one that follows. A diamond, ranked 10, can be scratched only by another diamond.

The Mohs scale, unlike the sclerometer, a more recently introduced precision instrument, does not measure *true* or *absolute hardness*. A diamond, at 10 on the Mohs scale, is actually four times harder than corundum (with a hardness of 9) and six times harder than topaz (with a hardness of 8). On the Mohs scale, a fingernail has a hardness of 2.5; a copper penny, about 3; a knife blade and window glass, 5.5; and a steel file, 6.5. Find the Mohs scale in Part IV.

moissanite A silicon carbide that simulates the diamond, made in the laboratory and discovered by and named after Dr. Henri Moissan (1852–1907), the French Nobel Prize–winning chemist. This transparent simulant has a Mohs scale hardness of 9. It was introduced as a gemstone to the jewelry market in 1998. It can be easily distinguished from a diamond under ultraviolet light. This durable simulant does not cloud over time.

mokume gane A metalworking technique, invented in 17th century Japan, that involves fusing metal sheets and forging or rolling them to create the appearance of wood grain or another pattern.

mold A cavity, often sculpted, carved, or otherwise impressed with a design, in which a substance, such as liquid glass, wax, clay, or metal, can be shaped. A mold can also be a frame on or around which an object can be constructed or shaped.

molded beads Molded beads are made from very thick glass rods heated into molten glass, stamped, and the hole pierced with a needle. To soften seam lines and remove any "flashing," the molded beads are rolled in hot sand. If striped or patterned canes are fed into the stamping machine, the resulting beads can be more elaborately colored than some other bead types. In the 19th and 20th centuries, various mold shapes, like seashells and coral, often mimicking more expensive beads, were commonly made by this process. *See also* pressed-glass beads.

momme An old Japanese measure of mass that continues in use for cultured pearls. Equivalent to 3.75 grams (about 0.132 ounce).

money belt In the Solomon Islands, various combinations of shells and beads are used as currency. On the island of Malaita, craftspeople fashion shell money from flattened shells made into disks about 10 mm in diameter and rolled and covered with plates of turtle shell. The shell money is strung as beads and worn as necklaces or belts, which function as money as well as decorative jewelry. (Another currency, not fashioned into beads, is red feather money.) The *tabu*, or shell-bead disks, are strung and typically worked like heishi. Teeth are also commonly used as both beads and currency, e.g., those of the porpoise, fruit bat, opossum, pig, and less often the dog. The use of human teeth is less common. These teeth, particularly the precious porpoise teeth, may be used as a bride price or burial payment or for other purposes.

monkstone Also called *monk's stone,* another name for the synthetic material goldstone.

moonstone A translucent colorless or yellow stone from the feldspar group with a pale sheen. Composed of potassium aluminum silicate, it demonstrates a weak bluish or orange fluorescence or adularescence. The stone's shimmer was compared to the moon's glow, from which the gemstone's name is derived. It has a vitreous luster and tends to be sensitive to pressure. The crystal system is monoclinic and prismatic and its Mohs scale hardness is 6 to 6.5. Moonstone may be confused with chalcedony, synthetic spinel, or glass. Other moonstones are found in the feldspar group. The traditional cabochon cutting shown below highlights moonstone's whitish-blue pearly or opalescent sheen.

Moretti beads Made from Moretti glass rods, a soft soda-lime glass characterized by a particularly low melting point. Moretti glass, also called Effetre glass, is manufactured in the Effetre factory in Venice, on the island of

Murano, where the Moretti beads are also manufactured.

morganite This transparent to opaque gemstone is the pink variety of precious beryl (aluminum berylium silicate); its namesake is for John Pierpont Morgan. With a Mohs scale hardness rating of 7.5, the stone's color varies from soft pink to peach to violet, owing to the amount of manganese embedded in it. It has weak fluorescence and pleochroism. Mined in Brazil, Italy, Madagascar, Mozambique, Namibia, Zimbabwe, Pakistan, and the United States, morganite may be heat-treated to remove a yellow discoloration. *See* beryl.

mosaic cane Also called millefiori cane. *See* millefiori cane.

mosaic glass beads These beads have an ornate composition determined by elements preformed from colorful mosaic-glass cane fused by heat to a glass core, which contributes to its often ornate composition. Mosaic glass beads come in many shapes—round, square, heart, star, oval, diamond, and tube. The Vikings had sophisticated glassmaking operations in Scandinavia for making millefiori beads by a similar process; the finished beads

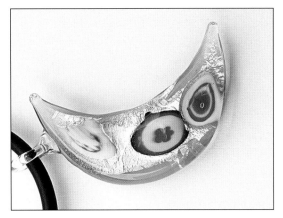

have been found in excavations of burial sites dating from A.D. 800 to 1000. Shown are a transparent, dark-blue-glass donut pendant accented with white and clear flowers, and a moon-shaped pendant lined with foil and embedded with pieces of cane. *See* millefiori beads.

Moslem prayer beads *See* Muslim prayer beads.

moss agate A transparent, colorless variety of chalcedony (silicon dioxide) with green, brown, or red inclusions. The green inclusions are hornblende or chlorite found in patterns resembling moss. Red and brown coloration is caused by oxidation of the iron found in the hornblende. It is preferred in thin slabs for cabochons, plates, pendants, and brooches. Its Mohs scale hardness is 6.5 to 7, and the crystal system is trigonal microcrystalline.

mother-of-pearl Also known by the acronym *MOP,* the inner nacreous layer of a mollusk shell or a snail shell, which has an iridescent play-of-color. The freshwater or saltwater mollusk's mantle secretes nacre, formed by successive coatings of calcium carbonate and conchiolin on the shell's inner surface. When the same nacre surrounds and entombs irritants or parasites found inside the shell, a pearl forms. Mother-of-pearl from pearl mollusks usually comes from pearl farms. While most mother-of-pearl is creamy white, dark varieties come from Tahiti. In New Zealand, the Maori people value mother-of-pearl from the paua seashell (*Haliotis australis*) for its blue-green iridescent color play and have popularly used it as the eyes of sculptures. Mother-of-pearl is sometimes called *sea opal*.

The European glass-bead industry, however, uses the same term for certain types of glass beads with a subtle sheen, similar to that of satin glass. One technique involves lining blown-glass beads with a fish-scale solution. A second technique involves introducing air bubbles to simulate the satin sheen. And a third involves coating the bead with an alabaster glass or pearly coating. Still another technique is to fashion large molded pearls (beads) from crushed small, but genuine pearls. Mother-of-pearl beads were made in Russia, Bohemia, and Murano, Italy, in the mid-18th to early 19th centuries. Shown is a popular form of the dyed bead in the shape of a bird fetish.

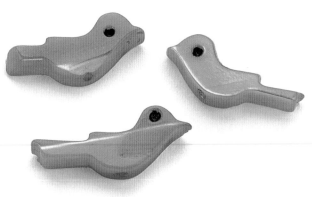

mother's ring or bracelet A piece of jewelry, introduced by jewelers in the 20th century, typically made as a ring or bracelet, that includes a birthstone for each of a woman's children.

mottled A bead finish usually applied to opaque glass to achieve a marbling effect by mixing several different colors. Mottling exhibits variations in color density, which gives it a somewhat textured appearance. Opaque glass may also be covered with marbled gold wash.

moukaite A cloudy pink to light red, plum, brown, and creamy jasper found in western Australia and mined near Mooka Creek, which means "running waters." It is also known as *bicorite, mook jasper,* or *Australian jasper,* as well as under various spellings, like *mookaite.* Moukaite is opaque, composed of silicon dioxide with impurities, and has a Mohs scale hardness of 6.5 to 7. Its crystal system is trigonal or microcrystalline aggregate. The word *moukaite* may derive from the Mooka clan of Australian aboriginal people who live in the area where the gemstone is found. *See* jasper.

mourning beads French glass seed beads strung on wire and sold on large spools, these beads are used to make beaded flowers to lay

on graves when mourning loved ones. French jet beads worn in jewelry by mourners are also called mourning beads. In the 1800s and 1900s, while black beads indicated mourning, these inexpensive and abundant beads were often used as fashionable ornamentation for nonmourners as well. *See also* French jet.

mousetail Satin cord that is 1.5 mm in diameter, commonly used for stringing beads.

mud beads Mud beads are actually bone beads that are dyed with an attractive relief design in dark brown with a creamy off-white background. The process for dyeing mud beads is similar to that used for making mud-cloth textile print designs and paintings. Mud cloth is still made today in parts of the African continent. (A similar process for making textiles is called lost-wax or batik in other parts of the world.) First the animal bones, usually from cattle or water buffalo, are bleached. The bead maker draws his design with wax on the beads and then submerges them in black dye. While the waxed areas do not receive the design, the remaining areas do, which creates an interesting pattern. Shown is a bracelet made with a barrel-shaped mud bead, small oval bone beads, and metal-based beads with tiny black glass marbles affixed to the surface.

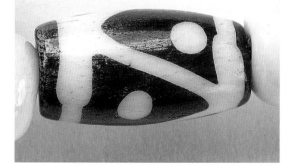

mulberry beads Also called *raspberry beads,* the name describes the shape characterized by surface bumps or knobs, resembling the fruit. The name was first noted in the late 1500s in Spanish lists of cargo taken to America.

multicolored beads A generic term for single beads having more than one color as well as for a strand or hank of beads of various colors. *Bead blends* can indicate beads of related colors in the same family or beads of contrasting colors. Shown is a hank of size-12 Czech glass seed beads in a beautiful monochromatic array of matte, copper-lined, opaque, and luster finishes.

mummy beads Beads of glass, gemstones, and brass have been found in ancient burial sites of many cultures, including Egyptian, Roman, Saxon, Viking, sub-Saharan African, and Native North and South American. Egyptian burial sites, such as that for King Tutankhamun, in particular have yielded enormous quantities of a variety of beads. Small ceramic beads are often found in such sites. The ancient Sumerians fashioned beads from steatite, a black, white, or gray ceramic. Egyptians used faience in a variety of earth tones ranging from light green to blue and soft red. Beaded netting has also been found covering the face and body of the deceased in tombs.

Murano glass Glassmakers on the island archipelago of Murano, near Venice, have since the late 13th century developed and refined various types of glass: crystalline, enameled or smalto, aventurine (gold threads run through it), multicolored or millefiori, and milk or lattimo. These artisans have created chandeliers, imitation gemstones, and contemporary artworks among the best in the world.

Murano glass beads Beads handmade from Moretti glass canes in the islands of Murano, Italy, in the Adriatic Sea. Glass furnaces were installed in the islands after 1291, when they had been banned in nearby Venice because of the danger of fires. Murano bead artists are known for their fine handcrafted glasswork; they produce a variety of bead types, often simply called Venetian glass beads. *See* lampwork beads.

murrine Another name for the glass canes or rods from which mosaic or millefiori beads are crafted; when cut into cross-sections, the slice reveals a pattern or image.

Muslim prayer beads Called *subha* or *tasbih,* "to exalt" or "to praise Allah," Muslim prayer beads consist of a string of 33, 66, or 99 beads. The 99 beads are said to symbolize the known names or attributes of God. A leader bead (the 100th in a strand of 99 beads) may be strung with two more beads dangling from the necklace and a tassel of gold or silk thread. Faithful Islamic practitioners especially prize beads fashioned from the sacred clay of Mecca or Medina. Muslim beads, carried by men in the Middle East, were established by the 9th century, but their use is not universal. *See also* prayer beads.

mutisalah Indo-Pacific beads, also called Indian reds, are small, opaque red or orange beads made of drawn glass. The red beads are also called earth beads since they are used by the lower class to give to brides at weddings. The orange beads called brick beads serve the same functions but are more expensive. Both types are considered heirlooms among the peoples of the Indonesian archipelago, but antique as well as newly manufactured beads are called *mutisalah*. They are also called *false pearls* or *false beads*. The king's beads are made from wound glass with significant lead content; these are very expensive and indicate the highest social status. *See also* Indo-Pacific beads.

myrrh beads Irregular yellowish to reddish brown berry-shaped beads made from the aromatic gum resin of the myrrh tree (genus *Commiphora*) found in eastern Africa and Arabia. Fashioned in Mali, these beads, when worn against the skin on hot days, release the myrrh's fragrance. Myrrh is burnt as incense. Also sometimes called myrrh beads are beads not made from the myrrh resin but from seeds of a different plant to which fragrance is added.

N

nacre The outside coating of a pearl, also called *mother-of-pearl*. Secreted by oysters and other mollusks, this substance lines the inside of their shells to make them smooth and hospitable. Mollusks also use nacre to coat and isolate within their shells any parasite or irritant that enters and cannot easily be expelled. A pearl will always have the same color as the lining of the shell in which it was created. Nacre consists of layers of calcium carbonate and conchiolin, an organic protein that serves as a bonding agent. The luster and iridescence of the nacre depend on the number and thickness of the layers, as well as on how the layers overlap.

nail head A glass bead with a dome shape; a metal finding that has prongs for attaching to leather or fabric; or a nail-head-shaped rhinestone that can be ironed onto a fabric or attached by an adhesive. All three uses of the term are independent.

nail polish Commonly used to coat fingernails for greater strength or shine, clear nail polish is handy for sealing knots in beadwork; a convenient brush allows for precise application of a small amount of adhesive to the thread. Jewelry cements are not recommended, because they can stiffen when dry and ruin the fluid quality of beadwork fabric.

naja Originating from the Navajo language, the *naja,* or *najahe,* is a crescent-shaped pendant often seen as the principal part of a squash-blossom necklace. Originally made from iron and used as decorative ornaments on horse bridals by the Spanish Conquistadors in the late 1500s, the design was also influenced by Moorish conquests in Spain. Usually crafted from silver today, the naja came to be symbolic of crop fertility. *See also* squash-blossom necklace.

name bracelet or necklace A piece of jewelry that fancifully displays the name, often in metal but sometimes in beads, of the wearer.

Native American prayer beads Although there is no commonly accepted set of prayer beads among Native American tribes, beads have always had a spiritual significance for them. Native North Americans often use beads in healing and other spiritual ceremonies. Creating peyote-stitch beadwork is an endeavor held to be sacred; such symbolic beadwork adorns much of the peyote ceremony paraphernalia associated with Native American religious practices. According to a folktale, when Europeans first introduced glass beads to Native Americans, they were called "little spirit seeds" because they were seen as spiritual gifts. One modern vestige of Native American prayer beads is the *rosario,* used by the Yoeme tribe of northern Mexico and the southwestern U.S. Similar in appearance to a Catholic rosary, the *rosario* is made with hand-carved wooden beads strung onto colorful yarn. It is customary to bless prayer beads by wearing them during a ceremonial dance. *See also* rosario.

natural Denotes gemstones that are known not to be treated in any way. Also refers to other stones or organic materials that have been left untreated.

natural beads Objects found in nature lend themselves to being incorporated into jewelry. Natural beads include seeds, nuts, animal teeth, and bones. In South America, many diverse groups found in the high Andes Mountains, who share the common language of Quechua, fashion beaded adornments from seeds and other objects found in nature. In the Amazon Basin of Ecuador, the Shuar people, who are related to the fearsome Jivaro (who had practiced shrinking heads of their enemies), make hand-woven dance belts decorated with beads, shells of nuts, and seashells that rattle when they dance.

In the Amazon rainforests of Venezuela, the Guahibo make beads from seeds and wood carvings and are known for their wood-carved pendants. The Piaroa people fashion necklaces from seeds, bones, and teeth of rainforest animals, such as tapirs, monkeys, or caimans. And the Yekuna are well known for complex beadwork, canoe-making, and basket-weaving. *See also* botanical beads.

Ndebele beadwork Beadwork, made with the notable bead netting or herringbone stitch by the Ndebele, a tribe living in Transvaal or Kwa Ndebele, northeast of Pretoria, South Africa. The Ndundza branch of the Ndebele have been widely recognized for their beadwork talents. In the late 1800s, the Dutch seized their farmlands and enslaved the people, which may have influenced their beadwork traditions. Contact with European traders who brought Czech seed beads may also have affected their beading style.

Ndebele flat netting Netted beadwork created by the Ndebele of South Africa. The flat-netted bracelet shown is typical of the beadwork sold to African traders, from which this bracelet was purchased. More exotic pieces may be

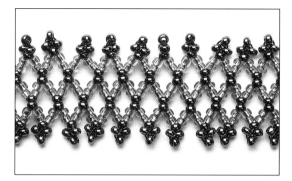

kept in the family for generations. *See also* Ndebele stitch.

Ndebele stitch Also called *herringbone stitch,* this stitch creates an interesting pattern formed by the path the thread takes as the beads are strung. It can be used flat or for three-dimensional work, such as a choker or rope. The technique has been credited to the Ndebele of South Africa, but the stitch has been used in other parts of the world as well.

The Zulu people describe this stitch as *feather stitch*. Shown is a beaded Ndebele belt from the collection of David Bingell. Find stitch diagrams in Part V.

necklace An ornament or piece of jewelry worn around the neck, often encircling it, that may feature a cord, chain, beads, or pendant. The standard pendant length for a woman is 18 inches (45 cm), and for a man it is 20 inches (50 cm). Popular lengths for necklaces, including the clasp, are the choker at 14 to 16 inches (35 to 40 cm), the opera at 28 to 32 inches (70 to 80 cm), the matinee at 30 to 35 inches (75 to 90 cm), and the rope at 40 to 45 inches (100 to 115 cm). *Metric equivalents were rounded off to the nearest 5 cm.*

needle Beading needles are specially designed to accommodate both a bead's hole and the material that threads or strings through it. The number of passes the thread must make through the bead will affect the needle size necessary. Peyote stitch, for example, can involve two or more passes of thread through each bead. Beading needle types include fine beading needles (long and short), and twisted-wire, big-eye, and glover's needles, used to

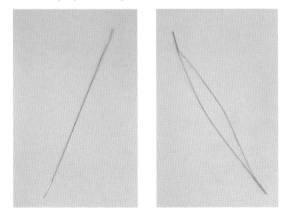

poke holes in leather for beading or lacing. In the Stone Age in Europe and the Americas, delicate sewing needles were made of bone and punched with eyeholes. Thread for stringing beads likely came from the same plant fibers or animal sinews used for fashioning clothing and constructing boats. Shown are an assortment of beading needles and two big-eye needles. Find needle size charts in Part IV.

needle-nose pliers A type of pliers used to bend or shape wire and to attach findings that has elongated, gradually narrowing jaws. The tool is also known as *long-nose* or *thin-nose pliers*. Needle-nose pliers tend to have more slender noses (jaws) than long-nose pliers. The pliers used in jewelry-making tend to be smaller and more lightweight, with slender jaws, good for working with delicate jewelry findings. Both round-nose and flat-nose pliers are also useful in jewelry crafting, for different purposes. Similar household pliers are too heavy for use on jewelry projects. *See* pliers.

needle threader A device designed to make threading a needle easier. It has an enlarged opening or eye, into which thread can be easily inserted, which can collapse when pulled through the smaller eye of a needle, deftly threading it.

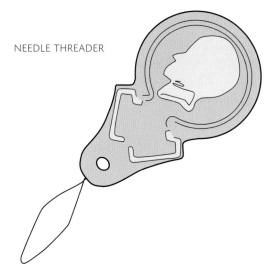

NEEDLE THREADER

needlepoint A technique for embellishing fabric with specialty yarns and threads; it may also include beads. A variety of colorful threads, such as cotton crochet, embroidery floss, or beading thread may be used for work done on needlepoint canvas, a fabric with a some-what open weave that typically has a printed design or graph with square cells (unseen in the finished work) to be used as guides.

negative The mold from which a positive is created in, for instance, the lost-wax process of casting metals.

neihua A Chinese glass bead that is painted from the inside.

nephrite The opaque green gemstone, popularly called jade, composed of basic calcium magnesium iron silicate. Nephrite is the more common of the two types of jade; the other gemstone is *jadeite* (sodium aluminum silicate). While it is found in colors other than green, often with a yellow undertone, green is the most valuable. Its crystal system is monoclinic and intergrown with a fine, fibrous aggregate,

and its Mohs scale hardness rating is 6 to 6.5. Nephrite has a vitreous luster. The gemstone is often made into cabochons and other jewelry as well as vases, small sculptures, and religious objects. China, Taiwan, and Hong Kong are major carving and cutting centers. The word *nephrite* derives from the Greek word for kidney. The creamy white nephrite is known in China as *mutton-fat jade*. The Maori of New Zealand consider it a protected treasure and make nephrite ornaments and weapons. The South Island of New Zealand was called Greenstone Water for the nephrite found in the rivers. Many imitations are made from glass and plastic. *See* jade and jade imitations.

netsuke Made in Japan, this bead, a miniature sculpture, was designed to be used with an *ojime* bead. The word *netsuke* comes from the Japanese words *ne* for "root" and *tsuke* "to hang." Since traditional kimonos have no pockets, Japanese men and women wore a compartmentalized box called an *inro*, which hung below the obi or kimono belt. At the top of the cord, a large carved bead called a *netsuke* acted as a toggle to anchor the *inro*. Today netsuke are collectible art objects with a long history that dates from the Edo period in Japan between the 1600s and 1800s. Although once considered a functional part of attire, netsuke has been elevated to an art form. Netsuke may be made of hornbill ivory; coral; fossilized wood or jet; bamboo; agate; tagua nut (ivory palm); walrus tusk; whale bone (usually used in scrimshaw); or bear, boar, tiger, or whale teeth. Trick netsuke may consist of two outer beads that form a sort of box that contains a third small sculpted bead. *See also* ojime beads.

netting A beadwork technique with flat, circular, round, horizontal, and vertical variations with subtle differences between them. *Circular netting* adapts well to covering three-dimensional objects like a gourd, pipe stem, or walking stick. The same beading technique can also produce a hollow rope. *Horizontal netting*, which is woven on a horizontal plane, can create a relatively two-dimensional flat necklace or a three-dimensional net surrounding a glass Christmas ornament. *Flat netting* is reserved for two-dimensional pieces, like bracelets. *Round* or *circular netting* can be woven flat and then cover an object like a vase since it assumes the shape of the object covered. *Vertical netting*, woven on a vertical plane, can fashion either two- or three-dimensional pieces. The decorative and fluid bag, an original design by Aurora Mathews, uses a variation on horizontal netting in the round.

niccolo An engraved layer stone with a very thin upper layer with translucent color tones due to diffused light and revealing the color of the base. This engraving technique was popular for creating seal rings, coats of arms, and monograms.

nickel This silvery white metallic element is hard, ductile, malleable, and can be highly polished. The metal is commonly used in alloys, such as that with silver. Nickel's use dates to at least 3500 B.C.; Syrian bronzes had nickel content. White copper or *baitung,* a name used in China, was another term for nickel. Nickel is an ingredient in stainless steel, magnets, and coins. It is used for plating and as a green tint in glass. It is used in nickel bronzes, nickel brasses, nickel steel, and nickel iron as well as in alloys with copper, aluminum, chromium, cobalt, silver, gold, and lead. So-called nickel silver or German silver does not contain silver. About 30% of the world's nickel is mined from the Sudbury Basin, impacted by a meteorite, in Ontario, Canada. Siberia, Australia, Cuba, New Caledonia, and Indonesia also have significant deposits.

nickel brass Alloys of copper, nickel, and zinc that sometimes may include tin, antimony, cadmium, or lead, are generally called "nickel silver" but might more properly be called nickel brass. These alloys may typically contain 65% copper, 18% nickel, and 17% zinc.

nickel-plated A base metal having a layer of nickel electroplated to its surface. The industry standard for gold, silver, or nickel plating is a thickness of 6 to 10 microinches (0.15 to 0.25 microns). The U.S. Federal Trade Commission requirement for plating thickness is expressed in both microinches (U.S. inches) and microns (metric). A microinch is equivalent to 1,000,000th (one millionth) of an inch. A micron is 1,000th (one thousandth) of a millimeter. The lustrous silvery-white plating, which can level and fill pores, serves as an undercoating for a precious metal. Nickel resists corrosion. In North America and Europe, nickel is the most common allergen among young women because of common exposure to nickel in close contact with skin. The green stain on the skin does not indicate allergy but rather a chemical reaction, oxidation of the metal with perspiration. The salt or sodium chloride in perspiration slightly corrodes the metal, making it inadvisable to wear the piece of jewelry to the gym. Concern about newly minted 1 and 2 euro coins containing nickel made headlines.

nickel silver Also called *new silver* or *German silver*. In Argentina and Peru it is known as *alpaca silver,* and in China as *paktong* or *pakfong* ("white bronze"). A silver-colored alloy of copper, nickel, and often zinc, the so-called nickel silver contains no silver. This imitation silver, which resists corrosion, may also contain antimony, tin, lead, or cadmium. Alpaca silver, an alloy of copper, nickel, zinc, and iron, does not rust or tarnish. Nickel silver's uses, besides those for costume jewelry, include zippers, keys, musical instruments, plumbing fixtures, and heating coils. Nickel silver alloys having a high amount of zinc may be stainless.

niobium Borrowed from the aerospace industry, this light-gray base metal can be anodized into six different colors. The anodization process involves putting a metal object in an acid bath and passing an electric current through the tank. The process causes oxygen atoms to bond to the metal object's surface, giving it a thin protective film and a lustrous sheen. Metals such as aluminum, titanium, and magnesium are often anodized. Many individuals whose skin is sensitive to certain metals can comfortably tolerate them when the metal is anodized with niobium.

noble metals Metals, like gold, platinum, palladium, rhodium, and silver, that are resistant to corrosion or oxidation. *Base metals,* in contrast, corrode or oxidize relatively easily.

nodule In geology or mineralogy, a spherical lump of a mineral or mixture of minerals often harder than surrounding sediments. Nodules may be hollow as geodes or vugs or be filled with crystals and have intricate geometric shrinkage patterns or bands. Volcanic rocks derived from silica (silicon dioxide) or silicon form nodules during cooling and recrystallization of obsidian and rhyolitic flows. (*Rhyolite* is a very acidic volcanic rock; the lava form of granite.) Thunder eggs are geodelike nodules that form in volcanic ash over time as a result of heat and pressure and chemical or physical change.

nomenclature A method of assigning unique names, using a scientific classification system to define characteristics. In regard to gemstones, modern naming may rely on ancient languages, such as Latin or Greek, to define, for instance, the stone's chemical composition, characteristics, place of origin or occurrence, or a person's name. The language of the region wherein the stone is found may also influence naming. Common names for bead types come from those myriad terms used in the marketplace.

non-tarnishing Not subject to corrosion through time and the environment; usually said of certain resistant metals, such as stainless steel.

nose rings In ancient India and Mexico, wearing a nose ring was considered a mark of distinction or prestige; today, nose rings are youthful fashion statements.

nose studs Commonly seen in India and other parts of Asia, these have been adopted as modern fashion by today's youths across many cultures. The side of the nose that has been pierced has significance to the women of India.

Nueva Càdiz A modern term for drawn-glass beads, usually tubular (long and thin) and often twisted and with a square cross-section, associated with Spanish conquest, exploration, and trade. These beads typically have three layers of glass: a blue, a white, and a lighter blue. Spanish Conquistador Francisco Vasquez de Coronado's journey of 1540–1542, which terrorized native populations of the American Southwest and began to establish Spanish colonies, brought chevrons and Nueva Càdiz beads with them. Distribution of Nueva Càdiz beads was limited to the Spanish New World, with the exception of those the Spaniards took to the Philippines. The beads have been found in Venezuela, Peru, Mexico, and the states of Texas, Pennsylvania, and Florida.

They were named for the location on the island Cubagua off the coast of Venezuela occupied by the Spanish from 1498 to 1545. The Spaniards did not have a significant bead-making tradition, so their origin is unclear. However, Columbus had named a Spanish town in Venezuela after Venice.

nuggets A term denoting chunky beads, often in irregular shapes, cut from natural gemstones.

nylon thread Ideal for beadwork, nylon thread comes on small bobbins in lengths of 60 to 80 yards (55 to 73 m) as well as on spools of various sizes. Many brands of beading thread are on the market, but Nymo is very popular and sets the standard for sizing. Size OO is the finest, most lightweight thread, and size F is the heaviest. For delicate jewelry using small beads (12/0, 13/0, 14/0, or 15/0), size OO thread is the most commonly used. Thread sizes A and O are commonly used with smaller seed beads. (Note that thread sizes are given in letters and bead sizes in numbers.) For general beadwork, thread size B is good with size 11/0, 12/0, and 13/0 beads. Size D is often used with size 10/0 and 11/0 beads, particularly for heavier projects, like loomwork, that need a lot of beads. Size 8/0,

9/0, and 10/0 beads, requiring extra strength, and stringing projects that use a great many heavy beads, call for thread size F. If limited thread sizes are available in stores near you, remember that the thread can be doubled to increase its thickness and strength.

Some nylon threads and cords are made expressly for pearl knotting and for macramé woven with large-holed beads. Be aware of the slight variations in bead and thread-hole sizes from one manufacturer to another. Also certain types of beads, such as white-heart beads made with two layers of glass, typically have smaller holes. When choosing stringing thread, the most important consideration is that the needle and thread fit through the bead hole. Also keep in mind that for certain stitches and weaving projects, the bead hole must accommodate two or more passes of thread. If the hole is too small, you risk breaking the bead. Most bead store personnel are happy to advise you on choosing materials for a particular project. *See also* stringing thread.

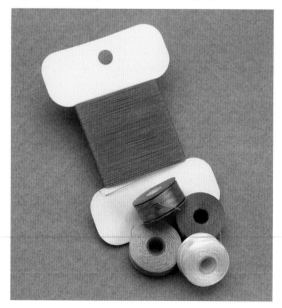

Nymo *See* nylon thread and stringing thread.

O

oblate A bead shape that is a squashed or flattened spheroid.

obsidian A transparent to opaque natural glass, composed of volcanic, amorphous, and siliceous glassy rock, found in areas of volcanic activity. Obsidian, largely silicon dioxide mixed with impurities, is formed with its glassy surface when volcanic molten lava comes into contact with water, such as when it flows into a lake or ocean, which rapidly cools it. Its Mohs scale hardness rating is 5 to 5.5. Because it is not crystalline, obsidian is not considered a true mineral. A few varieties are snowflake, spider web, sheen, and rainbow obsidian.

Iron and magnesium give obsidian a dark green, brown, gray, or black color. *Snowflake obsidian* contains inclusions of small grayish-white crystals of cristobalite arranged in radial clusters. Small rounded nuggets of obsidian, formed by droplets of molten lava in water, are called *Apache tears* (American Southwest) or *Pele's tears* (Hawaii). *Sheen obsidian* may have once contained gas bubbles or tiny crystals of mica, quartz, and feldspar. *Rainbow obsidian* may contain bands of feldspar, quartz, topaz, or tourmaline. Since the Stone Age, people have worked obsidian, which can achieve an extremely thin, sharp edge, to produce cutting tools, weapons, and ceremonial implements. Ancient Aztecs and Greeks polished it to create mirrors. The Moai, large stone statues on Easter Island, were constructed from obsidian. Since antiquity, obsidian has been used for necklaces and amulets and as a gemstone. In Mesopotamia around 4500 B.C., the city of Tell Hamoukar had industries dedicated to producing and exporting obsidian beads, tools, blades, and arrowheads from mines in Turkey, nearly 100 miles (160 km) away. Varieties may show a silver or golden sheen due to inclusions. Obsidian may be confused with hematite, jet, pyrolusite, gadolinite, and wolframite. Shown is an arrowhead once used as a cutting tool or weapon. Today such arrowheads may be wrapped in wire for use as pendants.

odd-count flat peyote stitch *See* odd-count peyote stitch.

odd-count peyote stitch This peyote-stitch variation begins with an odd number of beads. Unlike even-count peyote stitch, the beadwork spirals continuously rather than dropping down at the end of each row. Although it produces an attractive spiral form, with this stitch it is difficult to create a pattern more detailed than colored spirals. This stitch can be done either flat or round; the flat variation has the added problem of a special turnaround at the end of every other row.

odontolite Fossilized tooth from large prehistoric animals, such as mammoths, mastodons, or dinosaurs. This rare organic gemstone is also called *tooth turquoise* or may be dyed with *viviantite* to that color. The word *odontolite* comes from the Greek for "toothstone." While rare, it has been found in Siberia and the south of France.

off-loom weaving Many different methods of bead weaving are possible without a bead loom (a wooden or metal structure designed for fashioning beadwork fabric). Weaving is essentially the intertwining of two layers of thread (warp and weft), usually at 90-degree angles to each other, to form cloth or fabric. Although most off-loom beadwork techniques are technically not considered weaving, the term generally refers to beads attached together with a needle and thread and no loom. Common stitches in off-loom bead weaving are flat and round peyote stitch, gourd stitch, brick stitch, and right-angle weave. Less common are square stitch, herringbone, netting, and bead chains.

The "space creature" beaded zipper pull or key ring shown below, made by Drew Sutton, age 8, uses a basic cross-weave with artificial sinew. The sinew crosses in opposite directions

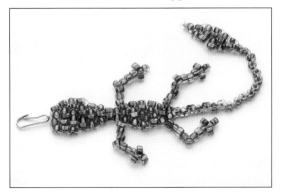

through the bead or beads to hold them securely in place. Although needles can be used, the holes in the triangle beads were large enough that no needles were required; they were threaded by hand. A good starter project for children, this type of cross-weave beadwork usually uses pony or crow beads. *See also* cross-weave.

Oglala butterfly   Named after the Native American Oglala Sioux tribe, this beading stitch or technique was published by Horace Goodhue in his classic book, *Indian Bead-Weaving Patterns,* along with many other techniques of Native North American beaders. Shown are a choker and bracelet by Aurora Mathews, using a variation of this technique.

oiling   A gemstone treatment involving the application of oil, colorless wax, or resin to improve the appearance of gemstones by filling in fine surface cracks or cavities.

ojime beads   Intricately hand-carved ivory beads originating in Japan, used with netsuke beads, allow items like an *inro* (a compartmentalized box, a sort of wallet) to be worn hung from the belt around the kimono. Since traditional kimonos, worn by both women and men, had no pockets, people wore the *inro,* attached to a cord hung from the kimono belt, called an *obi*. At the top of the cord was a large carved bead, the *netsuke,* which acted like a toggle to anchor the inro. The smaller ojime bead serves as a sliding closure to secure the lid of the inro. Ojime, since ivory has been outlawed, are now carved from boxwood, ironwood, horn, or bone.

olive shell   A natural marine seashell from the gastropod mollusks *Olividae,* found in tropical waters. To make beads, edges of the glossy olive shell, which has an oval or cylindrical shape, are squared off, drilled, and strung.

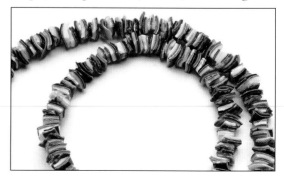

Several light to dark browns, blacks, grays, and whites, along with a rippled pattern, may appear in the finished beads. *See also* heishi.

olivine Also called *chrysolite,* a yellow to yellow-green transparent to translucent mineral, composed of magnesium iron silicate, with a vitreous and greasy luster. The ratio of iron to magnesium varies. Olivine, a variety of peridot, is in the orthorhombic crystal system and has a Mohs scale hardness rating of 6.5 to 7. *See* peridot.

onyx A variety of chalcedony, a crypto-crystalline quartz composed of silicon dioxide, and may bear bands of multiple colors. Some onyx is naturally black, but much of the gemstone on the market is stained. Its Mohs scale hardness factor is 7. It is commonly found in layer stones and may be used in cameos and intaglios. *Sard onyx* is reddish brown with black or white. Shown is a black onyx cabochon.

onyx marble A translucent to opaque rock formed by the minerals calcite and aragonite, found in yellowish green, white, brown, and striped. Also called *marble onyx,* it rates 3.5 to 4 on the Mohs scale of hardness, and can be carved. Onyx marble is formed from lime-containing water by layered deposits near warm springs or as stalactites or stalagmites in caves. The stone is always banded. It may be dyed to produce a variety of colors. It is sometimes called *Mexican onyx.* Although *onyx* is part of the name, it is unrelated to true onyx.

opacity The property of a material that prevents light from passing through it, or the quality of being opaque.

opal A transparent to opaque gemstone, composed of hydrous silicon dioxide, that demonstrates a play-of-color with rainbowlike hues that may vary according to the direction from which the stone is viewed. The word *opal* derives from the Sanskrit *upala* for "stone" or "jewel" or the Latin word *opalus* for "seeing jewel." This mineraloid gel has a water content of between 3% and 30%. Opal has an amorphous crystal system with kidney- or grape-shaped aggregates and has a Mohs scale hardness factor of 5.5 to 6.5. Light passing through the stone varies from reds and golds to greens and blues, known as *fire,* due to the reflection of shortwave, mainly blue, light. Opals may demonstrate white, bluish, greenish, or brownish fluorescence.

Opals are of three main types: *precious opals, yellowy-red fire opals,* and *common opals. Precious opals* include white (white or light with color play); black (with dark gray, dark blue, dark green, or grayish black, black, and play of color); opal matrix (banded or leafy inclusion of precious opal in matrix rock); boulder (occurs as pebble rock, dark base surface, color play); harlequin (mosaiclike color patterns); jelly (bluish gray); and crystal (transparent, colorless, vitreous with strong color play). Black opals are rarer than white opals; harlequin opals are desirable. *Fire opals* are orange, often with no color play, and may vary from clear and transparent to milky and turbid. Fire opals may be confused with garnet or rhodochrosite. *Common opals,* also called *potch,* have no color play and may be opaque and rarely, translucent. Varieties of common opal include agate (light and dark opal layers with agate); angel skin (palygorskite); wood (yellow or brownish like petrified wood); honey (honey yellow and translucent); hyalite (glass or water-stone; colorless); hydrophane (milk, turbid); porcelain (white, milky, opaque); moss (milk with dendrites); girasol (almost colorless, bluish opalescence); prase (chrysopal; apple green); and wax (yellow-brown with waxy luster).

Among the ancient Romans, the opal was considered a noble gem, ranking second to the emerald. Types of opal may have various common names, like Peruvian or blue opal. Opal is found in Australia, the Czech Republic, Brazil, Mexico, southern Africa, and the United States. *See* yellow opal and opalite.

opal beads Translucent beads with a slightly milky or pearly appearance and an iridescent play-of-color, similar to the glow of natural white opal. Today many of the colors in opal are the effect of dyes.

opal imitations Imitation opal, called *Slocum stone,* is made of laminated glass with bits of interspersed foil. *Ceylon opal* is a misleading name for glimmering moonstone. *See also* opalite.

opalescent Having a milky blue or pearly appearance, caused by reflection of short-wave, mainly blue, light. The term is usually applied to gemstones, but some glass beads may have a clouded or translucent appearance like that of the opal or opalite.

opalite A term both for a rock specimen bearing traces of opal, and for synthetic opal,

made of glass and sometimes called *opalescent glass.* Shown is a turtle fetish of synthetic opal, or opalite.

opaque Not transparent or translucent; not allowing light to pass through. The term is commonly applied to gemstones. It may refer to a bead type, generally of solid-color beads through which you cannot see light. The finished coatings of glass beads may have opaque luster, opaque matte, or other finishes in various combinations that make them opaque. *See* bead types and bead finishes.

open-face mold A bead and pendant mold sculpted for use molding a single side of the bead or pendant for easy removal.

operculum The arched lid of a snail found near the Australasian islands.

organic beads Beads made of natural materials, such as seeds, wood, horn, bone, shell, and resin. *See also* organic gemstones, amber, pearls, and coral.

organic gemstones These are materials of organic origin that have some of the qualities and characteristics of gemstones. Members of this group are amber, pearls, coral, ivory, bone, mother-of-pearl, abalone, jet cannel coal, and odontolite (fossilized tooth). Although not as durable as mineral gemstones, they are highly prized for their beauty and rarity.

orient The iridescence observed in natural pearls. the French expression "*essence d'orient*" refers to fish silver, another term for a solution of fish scales used to line blown-glass beads for making artificial pearls.

ornament cover A variety of methods for adding beads to embellish a decoration (often blown-glass globes) hung on a Christmas tree, or other decorative item intended primarily for display. Ornament covers are often seen with variations of the bead-netting technique. The beaded knitting ornament shown, made by Sylvia Elam, uses size 8 pearlized cotton thread

(a fine cord of twisted cotton fibers), silver-lined copper beads, and turquoise and amethyst chips as accents.

ostrich eggshell beads These beads originated in Africa from about 37,000 to 40,000 years ago, found in excavations of the Enkapune Ya Muto rock shelter in the Rift Valley of Kenya. Some evidence suggests they were made as long as 70,000 years ago. They have also been found in India and China to date over 20,000 years old. To make the beads, the ostrich eggshells (from which the bird was already hatched) are roughly cut, drilled, strung, and ground along a stone to smooth the edges in a method similar to that for producing heishi ("shell") beads. In East Africa, people usually broke shells into smaller pieces and chipped the tough shell into desired shapes (often disks) by using their fingers, stones, or teeth. They turned a drill in the palms of their hands to form a hole in the center of each bead. Finished beads were typically strung on twisted sinew.

Ostrich eggshell beads have been found in areas where the birds once lived or currently live and are used for necklaces, chokers, bracelets, bangles, headbands, earrings, belts, and apparel, such as aprons, skirts, bags, and powder puffs. They are sometimes combined with porcupine quills, horn, tambotie wood, and seeds. Dinosaur eggshells were put to the same purpose. Ostrich eggshell beads have been considered among the world's oldest beads.

ought A term used in seed bead sizes. *See* aught.

oxidation The darkening or antiqued appearance of metal that has undergone color changes by exposure to environmental conditions like humidity and salt air. High-karat gold and stainless steel resist oxidation (combining with oxygen) or surface corrosion.

oxidizing The flame used in glass beadmaking that is high in oxygen content may be called an oxidizing flame.

P

PMC An abbreviation for "precious metal clay." *See* precious metal clay.

padre beads Turquoise or sky-blue glass trade beads, sometimes streaked with white, made in China during the 17th and 18th centuries and reportedly brought into the American Southwest by Catholic priests from Spain. The priests were singly called *padre,* which means "father" in Spanish.

pagan prayer beads *Paganism* encompasses diverse belief systems; various cultural groups use what could be called prayer beads, often mixed with charms, amulets, or fetishes. Under this category fall diverse mythological and religious practices originating with, among others, the ancient Norse, Germanic, Celtic, or Saxon cultures, such as for witches, magicians, Druids, and others, perhaps stemming from ancient Egyptian and Greek cultures. Neo-pagan groups, such as the Wicca, may use healing gemstones or similar beads. *See also* prayer beads.

paillette A type of sequin with a hole drilled on its edge (rather than in the middle), such as a leaf or large circular bead, so that it can hang from a garment or jewelry. *See* sequins.

painted beads Surface dyes or pigments are occasionally applied to beads that are then baked. This process is common for obtaining certain colors, like purple and pink, which are notoriously sensitive to sunlight and heat. Body chemicals, like salts and perspiration, and normal wear may also affect the appearance of dyed beads. While the term *dyed* applies to transparent beads, *painted* usually refers to opaque beads. Treated beads are best kept away from strong fluorescent and natural light as well as solvents like water, hairspray, perfumes, and alcohol.

palladium A transition metallic element of the platinum group. This silvery white precious metal is soft and ductile when cooling (annealed) but increases strength and hardness when cold. It does not tarnish in normal air but tarnishes in moist atmospheres that contain sulfur and may dissolve slowly in sulfuric, nitric, and hydrochloric acid. It is used in watches, surgical instruments, and signs, among other medical and industrial uses. It may be found alloyed with other metals of the platinum group.

pancake beads Flat round beads, which may also be called tabular or coin-shaped beads.

papier-mâché beads *Papier-mâché,* a term adopted from the French language for the technique and finished object made of recycled paper, often newspaper, mixed with starch or an adhesive and layered over a mold or shaped.

After the paper dries, it can be varnished or painted to create a number of objects, including beads. These are novelty items.

parure A matching or coordinating set of jewelry, often made from gems. The set could include two or more of these items: necklace, earrings, brooch, comb, tiara, bandeau, bracelet, pin, and ring. The fashion of wearing a matched set of jewelry became popular in the 17th century. The English term, derived from the French *parer* ("to prepare" or "to adorn"), may also refer to matched ornaments.

paste A hard, brilliant glass that contains lead used for making imitation gemstones. The finished rhinestones and other faux gems made of this glass are also called paste.

pater bead A special bead, usually large, on a rosary that indicates that an "Our Father," or the Lord's Prayer is to be said. The Latin word *pater* means "father." *See also* paternoster beads.

paternoster beads Also called *Pater Noster beads*. Deriving from the Latin term *Pater Noster,* meaning "Our Father," the first words of the paternoster, or the Lord's prayer, this term refers to the entire string of prayer beads as well as the large individual rosary bead that calls for recitation of the Lord's prayer.

Medieval paternosters usually comprised 10, 50, or 150 beads, with or without marker beads. Most medieval prayer beads ended with a cross or crucifix, but many had silk tassels or religious medals hanging from them. Medieval prayer beads were sometimes worn as jewelry, depending on a person's station in life.

Often used synonymously with rosary, paternosters may be strings of wooden or bone beads; semiprecious gems like agate, jet, amber, and topaz; or precious materials like gold, emerald, and sapphire; or simply a series of knots in a cord. Today the beads are often made of glass. Paternosters may consist of a straight rope of beads, rather than a circular set, more commonly seen in modern rosaries. Unlike current paternosters, early examples did not have larger beads spaced throughout them. Eastern monks introduced the prayer rope to St. Dominic, who adapted it to the Dominican rosary used by most Catholics today. *See also* chaplet, rosary, chotki, and other prayer beads, such as the mala.

paternostrèri An Italian word for *beadmakers,* these were originally bead cutters, members first of the guild of rock crystal cutters and then of glass cutters. Beginning in the 15th century, the demand for prayer beads, fueled by Christians, encouraged the growth of the bead industry in Europe, which led to the establishment of a guild dedicated to the art. *See also* rosary beads and prayer beads.

paua shell A shell from the shellfish paua (genus *Haliotis*), also known as *abalone,* found in coastal waters around New Zealand, often cut into different shapes and drilled for use as beads. The name of the univalve mollusk comes from the Maori, who treasure the shellfish as food and use the shells as eyes in sculptures, among other uses. The opalescent oval shell has a natural, beautiful play-of-colors, including green, blue, pink, and cream. Three species of New Zealand paua are the silver (*australis*), virgin (*virginea*), and paua (*iris*). *See also* abalone. Shown is a polished piece of paua shell that can be used as a cabochon or pendant.

peacock A glass bead finish similar to aurora borealis or rainbow, with a blue and green luster.

peak bead The center bead in a netting project. For example, if you are adding five beads, the peak bead is the third, or middle, bead.

pearl A natural gemstone formed inside the shell of certain bivalve mollusks, usually oysters and mussels, living sea creatures found in both saltwater and freshwater environments. Pearls are recognized worldwide for their beautiful luster and iridescence. The oyster or mussel's mantle tissue normally secretes epithelial cells, what we know as *nacre* or *mother-of-pearl,* inside the shell. When irritated, such as when a foreign object is introduced, the mantle encrusts and contains the foreign object in a series of concentric layers of nacre, creating a pearl. Nacre consists of calcium

carbonate crystals, or aragonite, calcite, and conchiolin.

The numerous hexagonal platelets or layers of this translucent substance (the individual layer's thickness is comparable to that of the wavelength of visible light) create both the mother-of-pearl and the pearl's luster. Pearls created by this natural process are called *natural pearls* or *true pearls,* which are rare.

In the early 20th century in Japan, Tatsuhei Mise and Tokishi Nishikawa developed a way of introducing a nucleus and a bit of mantle shell into a mussel to induce pearl formation—what are called *cultured pearls.* They're of high quality and more affordable because they are less rare than natural pearls.

Pearls naturally come in a variety of colors and shapes, but many dyed pearls are also on the market. In India, the pearl was said to represent the moon as a symbol of perfection.

Keishi are saltwater pearls that have centers with portions of mantle material that separated from the implanted nucleus or bead. The term *marine pearls* refers to pearls found in saltwater as distinct from *freshwater pearls.* (*See also* freshwater pearls, cultured pearls, and glass pearls.) The names for pearls depend on geographic locales, the parent or mollusk genus and species, color, shape, and other distinctions. *Accidental pearls* are natural pearls that are not cultured. *Cyst pearls* form in a sac or pouch within a mollusk's tissues as distinct from one that grows outside the tissues or mantle, like the *blister pearl.* A *dead pearl* is lusterless, and a *fancy pearl* has a white, cream, or rose tone superimposed on the hue. The Portuguese word *barroco* ("baroque") was originally used to describe the elaborate or unpredictable shapes of natural pearls that were not round.

A mabé pearl is a large cultured pearl that forms only a half-sphere inside the oyster.

In some cultures, the word *pearl* is used interchangeably with the word *bead*. Indian reds (*mutisalah*) are called *false pearls*. Pearls are also crushed for use in cosmetics or paints. The terms *pearl, pearlized,* and *opaque luster* are used to describe a bead finish.

The elegant pearl necklace and earrings shown, designed by Linda Pennington, includes freshwater pearls mixed with graduated lapis lazuli beads and gold spacer beads.

pearl authenticity   To determine whether a pearl is real (natural or cultured) or fake (made of glass or plastic), one can examine it with a microscope or jeweler's loupe, weigh it, check for flaws, or compare its price with others on the market.

The quick *tooth test* may not be reliable if one is not familiar with the texture or sensation of natural pearls. But in general, authentic pearls will feel slightly gritty, like fine sandpaper, when rubbed against the teeth. Imitation pearls will feel smoother.

Examining pearls under the *microscope* or jeweler's loupe will reveal the nature of the surface and area inside the drill hole. Grainy or irregular (real pearls) rather than fine and smooth (fake pearls) surfaces will reveal whether the pearls are real. Again, experience helps in recognizing that distinctive quality.

Because natural pearls are somewhat dense and heavy, a *weight test* may be helpful. Plastic pearls are decidedly lightweight in comparison, but glass pearls can be heavy.

Flaws can be revealing. Natural pearls are rarely perfect in shape or texture, with minor flaws visible to the naked eye. If the "pearls" look perfect, they are very likely fake.

Finally, compare similar pearls with those of other dealers. Pearls very low in *price* could be fake. Glass beads with a pearlized finish are usually advertised as glass beads.

A reputable dealer will have the tools and experience to determine the pearls' authenticity. Buy costly gemstones, like pearls, only from reputable dealers.

pearl finish   A term often used to describe opaque-luster beads.

pearl grain   This metric weight is equivalent to approximately 50 milligrams or $^1/_4$ carat, as used in the pearl and diamond industry. Originally, one grain was the weight of a single grain seed taken from the middle of an ear of barley. *See also* carat (mass or weight).

pearl knotting   A stringing technique that features a knot between each pearl. The outer layer, or *nacre*, of a pearl is somewhat fragile; the knot prevents the pearls from scratching or abrading each other. In addition, if the string or cord should break, the risk of losing more than one pearl is minimized. Knotting between beads gives the necklace a very fluid character. The technique is common in stringing other precious materials, as shown here in knotted hematite beads.

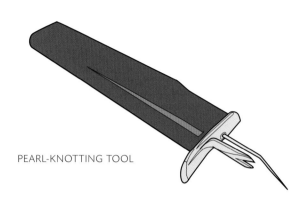

PEARL-KNOTTING TOOL

pearl-knotting cord A nylon or silk cord used to string pearls and other valuable beads. This cord is sometimes sold with a twisted-wire needle attached expressly for this purpose.

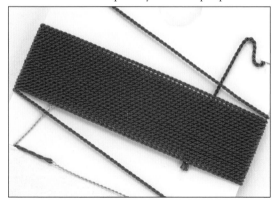

pearl-knotting tool A tool designed specifically for making knots between pearls. Tools such as tweezers and a T-pin are also used to knot pearls.

pearl sticks Pearls with an oblong shape that add an interesting dimension to jewelry designs. Pearl sticks, although somewhat untraditional, are popular as jewelry components, owing to their lustrous pearl coating, or *nacre*. Shown are pearl sticks in the typical white and in an apricot-peach variation.

pearlized glass An iridescent or "pearl" coating, typically applied to glass beads. *See* glass pearls.

pebbles Used to describe certain glass or gemstone beads similar in size and shape to small rocks or pebbles.

Peking glass Also called *Canton glass*; transparent to opaque glass first produced in mainland China in the Forbidden City, within Palace walls beginning in the late 17th century, and used to make wound-glass beads. Later an overlay glass with two layers of different colors was produced. The beads' colors tend to be more subtle than glass beads made elsewhere.

Pele's tears Small droplets of volcanic glass (obsidian) formed by droplets of molten lava that are airborne or that come into contact with water, fusing into volcanic glass. Pele is the Hawaiian fire goddess of volcanoes. While volcanologists and Hawaiians favor the term *Pele's tears,* mainland Native North Americans favor the term *Apache tears. See* obsidian.

penal rosary During an era of religious persecution in Ireland, notably between 1540 and 1731, penal rosaries emerged as a way believers could discreetly practice Roman Catholicism. The crucifix and a small set of prayer beads (a single decade, or ten beads) were easily hidden in a sleeve or the palm of a hand. A ring at one end acted as a marker to move from thumb to finger to finger as each of five decades was counted off. *See also* prayer beads.

pendant A bead, charm, or other ornament that hangs from a necklace or bracelet. The original design by Sylvia Elam shown features a goldstone donut framed by a bead crochet rope and flat peyote stitches.

pen shell The shell from a fan-shaped bivalve mollusk: the *Pinna noblis,* one of the world's largest, native to the Mediterranean, growing chiefly on the coasts of southern Italy, France, Yugoslavia, and north Africa. Its shell, found in various shades of brown, is squared off into beads used as heishi. Its soft pallial organ secretes a long stalk of strong golden or brown byssal threads that have been used in weaving textiles since ancient Roman times. The mollusk was also a source of natural pearls as early as the 300 B.C. It is also called *fan shell, noble pen shell,* and *Mediterranean pen shell. See also* heishi. A pen-shell necklace is shown on the next page.

pentagon A five-sided object; more specifically, a bead having five sides. *See* photo of pentagon bead shape under cinnebar beads.

perforation A groove or hole formed or drilled in a bead to facilitate stringing.

peridot Also called *olivine*; a transparent light to olive green, yellow-green, or brownish gemstone, composed of magnesium iron silicate, with a Mohs scale hardness rating of 6.5 to 7 and a greasy or vitreous luster. The crystal system is orthorhombic, with short, compact prisms and vertical striations. The word *peridot* comes from the Arabic *faridat,* which means "gem." The term *chrysolite* was once applied to peridot as well as many other gemstones of its color. In the Middle Ages, crusaders brought the stone to Europe, where it found ecclesiastical uses. During the Baroque period, peridot was at its height in popularity. The gemstone was mined on Zabargad Island in the Red Sea for over 3,500 years. Deposits are found in Australia, Brazil, China, Mexico, Pakistan, Sri Lanka, South Africa, Norway, and the state of Arizona, among other places. The stone is not resistant to acids and may burst under great stress, which is why some stones are metal-foiled. Green foil may enhance pale

stones, and imitations may be made of syntheses of corundum and spinel. *Peridot cat's-eye* and *star peridot* are rare versions. It is sometimes confused with chrysoberyl, emerald, prasiolite, and tourmaline. Shown are polished saucer-shaped beads that can be an attractive addition to any beaded design.

peridot imitations Evergreen bottle glass may be mistaken for peridot. *Siberian chrysolite* is a false or misleading name for demantoid (garnet).

period beads Relating to, representative of, or made during a particular historical era; the term usually refers to beads made or used by a specific culture within a well-defined time period. For example, 19th century millefiori beads, or Venetian beads, commonly would designate those beads mass-produced in Italy and other parts of Europe during that century. Mosaic beads made by the Vikings in a different era may also be called millefiori beads. They were used by the Norse in necklaces and found in burial sites dating from A.D. 800 to 1000.

perlen German word for "pearls" from mollusks, but the term can also refer to any bead.

Peruvian beads Hand-painted ceramic or clay beads in colorful designs and various shapes,

generally depicting the indigenous culture. Animal figures and popular images, like that of Santa Claus, are presumably fashioned to appeal to the tourist trade. The bisque-fired beads shown above have an image of a llama.

petrified wood Also sometimes called *fossilized wood,* composed of silicon dioxide and classified in the quartz group with a microcrystalline crystal structure, as a species of chalcedony. It ranges from browns to grays to reds or pinks and remains opaque even in thin slabs. Its Mohs scale hardness is 7. The outer structure and shape of the original wood is preserved. Some notable deposits are in Egypt, Patagonia in Argentina, Queensland in Australia, Mongolia, Madagascar, Alberta in Canada, and Arizona in the United States. Another form of so-called fossilized wood is *jet,* which is composed of lignite, or bituminous coal. *See also* quartz.

petroglyph An image or design, usually ancient, that is inscribed, carved, chiseled, etched, scratched, or pecked into rocks or rock formations; an alternative term is *rock art.* Beadwork popularly features such graphic elements. The small beaded pot shown is only 1¹/₄ inches

(3 cm) high; the petroglyph-maze design was created in peyote stitch with size 14 Japanese seed beads.

petrology The science of rocks, including their description, classification, origin, occurrence, structure, and chemical composition. This study defines minerals' distinctive optical, physical, and chemical properties.

pewter A silvery, bright, and shiny metal alloy with 85% to 99% tin and 1% to 15% copper, that may be mixed with various other metals, including antimony, bismuth, lead, and trace elements. *Fine pewter* contains 96% to 99% tin and 1% to 4% copper; *trifle pewter* tends to be duller, with 92% tin, 1% to 6% copper, and as much as 4% lead; and *lay (ley) pewter* contains up to 15% lead. Modern pewter includes tin, copper, antimony, and

bismuth and excludes lead, which had been used in earlier centuries. Low grades of pewter may have a bluish tint. When untreated, pewter oxidizes to a dull gray over time. Pewter may be a base metal for silver-plated objects. Shown are handmade pewter face beads.

peyote gourd rattle A ceremonial peyote rattle made from a gourd, used in peyote ceremonies and by gourd dancers in various ceremonies. Peyote is a cactus plant, from the word *pejuta,* which means medicine, traditionally used by Native North Americans in spiritual ceremonies. Shown is a beaded rattle made by Bonnie Gibson from a hard-shell gourd with walnut handle and plug, braided leather lace, horsehair, deerskin, and seed beads.

peyote stitch The word *peyote* derives from the Nahuatl *peyotl,* denoting the peyote cactus. Peyote cactus being sacred to many Native North American tribes, the peyote stitch has similar significance; among these groups, even doing peyote stitch is considered a sacred activity. Some native beaders accordingly feel

it is inappropriate for others to work this specific stitch. Not surprisingly, the stitch has come to be identified as *gourd stitch* when used in a secular, as opposed to a ceremonial, context.

Peyote stitch and its variations go by several names, including *gourd stitch, round peyote, circular peyote, odd-* and *even-count peyote, flat peyote, free-form peyote, twill, round flat peyote,* and *two-* and *three-drop peyote stitch.* In fact, what is commonly called peyote stitch may describe a number of different beadwork techniques. The various forms of peyote stitch span cultures as diverse as the ancient Egyptians, South Africans, and Native North and South Americans.

In truth, peyote and gourd stitches, although quite similar in appearance, have different methods of construction. Both are used to cover three-dimensional objects; however, what is commonly cited as peyote stitch in many beadwork publications is more appropriately called gourd stitch.

Understandably, most ceremonial objects feature what some refer to as "authentic" peyote stitch, in which beads are offset by two-thirds, meaning a bead is added every third bead. In gourd stitch, beads are offset by a half, meaning a bead is added every other (or second) bead. Consequently, peyote stitch tends to spiral more distinctly than does gourd stitch.

Shown are two fine examples of authentic peyote stitch. The key ring with a ball on the end (shown on opposite page, top right) is the creation of Thurman Bear, Jr. Made with size 13 charlotte beads, it demonstrates the fluidity possible with the stitch. The designer of the larger key ring (shown below), although unknown, is most likely an Apache beader. Assembled with size 13 opaque seed beads, its intricacy of design is incredible. Find peyote and gourd stitch distinctions in Part III. Find stitch diagrams in Part IV.

peyote tube A tube shape constructed with either flat or round peyote stitch. The cross shown consists of a long vertical tube adjoined to two shorter tubes. They were assembled flat and then seamed to close the tube. *See also* tubular peyote.

phallic beads Representing male sex organs, such beads are used more often as amulets for luck, fertility, or protection against the evil eye than for anything blatantly sexual.

philosopher's stone In alchemy, this stone was thought to be able to turn lead or base metal into gold or to aid in the achievement of spiritual enlightenment. The philosopher's stone was sought in ancient Egypt, the Middle East, China, and in medieval Europe, notably by alchemists. In some folklore, it was said to create an elixir to make humans younger. It has been called the astral body, living stone, diamond soul, soul body, and golden wedding garment.

phosphorescent Exhibiting luminescence or emitting light under certain circumstances without emitting heat, qualities which may be tested under ultraviolet light. The term comes from the mineral fluorite, in which fluorescence was first observed. Among minerals that may produce it are aragonite, calcite, fluorite, halite, and willemite.

phosphorescent beads Glow-in-the-dark beads that exhibit luminescence for some time following the absorption of radiation (in the form of light or electrons), without producing any noticeable heat. Luminous beads, with similar qualities, are common in fishing lures.

Picasso beads A finish with swirls or a marbled effect on opaque glass beads or multi-colored glass beads with internal or external marbling. The term is thought to derive from Picasso marble, a natural gemstone found in a conglomeration of textures and colors, probably in recognition of the Spanish artist Pablo Picasso.

Picasso marble Found in Utah, this marble has striking browns, blacks, grays, and white and can appear like landscapes when carefully cut into cabochons.

pick stitch Also called *seed stitch,* a stitch for embellishing a garment or fastening beads to the surface of a garment, accomplished by passing the needle from the back of the fabric through the front or edge of the fabric. Pick stitch may use decorative threads or beads to accent the finished clothing.

picot edging A three-bead edging used on clothing, amulet bags, and leather as well as around cabochons. Picot edging adds a nice decorative finishing touch to beaded objects and fabric accessories. *See also* appliqué.

piercing *See* body piercing.

Pietersite A trade name for breccia aggregate of hawk's-eye and tiger's-eye, that's dark bluish gray. *Brecciation* occurs when the fibrous structure of two different stones are broken down and the tiny fragments become cemented together during geological processes by quartz, which creates a finished stone with multiple hues and chatoyancy. Its Mohs scale hardness is 7. Pietersite, discovered in 1962, can only be found in Namibia. A similar stone found in Hunan China, sometimes called eagle's-eye, is a magnesium-rich alkalic amphibole and has combinations of gold, red, blue, and golden brown.

piezoelectricity A quality that may be generated by a mineral crystal that has the ability to give off an electrical charge strong enough to have a readable voltage in response to mechanical stress. It defines both mechanical and electrical properties, such that when a piezoelectric material is squeezed, an electric charge forms on its surface.

pin back Simple metal hardware that can be affixed to the back of beaded or other jewelry. The pin allows the jewelry to be attached to clothing or accessories, like a purse, hat, strap, or belt.

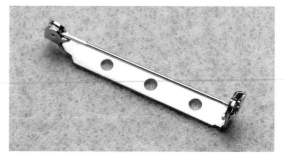

pinch beads Also called *hot-pinched beads,* glass beads that are pinched or squeezed by a tool used to manipulate their shape when the glass is still hot. The technique may have originated in Alexandria, Egypt, around 300 B.C. Sometimes the resulting beads are called *triangular melon beads* since they tend to be both oval and three-sided.

pineapple beads Originating in Venice in the late 19th century, these glass beads resemble the fruit of the same name.

pink coral A pink variety of coral. Coral beads and rhinestones decorate the barrette shown. *See also* coral.

pink quartz Known primarily as *rose quartz,* this gemstone is popular for its delicate color. *See also* rose quartz.

pipestone Native North Americans use this highly prized red stone, also called *catlinite,* to carve ceremonial pipe bowls. The pipe bowl represents the female aspects of creation, and the pipe stem, the male aspects. Reserved for ceremonial use, respect for their symbolism obliges that the pipe bowl and stem be stored separately. The pipe is deemed holy owing to a legendary event described by Black Elk in *The Seven Sacred Rites of the Lakota Sioux,* wherein White Buffalo Calf Woman bestows the pipe to tribal representatives. She explains that the pipe bowl of red stone represents the earth, who is our mother and grandmother. The pipe stem, made of wood, represents all that grows upon the earth. She describes the sacred pipe as primarily a tool of prayer. Pipes sculpted from the stone can have many different variations.

plaited beadwork Strung beads can be plaited or braided to display a textured effect. The white plaited bead necklace from Czechoslovakia shown dates from the 1950s

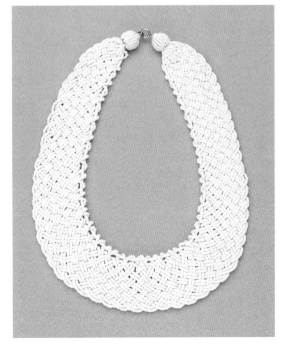

period of Communist domination. From the collection of David Bingell. *See also* braid.

plastic A generic term for a petroleum-based synthetic material. Over 40 major groups of plastics have been used to make beads; among the most popular are casein, celluloid, Bakelite, and polystyrene. Plastic beads are relatively inexpensive and tend to be lightweight compared with glass or gemstones. Plastic is commonly used to imitate exotic beads like dZi beads and crystal beads. *See also* polymer clay.

plating Covering with a metallic layer over another metal or base. In the process of *electroplating,* a conductive surface is covered with another metal to lend the finished object the appearance of the plated metal, whether gold, silver, or something else. The result may be gold (usually on copper or silver), silver (on copper or another metal), palladium, rhodium, chrome, zinc, or tin plate, as desired. Other types of plating include alloys (nickel-cobalt) or composite metals or metal matrix (mixed with ceramics). In *Sheffield plate,* a metal sheet may be fused with another metal sheet. *Vapor deposition* and *non-galvanic* are other methods of plating. *Gilding* is the general term for applying a thin layer of gold on another metal surface. *Metallizing* is the process of coating metal on nonmetallic objects.

platinum A rare precious metal, considered more precious than gold. This malleable and ductile grayish-white transition metal resists corrosion. It is relatively heavy. Since it can be worn without tarnishing, it has been desirable for jewelry. Platinum was commonly used in pre-Columbian Central America, but had been previously unknown in Europe. The word *platinum* comes from the Spanish *platina,* or "little silver." It has a high melting point. Metals considered members of "the platinum group" are *palladium, iridium, rhodium, ruthenium, osmium,* and *platinum.* These have similar chemical and physical properties and may occur together in the same mineral deposits. It is generally sold by the troy ounce. All jewelry made of platinum must have a stamp that indicates its percentage of platinum. For instance, PT 999 indicates 99.9% pure platinum, PT 950 contains 95%, PT 900 contains 90%, and PT 850 contains 85%. Platinum may acquire a patina over time but can be polished by a jeweler. Like other metals, platinum can be scratched.

platinum imitations Also called *faux platinum* if imitation rhodium, which has a silver color similar to sterling but that does not tarnish the way sterling or silver plate would. Many jewelry components and beads have a silver tone that may be the result of plating with imitation rhodium or faux platinum.

play-of-color Flashes of rainbow colors observed in opals and other gemstones, due to rays of light refracted within the stone. The colors change depending on angle of observation.

pleochroic A gemstone or crystal that displays pleochroism. *See* pleochroism.

pleochroism The property of certain colored gemstones or crystals that appear to change color, depending on the angle from which they are viewed. This effect is caused by light vibrating parallel to different axes in the given crystal or stone. This may be caused by the difference in absorption of light rays or wavelengths in doubly refractive crystals. Stones that show two colors or shades are called *dichroic*; those that show three colors are *trichroic*. Gemstones may be cut to display or conceal their pleochroism, depending on which is the more attractive. See, for example, the gemstone iolite. *See also* dichroism and trichroism.

pliers A tool with curved handles and a jaw or nose used to grab and secure an object. Many types of pliers, such as *chain-nose, flat-nose, rosary, needle-nose,* and *round-nose,* are used for specific jewelry-making and beading tasks. Sometimes called *jewelry pliers,* they are more delicate and lightweight than the common household pliers found in hardware stores. *See also* specific types of pliers. The photo below shows from left to right: chain-nose, round-nose, and flat-nose pliers.

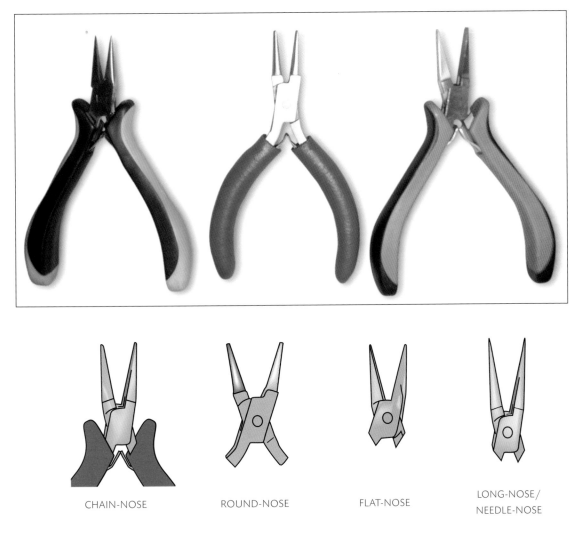

CHAIN-NOSE   ROUND-NOSE   FLAT-NOSE   LONG-NOSE/ NEEDLE-NOSE

points Gemologists and jewelers use this term to describe a diamond. The term does not refer to the number of facets on a diamond, but rather to its weight. A carat, the most common unit of weight, is divided into 100 points. Each point is one-hundredth of a carat. *See also* carat (weight or mass).

polishing Usually the last stage in beadmaking, in which the bead surface is made shiny or bright by using another chemical or substance or by agitating it with friction to increase its sheen and minimize optical or other flaws. But various methods, depending on the bead material, are used to create a desirable sheen. Fire-polished beads are placed in an oven (furnace or kiln) and heated to a high temperature, which smoothes out any sharp facets. Metal beads are usually burnished with a chemical compound.

polishing cloth A special jewelry cloth impregnated with chemical cleansing agents, nonscratching microabrasives, and tarnish inhibitors. Different kinds of cloths, often with a velvety texture, are designed to clean, remove dust or tarnish, and polish items of precious metal or to brighten chrome, wood, ceramic, and glass. Some polishing cloths, called *rouge* or *rose cloths,* are impregnated with a jeweler's rouge and must not be used on plated items since the cloth can rub off the finish. Generally, it is advised not to wash polishing cloths; they retain cleaning power even when blackened. Exercise caution and carefully read the manufacturer's instructions and note all the materials used in a piece of jewelry; what is fine when used for a precious metal, for instance, may damage another bead type or component. Most jewelry cloths are not designed for use on 24-karat gold, ivory, pearls, opals, coral, lapis lazuli, malachite, turquoise, and soft or porous stones, or lacquered surfaces.

poly cord Polyester cord is a durable material used for stringing heavier beads. *See also* poly thread.

poly thread Made of polyester, this thread comes in very fine gauges that can be used for delicate seed beadwork. Poly cord, in contrast, is used for heavier stringing projects.

polychrome Having a surface with three or more colors, usually in reference to pottery or ceramic bead surfaces.

polyester Usually shortened in the industry to "poly." *See* poly cord and poly thread.

polymer clay Not truly clay at all, this plastic material has a base of fine particles of polyvinyl chloride (PVC) suspended in a pliable binder, giving it the moldable quality of clay and the intense colors of plastic. Shown is a butterfly pin handmade by Linda Pedersen; its vegetable design features carrots, peas, chili peppers, tomatoes, oranges, and corn.

pom *See* copal.

pony beads Also called *6/0* or *E beads,* pony beads are manufactured in Japan, France, and the Czech Republic. The term *pony bead* may have originated from traders who used pack animals, like horses or ponies, to carry their merchandise and who introduced this particular bead type. Pony beads are larger than most seed beads and smaller than crow beads, so they are very multipurpose and used for stringing such things as eyeglass holders, chokers, and key chains. They may also function as spacer beads. Shown are silver-lined square-holed blue beads.

pop beads Also called *pop-in, pop-it,* or *snap beads,* these soft plastic beads snap together and are designed primarily for children's use. A ball knob at one end fits into a corresponding hole in another bead, allowing them to be joined together in a chain. Since they cannot be strung, technically, pop beads are not beads. Some Mardi Gras beads are similar in construction and molded directly into necklaces by machines. They date from the 1950s, and later served as retro jewelry or children's toys.

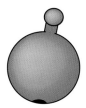

pop-up beads In peyote stitch or gourd stitch, when you add one bead every other bead, the newly added beads will pop up or stick out more than those in the previous row. When you begin the next row, it is easy to identify the beads to which you will attach new ones, as they are the "pop-up" beads.

porcelain A hard, nonporous, white ceramic ware, usually translucent, made from kaolin (a fine clay), quartz, and other rock, and fired at a high temperature. It is similar to earthenware, but harder, more translucent, and less porous. Stoneware is another category of ceramic, falling somewhere between earthenware and porcelain.

porcelain beads Porcelain beads are typically shaped on a potter's wheel, fired, and then painted by hand. Hand-painted Chinese porcelain may be the most highly recognized, especially that which is cobalt blue on a white background. The hand-painted Chinese porcelain beads here feature a sun face.

porcupine quill A quill from the large rodent, the porcupine, is a very sharp needlelike or hairlike structure barbed on the tip. Porcupines inhabit temperate areas of Italy, Asia, Africa, and North and South America; 27 species are known. The quills are carefully collected, treated, and dyed for use in quill embroidery and beadwork. Their natural color is off-white with brown or black tips. In preparation for stringing, the barbed tip and the follicle end are both trimmed with sharp scissors. The quills are sanitized before use with a soft cloth that removes debris, and are then wiped with alcohol. Avoid soaking them too long, because the alcohol will make the quills brittle and prone to splitting. The quill's center is pithy, which makes it easy to string when pierced by a sharp beading needle. Porcupine quills are used for making beaded bracelets, chokers, and earrings. In Native North American crafts, such as that of the Paiute, they have been used in loom projects, to decorate birch bark, wrap rawhide, or in other quillwork.

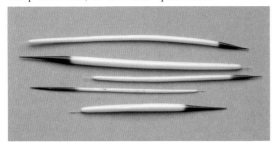

porphyr beads Glass beads with two or more colors in a pattern of stripes or swirls. One of the colors is usually white.

porpoise teeth Like other kinds of teeth, these are sometimes made into beads, which become part of a necklace, crown, or other decorative object. Each porpoise has about 150 teeth, which are considered valuable and are used for beaded objects, especially in New Guinea. A Polynesian crown, such as that fashioned in the Marquesa Islands, that includes porpoise (or indeed dolphin or whale)

teeth with other beads would indicate wealth. About 300 to 400 porpoise teeth were used along with dog teeth to make a necklace as part of bride's dowry on Malaita. This type of necklace is also sometimes used for burial ceremonies. Proper distinctions between Cetaceans—the porpoise, dolphin, and whale— are generally ignored by collectors, who may call the teeth by any number of names.

Portrait Beads These trademarked, custom-made face beads use photographs as a guide; the process uses the millefiori cane technique with polymer clay. The facial features, sculpted individually from thin sheets of polymer clay, are made into tubes; the successive layers are built up from the center to the outside to render the face or hair. *See also* face beads and portrait beads (generic type).

portrait beads Also called *face beads,* these beads with an image of the human face have been produced for over 1,600 years. Antique portrait or face beads are thought to have originated in the late Roman period, A.D. 400–600. These beads, made with glass canes used to detail facial features, have been found by archaeologists in Scandinavia, Poland, northern Hungary, and southern Germany. *See* face beads.

positive The resulting shape when wax or metal is poured into a mold (the negative) in the lost-wax process.

potato pearls *See* freshwater pearls.

pottery A generic term for ceramic or clay-ware, but chiefly applied to earthenware, as distinguished from stoneware and porcelain. Ceramic pendants with intricate designs are made from local clays in Peru and other countries of South America.

pottery shard A fragment or broken piece of clayware; antique pieces of these materials make interesting jewelry components.

pouch A small bag, made of soft cloth or leather, used as a gift or for storing valuable jewelry, and to help prevent it from being misplaced. Most are designed to protect jewelry from scratches or metals from tarnishing.

pouncing A method for transferring a pattern to fabric for beading. Pouncing entails pricking pinholes through a paper, plastic, or other lightweight pattern or stencil. Afterward, colored chalk inside an old sock or fabric bag serves as the pounce pad, which is rubbed in a circular motion to mark the stencil holes and thereby define the pattern.

pound beads An old term for drawn-glass beads that traders sold by weight (the pound) rather than by number.

powder beads *See* powder-glass beads.

powder-glass beads Also called *sand-cast* or *sugar beads,* they are made from recycled glass today primarily in West Africa, by Ashanti and Krobo craftspeople, most notably in Ghana. Early archaeological evidence dates the earliest powder-glass beads from 970 to 1000 B.C. in what is today Zimbabwe. *See* Akosu, bodom, kiffa, Krobo, and sand-cast beads.

power beads Sometimes known as *earth beads,* a modern commercial exploitation of the concepts of prayer beads, healing gems, and an eclectic conglomeration of religions, mythology, mysticism, folklore, or alternative health practices. The beads function as talismans, empowering the wearer; turquoise is worn for good health or rose quartz for attracting love, for instance. The beads themselves, typically used in bracelets and necklaces, may be made of anything from gemstones to glass to plastic or wood. Healing gemstones and crystals, sometimes strung and called power beads, have a strong following among alternative-health practitioners and believers. The term *power beads* may also be used in reference to Buddhist and Hindu mala beads.

Power Pro *See* stringing thread.

prasiolite A synthetic, transparent, leek-green quartz, composed of silicon dioxide, produced by subjecting amethyst (violet) or a yellowish quartz to high temperatures.

prayer beads The practice of counting prayers using a string of beads is very old, tracing back to Hindu religious practice in the 8th century B.C. Although differing in appearance and materials, prayer beads exist throughout the world, used by diverse peoples and cultures who all share the purpose of counting off prayers or meditations. The earliest known prayer beads are said to have been pebbles that were moved from one bag to another as prayers were said. One early practice used knots on a cord, for illiterate people to keep track of their prayer count. Even today, knots form the basis of some rosaries. It is unclear whether the concept of prayer beads developed independently or was borrowed from one culture by another. Here are a few of the common types of prayer beads.

Today Christians, Hindus, Buddhists, and Muslims all use prayer beads. Among Christians, prayer beads are associated primarily with the Roman Catholic, and Greek and Russian Orthodox traditions. John Calvin, the 16th century French theologian, reportedly discouraged their use by Protestant believers, rejecting what he felt was materialism and ritual in favor of reading and analyzing spiritual texts in direct relationship to God.

The *chotki,* or Russian Orthodox prayer rope, has its origins in Egypt, where St. Pachomius devised it in the 4th century to aid illiterate monks. St. Dominic is credited with popularizing the use of the rosary among Christians, encouraging them to pray with the rosary for the conversion of sinners and those who had left the faith. Rosaries came into mass production in the 15th century, being in demand by Christians around the world. The Anglican rosary was developed in the late 20th century; interestingly, it has found favor among Protestants.

Hindus and Buddhists in India and Tibet use a prayer-bead set called a *mala,* which uses as beads the seeds of the rudraksha tree, a species native to Java; malas comprise 108 beads, that number having particular religious significance for Hindu adherents. They are used to count repetitions of a mantra and so facilitate meditation. The same item used by Buddhists in Japan is called *juzo.*

Among diverse African cultures, beads have long been associated with wealth and power. Diviners wear special beads to identify themselves as spiritual leaders, and beads are often called *ambassador beads,* used as gifts to witch doctors or shamans to elicit divine favor. The power of the beads is enhanced by their use in rituals. Beads in many cultures represent the qualities of spiritual wisdom and spiritual power.

Shown are three different forms of prayer beads: a Yoeme rosario, a wristlet mala, and a chaplet made of rose beads. *See also* chotki, Native American prayer beads, penal rosary, rosary, rosary beads, rosario, rose beads, Muslim prayer beads, mala, and rudraksha.

prayer box *See* gahu.

prayer rope Originally designed to assist illiterate monks in keeping track of their prayers, the prayer rope dating from the 7th century was made of a series of knots at intervals and a knotted cross at one end. As it evolved and was commonly used as a wristlet, beads replaced the knots and a tassel was added to the opposite end to wipe one's tears. The oldest prayer ropes were hand-crafted from wooden beads in the Carpathian mountains of Eastern Europe. Variations of prayer ropes have evolved into the modern rosary and other types of prayer beads. Greek and Russian Orthodox Christians call their beaded prayer rope the *chotki*. In general, prayer ropes can consist of a set of 25, 33, 50, 200, or 103 beads or knots.

prayer-wheel bead Used in southern India during the chanting of prayers, a rotated bead, which could be attached to a sacred bull's collar or necklace.

precious beryl Transparent to opaque gemstones composed of aluminum beryllium silicate and found in golden yellow, yellowish green, yellow, pink, or colorless. Green beryl is called emerald, and blue beryl is called aquamarine, while all other varieties are called precious beryl. Depending on the color of the stone, precious beryl may also be known as *bixbite* (raspberry red), *golden beryl* (lemon to golden yellow), *goshenite* (colorless), *heliodor* (light yellow-green), or *morganite* (soft pink or salmon to violet). All varieties have a Mohs scale hardness factor of 7.5 to 8. The crystal system consists of hexagonal prisms. What is called greenish or bluish precious beryl and what is called emerald or aquamarine depends on the individual stone's intensity, depth, and hue.

precious gemstones Also called *cardinal gems,* this term developed in ecclesiastic and devotional circles, and traditionally referred to diamonds, emeralds, rubies, sapphires, and amethyst. Today, amethyst has been omitted from this arbitrary group since it has been found to be more abundant than once thought. A gemstone's value is related not simply to its supply or availability but to its hardness rating, color, clarity, size, and visual appeal based on certain enhancements like its overall shape, cuts, or facets. A diamond, for example, has a Mohs scale hardness rating of 10. A sapphire that's admired for its deep blue color is rated at 9, while a red sapphire, usually called a ruby, also has a hardness rating of 9. An emerald may have a hardness rating of 7.5 to 8. Not all diamonds, emeralds, rubies, and sapphires can qualify as desirable, high-quality precious gemstones. *See also* cardinal gemstones, gemstones, and semiprecious gemstones.

precious metal clay A team of Japanese scientists developed and patented a process that transforms precious metals into a pliable substance that can be molded like clay. Very small particles of precious metals, such as silver, gold, or platinum, are mixed with an organic binder and water. After the clay is shaped and dried, it is fired in a kiln or by a hand-held torch. The binder burns off in the firing, leaving just the metal. Abbreviated *PMC,* this versatile material can be shaped by hand, molded, delicately textured, and extruded.

Like ceramics, it can be fired, glazed, and treated with oxides to produce interesting surface colors. Like metals, it can be enameled.

Shown is a necklace designed by Gabie Warmuth with PMC components, fine silver charms, and briolettes of garnet, peridot, and mandarin spessartite, on a sterling-silver chain; a large heart-shape charm has a ruby (corundum) inlay.

precious metals Gold, platinum, silver, palladium, rhodium, and iridium; these metals are rare and highly valued and used to make coins and jewelry.

precision knife Also called hobby knife or X-ACTO knife. *See also* X-ACTO knife.

press-molded beads Pressed-glass beads as well as beads made of other materials, such as ceramics, that are molded or pressed into a desired shape. *See also* marver.

pressed-glass beads Also called *press-molded beads,* these are formed by pressing hot glass into a mold to create the desired bead shape. Machine-pressing methods developed in the 19th century, and pressed glass was the most novel change in glassmaking in over 2,000 years. Raised seams on their sides reveal the process by which these beads are made. However, various peoples in Africa and other parts of the world had been making pressed-glass beads without the use of machines for centuries. *See also* marver.

prison prayer beads Assorted types of prayer beads, such as rosaries, malas, and more, are distinctive because prison facility managers dictate the types of bead materials, usually limited to plastic beads strung on cotton cord, because glass or metal objects can be misused or fashioned into a weapon or other device that could threaten prison security. *See also* prayer beads.

prosser beads These trade beads can be recognized by their raised equatorial ridge or band. These glass and ceramic beads were produced by technology invented by the Prosser brothers in 1830s Bohemia: a button-making machine. Their characteristic thin seam formed the equatorial band. Native North Americans incorporated the beads into their crafts, and in Africa, they were also called *kancamba* or *kankanmba*.

puffy rondelles Beads with a circular shape essentially the same as the rondelle, but with rounder, rather than sharp-edged, sides. These luster-finish amber glass beads are faceted.

puka-shell beads Smooth round beads from Hawaii made from the shell of a cone snail, these beads generally have a natural hole. The Hawaiian word *puka* refers to the naturally occurring hole found in the middle of the shell fragment. Although the natural shape of this shell is conical, the action of surf and sand may grind off the shell's pointed end. Usually white, puka-shell jewelry is a favorite of tourists.

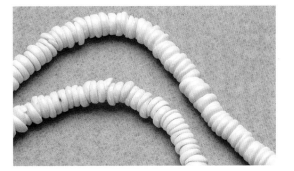

pukalets Disk-shape beads similar to those of puka shell, pukalets are made of shells and other materials, including wood. They can be ground smooth to a consistent diameter like heishi. Much of the world's seashell beads and heishi originate in the Philippines. The beads shown above are of abalone shell and can be used like sequins on beaded clothing or embroidery designs.

pumtek beads *Pumtek* means "buried thunderbolt." These beads were made over 1,000 years ago by the ancestors of the Chin people who live in western Myanmar, formerly Burma. Made of opalized wood from the palm tree *Borassus flabellifer*, they are noted for fluorescing under a short-wave ultraviolet lamp. These local heirloom beads are collectible by world travelers. Imitation pumtek beads are made from fossilized wood from a different tree.

purple jade A natural rock, composed of the minerals jadeite, acmite, quartz, and plagioclase, that displays colors ranging from lavender to purple and mahogany. Genuine purple jade is not heat-treated, polymerized, or dyed. It has a Mohs scale hardness of 6. Found in Turkey, it may be confused with charoite or sugilite. What is sometimes sold as purple jade may be bleached, impregnated with polymers, and dyed to imitate natural colors.

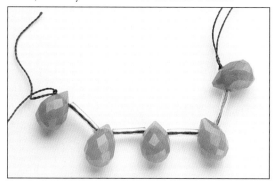

pyramid beads Beads in the shape of a pyramid, flat on the bottom and pointed at the top, with four sides. These beads are typically drilled from top to bottom.

pyrite Also called *fool's gold,* really iron sulfide, an opaque brassy yellow or grayish yellow mineral with a metallic luster. It has a Mohs scale hardness of 6 to 6.5 and a cubic, pentagonal, dodecahedral, or octahedral crystal system.

The word *pyrite* is related to fire; the mineral produces sparks when knocked. It may be mistakenly called marcasite, but true marcasite turns to powder in the air and is unsuitable for beads.

pyrites Various metallic-appearing sulfides, of which pyrite is the most common.

pyrometer A high-temperature thermometer, used to read the internal temperature of a kiln.

pyrope A member of the garnet group of gemstones, pyrope has a chemical composition of magnesium aluminum silicate. The Greek word *pyrope* means "fiery"; the red stone often has a hint of brown. In the 18th and 19th centuries, the very fashionable pyrope was called *Bohemian garnet*. Imitations may be made of red glass.

Q

Q-tip A name-brand product consisting of a short plastic, paper, or wooden stick with a cotton-wrapped tip. It is very useful for applying adhesive when joining leather or fabric backing to beadwork.

quartz A rock-forming group of minerals composed of silicon dioxide or silica, commonly found on the earth's continental crust. The crystal system is hexagonal or trigonal prisms that can be compact, massive, or fibrous.

Macrocrystalline quartz is vitreous (glassy) and transparent to translucent, with individual crystals visible to the naked eye; *microcrystalline (cryptocrystalline) quartz* is waxy, dull, or vitreous and translucent or opaque, with individual crystals that can be seen only under high magnification. The word *quartz* is derived from a Slavic term that means "hard"; it rates a 7 on the Mohs scale of hardness. The appearance and properties of quartz are determined by the pressure and temperature during its formation that influenced the chemical organization of molecules. The colors of quartz are as variable as the spectrum. The four main groups of the quartz family of gemstones are *crystalline quartz, chalcedony, jasper,* and *opal* (although the latter is hydrous silicon dioxide).

Macrocrystalline quartz includes *amethyst, citrine, rock crystal, smoky quartz,* and *rose quartz,* and colors, among others, may be clear, milky, smoky, pink, lavender, lemon, snow, tourmalinated (have mixed colors), or rutilated (have rutile inclusions).

Cryptocrystalline quartz includes members of the *chalcedony* or *agate group,* which in turn has many types: *chrysoprase* (green), *carnelian* (yellow to orange), *onyx* (black and white agate), *sard* (yellow to brown), *sardonyx* (banded sard), *bloodstone* (green with red specks), *tiger's-eye* (demonstrates chatoyancy), *flint, jasper* (colorful impure agate), and *petrified wood* (also called *fossilized wood*). *Prasiolite* is synthetic; the leek-green color is achieved by heating amethyst or a yellow quartz. *See also* agate, chalcedony, flint, geode, jasper, and silica.

Quartz crystals have been called the "ice of the gods" and were traditionally used for healing or magical purposes by diverse cultures.

The bracelet shown here is made of quartz crystal beads accented with rosaline, faceted, puffy rondelles; rose luster pony beads; 3-mm crystal glass fire-polish beads; a two-tone glass butterfly bead; Czech glass leaf pendants; and a sterling-silver magnetic clasp.

quartz cat's-eye A white, gray, green, yellow, or brown semitransparent to translucent species of quartz, composed of silicon dioxide. Its Mohs scale hardness is 7, and the crystal system is trigonal and usually massive. When cut *en cabochon,* fiberlike inclusions of rutile cause chatoyancy in the quartz. It is sometimes confused with chrysoberyl cat's-eye. See also *hawk's-eye* and *tiger's-eye.*

quartz imitations Synthetic quartz is produced by a hydrothermal process in an autoclave. Many dyed quartz and dyed-glass imitations are on the market.

quill The sharp hollow spines that a porcupine uses for self-defense. A porcupine quill has a very sharp end, with a barbed tip; it is trimmed on both ends for use as a bead. The quill's center is quite pithy, allowing a beading needle to pierce it easily. The porcupine quill is commonly used in Native North American beadwork or quillwork. The quill of a bird's feather is not used in beading. *See* porcupine quill.

quillwork Also called quill embroidery, this is a decorative stitch using porcupine quills sewn onto animal hide or birch bark. Awls or needles, along with sinew or thread, are used to stitch the quills. Many embroidery techniques require that the quill to first be flattened so that it will lay flat in the finished work. Quillwork is often seen in combination with beadwork.

quipu An Inca counting device; a rope consisting of strings which are knotted to represent whole numbers. Spaces between the particular number of knots represent figures or digits, the ones, tens, and hundreds. The quipu may also have subsidiary cords with strings distinguished by different colors.

R

rain stones Tribes in Queensland, Australia, used white quartz crystals, which they called rain stones, attached to sticks in rain-making ceremonies or used them as a powder.

rainbow finish A permanent, translucent, iridescent coating, usually applied to the entire surface of a bead. It is often called an *aurora borealis* or *AB* finish.

raisin beads A somewhat oval bead, with a wrinkled surface, bearing a resemblance to the dried fruit. The beads shown are a mixture of light and dark amber glass.

raking Applying textured surface to the still-hot glass bead with a tool like a bead rake, mandrel, or paddle; combing, feathering, or trailing. *See* bead rake and feathering.

raku A Japanese pottery technique that produces somewhat porous beads with a unique matte finish. The use of lead in the glaze and the combination of smoke, fire, and water in firing and cooling creates clayware with unusual and striking surface effects in hues of copper, blue, and magenta. The process requires firing

the pieces at relatively low temperatures, the first (or bisque) firing at 1,650° F (900° C) and the second (or glaze) firing between 1,450° and 1,800° F (800° and 1000° C). The still-glowing piece is cooled quickly by immersion in water.

Handmade raku beads are in great demand among collectors. Shown opposite is a necklace featuring three raku pendants accented by raku and turquoise beads, peacock blue glass rondelles, copper spacers, gray and teal pearls, and abalone pieces.

rattail A round satin stringing cord, 2 mm in diameter, that comes in a wide array of colors. Rattail is particularly useful for stringing beads with larger holes and is favored for Chinese knotting that may incorporate beads. The pale turquoise shown is a popular color.

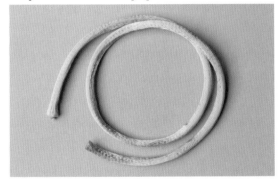

rayon thread One of many fibers used in sewing, beading, and other crafts. The cellulose for rayon production usually comes from specially processed wood pulp. The rayon fiber's characteristic strength makes it a useful and versatile fiber for beadwork and other crafts.

reconstituted Created from small stone chips or powder that is ground up, bound or fused with a plastic resin or epoxy, and compressed into blocks that may be cut and polished to

create low-quality but inexpensive stones. Such imitation stones, such as reconstituted turquoise, may appear shiny and flawless. Reconstituted stone is typically used for inlays, cabochons, and making beads.

rectangular A bead shape with four sides in which two sides are longer than the other two.

red brass A brass alloy which contains enough copper to give the metal a reddish tint. The metal includes tin and about 15% zinc. It is often used in inexpensive jewelry and brass hardware. It was once used as *gunmetal*; hence it is also known by that name.

red jasper An opaque variety of quartz, silicon dioxide, that contains iron oxides and mineral impurities. A species of chalcedony, (red) jasper appears richly colored with brownish red and other reds, but may also be in yellows and greens and other colors. Its Mohs scale

hardness is 6.5 to 7. The stone breaks with a smooth surface, can be easily carved, and takes a high polish—qualities that make it ideal for jewelry designers. It may be striped or banded. Shown on previous page are earrings with octagonal donuts of red jasper, accented with 4-mm fire-polish and copper beads. *See also* jasper.

red lip Various species of shell beads of a pinkish red color, mixed with white. The shells are often made into heishi.

reducing flame A flame used in glass beadmaking that has a reduced amount of oxygen in proportion to the propane.

reduction frit Ground bits of glass specially formulated to react chemically in a reducing flame; the process pulls metals from within the glass to the surface, to give it a metallic surface sheen. *See also* frit and reducing flame.

reed beads Organic beads made from tall, woody, perennial grasses with slender hollow stems. *See also* bamboo.

refraction When a ray of light exits from one medium and enters another, it tends to bend; the degree of the bending the light undergoes

(refraction) can be measured. A light ray traveling from air into water typically bends in a way visible to the naked eye. Gemologists use the term to describe the way light bends when entering a crystal. The amount of refraction found within a specific type of gemstone remains constant and can therefore help identify the stone.

refractive index The proportional relation between the speed of light through the air to that found within a gemstone. The visual effect results from the decrease in the velocity of light within the stone, which causes a deviation in the light rays, apparently bending it, known as refraction. The speed of light in air divided by the speed of light within a diamond equals its refractive index, which in the case of a diamond is 2.415. Thus the speed of light in air is 2.4 times as fast as it is in the denser substance of the diamond.

relative density In reference to gemstones, *relative density* is measured rather than *specific gravity* (a measure of the ratio of a specific material to the weight of the same volume of water, typically expressed in grams per cubic centimeter). Both density and gravity measure weight per volume. In general, more valuable gemstones, like the diamond, ruby, and sapphire, have densities greater than those of more common minerals, like quartz and feldspar. Therefore, the denser stones' weight and displacement of water would also be expected to be greater and their buoyancy less than those of the less dense minerals.

repoussé The technique of shaping or ornamenting a material, such as a metal, with a relief pattern by hammering or pressing on the reverse side.

resin A translucent to transparent substance in plant secretions, usually golden yellowish to brown. Insoluble in water (though soluble in organic solvents, like ether and turpentine) and an electrical nonconductor, resins, among other purposes, are used as varnish, glue, and incense. One of the best known resins in jewelry and beadmaking is a petrified form of resin called amber. Many synthetic products, also called resins, have some of natural resin's physical properties; they are used chiefly in plastics. *See also* amber, copal, and lac.

resin beads Beads made from synthetic material, generally a variety of plastic. One of the most common resin beads is imitation amber, shown here. Resin beads come in natural-looking as well as bright colors with a range of finishes. Resin beads' greatest selling point is their light weight.

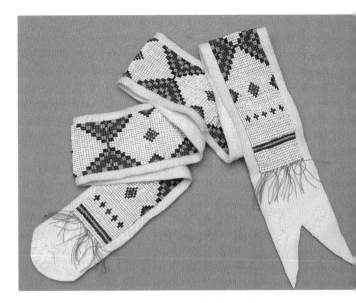

restoration Restoring to a sound or former condition; renewing or revitalizing. In beadwork, restoration may be as simple as replacing a broken clasp or lost ear wire to make it functional again. In antique or highly valuable beadwork, it might be a general intervention to preserve a piece and prevent further damage. For restoration, it is generally preferable to use the same materials as in the original, including the beads, thread, and backing material. This may involve harvesting beads from the original piece to replace missing ones. For example, if beads are missing in the body of the beadwork, they can be collected from the ends of fringe, making their absence less noticeable. The restoration of antique beadwork should be attempted only by knowledgeable and experienced beaders. Find the care and preservation of beadwork in Part IV.

The loom-woven beaded item shown, originally a belt, was sewn onto deerskin. It has been restored, repaired, and stabilized.

retorte An Italian term for "twisted" in reference to twisted glass.

rhinestone Genuine gemstones, affordable only to the wealthy, have been used throughout the centuries for ornamentation, personal adornment, and prestige. The introduction of

rhinestone, a hard, brilliant leaded glass sometimes called *paste* or *strass,* meant that more people could enjoy the sparkle and glitter of gemstone look-alikes at affordable prices. The word *rhinestone* derives from the Rhine River; along its banks bits of rock crystal were once gathered to fashion rhinestones. In 1775, the Alsatian jeweler George Frederic Strass perfected the art of applying metallic powder or foil on the backs of his handcrafted "diamonds," making them still more light-reflective. These faux gems, because handmade, were still very expensive. A century later, Daniel Swarovski patented a glass-cutting machine that could make imitation diamonds, rubies, emeralds, and sapphires at relatively low cost to consumers. Rhinestone colors were typically named after the gems they mimicked. Commonly known as rhinestones, these small

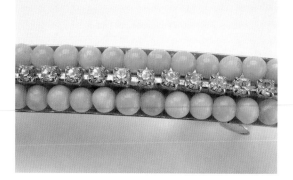

glass or crystal decorations are typically held in place by metal prongs, but the backing has a channel so that the rhinestone can be sewn onto fabric. Fancy evening wear, wedding attire, dance costumes, or skating outfits may be adorned with rhinestones, sequins, and beads. Different types of rhinestones are more adaptable to beading and jewelry. Shown are "ruby" rhinestones and a barrette with rhinestones and pink coral beads. *See also* paste and Swarovski crystals.

rhodium A silvery white, highly reflective transition metal. This hard, durable, tarnish-resistant metal can be made into an alloy with platinum. When rhodium is electroplated onto other metals, notably white gold or platinum, to provide corrosion resistance and a white shiny surface, this is called *rhodium flashing.* It is the whitest of the platinum group of metals, with which it shares many qualities. About 6% of rhodium is used in jewelry manufacturing. Rhodium is among the most expensive precious metals, worth as much as six times its weight in gold. It usually occurs in ores mixed with other metals such as palladium, silver, platinum, and gold. It is found in the Ural Mountains, South Africa, and parts of North and South America. Extraction can be complex and expensive.

rhodochrosite Named after the Greek term for "rose colored," a transparent to opaque rosy pink, striped gemstone with a pearly luster, composed chiefly of manganese carbonate. The crystal system consists of trigonal rhombohedra, usually found in compact aggregates, which have light to dark stripes with zigzag bands. Also called *manganesespar* and *raspberryspar,* it has a Mohs scale hardness rating of 4. Rhodochrosite formed as stalagmites over a 700-year period in abandoned silver mines of the Incas. It is found in Argentina, Chile, Peru, Mexico, South Africa, and the United States. The stone may be confused with fire opal, rhodonite, and tourmaline.

rhodolite A member of the garnet group of gemstones, this is a purplish red to rose-colored garnet with a chemical composition between that of *pyrope* (magnesium aluminum silicate) and *almandite* (iron aluminum silicate). Its Mohs scale hardness is 6.5 to 7.5.

rhodonite Also called *manganese gravel,* a transparent to opaque dark or fleshy red gemstone, composed of manganese silicate, with a matrix of gray to black dendritic inclusions of manganese oxide. It has a vitreous to pearly luster and demonstrates pleochroism. Its crystal structure is triclinic, platy, columnar, and usually compact aggregates, and the Mohs scale hardness is 5.5 to 6.5. *Fowlerite* is a variety of rhodonite with a brown or yellow undertone. Subway tiles in Moscow are made of rhodonite. It is found in Finland, Sweden, Japan, Canada, Mexico, Tanzania, South Africa, Madagascar, Australia, and the state of New

Jersey. It may be confused with rhodochrosite, spinel, and tourmaline. Shown below left is an assortment of rhodonite cabochons in light and dark pink with varying degrees of matrix.

ribbed beads Having raised vertical lines radiating from the hole.

ribbon cane A glass rod comprised of several colors that can be used to add decorations, like trails or trailers, to a glass bead.

rice pearls *See* freshwater pearls.

right-angle weave Stitching characterized by a thread path of four 90-degree angles, resulting in a square or diamond shape. Often seen in Russian and Czechoslovakian beadwork, this technique can be done with either one or two needles. It produces a very flexible and fluid bead fabric, depending on the thread and bead size used. A three-dimensional variant, known as *right-angle weave 3-D* or *dimensional right-angle weave,* creates three-dimensional beaded pieces. Beadwork using the 3-D stitch can cover objects like bottles and vases. Shown is a simple bracelet made with a single row of right-angle weave, using 4-mm fire-polish beads and metallized rose beads.

right-angle weave 3-D *See* right-angle weave.

Riker mounts Also known as *butterfly boxes,* display cases specially designed to show products without distortion. Riker mounts also provide a way of displaying and storing sensitive or valuable objects like insects, cut gems, minerals, museum specimens, and other collectibles, such as coins, military medals, jewelry, beads, or memorabilia.

ring bead A round, flat bead with a large hole and shaped like a finger ring. It is also called an *annular bead.*

roach A type of Native North American men's dance headdress or headgear typically made from tied porcupine guard hairs (usually not quills); deer fur, skin, or the white tail; a beaded spreader; and sometimes turkey feathers. After the 19th century, the roach was traditionally worn by male dancers and by other males from various tribes (such as the Crow, Pawnee, Cheyenne, Apache, and Missouri River tribes) during modern powwows. The Mohicans and Mohawk shaved the head except for a middle crest or scalp lock before going to war. The roach replicates this hairstyle that has been copied by other groups, such as the Potawatomi, Wyandot, or Huron. The roach "hairs" may be separated by a roach spreader. The roach is usually secured with a scalp lock, held in place with a roach pin, or tied with strings under the chin. The roach may be decorated with beads, beadwork, cloth ribbons, and feathers.

roach pin A dowel that holds the roach (a type of headdress) in place on the head.

Sometimes string is attached to the roach pin. *See* roach.

rocailles Glass seed beads. The term comes from the French word *rocaille,* meaning loose or tiny pebble. Rocailles are manufactured in Japan, the Czech Republic, Taiwan, Italy, and parts of France. Each seed-bead size has a corresponding glass rod, cane, or stick. The cane is sliced into beads of uniform size that are put in a furnace to smooth the edges. After cooling, the glass seed beads are washed, dried, and checked for imperfections. Then they are lined and coated. *See also* seed beads.

rock Most gemstones are minerals; only a few belong to the rock family. Rock families include igneous, sedimentary, metamorphic, and meteorites and tektites. In the context of gemstones, a rock loosely refers to an aggregate of two or more minerals. Examples of rocks that serve as gemstones are onyx marble, also called Mexican marble; landscape or ruin marble; obsidian and snowflake obsidian; orbicular diorite; and moldavite, also called bouteille stone.

rock crystal   Also called rock quartz or quartz crystal; a transparent, colorless natural gemstone, a type of quartz, silicon dioxide, with a vitreous luster. The crystal system is trigonal with hexagonal prisms, and its Mohs scale of hardness is 7. The term *crystal* comes from the Greek for "ice," since it was once thought that rock crystal was frozen. Inclusions may be of goethite (star crystal), gold, pyrite, rutile, and tourmaline. It is sometimes called Alaska diamond, Arkansas diamond, Bohemian diamond, German diamond, Marmarosch diamond, and Mexican diamond, terms that can be misleading. Rock crystal is found all over the world; notable deposits are in the Alps and in Brazil, Madagascar, and the United States. A few of the other varieties of quartz are rose quartz, citrine, amethyst. *See also* crystal and quartz.

rock quartz   *See* rock crystal.

rock-salt beads   These somewhat unusual beads, made from rock salt, are more of a curiosity than a practical bead, because they are subject to the stress of weather and humidity. Like most organic beads, they are biodegradable and therefore fairly fragile. In some cultures, salt is considered a symbol of good luck. The rock-salt beads shown below left are from Poland.

rod rest   A grooved metal shelf that prevents glass rods from rolling around on the work surface and keeps their hot ends pointed away from the bead maker. A slight elevation on the rod rest also keeps the rods from picking up worktable debris.

rolled-paper beads   Beads made from tightly rolled pieces of paper, often recycled paper printed with colored ink, such as glossy advertising material. The paper forms nice oval or tubular shapes that can be painted, lacquered, or sealed. *See also* flour beads.

roller beads   A bead type, produced by the Czech Republic and usually made of glass, similar in shape and size to a crow bead. In ancient times, what are called roller beads were made of bone or stone and used to create seals that could transfer a design or other imprint when first rolled in wax, clay, or ink and then rolled onto paper or cloth. *See* seals.

rondelle   A bead shape that's essentially round but has flattened ends. Sometimes called *belly beads,* rondelles are commonly made with

smooth or faceted finishes in glass or gem-stones. Finished with a magnetic clasp, the bracelet shown on previous page features faceted red-coral rondelles, black 10-mm fire-polish beads, and Bali sterling-silver accent spacers.

rosario The Yoeme (Yaqui), a Native North American tribe, call the rosary *rosario,* a Spanish-language derivative. Similar in appear-ance to a Catholic rosary, the rosario is made of hand-carved wooden beads strung on colorful yarn, with a wooden cross and a yarn tassel at the end. It is more valuable after being worn by a dancer in a ceremony, which serves to bless it. Residing in the southwestern United States and northern Mexico, the Yoeme consider the smell of the rose capable of transporting humans into the "flower world," a spiritual concept of a place where humans

are happy and healthy, and live in harmony with all of nature. While Native North Americans do not have a commonly accepted set of prayer beads, they have traditionally accorded spiritual significance to beads, which are often used in healing ceremonies. The beads shown feature a wooden cross accented with a yarn tassel. *See also* prayer beads.

rosary A set of prayer beads in a strand com-mon to a vast number of the world's Christians. The term *rosary* is derived from the Latin word *rosarium,* meaning "rose garden." While not all prayer beads are alike, they are generally used to count prayers or mantras so as to achieve spiritual understanding or repentance. Rosaries have, at various times, been worn as badges of respectability; elaborate pieces have been used as jewelry. While established among Roman Catholic and Greek Orthodox practi-tioners, many Protestant groups do not use these or other prayer beads. *See also* rosary beads and prayer beads.

rosary beads Any beads used to make a rosary, a set of prayer beads common to a vast number of the world's Christians, notably Roman Catholics and Greek Orthodox practi-tioners, as well as some but not all Anglicans, Episcopalians, and Lutherans. Early rosary beads were made of rose petals, suggestive of the Virgin Mary, who was identified with the rose's natural perfection.

The beads generally signify prayers, as in the "Our Father" (*Pater Noster* in Latin) or *pater bead* that signifies the Lord's Prayer. The *ave bead* is named after the first word (*"Ave Maria"*) of the Hail Mary prayer. Rosaries are typically constructed with five sets of ten ave beads separated by a pater bead. One such sequence is known as a decade. The standard rosary has 53 beads, but other forms may have 100 or 150 beads. An abbreviated rosary called a chaplet, usually worn on the wrist or in a pocket, consists of one decade. Rosaries are generally formed in the shape of a ring with a tail of more beads and a crucifix or cross.

In various religious orders, they are used by both men and women and often prescribed as part of the religious garb, frequently worn around the neck or waist. Various versions are used, such as the Dominican rosary, the Marian Psalter, Brigantine beads, Dolour beads, Immaculate Conception beads, Crown of Our Saviour, Chaplet of Five Wounds, Crosier beads, and others too numerous to mention. In all these devotions, the beads serve the purpose of distinguishing and numbering the essential prayers.

In the 8th century, some evidence suggests, penitents were prescribed various penances of 20, 50, or more prayers, so the early function was to count prayers in order to fulfill the required number. Lay brothers and sisters were obliged to say a number of prayers equivalent to the clerical obligation, so rosaries or paternoster beads were commonly used by the members of a religious order, laypeople, and penitents.

In the early Latin church of the Middle Ages, many names were given to prayer beads such as devotions, *signacula, oracula, precaria, patriloquium, serta, preculae, numeralia, computum,* and *calculi.* The Old English term *bedes,* or *bedys,* translates as "prayers" and has become today's term *bead(s).* From the late 15th century to the early 16th century, the name *paternoster beads* were gradually replaced by the names *ave beads, rosary, chaplet,* or *crown.*

Rosaries can be made out of a variety of materials; by the 18th century, glass beads had become the predominant rosary bead type. *See also* chaplet, mala, bodhi, chotki, rose-petal beads, and prayer beads.

rosary pliers Needle-nose or chain-nose pliers, sometimes with a wire cutter as part of the tool. Rosary pliers are used for making and attaching links in rosary and chain construction. *See* pliers.

rose beads A bead molded, painted, or pressed to resemble a rose; such beads may be of metal, plastic, gemstones, or other materials. Rose-shaped beads are favored for rosaries. *See also* chaplet (photo), prayer beads, and rosary.

rose gold An alloy of gold and copper that is reddish or pinkish yellow. Here are two common formulas for making rose gold. For 12-kt rose gold, 58% gold + 10% silver + 32% copper. For 18-kt rose gold, 75% gold + 5% silver + 20% copper.

rose montée A rhinestone that has a metal backing with channels in it for sewing onto fabric. *See also* rhinestone.

rose-petal beads Made of real rose petals, the beads have a delightful fragrance. They inspired the original rosaries and rose-shaped beads that followed. The Virgin Mary in Catholic tradition is associated with the rose in perfection. The rosary shown came from Israel.

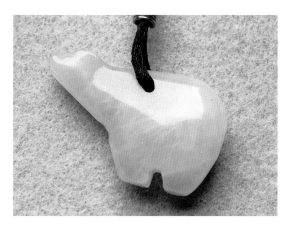

rose quartz A semiprecious pale to strong pink, semitransparent to translucent gemstone that often appears somewhat cloudy or milky. It is also called *pink quartz*. Its crystal system is compact with trigonal prisms, and its Mohs scale hardness factor is 7. Titanium is the coloring agent added to the natural quartz chemical composition, silicon dioxide. Traces of rutile needles may create six-rayed stars when the gems are cut into a cabochon. Rarer than other types of quartz, rose quartz is greatly favored by jewelry designers. Only

the large clear stones can be faceted. Natural deposits are found in Brazil, India, Madagascar, Mozambique, Namibia, Sri Lanka, and the United States. It may be confused with topaz, morganite, and kunzite. Shown is a bear fetish carved from rose quartz.

rosebud beads A lampwork bead with the image of a rosebud painted on it with glass. Shown below is a bracelet of such beads; they have solid colors at the core and clear glass on the outside, embellished with gold swirls and rosebuds painted with colored glass on the surface. Cobalt and gold fire-polish beads serve as spacers.

rosetta beads More popularly known as *chevron beads,* rosetta beads are also called *rosary* or *star beads. See* chevron beads.

rosette (concentric circles) Concentric circles sewn with an appliqué or couching stitch onto leather or fabric, typically used for Native North American dance regalia or pendants. Others may decorate gourds, hair ornaments, or neckties. The necklace and earrings shown below have rosettes beaded on both sides. The neck strap shown is made using the daisy-chain stitch.

The beaded band around the gourd shown includes rosettes.

rosette A round, usually stylized flower design, usually of a small, simple three-dimensional rose, commonly found in metalwork and jewelry design. The term *rosette* is a diminutive word for *rose*. Shown are rosettes beaded by Aurora Mathews. *See also* rosette necklace.

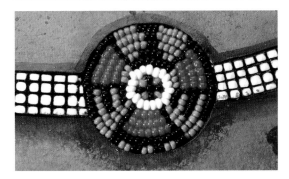

rosette necklace A necklace in which a rosette is part of the design, used as a pendant or focal piece. The black necklace shown to the right is an older piece whose date and origin are unknown; it has a beautiful floral-pattern rosette and a neck strap of fire-polish, brass, and bone hairpipe beads strung on leather. The dangles include the same beads, plus cowrie shell. The blue necklace shown below has a rosette set on the side, on multiple single strands of beads, separated by a leather spacer bar. Finished with metal cones, a hook-and-eye clasp, and a combination of seed beads and bone beads, it too is an older piece, of unknown date and origin.

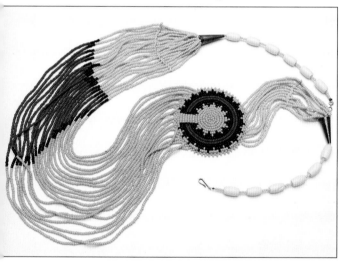

rouge Ferric oxide made into a very fine powder, used by jewelers and opticians to put a final polish on metallic jewelry or glass lenses. It is sold as a powder, paste, applied to polishing cloths, or as a solid bar and tends to cut more slowly than many modern polishes. It slightly stains gold when used as a polish, creating a desired effect. It is also called *jeweler's rouge* or *red rouge*. Other polishing compounds are also loosely called "rouge."

The fine powder was once used as a cosmetic to redden cheeks and lips. Today other substances are favored.

rough A gemstone as it is found in nature, prior to any cutting or polishing. Shown is an example of emerald rough.

roughouts This is a part of the beadmaking process in which a stone is chipped into a rough shape and then ground into a blank, creating a crude prototype of the finished bead. Perforating, polishing, and heating are some of the steps that follow.

round flat peyote stitch *See* flat round peyote stitch.

round-nose pliers A tool designed to turn or shape wire, not just to hold onto a jewelry component. Round-nose pliers used for jewelry-making usually have a narrow, round, and often long nose or jaw. The smooth round surface of the jaw is used for delicate work, such as making loops, holding small components, closing jump rings, wrapping wire, and making chains. Photo by JG. *See also* pliers for jaw close-ups.

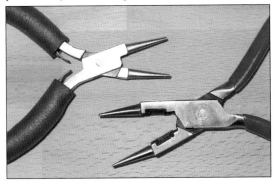

round peyote stitch A stitching technique for covering a three-dimensional object. The beads can be attached around an object, such as a fan handle or gourd rattle; or a flat fabric can

be beaded and then seamed to make a tubular amulet bag. Also used to make beaded beads, this stitch is sometimes called *circular peyote* or *gourd stitch*. Find stitch diagrams in Part V.

round stitch Also called *square stitch* and *corn stitch,* this off-loom beading technique is done by hand without the assistance of any mechanical devices or structures. Beaded by Janet Schumacker, the feather earrings below were made with a pattern designed by Peggy Wilson.

royal beadwork Royalty and beadwork have had close associations throughout Africa. Central and West African chiefs or kings commission artists to create beaded masterpieces of clothing, adornment, and ceremonial objects. Rulers from Cameroon and Zaire likewise commission ceremonial clothing, beaded sculptures, and other objects, including fly whisks, headdresses, shoes, belts, necklaces, and staffs featuring elegant and intricate designs. In Cameroon, beaded stools, seats, and thrones are reserved for royalty or very important individuals; only a ruler is allowed to sit on a seat depicting an animal. Such beaded chairs are collectors' items, although it is forbidden to sell or dispose of royal paraphernalia. The Bamileke, also from Cameroon, made beaded bird helmets and elaborate elephant masks beaded on long fabric as tall as a man. The crowns of Yoruba kings, from Nigeria, represent some of the most extravagant beadwork on the continent. The beadwork in a king's typical regalia can weigh upwards of 200 pounds; kings are typically buried in their ceremonial dress.

Embroidered beadwork has been a part of royal regalia at least since the Dark Ages. Cuff details from the insignia of the Holy Roman Empire feature intricate beadwork with seed pearls embroidered on purple silk with gold thread. The royalty of Europe wore garments encrusted with jewels and delicate beadwork. King Henry VIII and Elizabeth I of England are popularly remembered in their elaborate costumes.

ruby A transparent to opaque precious gemstone, composed of aluminum oxide, found in varying reds. The name *ruby* comes from the Latin word *ruber,* meaning "red." Ruby is the red variety of corundum; the sapphire is its blue equivalent. Chromium provides the red color, and iron, if present, makes the stone tend toward a brownish red. Its crystal system is trigonal with hexagonal prisms, tables, or rhombohedrons, and it has a Mohs scale hardness rating of 9. It demonstrates strong pleochroism and fluorescence. Rubies are found in Sri Lanka, Myanmar, Thailand, Tanzania, Brazil, India, Kenya, Malawi, Nepal, Pakistan, Tajikistan, Vietnam, Cambodia, Afghanistan, Australia, Norway, Greenland, and the United States, and may occur in bright red to purple and dark brown. The stone may be heat-treated to improve the color. While rough stones may appear dull and greasy, when polished, rubies can appear as brilliant as diamonds. Corundum is brittle, so care must be taken when cutting into it. The terms *Burma ruby* and *Siam ruby* do not originate from those regions but designate a particular quality of ruby. The *star ruby* displays asterism caused by rutile needles. Shown is a heart-shape charm that holds a ruby.

ruby imitations *Brazilian ruby* is a false or misleading name for red or pink topaz. *Siberian ruby* is a false or misleading name for red tourmaline.

rudraksha Hindu adherents in India and Tibet use these interesting textured seeds as prayer beads. The seeds are from the rudraksha tree (*Elaeocarpus ganitrus* and some other species) that grows in a wide range from the Ganges to the foothills of the Himalayas and is found in parts of India,

Pakistan, Bangladesh, Tibet, and Nepal; they have a natural hole for stringing. Indian yogis and Hindu monks have worn rudraksha beads at least since the 11th century; devotees often wear a single bead hanging from a cord around the neck. Nicknamed "miracle beads" in India, rudraksha are ascribed numerous mystical powers; they are also called "blueberry beads" because the seeds are blue when fully ripe. The Sanscrit words *Rudra* (Lord Shiva) and *aksha* (teardrop) suggest that the seed and plant were born of Shiva's tears. Wonderful powers have been attributed to the rudraksha seeds and beads, which have adorned saints and sages.

running stitch A bead embroidery stitch suitable for both bugle and seed beads. A top-stitch and an under-stitch are made in one movement after the bead is added.

Russian blues Faceted cobalt-blue beads used by Russian fur traders, who exchanged them for sea otter and other pelts. Although they are called Russian blues, they probably originated in Bohemia (today's Czech Republic). Today they are also made in Venice, Germany, Taiwan, and Mexico. They have been found widely distributed throughout the United States and Canada. When purchased in Alaska,

the beads are commonly strung on raffia palm leaves grown in West Africa. Because of the complicated trade networks worldwide, their place of origin is uncertain. A distinctive trait of the so-called Russian blues is their six-, seven-, or eight-sided drawn tubes hand-faceted at each of the twelve corners. The beads are also called cornerless hexagons or cut blues. However, they were also produced in clear and milky varieties and in the colors amber, green, black, and light blue. The most popular color was cobalt blue. These beads are still made today, but the antique hand-faceted beads are collectible.

Russian leaf The earrings shown here exemplify an interesting method of assembling beads with flat peyote stitch to create a three-dimensional object. They were beaded by Donna Haig from a pattern by Barbara S. Henthorn. Donna used cylinder beads to make these unique earrings, which have an American flag design. The pattern is a variation on an old Russian beadwork design called Russian leaf.

Russian spiral This beading technique produces a beaded rope with a hollow center. Shown is a pink and silver choker, beaded by Shelia Vinson.

ruthenium A hard, white metal, a member of the platinum group of metals. While it does not easily tarnish, it oxidizes explosively. As an alloy, it hardens platinum and palladium and improves the corrosion resistance of titanium. Fountain pen nibs have contained alloys of ruthenium. It is sometimes alloyed with gold in jewelry. However, the metal strongly stains human skin, accumulates in bone, and could possibly be carcinogenic.

rutile The mineral rutile, composed primarily of titanium dioxide, and often brookite and anatase. Needles of rutile, usually appearing as white inclusions, found in some gemstones are responsible for the optical phenomenon called *asterism*. Rutile has one of the highest refractive indexes of any mineral, which causes high dispersion of light. These gems are known as star gems, notably *star sapphires* and *star rubies*. Such gems are highly prized and often more valuable than the gem without such an inclusion. It rates 5.5 to 6.5 on the Mohs scale of hardness. *Titania,* the name of synthetic rutile, developed in 1948, is used as a diamond substitute. But it rates only a 6 on the Mohs scale of hardness.

S

S-hook clasp Used to attach one end of a necklace to another, a clasp with the characteristic S shape and a ring into which it can fit or be hooked in order to secure each end of the necklace together to be worn around the neck. Shown is a handmade clasp of Bali silver.

sacrifice beads St. Thérèse, the Little Flower, popularized the concept of sacrifice beads, also called *vices and virtues beads.* Each time you practice a virtue, like avoiding gossiping, you move a bead on the string, with the goal of moving ten beads throughout the day. Some sacrifice bead strands have 15 beads, with three beads of a different color interspersed evenly among them, each representing a member of the Holy Trinity.

safety clasp This type of closure or finding comes in many different designs. The essential feature is some type of catch or lock that makes the clasp more secure and less likely to open or malfunction, resulting in the loss or breakage of the jewelry.

salt rock beads *See* rock-salt beads.

salwag-palm beads Natural beads carved from the nuts of the salwag palm tree, native to the Philippines. Creamy white with black specks or veining, the beads can also be dyed many different colors. Shown are salwag-palm beads in the rondelle shape.

sand-cast beads Also called *sugar beads* or *powder-glass beads* for their rough, grainy texture, African trade beads made of recycled glass. The bead colors come from glass items used in their making, such as soda-pop or beer bottles. Ghana began making sand-cast beads in the 16th century, but they were later produced in other parts of Africa and other countries as well. The term *sand-cast* is not quite accurate because clay molds, rather than sand, give these beads their shape. *See also* Krobo beads.

sandwich-glass beads Made from two layers of usually clear glass, typically separated by a layer of gold foil, silver foil, or other material.

Sangoma bead doll Zulu healers, called *sangomas,* serve as community herbalists and healers, performing ceremonies intended to drive out the forces causing all nature of ills. Mothers make these traditional Zulu dolls for their children by wrapping cloth and beads around corn cobs or pieces of wood. *See also* bride bead doll, fertility bead dolls, gourd doll, and initiation bead doll.

sapphire A transparent to opaque precious gemstone, the crystal form of aluminum oxide known as *corundum.* Sapphire, one of the most prized gemstones, has a Mohs scale hardness rating of 9. The crystal system is trigonal or with double-points, hexagonal pyramids, tabloid-shaped, or barrel-shaped. Although many people think of sapphires as blue, they also can be colorless, pink, orange, green, golden, yellow, purple, and black. The pink and reddish colors are called *ruby.* Most sapphires are heat-treated to improve or darken the color. Cloudy sapphires may change to a bright blue permanent color.

Blue sapphires have inclusions of titanium and iron in the aluminum oxide that make them blue. Red or ruby sapphires, also simply called rubies, contain chromium. Violet stones have vanadium. Other than color, which depends on the viewer's perception, no definite division exists between the blue sapphire and the ruby. *Fancy sapphires* are any sapphires that are not blue or red. Purple sapphires contain trace elements of vanadium. Yellow and green have traces of iron, and pink have traces of chromium. White sapphires, which are mined as light gray or brown, are usually heated to make them clear. The most desired color is cornflower blue.

In the ancient world, various blue stones, such as lapis lazuli, were called sapphire. Today the term is reserved for blue corundum and loosely for other varieties of sapphire. Around 1800, sapphires and rubies were recognized as varieties of corundum. Misleading names persisted for other colors, such as Oriental peridot for the green corundum and Oriental topaz for the yellow corundum. Today they are called according to color *green sapphire* or *yellow sapphire*. Colorless sapphire is *leuko-sapphire*; *leuko* is Greek for "white." Some sapphires may have inclusions of rutile needles that create a shiny star. In artificial incandescent light, some sapphires may appear inky or blue-black.

Sapphires occur throughout the world, but those with the highest value come from Kashmir. The second most precious fancy sapphire is *padparadscha* ("lotus flower"), a pinkish-orange gemstone. Sri Lanka, Thailand, Australia, Myanmar (Burma), Brazil, and Tanzania also have high-quality sapphire. Other sources of sapphires are Afghanistan, Cambodia, Vietnam, Malawi, India, Pakistan, Nigeria, Rwanda, Zimbabwe, Kenya, China, and the United States. They are found in host rocks of limestone, marble, basalt, and pegmatite. *See also* corundum, star sapphire, and ruby.

sapphire imitations *Brazilian sapphire* is a false or misleading name for blue tourmaline. *Water sapphire* is a misleading name for blue iolite. Spinel and kyanite are sometimes mis-taken for sapphire. Synthetic and laser-produced sapphires are also on the market.

sard A reddish-brown dull to translucent variety of chalcedony, composed of silicon dioxide. This cryptocrystalline quartz has a Mohs scale hardness of 6.5 to 7. The lighter reddish orange or brown chalcedony is called *carnelian*; no strict separation exists between the two. *See* carnelian, chalcedony, and sard onyx.

sard onyx A variety of chalcedony, a type of cryptocrystalline quartz, composed of silicon dioxide; a layer stone with a brown base and upper layer of white, often used for carving or engraving and creating cameos. Its Mohs scale hardness is 6.5 to 7. The gemstone is found worldwide. Its name derives from its chief components, *sard*, a reddish-brown chalcedony similar to carnelian, and *onyx*. It appears as parallel bands of the two minerals. This translucent stone is frequently dyed. *See* sard and onyx.

sashiko This term applies to a Japanese method that uses running stitches to make designs on fabric. With the addition of beads, the stitch makes an interesting clothing embellishment. The Japanese word *sashiko* means "stab stitch." This traditional needlework technique creates beautiful decorative quilt patterns; it is also functional for patching torn clothing.

satin bead A bead type with a smooth, lustrous, striated surface, similar to satin fabric, producing varying color shades. Its unique, changeable appearance results from mixing air bubbles into the molten glass; the bubbles

arrange themselves in parallel lines that absorb color. Made chiefly in Japan and the Czech Republic, the beads shown above are Delica cylinder beads.

satin finish A matte or unreflective surface of a bead or metal.

satin stitch An embroidery stitch also used in beadwork. Similar to *lane stitch,* it nicely covers a large surface area. The beads are added in rows laid side by side so that no fabric shows. Find satin stitch in Part V.

Saturn bead This consists of two beads, not a single bead, assembled together, suggesting the planet Saturn with its many rings. A round or spherical bead spins inside another round, flat bead that encircles it. The term also refers to round Bali-style, saucer-shaped beads or bicone beads with decoration along the center seam that resembles the planet.

saucer beads A round bead, flattened somewhat to resemble a flying saucer.

scarab A figure in the shape of a scarabaeid beetle (*Scarabaeus sacer*), or dung beetle, which rolls dung or dirt with its hind legs for

long distances and was associated with the diurnal movement of the sun. Fashioned from clay, rock, or gemstone, ancient scarab figures often bore etched hieroglyphic designs. An important symbol in ancient Egyptian culture, found in ancient tombs, scarabs were thought to signify the soul's immortality. *See also* scarabee.

scarabee A bead finish named after the iridescent greenish-blue color peculiar to the scarab beetle, this is an aurora borealis finish generally applied to a jet bead.

scented beads These beads have fragrances, usually imparted by essential oils from flower petals or other natural concentrates. Cloves and other spices as well as scented resins like myrrh may be combined with aromatic leaves and flower petals to form a paste for molding beads. Sandalwood is a popular choice. *See also* rose-petal beads.

schiller effect Also called labradorescence, iridescence in metallic hues, caused by the scattering of light in a rock or mineral, notably labradorite or spectrolite. In feldspar, for instance, lamellae, which are thin platelike layers within the crystalline structure, cause this effect by scattering light between the layers. Similar flashing-color effects are found in aventurine quartz, moonstone, and sunstone. *See* adularescence, adventurescence, and labradorescence.

scissors Varieties of cutting instruments abound, but beading scissors are generally small—about 4 inches (10 cm) long—with edges honed to cut thread. Embroidery scissors do just as well, because they meet similar standards. For cutting backing fabrics like leather and faux suede, longer shears offer better leverage and control.

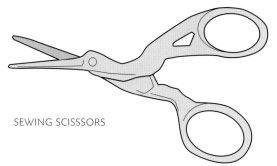

SEWING SCISSSORS

sclerometer This modern precision instrument can measure *absolute hardness* of a rock, mineral, gemstone, or other substance with a range of about 1 to 1600. The diamond is 1500 to 1600 compared with corundum, which has an absolute hardness of 400. The absolute hardness of quartz is 100 and of calcite 9. Compare the Mohs scale of hardness, which measures relative hardness and has the advantage of being able to test rocks or minerals in the field. Find Mohs scale of hardness in Part IV.

scoop A tool specially designed for picking up beads and gemstones. The scoop makes it fast and easy to clean up a work area and safely stow valuable beading supplies. Other household items, such as plastic spoons, also serve the purpose.

scorzalite A rare transparent to opaque mineral, iron magnesium aluminum phosphate hydroxide, often associated with lazulite, but more iron-rich. Its crystal system is monoclinic, and it has a Mohs scale hardness of 5.5 to 6. The gemstone may be dark azure blue, blue green, or violet. It may be confused with lapis lazuli.

screw eyes Small screws designed to attach to a bead with jewelry cement or other adhesive. The screw penetrates the gemstone or bead only partway.

scrimshaw A carved, engraved, or pierced bone or ivory. The term *scrimshaw* may have derived from a Dutch phrase meaning "to fritter time away." While scrimshaw reportedly began on whaling ships around 1817 on the Pacific Ocean, for centuries the Inuit and other native peoples of the Pacific Northwest coast of the United States and Canada have etched images, sometimes quite intricate ones, using a sharp knife or needle, on bone and ivory. For color, the sailors used lampblack, whale oil, sepia or squid ink, fruit juice, and tobacco juices. In the early 1800s, whalers from other nations adopted the technique, working on whale teeth and jawbones. On many ships, the valued whale teeth were part of seamen's pay that could be traded with port shopkeepers for goods and services. Today scrimshaw may be machine-engraved, and durable modern pigments and dyes are favored over the application of oils, inks, and juices.

Because of import-export bans, the bone and ivory available for scrimshaw are limited. In the United States, the Marine Mammal Protection and Endangered Species Acts protect whale ivory. Consequently, modern "scrimshanders" use such materials as naturally shed deer, elk, and moose antlers, as well as old piano keys (at one time made of real elephant ivory); fossilized walrus, mastodon, and mammoth ivory are also suitable for scrimshaw. Walrus tusks periodically wash ashore. The Alaska Fish and Game Commission distributes fossilized artifacts and fresh ivory from species hunted legally by the Inuit. The whale scrimshaw shown is the work of an unidentified Alaskan artist.

sculpted beads Handmade beads created with a free-form shape rather than those produced with a mold or in basic shapes like the sphere, cylinder, ovoid, or cube. Examples are beads in heart, abstract, face, flower, animal, mermaid, or dragon shapes. Sculpted beads are generally unique, more expensive, and considered works of art.

Sculpted beads can also be formed in the lost-wax process. A wax mold is first sculpted, the wax melted, and then molten metal poured inside the mold, assuming the original shape of the desired reverse sculpture. Since the clay shaped around the outside of the wax must be removed after the metal is poured, the product is one of a kind. *See also* investment.

scrying Crystal gazing for the purpose of divination, practiced in ancient Greece, Egypt, British Isles (notably by the Druids), Polynesians, and later by the Zulus, Siberians, Incas, Huille-che of South America, and Euahlayi of Australia, among other peoples. The stones preferred were beryl and polished quartz, but black glass, water, mirrors, and other transparent media that caught light were also used.

sea-urchin spines Here is another interesting gift of nature that is drilled and used as a bead. These sea creatures use their spines to defend themselves from predators. The spines, connected to the skeleton by a ball joint, inject very irritating poisons. The exotic necklace shown was made by Joaquin Flores. The design

uses sea urchin spines and glass druk beads of many colors, including earth brown, orange, beige, and blue.

seals Most early seals were made as beads with one flat end that was engraved with the desired initials, logo, or design. When pressed into sealing wax, lac, or clay or pressed into ink, it could imprint a design on paper. Seals have served as notary marks, talismans, padlocks, letterheads, signatures, and more. For more than 5,000 years, other seals were shaped as bone or stone rollers or stamps that could be rolled in clay and used to make an impression. These were once important possessions.

seashells The hard exterior skeletons of seadwellers, many shells have natural crevices or holes easily adapted for stringing as ornaments. Most seashells are drilled and cut into a variety of shapes and sizes. Some shells have been used as money by various cultures. These are the dentalium (*Dentalium pretiosum*), money cowrie (*Cypraea moneta*), wampum (*Busycon carica*), Atlantic knobbed whelk, and North Atlantic quahog hard-shelled clam (*Venus mercenaria*). Shown are seashells in a variety of shapes, colors, and sizes. *See also* wampum.

sectile Easily cut with a knife, which may apply to certain minerals or metals.

seed beads This term originally applied to a natural, organic seed drilled and used as a bead. Plant seeds, shells, small freshwater pearls, coral, wood, and other types of clay, or faience beads have been found in ancient tombs. Today, small glass beads (available for over 600 years) are called seed beads as well as any bead, such as seed pearls, small enough to be used for fine work in fabric ornamentation. The particular seed shown is called an *ojo de venado*, or deer's-eye bead, by the Pascua Yaqui from Arizona and the Sonoran region of Mexico. It is used as a necklace pendant for protection against evil forces. *See also* rudraksha, cedar seeds, mescal beans, and seed stitch.

seed beads (rocailles) Small glass beads, often called by the French word *rocailles,* that are 2 mm or smaller in diameter and range from size 8 to 22. (Remember, the higher the size number, the smaller the bead.) They are made on a gauged glass rod or stick, cut according to size and then fired or put inside a furnace to round the edges. After firing, the beads are cooled, checked for uniformity, washed, and dried. Beads are then ready for special linings, coatings, or finishes.

Commonly available beads range from size 10, 11, 12, 13 to 14. Japanese seed beads are usually sold loose in plastic bead tubes or containers. Czech beads are typically sold in bundles of strands called hanks, which consist of twelve strands about 10 inches (25 cm) long. They both weigh approximately 1 ounce (28 g). Literature on the naming of seed beads refers to a Native North American woman naming small glass beads "little spirit seeds" when she saw them for the first time. Find the bead sizes chart in Part IV.

seed pearls These natural pearls occur in a rounded irregular shape and weigh less than one-fourth pearl grain. Their most significant characteristic is their tiny size, usually less than 2 mm in diameter, which presents a challenge for drilling. Seed pearls are typically used for beading designs on clothing and other fabrics. They are also common in ornate necklaces. Glass or plastic beads with a pearlized finish are sometimes referred to as seed pearls. While they are not real pearls, these glass or plastic imitations are less expensive and easier to obtain for intricate beadwork, especially for replicas of period clothing or for embellishment of wedding gowns and evening attire. *See also* pearl and pearl grain.

seed stitch A basic bead embroidery stitch that sews a single bead to fabric by running the needle and thread from the back of the fabric to the front. This stitch is repeated randomly over the fabric's surface. It is also called *stab* or *pick stitch*. *See also* sashiko. Find stitches in Part V.

segi beads Translucent tubular beads, usually in blues and greens, handmade in Africa, notably in Nigeria and Ghana, and related to the older aggrey beads. The word *segi,* used by the Yoruba, means "blue." *See also* aggrey beads.

segment A demarcated section, lobe, seam, or other mark. *See* segmented beads.

segmented beads Some antique beads have surface seams or indentations that mark segments. Some speculate that they were tube beads or glass rods marked for cutting, while others believe the beadmakers were creating a deliberate bead design. The term can also indicate any bead with lobes or sections.

semi-matte A matte finish with a slight sheen, falling between polished and matte. Beads with this finish are not as shiny as regular opaque beads.

semiprecious gemstones A general term for gemstones other than diamonds, emeralds, rubies, and sapphires. The term *semiprecious* should be used with caution because it implies that a given stone has less value; in other words, it's bad salesmanship. The greatest influences on a gemstone's value are supply and demand. Apart from these, color, cut, clarity, and size are the main determinants; the popular appeal, hardness, enhancing treatments, and other factors have less effect. *See also* gemstones.

sequins   Made of very thin plastic, usually with a metallic or fancy finish, sequins are technically considered beads because they have a hole and can be strung, threaded, or sewn together in a variety of ways. Sequins are most often used to embellish clothing and accessories. Note that the thread hole is at the top of some beads and in the middle of others; a few sequins have two for attaching to fabric. Shown are common round and cup shapes along with a sample of others, like stars, leaves, coins, and flowers. A *paillette,* such as the leaf sequin shown, has a thread hole near the sequin's edge (rather than in the middle) so that it can hang from the garment or jewelry. *See also* paillette and spangles.

serafinite   Rare deep green gemstone with feathery or silver-colored inclusions that create chatoyant or starlike patterns. Found in Siberia and sometimes called *angel stone,* serafinite is considered a healing stone.

serpentine   A semitransparent to opaque gemstone, composed of magnesium silicate, that is green, yellowish, or brown with a greasy to silky luster. From the Latin *serpens,* meaning "snake," in reference to its coloring, serpentine comes in two aggregate structures: *leafy* (antigorite) and *fibrous* (chrysotile). *Asbestos serpentine* is a finely fibrous variety. Other varieties are *bastite* (enstatite), *bowenite* (light green with light spots), *Connemara* (intergrown with marble), *verd-antique* (interspersed with calcite or dolomite veins), and *Williamsite* (oily green, often with black inclusions). Serpentine has a microcrystalline crystal system and a Mohs scale hardness of 2.5 to 5.5. It is found in Afghanistan, China, New Zealand, and the United States. The stone is vulnerable to acids. It may be confused with jade, onyx marble, verdite, or turquoise. The fibrous variety of serpentine, an asbestos, is toxic.

sharps   Short, stiff needles used for sewing through material as well as for bead embroidery.

shekere   *See* gourd shekere.

shell money   Various kinds of marine and snail shells have been used in diverse ancient civilizations around the world as money. The shells were often strung and worn as beads. *See* seashells, land-snail shell beads, and wampum.

Sherpa coral   Red or orange glass, approximately 200 to 400 years old, originally made in China and prized in Tibetan culture. Red is a significant color, and the beads made of this material were valuable since most Tibetans could not afford genuine coral.

shisha Small, round mirrors used along with beads for fabric embellishment and embroidery, considered a hallmark of Indian textile handiwork, notably in Gujarat. It appears to be related to the practice of sewing metallic plates or spangles on clothing. These mirrors are thought to deflect the evil eye and are associated with vitality, mystical, magical beauty. Middle Eastern desert peoples sewed shisha embroidery on a camel's headpiece for when it was ridden by the groom to meet his bride. This type of embellishment is over 2,000 years old and may be related to the use of gold medallions and other shiny objects sewn onto clothing. Shisha embroidery is commonly used in the Middle East, India, Russia, China, and other parts of Asia. The mirrors also come in diamond, triangular, and square shapes.

sibucao Seeds or nuts from the tree *Caesalpinia sappan,* sometimes called sibukaw, found in the Philippines, that are made into beads. The shiny seeds are almost black and reddish brown with marbling or similar markings.

side-cutter pliers Also called *side-cutters,* jewelry pliers used for general trimming and cutting of wire and cord.

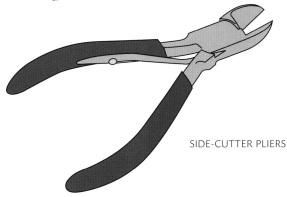

SIDE-CUTTER PLIERS

Silamide A brand name for a prewaxed, two-ply twisted nylon thread ideal for certain bead projects, especially those with seed beads. Silamide generally comes in white, black, and gray on thread cards and spools but may be available in a wider variety of colors, depending on the merchant.

silex Another name for *flintstone* or *flint. See also* flint.

silica Silicon dioxide, which may occur in crystalline (quartz), amorphous (opal), and impure (sand) forms.

silk Inclusions of rutile needles, such as those common to natural rubies, sometimes considered impurities and sometimes adding interest to the given gemstone.

The reflection of fibrous or crystal inclusions or canals give a gemstone a silky appearance. When numerous, metal oxides, rutile needles, or other materials may produce chatoyancy in the stone. Heat-treatment can reduce the silk and improve the stone's appearance; generally, silk visible within a stone attests that it has not been treated. Silk, while considered a flaw in some gems, is very desirable in others, such as sapphires and rubies that display asterism.

silk beads Made with a wood, plastic, or Styrofoam base with silk threads wound around them, silk beads are an old Korean craft, practiced by women. The beads are somewhat uncommon.

silk cord Braided and twisted strands of silk, used for tying, sewing, or stringing beads. Made from unraveled silkworm cocoons, silk is wonderfully soft and strong. The major drawback of such natural fibers when used for stringing beads is that they are biodegradable and do not last as long as synthetic fibers.

silky A soft bead finish resembling the natural fabric silk.

silver *See* sterling silver.

silver finish Also called *silver color,* a base metal of brass or steel that is electroplated with a layer of silver or nickel, the thickness of which is not standardized.

silver imitations *Alpaca silver* (copper, nickel, zinc, and iron), *German silver* (copper, nickel, and often zinc), *white bronze* (copper, nickel, and often zinc), and *nickel silver* (copper, nickel, and often zinc; sometimes also antimony, tin, lead, or cadmium) are metal alloys with no silver content. Alpaca silver is commonly sold in Peru and Argentina but labeled as such; most store owners will tell you that it is not real silver (*plata*). German silver, also sometimes called nickel silver, contains no silver. White bronze is called *paktong* or *pakfong* in China. Genuine sterling silver sold in the United States and Canada usually has the tiny words *sterling silver* incised on the back of the object. *See also* silver-lined, silver finish, and silver-plate.

silver-lined Glass beads having a reflective silver lining, which gives them extra sparkle. Beads also come lined with gold and copper. Shown above right is a hank of silver-lined teal beads made in the Czech Republic.

silver plate *See* silver-plated.

silver-plated Having a coating of silver electroplated onto the surface of a base metal. The industry standard for gold, silver, or nickel plating is a thickness of between 15 to 25 microns. (A micron is 1,000th of a millimeter.) This term may be applied to plastic beads plated with silver. While the outward appearance is similar to that of sterling silver, the product is less expensive than pure sterling silver. Note the U.S. Federal Trade Commission requirements for silver plating thickness on their Web site.

simulant *See* synthetic gemstones and imitation gemstones.

sizer A mandrel or long tube with a progressively widening base for measuring the diameter, length, or size of a ring, bracelet, or necklace.

skunk beads Usually black wound-glass beads with white, blue, or pink stripes, spots, or other markings. Skunk beads are made using one of the oldest ways of making a glass bead: twisting or wrapping hot glass around a rod or mandrel.

slave beads Yet another name for the so-called trade or African trade beads, any one of many kinds of decorative glass beads made in Europe that European traders and merchants (or indeed slavers) used from roughly 1500 to 1900 as a medium of exchange in Africa and other parts of the world for the purchase of goods and services and, in some cases, slaves—human cargo forcibly taken to the New World. During this era, the glass beads produced in Venice were among the most desirable trade beads. *See* African trade beads.

slave bracelets Costume jewelry, usually with elaborate chains or metalwork and attractive stones to be worn on the wrist, attached with a chain to a finger ring. These so-called slave bracelets are of course items of fashion.

slip-joint pliers This conventional tool has expandable jaws and teeth that are serrated to firmly grasp objects of different shapes. The small jaw setting is good for objects like jewelry components. A beading or jewelry-supply store should sell a type made especially for handling jewelry.

slip knot This knot, also sometimes called a granny knot, is not advised for beadwork because, as the name suggests, it easily becomes untied. Find knotting diagrams in Part V.

slip stitch A very fine stitch used to join two edges of fabric. If the thread is a close match, when joining fabric backing to beadwork, the tiny slip stitches can be nearly invisible. Find stitch diagrams in Part V; slip stitch is not included.

slurry In beadmaking, the thick suspension of solids in a liquid that is a by-product of bead-hole perforation or drilling.

smith An artisan who works with metals, forging and otherwise shaping them. Also called a metalsmith, or, depending on the metal worked, a silversmith, goldsmith, pewtersmith, tinsmith, coppersmith, and more. A whitesmith works on light-colored metals or finishing and polishing cold-metal pieces, while a blacksmith works with hot metals.

smoky quartz A transparent gemstone, composed of silicon dioxide; quartz that is smoky gray or brown to black. The color is caused by gamma rays that alter the color naturally or artificially. Smoky quartz may have inclusions of rutile needles; it is used as rock crystal. The crystal system is trigonal or with hexagonal prisms, and it has a Mohs scale hardness of 7. Dark stones are sometimes called *morion* or *cairngorm*. Deposits are found in Brazil, Madagascar, Russia, Ukraine, Scotland, and Switzerland. It is sometimes mistakenly and improperly called smoky topaz, which has a different chemical composition. It may be confused with andalusite, idocrase, sanidine, and tourmaline. *See also* quartz.

snake beads Pressed glass beads that interlock and are made to resemble snake vertebrae when strung. They have a somewhat zigzag cut and are much more uniform than actual snake vertebrae. Real snake vertebrae were traditionally used by the Cherokee and Seri people as beads.

snake's eye A fiber-optic glass cabochon with an S-shaped line running through it. *See* cat's-eye and fiber-optic beads.

soapstone Among the softest minerals, composed of talc (a hydrated magnesium silicate) with chlorite and traces of iron chromium oxides, that feels soapy to the touch. Soapstone, also called *steatite,* is relatively easy to carve and has a Mohs scale hardness rating of 1. Soapstone is very dense, nonporous, heat-resistant, and durable. Soapstone's dual nature (both soft and dense) makes it ideal for a range of uses from bead and fetish carving to inlays. The ancient city of Tepe Yahya (in what is today Iran) was a trading center for the production and distribution of soapstone from 5000 to 3000 B.C. Soapstone has been carved for thousands of years by populations as diverse and distant as the Inuit in the icy regions of North America and the architects of the Hoysala Empire (1026–1343) of the Indian subcontinent. Soapstone is commonly used to create molds for casting pewter objects. It is known as *palewa* and *gorara stone* in India, *Kisii stone* (*pyrophillite*) in Kenya, and *combarbalite stone,* found in many colors, in Chile. The assortment of soapstone beads here can

add a delightful earthy element to beadwork designs. *See also* steatite and talc.

social-status beads Throughout the world, beads have served to identify cultures, families, lineage, occupations, and age. The size, shape, and color of the beads can signify personal achievement, ethnic association, marital standing, or wealth. Beads can serve to distinguish male from female, youth from adult, married from single. (In Medieval Germany, Poland, Hungary, and Bohemia, for instance, red beads signaled that the young women were unmarried while blue beads were worn by married women.) They denote royalty, diviners, and healers. Of course, they also act as simple adornment.

In Africa, for instance, beads are part of a complicated communication system. Zulu females wear beads that unmistakably identify their marital status, as well as the region in which they live. Maasai women in Kenya and Tanzania wear wonderful beads, but only those who are married can wear the blue beads called *nborro.* Young Maasai girls pierce their upper ears but they are not permitted to decorate their lobes. After marriage, the lobe is pierced, and bead ornaments gradually accumulate until the earlobe sags with their weight. Women of the Turkana tribe in Kenya wear beads that indicate their wealth and marital status. Ndebele women in Africa wear beaded aprons that convey their changing status from girlhood to womanhood; *jocolo,* fingerlike extensions that hang from the apron, are reserved for married women. Among the Kirdi of Cameroon, beaded aprons denote age, status, and social condition. During an initiation ceremony for young Ndebele males, their mothers wear bead strips called *linga koba,* meaning "long tears," that reflect the sorrow of losing a boy and joy at gaining a man; they are also called mother's tears.

The Bamileke of Cameroon wear beaded-cloth elephant masks, an important icon of royalty, with other regalia at court ceremonies to reveal the wealth of the Bamileke kingdom. Other motifs include leopards, human figures and animal heads, spiders, lizards, birds, and other abstract designs, found in headdresses, caps, masks, and worn or displayed on other objects. The spider design serves as a symbol of wisdom, while the leopard suggests cunning, speed, mobility, and aggressive qualities important to survival. Glass beads embellish the most important royal objects.

Yoruba diviners in Nigeria traditionally wore beaded sashes that indicated their spiritual position and carried beaded bags that held divination objects or tools. Yoruba Oba, a king or chief, wore a beaded veil and costumes embellished with beads in symbolic designs, indicative of his status and wealth.

Shown are two Yoruba beaded panels on bags. Courtesy of Peg Alston of Peg Alston Fine Arts Gallery, Inc.; photos by JG.

sodalite A transparent to opaque white, deep royal blue, or gray stone, sodium aluminum silicate with chlorine, sometimes with white veins of calcite. The gemstone has a vitreous luster and may display orange fluorescence. Sodalite has a cubic, rhombic dodecahedral crystal system, and its Mohs scale hardness rating is 5.5 to 6. The stone is found in Greenland, India, Namibia, Russia, Brazil, Canada, and the United States. The sodalite

group includes sodalite, hauynite, nosean, and lazurite, a common constituent of lapis lazuli. It is not typically dyed. *Hackmanite* is a pink sodalite variety found in Quebec that fades in sunlight. For jewelry the blue stones are preferred and typically cut into cabochons. It may be confused with azurite, lapis lazuli, and lazulite. Synthetic sodalite has been made since 1975.

Soft Flex wire *See* stringing wire.

soft glass A kind of glass that contains lead or soda-lime as flux and has a much higher coefficient of expansion (COE) than hard glass is called soft glass. The proportion of silica to oxides affects the melting temperature of the glass. Many bead makers favor soft glass because of its lower melting temperature than hard glass and because it is easier to work with. It is, however, more sensitive to temperature change and more likely to crack and pop. *Borosilicate glass,* in contrast, is a hard glass. *See also* COE, hard glass, and borosilicate glass.

soft stones Aside from mud brick, soft stone was the most frequently used long-term building material in ancient Egypt. This broad category including limestone, chalk, soapstone, pumice, and sandstone, dominated Egyptian architecture. When compared with hard stones like granite, quarrying soft stone was often less expensive, time-consuming, and dangerous. Soft stones are less difficult to cut than hard stones. The cutting of gemstones is referred to as *lapidary,* in which stones are carved and cut into delicate shapes like beads, cabochons, and donuts. *See* Mohs scale of hardness.

Soft Touch wire *See* stringing wire.

software Computer software can enable beaders to design their own patterns. Find software through the Internet and bead magazines.

soldering Fusing two metals or metal alloys together with the use of a third, "wettable" metal or alloy with a relatively low melting point, commonly with a hand-held soldering iron (although many other tools are available) that applies heat to the third metal used to join the original two. The two original metals remain unmelted, while they are joined with the use of a solder and a flux, such as Borax. No visible gaps should appear between the two original pieces in the finished piece. Silver and other metal chains, pendants, and other jewelry are commonly soldered. Lead-free solders contain tin, copper, silver, and sometimes bismuth, indium, zinc, and antimony.

sommerso beads Murano glass beads named for the technique in which different colors and tiny flakes of copper or other metals are submerged or suspended beneath clear glass. The Italian word *sommerso* means "sunken." *See also* aventurine effect.

spacer bars Designed to separate multiple strands of beads and make them lie flat, these bars usually have two or more holes. These components provide precise spacing for multistrand bracelets or necklaces. The spacer bars shown opposite, top right, are of bone and horn, but they are also commonly made in leather, bone, wood, and metal.

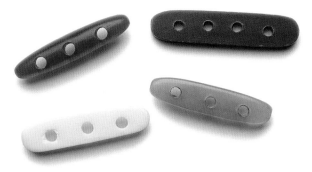

spacer beads Similar to spacer bars, these beads are designed with two or more holes so that several strings can pass through them in separate paths.

spacers Decorative links used primarily to fill in a design featuring larger or more expensive beads. Spacers come in a variety of materials, sizes, and colors; ideally they should complement the main bead material. Metal spacers are fairly common. The bracelet shown features faceted red-coral rondelles, black 10-mm fire-polish beads, and Bali sterling-silver accent spacers. *See also* spotted lampwork beads for another typical spacer bead type.

spaghetti beads Tubular beads with the same shape as bone hairpipe beads. The name can be confusing because the beads do not resemble spaghetti at all. Native North American replicas frequently use plastic spaghetti beads, which are much cheaper than those shaped from bone. *See* bone hairpipe beads.

spaghetti glass *See* stringer.

spangles Also called *beaded spangles,* these are used at the ends of lace bobbins to aid in identifying the correct thread. See also *spindle whorls.*

The term *spangle* may also describe a small, shiny object; it is sometimes used interchangeably with the word *sequin(s).* The Tiboli people of the Philippines use triangular-shaped shell spangles to decorate clothing.

Spanish topaz A false or misleading name for citrine (quartz).

spectra A textured glass or acrylic bead with a multicolored satiny metallic finish, suggestive of the color spectrum.

spectrolite Labradorite found in Finland, that shows spectral colors (schiller effect) effectively. *See also* labradorite and schiller effect.

spessartite A transparent to translucent bright orange-yellow to reddish brown gemstone, a member of the garnet group, composed of magnesium aluminum silicate. Named after the Spessart forested mountain range in Germany, it is also known as *spessartine.* The stone has a Mohs scale hardness rating of 7 to 7.5. It is also found in Namibia, Brazil, China, Kenya, Madagascar, Sri Lanka, Myanmar, Tanzania, and the United States. Spessartite stones are the orange briolettes that dangle from the top of the necklace on next page designed by Gabie Warmuth. *See also* garnet.

spindle whorls Originally designed as hand tools (first use uncertain), *spindle beads* or spindle whorls are commonly used weights to aid in spinning thread. The beads have also served as a potter's tool for burnishing the surface of ceramics. The spindle-whorl bead with a hole for stringing has also functioned as a seal for signatures, letterheads, or notary services. However, its primary purpose is not as a bead. Found worldwide, examples from Ecuador, used to spin llama hair and cotton, are typically decorated with fanciful fauna or geometric carvings.

spinel Also sometimes spelled *spinelle*, transparent to opaque gemstone composed of magnesium aluminum oxide, that comes in a variety of colors. Its crystal system is (cubic), octahedron, twin, or rhombic dodecahedron,

and its Mohs scale hardness is 8. A few varieties are flame or rubicelle (orange to orange-red); balas (pale red); pleonaste or hercynite (dark green to black with iron); gahnite or zinc spinel (blue, violet, or dark geen); gahnospinel (blue to dark blue or green with spinel and gahnite, iron); and picotite or chrome spinel (brown, dark green, black, with iron). Spinel is sometimes mistaken for ruby, sapphire, garnet, amethyst, and topaz. It is found in Australia, Madagascar, Sweden, Turkey, Pakistan, Brazil, Italy, Sri Lanka, and the United States. Spinel occurs in a wide spectrum of colors from red, orange, yellow, dark green, blue, purple, brown, to black. The name may originate from the Greek for "spark" or the Italian *spinella* for "little thorn"; it has sharply pointed crystals. The favored variety is ruby red. The term *spinel* is also used for a broad group of related minerals, not all of which are of gemstone quality. These stones may also include zinc, iron, manganese, chromium, titanium, and silicon.

spiny oyster Also called by its genus *spondylus,* a bivalve mollusk. This marine shellfish has beautiful coloring on its shell, ranging from orange-red to purple. The necklace with multiple strands is made of orange and purple

spiny oyster chips embellished with turquoise, mother-of-pearl, assorted gemstone beads, and sterling-silver spacers.

spiral stitch Spiral stitch produces a very sturdy rope for use in jewelry; it can make bracelets, bag straps, chokers, and long rope necklaces. Shown here is a spiral stitch necklace accented with purple jade briolettes.

split ring This metal ring is a durable jewelry component, often used to attach a clasp to a necklace or bracelet. It comes in a good range of sizes and may also be called a *key ring,* since it can keep several keys together to prevent loss. *See also* jump ring.

split-ring pliers A tool used in jewelry-making and beading to open split rings, especially useful in a repetitive project, such as making chains.

SPLIT-RING PLIERS

spotted lampwork beads Handmade glass beads that have glass dots or spots on the surface.

spring-ring clasp A circular metal fastener with a tiny catch that pulls back a small tongue in the ring. A built-in spring puts tension on the tongue to ensure that it closes snugly when released. For security, the heavier, more durable spring-ring clasps are preferable.

square beads Cube-shaped beads with six equal sides or tabular beads that are essentially flattened squares. Widely manufactured, they come in all sorts of materials. The glass beads shown were made in Japan.

square-holed beads Beads with square, rather than round, holes. Silver-lined and gold-lined beads are often square-holed because the holes are roomier and permit more light reflection and sparkle.

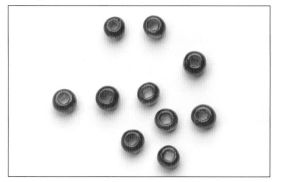

square knot A common knot used in beadwork for attaching a new thread to a beadwork project when the original thread runs out. The sequence for tying the square knot is right over left (twisting the threads together); then left over right, under, then through. Or you could begin left over right and then right over left. When pulled tight, strands from each thread come back out of the knot together in the same direction. Still more secure is the *surgeon's knot*. Find knotting diagrams in Part V.

square stitch Also called *round stitch* and *corn stitch* and almost identical in appearance to loom-stitch beadwork, in which the beadwork piece is square or rectangular. Square-stitch beadwork is often done in even rows, horizontally and vertically, to make bead strips to attach to fabric, or to use as hatbands, belts, necklaces, barrettes, or the like. However, the earrings shown here are an interesting demonstration of how, by careful color design, you can use square stitch to make uneven edges and textures. This is accomplished by increasing and decreasing the number of beads with square stitch.

Beaded by Janet Schmucker, the feather earrings use a pattern designed by Peggy Wilson. The corncob earring has a "husk" of leather. Find stitch diagrams in Part V.

squash-blossom necklace A necklace design found in Native North American jewelry, particularly in the Southwest of the United States, probably influenced by Spanish or Mexican contact. The crescent-shaped pendant is called the *naja* or *najahe* in the Navajo language for "bead that spreads out." Originally, similar decorative ornaments were used on horse bridles by the Spanish Conquistadors in the late 1500s, in turn influenced by the Moors who had settled in Spain centuries earlier. Once made of iron, these squash-blossom or pomegranate-blossom shapes were later crafted in silver. The naja symbolizes crop fertility. *See also* naja.

stacking brick stitch A variation of the brick stitch using two or more beads at a time in place of just one. Except for that, the stitch is identical to ordinary brick stitch. This very useful technique allows for more shaping of a beaded object, and the project can be completed faster. The beaded feather shown uses increasing and decreasing brick stitch to produce uneven edges, making it look more like a real feather. Find stitch diagrams in Part V.

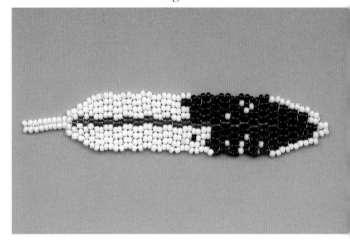

stainless steel An alloy of iron, carbon, and chromium (minimum 10.5%) that resists corrosion and scratching. It has a silvery metallic luster. Chlorine and saltwater may cause it to corrode or pit (known as *galling*). The typical 18/10 stainless steel used in flatware contains 18% chromium and 10% nickel. Other formulas for stainless steel may include molybdenum, manganese, aluminum, vanadium, or titanium. Stainless steels are classified by their crystalline structures: austenitic, ferritic, martensitic, and duplex, or combinations of these.

stamp In metalwork, a punch or other tool can press or stamp a design, texture, or shape (raised or somewhat flattened) into a metal object. Malleable or soft surfaces, such as unfired clay, can also be impressed with a harder object to create the desired image or design. Ink may be pressed onto wood with the use of a rubber stamp, for instance. The stamp can be the tool doing the stamping, the impression made, or the act of stamping.

star beads Also called *chevron* or *rosetta beads,* they are made with multiple layers of different colors of glass and were originally manufactured in Venice. The term *star beads* is also used to identify any star-shaped beads. *See also* chevron beads.

star crystal Rock crystal with inclusion of goethite.

star ruby *See* star sapphire.

star sapphire The transparent to opaque gemstone sapphire, composed of aluminum oxide; a corundum species, exhibiting pleochroism and available in various colors. Coloring agents come from the addition of elements or minerals. Needlelike inclusions of the mineral rutile (titanium dioxide) can align in rays to create the starlike occurrence in the stone known as *asterism*. The stars give the stone a silky sheen. Prized for its high

Mohs scale hardness rating of 9 and six-rayed star (sometimes four or twelve rays), the star gemstone is quite expensive. The favored blue star sapphires are found in Australia, Brazil, Cambodia, Pakistan, the United States (Montana and North Carolina), and Zimbabwe. A few isolated star sapphires have also been found in Finland. The gemstone is typically heat-treated to improve its color and appearance. The blue color may result from the titanium and iron inclusions in the aluminum oxide. Red sapphires, known as rubies, are made red from chromium and sometimes iron and may also display asterism.

Shown is a pair of dainty beaded earrings with sapphire cabochons made by Sylvia Elam, who trimmed them with appliquéd beads. *See also* corundum, sapphire, and ruby.

star stone Quartz pebbles in early British folklore were called star stones, sought for their curative powers.

starflake beads Acrylic or plastic beads with six or more points, making them look like a cross between a star and a snowflake. They are also sometimes called paddle-wheel or sunburst beads. They are good for children and those with little dexterity, because they have large holes and a low price.

station Also known as a focal bead, the central or main bead in a piece of jewelry.

steatite Also known as *soapstone,* composed mostly of dense aggregates of talc, a very soft translucent to opaque material used for carving. *Steatite* is also a term used for a type of ceramic material made of soapstone with additives, heated and fused into a glassy or vitreous substance. For thousands of years, ancient civilizations have produced steatite to be pressed into beads and other materials. The Egyptians made scarab amulets from steatite, which they carved and glazed. Its Mohs scale hardness is 1. *See also* soapstone.

step-up If, for instance, you are working a round peyote-stitch pattern from the bottom up, at the end of each row you will need to pass your needle through the first bead added from the previous row. This movement is called *drop down* if you are working from the top down. Find stitch diagrams in Part V.

sterling silver *Sterling* is an industry standard; it calls for metal that is 92.5% pure silver. Other metals, chiefly copper, are added in the amount of 7.5%, to increase its hardness (durability). Sterling silver usually has a stamp showing "925," which guarantees its metal content. It is also known as *925 silver* and *92.5% silver.*

Silver is sold by the troy ounce; prices fluctuate with the world commodities market. *Hilltribe silver,* handmade by the Karen tribe of Thailand, contains 95% to 99% silver; this softer metal can be easily bent and shaped. *Britannia silver* contains 95.84% silver, *Mexican silver* has 95% silver and 5% copper, and so-

called *coin silver* is 90% silver. *See also* Argentium Sterling Silver, a patented process, made with germanium. Shown is a sampling of Bali sterling-silver beads.

stone In gemstone terminology, the word *stone* is synonymous with (semiprecious or precious) *gemstone.* Even glass imitations of gemstones are sometimes called stones or stone beads. Geologists, however, tend to be stricter in making distinctions between rocks and minerals and other elements found in the earth. *See also* glass pearls.

stone beads As early as 38,000 B.C. or even 100,000 B.C. (*National Geographic,* April 2007, p. 14), Stone Age humans used animal bones, teeth, eggshells, and seashells as beads. In the Bronze Age they traded and produced stone beads from native raw materials. Later soft stones, like soapstone, limestone, marble, and sandstone (with a Mohs scale hardness of 1 to 3), were most likely preferred, since they were easier to drill and carve, for about 25,000 years.

According to the timeline in Lois Sherr Dubin's *The History of Beads* (2000), white calcite beads were found in Nevada dating from 11,000 B.C. Here is a sampling from other parts of the world, revealed in excavations. In the Indus Valley and Pakistan, beads were made from alabaster, turquoise, steatite, and lapis lazuli in 7000 B.C. In Cyprus the stone was carnelian from 5800 to 5200 B.C.; in Syria agate, serpentine, and turquoise in 6500 B.C.; in Turkmenistan unnamed stones in 5000 B.C.; in Yugoslavia azurite and malachite in 6000 to 4500 B.C.; and in Mesopotamia, turquoise, lapis lazuli, beryl, and amethyst in 4200 B.C. *See also* various stones, such as soapstone.

stone-setting tool A tool used to tighten prongs on gemstones set into jewelry.

stop beads A bead tied to the end of stringing material to keep the beads from falling off until stringing is complete and the clasp is added. A crimp bead is sometimes used in the same way and then cut off when finished. A rubber earring-back or a piece of adhesive tape also works.

strass *See* rhinestone.

strawberry quartz Also called *cherry quartz,* typically a natural quartz, silicon dioxide, dyed a translucent pink. Its crystal system is trigonal with hexagonal prisms, and it has a Mohs

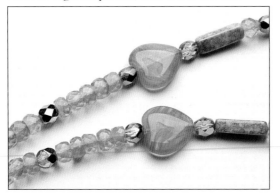

scale hardness of 7. However, imitation glass beads are sold by the same name; verify its authenticity with a reputable gemologist or bead dealer. Shown is a 16-inch (40-cm) choker made with faceted strawberry quartz (not imitation glass) rondelles, accented with fire-polish beads, glass hearts, and floral lampwork beads. *See also* quartz.

streak In strict scientific terms, the color of the powder a mineral leaves when it has been rubbed on an unglazed porcelain streak plate. This may not be the same color as that of the original material. The streak a mineral or gemstone creates is used by gemologists and geologists to help identify it.

The layman's usage, however, tends to be rather loose, however, and may refer to a "streak of color" within a given stone, such as that caused by an inclusion of other elements. The gemologist, however, may refer to such color differentiations as veins, bands, webbing, striations, marbling, mottling, or any of a number of more exacting terms.

striated Decorated with a pattern of lines, strands, threads, or swirls often of a different color.

striking colors Glass-rod colors are called *striking* or *reheat colors* because they change colors when heated, cooled or annealed, and then reheated to a molten state.

stringer Also called *spaghetti cane,* a very thin strand of glass (often only about 1.5 mm thick) applied in its molten state to bead surfaces to create dots, stripes, trails, squiggles, and other decorations. *See also* dot beads.

stringing thread Of all the threads on the market for sewing, quilting, knitting, crochet, and the like, the ones most appropriate for beadwork—owing to their greater strength and durability—are probably those of synthetic, rather than natural, fibers. The chemical compositions of these materials are trade secrets, but they presumably feature nylon or polyester derivatives. Aside from stringing beads, such thread is useful in sewing and in making hats, purses, bags, shoes, and other articles of thick or stiff materials, like bulletproof or upholstery fibers. Here are a few of the reliable trademarked brands (C-LON, Conso, FireLine, Nymo, Power Pro, Strength) good for beadwork. Definitions are drawn from the manufacturers' descriptions. Also find Stringing Materials in Part IV.

C-LON nylon monofilament thread, roughly equivalent to thread size D Nymo thread, available in many colors. It has a silky texture.

Conso thread, used for upholstering because of its durability. Comparable to Nymo thread size F, this supple heavy, twisted thread is a good choice for stringing large glass beads that may break relatively lightweight threads. It may be difficult to use with a traditional beading needle; a big-eye or twisted-wire needle is recommended. Other uses for Conso thread are bead crochet and netted beadwork that is not mounted on a sturdy backing, like leather or cloth, and as a warp-thread on loom projects.

FireLine has the consistency of a heavy thread and comes in 4-pound to 10-pound (1.8-g to 4.5-g) test weights. It is smoke gray in color and has a thickness of 0.006 inch to 0.008 inch (0.2 mm) diameter. It is a spun polyethylene, fused into a very strong fiber, and braided.

Nymo thread comes in standard sizes that are useful for many bead projects. It also comes in many colors. *See* nylon thread.

Power Pro, according to the manufacturer, has the consistency of a heavy thread and the strength of a coated cable wire. It has the durability of a braided bead thread and has up to a 10-pound (4.5-kg) test weight. This white thread is useful with certain types of glass, metal, and gemstone beads that are known to have holes with sharp edges that often cut nylon thread.

Strength is a strong bead cord that comes in many different sizes. Made from bonded nylon, it is good for stringing and knotting a variety of bead projects. Nylon products in general do not fray or stretch much. The suppliers usually recommend that a bit of glue be placed on the end of the cord to let dry to serve as a stringing needle.

stringing wire Jewelers use this metal wire to string beads and wire-wrap jewelry components. Most often a nylon-coated wire cable, it is available in a variety of sizes and test weights. This wire is of base metal, coated with copper, silver, gold, or other materials. The number of wires bundled into a cable determines its flexibility and strength. Stringing wire is most often preferred with heavier beads, but the smaller gauges are quite useful with seed beads. Stringing wire is generally sold on spools. The term *stringing wire* can also refer to metal chain used for stringing. Definitions are drawn from the manufacturers' descriptions. Note that sizes are based on diameter inches; the usual household wire gauges do not apply to beading wire. Also find Stringing Materials in Part IV.

Soft Flex is a brand name of nylon-coated wire cable, designed for maximum durability and flexibility, with a construction of either 21 or 49 strands of woven stainless-steel microwires. The smallest size (0.014 inch diameter) has 21 strands and a 10-pound (4.5-kg) test weight. It is recommended for stringing freshwater pearls (notorious for their small holes) and lightweight beads like shells and small glass beads. The wire can pass through a size 14/0 seed bead. The versatile 0.019-inch (0.5-mm) size with 49 strands has a 26-pound (11.7-kg) test weight. (It consists of 7 braided strands of 7 wires each for a total of 49 stainless-steel microwires.) It is recommended for eyeglass holders, bracelets, necklaces, watch bands, and ankle bracelets. It can be used with glass, gemstones, metal beads, and some pearls. The wire will fit inside a seed bead as small as 13/0. The 0.024-inch (0.6-mm) size also has 49 strands, with a 40-pound (18-kg) test weight. Although recommended for use with large, heavy beads like silver and chunky gemstones, it will accommodate a seed bead as small as size 11/0. Soft Flex comes in a variety of colors and metals.

Soft Touch is the brand name of a stringing wire notable for its sturdiness and flexibility; the product is based on Soft Flex technology. Sizes are based on diameter in inches. Available in four diameters, the 0.010-inch (0.25-mm) size is so delicate, it almost has the appearance of thread; wire of this size has 7 strands, but it can pass through a size 22/0 antique seed bead. The 0.014-inch (0.35-mm) size has 21 strands, and both the 0.019-inch and 0.024-inch sizes have 49 strands. It resists kinks and can be knotted.

Tigertail is a nylon-coated wire cable. It is sold under the brand name Accu-Flex as well as under the brand names Acculon and 19-Strand Jewelry Wire by Griffin. It hangs nicely if the weight of the beads is considered when selecting the appropriate wire gauge for the beading project. Tigertail, if passed through the hole just once, should fit inside the hole snugly with little play. The wire is stiff enough to serve as its own needle, which eliminates the need for threading a beading needle. While smaller, lightweight tigertail can be knotted, use of a crimp bead is recommended. Lightweight sizes (0.012 to 0.018 inch in thickness or diameter) can be used with small beads, like seed beads and liquid-silver beads for bracelets and necklaces. Larger sizes (0.018 to 0.024 inch thickness or diameter) are more appropriate for heavier glass, metal, or gemstone beads. Tigertail is available in stainless steel, 24-karat gold plate, silver plate, sterling silver, brass, and clear as well as numerous colors, which are visible beneath the clear nylon coating. Note that the tigertail sizes do not correspond to standard wire-gauge sizes.

Strength *See* stringing thread.

striped beads Usually glass beads with a surface featuring stripes of a color complementary with the bead base. They come in a variety of sizes, shapes, and colors, as shown.

stripes Generally, lines drawn on a glass bead with a trail of hot glass. Stripes can also be painted on or otherwise fashioned with dyes and molds in ceramic, plastic, or metal beads.

Stunz Classification System A system for classifying minerals that divides them into nine groups: (1) elements; (2) sulfides; (3) halogenides; (4) oxides and hydroxides; (5) nitrates, carbonates, and borates; (6) sulfates, chromates, molybdates, and tungstates; (7) phosphates, arsenates, and vanadates; (8) silicates; and (9) organic compounds. *See also* Dana Classification System.

suede lace Also called *thong*, a natural leather cut into long strips and used for stringing. It is usually dyed. It may also be referred to as *leather lace*.

sugar beads *See* sand-cast beads, powder-glass beads, or Krobo beads.

sugilite A translucent to translucent violet (pink to purple) cyclosilicate mineral that may be lightly banded. Sugilite crystals are in the hexagonal crystal system with prismatic crystals, and the Mohs scale of hardness is 6 to 6.5. The chemical composition is complex and includes potassium, sodium, lithium, manganese, aluminum, iron, silicon, and oxygen. Also called *luvulite,* the gemstone was reportedly discovered in 1944. Often combined with manganese or quartz, it is found in Japan, Canada, Italy, India, Bangladesh, South Africa, and Australia. Sugilite may be attractively set with turquoise and lapis lazuli in jewelry.

sunstone A natural gemstone, a translucent to opaque feldspar, composed of sodium calcium aluminum silicate, with a brilliant deep golden-orange sparkle caused by enclosures of red hematite in minute scales or goethite platelets. Also called *aventurine feldspar,* it is found in Norway, Siberia, the United States, and India. Sunstone has a deep golden orange to reddish brown sparkle. The crystal system consists of triclinic, rare, solid aggregates, and its Mohs scale hardness rating is 6 to 6.5. It has a metallic appearance due to reflective inclusions of red, orange, and green crystals. The Vikings are thought to have used sunstone as a navigation aid since it could polarize a patch of skylight. It displays a dark brownish red fluorescence. It is sometimes called *heliolite*. Do not confuse it with aventurine quartz (silicon dioxide) or artificial glass known as goldstone. *See also* aventurine effect.

supra-metallic A durable, baked-on bead finish that has a metallic, dull, or matte appearance. This finish, more durable than sprayed-on coatings, reportedly lasts for decades.

supra-pearl A baked-on pearlescent finish known for its durability. Supra-pearl color finishes wear without fading and resist chipping.

Its durability reportedly matches that of supra-metallic bead finishes, which are reported to last for over 30 years.

surgeon's knot A knot used by surgeons and other physicians that works well in beadwork because this secure knot will not slip. Find knotting diagrams in Part V.

surgical steel A type of stainless steel that is hypoallergenic when not plated; the metal resists corrosion and scratching. Although many different formulas exist, it is typically an alloy of the metals steel (iron-carbon), chromium (12% to 20%) for scratch-resistance, molybdenum (0.2% to 3%) for hardness, and sometimes nickel (8% to 12%) for a polished appearance. Because it can be sterilized, it is suitable for surgical instruments. In appearance, it is darker and grayer than sterling silver. Jewelry made of surgical steel when including nickel can cause allergic reactions. For implants and new body piercings, titanium is recommended instead. *See also* stainless steel.

Swarovski crystals In 1892, Austrian Daniel Swarovski, born in Bohemia, invented an automated process for precision-cutting exquisite facets into lead-crystal glass. The Austrian company he founded has been producing a

majority of the world's high-quality glass beads and ornaments since the late 1800s. Defined by their 32% lead content, the multiple sharp facets in this glass produce hard-edged refractive surfaces, which are often enhanced by means of numerous coatings or finishes, some of which are metallic and designed to admit a rainbow spectrum (aurora borealis, or AB). Shown are Swarovski crystals in a variety of shapes.

Swarovski pearls The manufacturer of Swarovski crystals also produces crystal-based pearls in a wide range of colors.

swirl-glass beads A glittery golden swirl that is hand-painted on the surface of a glass bead. Also, two or more colors of glass swirled together on the bead surface to produce a multicolored bead.

synthetic gemstones Made in a laboratory, these stones have physical, optical, and chemical properties, including their crystal structure, in common with naturally occurring gemstones mined from the earth.

The term may also be applied to gemstones introduced to the trade that do not have a counterpart in nature. Cubic zirconia (zirconium oxide), for instance, on the Mohs scale of hardness rates an 8.5, and resembles the diamond (10 on the Mohs scale of hardness), although it is not as brilliant in its reflection of light.

An *imitation gemstone,* also called a *simulant,* in contrast, appears much like its counterpart in nature, sometimes with similar physical and optical properties, but does not share its chemical properties. An imitation ruby, for instance, may simply be colored glass.

T

T-necklace A choker that appears T-shaped when laid out flat, having a band or strands of beads hung from its center. The Apache T-necklace has loomed beadwork in the choker encircling the neck and another loomed piece hanging from the front middle. The necklace was worn in the Sunrise dance and ceremony, in a puberty rite for young women.

Traditionally, the T-necklace was made in the Apache colors of white, green, yellow, and black. Sometimes a few strands of beads adorn the main piece, and ribbon ties may go around the neck. Other traditional components, such as the sacred abalone shell, used in daily prayers, or dentalium, may serve as accents.

The T-necklace shown demonstrates the artist David Bingell's interpretive style and the influence of the San Carlos Apache and White Mountain Apache. The base uses an off-loom right-angle weave with bugle and seed beads. The three-dimensional flowers were done with a herringbone or Ndebele stitch, and the hummingbirds draw on Barbara Elbe's pattern. Veins, incorporating leaf-shaped glass beads, are embroidered over the necklace surface.

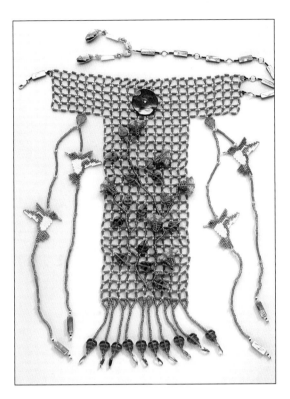

T pin A straight pin with a bar at the top; a useful tool for spacing knots in pearl-knotting projects. This T-shaped pin can also hold beadwork in place on a beading mat or cloth.

taali In southern India, a wedding chain, which may include gold or silver beads and anthropomorphic pendants, is a traditional wedding gift from the groom to his bride, who usually wears it until her husband's death, much like the Western wedding ring. Orange-colored thread may replace the gold. The desired pendant shapes depend on the region or communities where they are made and function something like good-luck charms. A turmeric root may replace the pendant. During the traditional Hindu wedding ceremony, the groom ties the taali around the bride's neck. *See also* mangal sutra and wedding beads.

table-cut beads Made of glass, these beads have a smooth, flat surface and rough edges that are unpolished or matte. They come in a variety of shapes; one of the most popular is the heart. They often appear as slabs.

tabular beads Originating from the Latin word *tabula* for "board" or "tablet," the term *tabular* describes beads with a flattened surface. The flattened beads may be of any shape— round, oval, rectangular, or any other. The term also denotes items that can be arranged in a table or set up in rows and columns or computed in such a table. Such beads were once on ancient counting boards, used in market places. Old African-trade and metal beads often have this shape. *See also* marver.

tagua nut Also called *vegetable ivory,* the dried nut (endosperm) from various palm trees, like the *Phytelephas macrocarpa palmae* that grows in Ecuador, Colombia, Peru, and Panama. In various parts of the world. tagua nut is carved into netsuke, scrimshaw, chess figures, dice, beads, buttons, and other items. It substitutes nicely for ivory from mammals (such as elephant or walrus), having similar carving characteristics, texture, appearance, and color. In Colombia it is called *anta,* in Peru *pullipunta* or *homero,* in Britain *corozo,* and in Japan *binroji nut.*

Tairona beads Ancient beads made by the Tairona (also spelled *Tayrona*) peoples from Colombia are represented in bead museums; fine specimens have been recovered from burial sites. These wonderful beads, dating from the 11th to 15th centuries, are made of jade, gold, jasper, agate, carnelian, and shell.

talc A translucent to opaque soft stone found in pearly white, yellowish, or blue-green. It has a Mohs scale hardness of 1, the lowest on the mineral scale. Dense aggregates of talc-schist are called *soapstone* and *steatite,* which are commonly used for carving. Talc is a hydrated magnesium silicate with a monoclinic crystal structure. It feels soft and soapy to the touch and is used for cosmetic, baby, and astringent powders, or as talcum powder.

talhakimt Triangular or arrow-shaped pendants of agate or molded glass used as amulets, necklace pendants, and hair ornaments in India and Africa. Talhakimt were also manufactured in Europe and made of glass or plastic.

talisman From the Arabic *tilam* or Greek *talein,* which means "to initiate into the mysteries," an object intended to bring good fortune to its bearer, transforming him so that he can accomplish great deeds. The *amulet,* however, is thought to protect from harm and to ward off evil. Often the two terms are confused. The influence of the talisman depends on the social, spiritual, and emotional relevance to the particular culture and person. *See also* amulet.

tambour An embroidery technique that adapts well to embellishing the surface of fabric with beads, tambour uses a tool similar to a delicate crochet hook to stitch a continuous chain on the wrong side of the fabric; the beads show on the surface. Its chief advantage is that it can be done very fast. This technique requires that the beads be prestrung on the thread.

tanzanite A transparent sapphire blue to amethyst-violet gemstone composed of calcium aluminum silicate. It has an orthorhombic, multifaceted prism and striated crystal system, and its Mohs scale hardness is 6.5 to 7. It displays strong pleochroism and a vitreous or pearly luster. Discovered in 1967 in Tanzania, this zoisite gemstone species sometimes has tanzanite cat's-eye variations. The gemstone's apparent color may vary with natural and artificial light. The stone tends to be brittle. Tanzanite may be confused with amethyst, lazulite, iolite, sapphire, and spinel.

tanzanite imitations Glass imitations of tanzanite may have a tanzanite crown or be made from synthetic spinel pieces glued together with a colored glue. Tanzinique originates from the mineral fosterite and does not have the same pleochrism as natural tanzanite from zoisite. A cubic zirconia imitation in periwinkle or lavender is also on the market. Heat-treated beryl with a dark blue color, vanadium, simulates tanzanite.

tassel A decorative dangle or fringe tied together at one end that includes loosely hanging multiple braids, cords, or beaded fringe at the other. Tassels can be used to decorate not only jewelry but clothing, bags, purses, cushions, lampshades, hats, fans, drapery, and more.

tatting A textile art also used with beads. Tatting is formed with a series of lark's-head knots, half-hitch knots, loops, rings, and chains to create a lacy appearance. It may also be embellished with beads that are pre-strung prior to tatatting.

teardrop A bead shape also known as *drop,* these beads resemble teardrops in being rounded at the bottom and somewhat pointed at the top. Teardrops can be of any material and are usually drilled at the top, narrow end, from side to side.

teeth Animal teeth, sometimes fossilized, such as those of the bear, sloth, fruit bat, large cats, donkey, porpoise (dolphin, whale), shark, and even dogs or humans, have been fashioned into beads, usually strung through a hole across the top or root that allows them to display their length, menace, or beauty. Found all over the world, these tooth beads are more common in the Pacific islands or sub-Saharan Africa. The Penare people of the Amazon Basin make exotic beadwork that features the teeth or nails of animals found in the rainforest, like tapirs, monkeys, or caimans.

Beads shaped like animal teeth, and called tooth or teeth beads, although made of glass or gemstones, are used as pendants or amulets.

tenacity A mineral's resistance to breaking, bending, cutting, crushing, or being deformed by mechanical means. When a mineral breaks, its tenacity has been exceeded; the break is called a *fracture.*

Tennessee River shell A shell from various mussels living in the rivers of the eastern central United States, notably the Tennessee River, used to make beautiful beads. The mussels are also used in the farming of freshwater cultured pearls. Both the shell and the beads shown on the next page reveal the natural sheen and striations of color.

tennis bracelet Usually a thin, lightweight band worn on the wrist that has small diamonds or other gemstones linked in line, like that reportedly worn by tennis star Christine Evert in 1987 during a tennis match. It is sometimes called an eternity bracelet. Today rhinestones and crystals may be used instead of gemstones.

terbium A rare-earth metal that's silvery gray or white, malleable, ductile, and soft. Known for its brilliant fluorescence when added to glass, its addition creates brilliant crystal-like beads.

terra-cotta beads The Italian word *terra-cotta* means "baked earth." Terra-cotta beads are made of a brownish orange, waterproof ceramic. Since ancient times, terra-cotta has been used to make not just beads but vessels, water pipes, tiles, roof shingles, sculpture, and pottery as well as decorative motifs or details used in building construction.

test weight A standard calibration indicating the weight a product can withstand without breaking. To avoid breaking a string and possibly losing beads, it is important to use stringing material, such as wire of a sufficiently high test weight, to support the beads. Heavy or chunky gemstones or metal beads may require a higher than average stringing wire. *See* stringing thread and stringing wire.

textured beads Beads with a textured surface, such as rough, grainy, fuzzy, or silky, giving them added dimension and interest. Textured beads may have a distinctive underlying pattern or structure. Shown are some rich red textured heart beads.

Thai silver In Thailand, the standard of purity of Thai silver is 0.950 (95%); in the United States, the standard for sterling silver is 0.925 (92.5%). Silver, a relatively soft metal, is often produced with alloys that help it retain its shape and resist scratching. The Thai silver beads shown are handmade, with intricate patterns stamped on the surface, and have a type of pitch found inside the bead.

thaler Also known as a *taler,* a large silver coin that appeared in the 1518 and was soon commonly used as currency in Europe. The word *thaler* was taken from the city name Joachimstahl, Bohemia, where it was first minted. Silver coinage in Europe began with the 1472 introduction of the lira of over 6 grams; before that, the metal content of coins tended to be debased. Austrian, Dutch, German, Scandinavian, and various other mintings of coins called the thaler followed in the next four centuries. It was a popular European medium of exchange. The American dollar borrows its name from the sound of the term (in *thaler,* the emphasis is on the first syllable).

Later coins were minted with the date 1780, the year of the death of Hapsburg (or Habsburg) Empress Maria Theresa. She ruled Austria, Hungary, and Bohemia from 1740 to 1780. During her life she had insisted that the thaler coin be minted according to high-quality design, standard weight, and with a strict silver content. Scholars call the coin the MTT or Maria Theresa thaler, which has been called the most beautiful coin in the world. Although the thaler is no longer circulated as currency, many replicas have been struck by various European cities since that time, with the date 1780.

It has been a component in Arabian jewelry, often drilled to be hung as a pendant and embellished with stones, bells, and chains. The coins have also been melted down to create other silver jewelry and components.

thermal shock In glassmaking or ceramics, when the glass or ceramic is heated or cooled too quickly, the sudden temperature change may cause stress within the glass or ceramic that causes it to break, crack, or pop. This is caused when different parts of an object expand by different amounts when heated. *See also* COE (coefficient of expansion).

thin-nose pliers *See* needle-nose pliers.

thong Another term for *suede lace* or *leather lace,* leather cord used for stringing beads.

thread In sewing, thread is used to attach pieces of fabric together. In beading, it is used to attach beads to each other or to something else, to weave beads into a fabric, or to string them. Thread designed specifically for beadwork must be able to accommodate beads of a given type, size, and weight, so beading thread comes in a variety of types and sizes for different uses. Cotton, linen, silk, or other natural threads, which deteriorate more quickly than synthetics, are not recommended for beadwork projects unless the thread is required to match a particular fabric for clothing designs, especially for restoration of antiques. The most durable beading threads are synthetics, like polyester and nylon. If necessary, a cotton thread wrapped with a synthetic (like polyester) is a good compromise. Metallic thread has fine metal filament entwined in it. Thicker threads, often called cord or string, are used for stringing projects. *See* stringing thread and stringing wire.

thread conditioner A substance similar to beeswax that helps prevent tangles and knots in thread. Various manufacturers use different formulas of substances that make thread more manageable, some even reducing static electricity.

thread hole Sometimes spelled *threadhole*. This is more appropriately described as a bead hole or just a hole. The hole is an aperture, usually running the length of the bead, through which thread is passed (called the *thread path*). The area near the hole is sometimes called the lip.

thread path The route the thread or other stringing material takes through the bead, beginning with the first aperture or hole in the bead until it exits on the opposite side.

three-cut beads Seed beads with three or more irregular cuts, or facets, that add light reflection and sparkle. Three-cut beads are not the same as triangle beads. *See also* cut beads, two-cut beads, charlotte beads or true-cut beads, and hex beads.

three-dimensional beadwork A relative term for techniques or projects that produce three-dimensional rather than flat or seemingly two-dimensional items. *See also* free-form peyote stitch, beaded rosette, circular netting stitch, and three-dimensional gourd stitch.

Shown is a cardinal pajama fish, designed by Karin Houben, with carnelian eyes and a mouth stuffed with freshwater pearls. The body consists of Delica beads strung on silk-

nylon blend thread, shaped into three dimensions with modified brick and peyote stitches.

The three-dimensional doll of a man, created by a woman in the MonkeyBiz bead cooperative in South Africa, was beaded around a central core. Courtesy of MonkeyBiz.

three-dimensional gourd stitch This exquisite turquoise-blue bottle, done in three-dimensional gourd stitch by David Bingell, illustrates the use of this technique to cover three-dimensional objects. *See also* circular gourd stitch. Find stitch diagrams in Part V.

three-drop peyote stitch A technique similar to peyote stitch, but using three beads in the place of one when weaving beadwork fabric. Find stitch diagrams in Part V.

through hole The hole in a bead that passes all the way through it, defining the thread path, also used to describe such holes in pendants.

throw beads *See* Mardi Gras beads.

thulite An opaque pink variety of zoisite, sometimes called pink zoisite, composed of calcium aluminum silicate and rich in man-

ganese. Its Mohs scale hardness if 6.5 to 7 and its crystal system is orthorhombic with multi-faceted crystals that are striated. It may be mottled with white calcite. The gemstone demonstrates pleochroism and has a vitreous luster. The luster may be pearly on surfaces of cleavage. Typically cut into cabochons, it is found in Australia, Namibia, Norway, and the United States. It was discovered in 1820 in Norway and named after a mythical island, Thule.

thunderegg A spherical nodule that occurs in rhyolite (very acidic volcanic rock; the lava form of granite), welded tuff (rock consisting of consolidated volcanic ash), or perlitic (volcanic glass with concentric shell-like structure) rocks found in areas of volcanic activity. Similar to geodes, thundereggs are also called *agate eggs, star agate,* and *volcanic geodes.* Although not really a rock or a geode, their external appearance is unremarkable, while the inside is filled with opal, agate, chalcedony, jasper, amethyst, or quartz crystal.

According to Native North American folktales, when the Thunder Spirits living on top of Mount Hood and Mount Jefferson (sometimes modern place names are given) became angry with one another, they stole eggs from the thunderbird's nest and hurled them at each other during turbulent thunder and lightning storms. Thundereggs are sliced, polished, and made into jewelry, bolo ties, pendants, or used for bookends or attractive collector's items.

thunderstones A mineral concretion, such as belemnite, once thought in popular lore to be the result of thunderbolts and often associated with a thunder god. In ancient Greece, China, and other parts of the world, these apparently worked stone objects were thought to have fallen from the sky. They are also called thunder axes, storm stones, sky arrows, sky axes, thunderbolts, lightning stones, or thunder teeth; in Brazil, the favored term is *raio*, which means "lightning flash." They were fashioned by cultures in all parts of the world, according to the prevailing folklore, into protective amulets with various uses.

In Britain, from ancient times up to the 19th century, the so-called thunderstones were usually fossilized sea urchins. Made into beads or amulets, they were worn during thunderstorms with the thought of protecting the wearer from lightning.

Thuringian glass A glass made in the Thuringian Forest region of Germany, well known for its glass beads and hand-blown glass Christmas ornaments. A major glass-producing area since the 1500s, in the mid-1800s, beadmaking began as well as the cottage industry of glass ornaments. Delicate glass ornaments were made from glass molds. Their glassblowing skills presumably came from wandering Venetian traders.

Tibetan beads A general term for beads produced in Tibet that can include a variety of materials. Notable beads are made of silver or gemstones like turquoise, coral, agate, and carnelian. Tibet is thought to be the origin of dZi beads. *See also* etched carnelian.

tic-tac-toe beads Resembling the pattern of the age-old children's game, these Venetian beads have a characteristic design of intersecting horizontal and vertical lines filled with O's

(but no X's). In essence, the bead surface features white trails that form boxes that are filled with eyes.

tie-dye beads Glass beads that have bright, randomly mixed color patterns, similar to those resulting from tie-dyeing. They often have two or more colors.

Tiffany glass The studios of stained-glass artist Louis Comfort Tiffany (1848–1933) used many different kinds of glass to fashion lamps and other stained-glass artworks, later copied by other glassworkers and artisans. Here are a few of them: *Beveled glass* is clear glass with a bevel around the periphery that causes sunlight to create interesting color diffraction. *Drapery glass* has heavy folds that suggest fabric folds. *Fracture glass* has a pattern of irregular, thin glass wafers affixed to its surface. *Fracture-streamer glass* has a pattern of strings and thin glass wafers affixed to its surface. *Ring-mottle glass* has a pronounced mottled effect caused by heat and crystal growth. *Rippled glass* has a textured surface marked with waves. *Streamer glass* has strings that make up patterns affixed to the surface. Louis Comfort Tiffany was the son of the jeweler Charles Lewis Tiffany (1812–1902). Small pieces of these glass types can be made into pendants.

tiger stripe A type of glass bead that is usually amber with dark brown or black swirls. Shown is a turtle bead with tiger-stripe coloring.

tiger's-eye Also called *tiger eye;* a golden yellow or golden brown opaque gemstone, a variety of quartz (silicon dioxide). Crocidolite oxidized to a brown color with a silky luster on fractures display chatoyant stripes because the structural fibers are crooked or bent. The golden yellow reflections in the brown stone are caused by parallel fibrous inclusions that mimic the band of light in a cat's eye. Tiger's-eye has a Mohs scale of hardness rating of 6.5 to 7, and its trigonal crystal system has fibrous aggregates. It can be sensitive to some acids. The greenish gray stone is called *cat's-eye;* when bluish gray, it is called *hawk's eye;* and when brown, *bull's-eye* or *ox-eye quartz.* Red tiger's-eye is dyed. Natural tiger's-eye is found in South Africa, Sri Lanka, Brazil, Australia, and the United States. *See also* chatoyancy.

tigertail Clear nylon-coated steel wire that can be knotted and tied and will not stretch. This tough wire is especially useful for bead-stringing projects that involve heavy beads. Tigertail, originally a brand name, has become a generic term. Today the wire is produced under various brand names. *See also* stringing wire.

tile beads Tile beads are made of glass and similar in shape to pony beads, although a bit smaller, with thinner walls. The thinner wall makes for a larger hole; these beads are great for projects using leather lace and heavier cords.

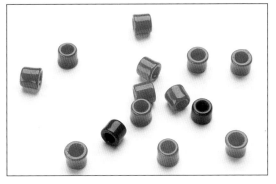

tin A silvery gray, lustrous metal that is malleable and ductile and can receive a high polish. It resists corrosion from seawater and freshwater and may serve as a protective coating for other metals. Acids and alkalis or their salts may cause it to corrode, however. The metal is highly crystalline, and forms known as *gray tin* or *white tin* are temperature dependent. Many tin alloys include bronze, phosphor bronze, pewter, soft solder, and white metal. In glassmaking, molten glass is floated above molten tin to achieve a smooth surface. Today tin foil is usually replaced by aluminum foil. Sometimes the term is improperly used to refer to various silvery metals that come in sheets. Important tin deposits are found in Southeast Asia and Tasmania. In Thailand, tin was first added to copper to make bronze in 3600 B.C., heralding the Bronze Age. Thai bronze was superior to the Mesopotamian bronze that contained the toxic substance arsenic rather than zinc. The Chinese learned the craft from the Thai artisans.

tin-cut *See* cut beads.

tin snips A common tool designed for cutting thin metal. It's advisable to use gloves when cutting metal because the cut edges may be very sharp. Various types suit specific purposes. The straight and duckbill types are used for cutting straight lines, the hawk's bill for cutting tight circles with little distortion, and the aviation and the universal for cutting straight and curved lines. Offset snips may be easier to use than the large, heavy, straight snips. The smaller, lighter types usually called *shears,* are preferable. Hardware-store varieties are likely to be too unwieldy for fine work. Shown are standard heavy-duty tin snips; photo by JG.

titania Synthetic rutile, developed in 1948.

titanite Also called *sphene,* a yellow, brown, green, or red transparent to opaque gemstone, composed of calcium titanium silicate with trace impurities of iron and aluminum and often cerium and yttrium. It is brittle, has an adamantine luster, and demonstrates strong pleochroism (trichroic). Its ability to disperse light is greater than that of a diamond. The crystal system is platy and its crystals are often wedged and twinned. Its Mohs scale hardness is 5 to 5.5. It is found in Brazil Mexico, Sri Lanka, Myanmar, Austria, and the United States.

titanium A lightweight, strong, opaque, lustrous metallic element with a white silvery or gray appearance found in abundance on earth. It resists corrosion (notably from acids, salts, and chlorine) and may be alloyed with other elements, such as aluminum, iron, copper, and vanadium, to produce lightweight objects. The metal resists tarnishing. Items manufactured of titanium can be anodized into six colors. Although titanium findings are not certified hypoallergenic, many people with sensitivities can wear them comfortably.

titanium dioxide Titanium dioxide creates a white permanent pigment used in gemstones, paints, plastics, and even toothpaste. Rutile, composed primarily of titanium dioxide, occurs naturally as inclusions in star sapphires and rubies and gives them their asterism.

toggle beads Elongated beads with a hole in the center. When strung, half of the bead projects above the string and half below. Common toggle-bead shapes include *dumbbells, rice grains,* and *dog bones.*

toggle clasp A type of clasp with a ring on one end and a crosspiece or bar on the other; the crosspiece fits through the ring to fasten a

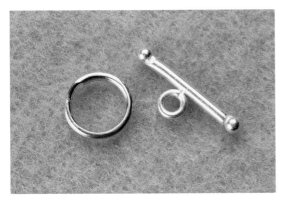

bracelet or necklace. Although the photo shows a sterling-silver toggle clasp, they are sometimes made of beads.

top hole Also called an *end hole,* a hole half-drilled into the top of a pendant or drop bead so that a glued or screwed-in finding can secure the pendant or bead when it is hung. A half-drilled bead can secure an eye screw for an earring, for instance.

topaz A transparent or translucent gemstone, composed of neosilicate of aluminum and fluorine, with a vitreous luster. Its crystal structure is orthorhombic, and it has a Mohs scale hardness of 8. The stone may be subject to cleavage flaws and requires care in cutting, polishing, and setting. Generally considered yellow or golden in color and sometimes referred to as *precious topaz,* pure topaz is transparent but may be tinted by impurities. Heat-treated yellow topaz will appear pink. *Imperial topaz* is reddish orange; the colors may come from iron and chromium. Some yellowish brown varieties may fade in sunlight. Different varieties of the gemstone topaz are subjected to enhancements, such as heat treatments, irradiation, or coating to produce blue, green, pink, red, peacock, teal, rainbow,

and silver topaz. For instance, titanium oxide thinly applied to the surface of topaz causes it to display iridescent colors. It is found in Afghanistan, Australia, Brazil, the British Isles, China, the Czech Republic, Germany, Italy, Japan, Madagascar, Namibia, Nigeria, Norway, Mexico, Myanmar (Burma), Pakistan, Russia, Sri Lanka, Sweden, the United States, and Zimbabwe. Blue synthetic topaz has been produced from colorless topaz. Topaz may be confused with apatite, aquamarine, chrysoberyl, citrine, precious beryl, fluorite, spinel, sapphire, tourmaline, zircon, and other gemstones.

topaz imitations Citrine, a variety of quartz, has been mistakenly called gold topaz or Madeira topaz.

torch A tool, also called a *burner,* employed in glass beadmaking or in metalwork that typically uses propane fuel surface-mixed with oxygen to produce a flame for melting and shaping glass or metals. Torches for glasswork or metalwork are available for beginners as well as those more advanced in jewelry-making. Some torches, for instance, are designed to work with soft glass, which melts at a lower temperature, but more expensive torches are available to work with hard (borosilicate) glass. In the lampworking industry, the torch usually remains stationary while the lamp-worker moves or manipulates the glass through the flame to shape it. *See also* fuel.

tortoise beads Amber-colored beads that have black stripes, or any translucent bead with usually horizontal, dark parallel stripes. Such beads in different base colors, such as blue or green, may be called tortoise beads.

tortoiseshell   The hawksbill turtle, an endangered species protected by the United Nations since the late 1970s, was once the preferred source of tortoiseshell. Today many imitations, such as Tortex, are on the market. The hard protective shell of the tortoise or turtle, composed of keratin, has been used for rattles and sculpted into fetishes. Tortoiseshell beads are rare, but the term is popularly used to describe beads made from glass, Bakelite, Lucite, resins, and plastic materials. Also called *pen shell,* a seashell that resembles tortoiseshell in olive greens, browns, and blacks with a spotted, striped, or mottled pattern has been used to make heishi. To distinguish genuine tortoiseshell from imitations, touch a particular spot on the surface with a hot point. Tortoiseshell gives off a musty natural odor like that of burning hair, whereas plastic will emit a more chemical odor. The same procedure works for testing amber.

tourmaline   A complicated group of transparent to opaque silicate minerals with a number of related species and varieties. Its Mohs scale hardness is 7 to 7.5, and the crystal system is trigonal with long crystals with a triangular cross-section and rounded sides and definite striation parallel to the main axis. Many varieties display pleochroism. These silicates of aluminum and boron may contain sodium, calcium, iron, magnesium, lithium, or other elements. The name *tourmaline* from the word *turamali* in Sinhalese means "stone with mixed colors." It may be colorless, pink, red, yellow, brown, green, blue, violet, black, or multicolored. Widely recognized varieties are *achroite* (colorless), *dravite* (yellowish brown to dark brown), *indicolite* (blue shades),

rubellite (pink, red, ruby, or violet tint), *schorl* (black), *siberite* (lilac to violet), and *verdelite* (green). Noted by composition are *buergerite* (iron tourmaline), *dravite* (magnesium tourmaline), *elbaite* (lithium tourmaline), *liddicoatite* (calcium tourmaline), *schorl* (iron tourmaline), *tsilaisite* (manganese tourmaline), and *uvite* (magnesium tourmaline). *Watermelon tourmaline* is pink in the middle followed by a layer of white, then green, similar to the fruit.

Shown is a gem-chip choker, designed by Melba Flores, strung with tourmaline chips, olive-colored 4-mm fire-polish beads, and bronze spacer beads.

trade beads   *Trade beads* generally refers to beads used for trade, especially by Europeans and Arabs, from about 1500 to 1800 for trading in Africa and Asia as well as in the New World. Trade beads also sometimes served as ballast to stabilize the weight of ships on outgoing journeys. Various beads, including Russian blues, Dutch or dogon donuts, aggrey, chevrons, padre, ambassador, and white-heart beads were used as trade beads. Popularly traded were glass beads made in Venice. Another general name for these various bead types that were traded is *African trade beads*. Some are still valued as trade beads today.

trade-wind beads Also called *trade beads,* old beads made in Europe and India and then transported by sailing ships to Arab traders, across to West Africa and then to the West Indies. The so-called trade winds defined the triangular trading routes from Europe to Africa and then to the West Indies. Naturally, the merchants and sailors onboard these sailing vessels, dating at least from the 1500s, traded for other goods besides beads at every port and finally returned home with cargoes of gold, ivory, palm oil, food, and more.

trail beads Beads made with molten canes of colored glass and having lines, threads, or *trails* of different-colored glass on the surface. *See also* wedding-cake beads.

trailing The process of applying threads or trails (or trailers) of hot glass over a glass bead to create a decorative pattern.

translucent A translucent stone or bead transmits weakened, diffused, distorted, or blurry light, so you cannot see through the object clearly, although light comes through. The material distorts the image.

transparent A transparent stone or bead allows you to see clearly through it. Light passes through it unobstructed.

transposition A simulant. *See* synthetic gemstones and imitation gemstones.

treasure necklace A necklace that features a variety of interesting and colorful beads and fetishes. Bear and fish fetishes, pearls, and beads of glass, bone, coral, turquoise, carnelian, abalone, and cowrie shell decorate the necklace shown here. The glass beads include fire-polish, chevron, pony, foil, and teardrop.

tremolite A transparent to opaque colorless, white, gray-brown, or pink stone composed of calcium magnesium silicate hydroxide. It has a vitreous, silky, or dull luster. It is a member of the actinolite and ferro-actinolite mineral series in which two or more ions can substitute for each other. It is composed of microscopically fibrous crystals called *asbestos.* It has a Mohs scale hardness of 5 to 6. The green variety of actinolite is nephrite and the other is jadeite. One variety is called mountain leather or mountain cork, which appears to form a feltlike mass. Violet tremolite is called hexagonite. The fibrous variety used as asbestos is toxic.

tri beads These are plastic beads with three points or "spokes," which make them look like little propellers. *See also* interlocking beads.

triangle beads Three-sided or triangular-shaped beads come in many sizes and materials. The light reflected by the three sides can add sparkle and texture to a jewelry design.

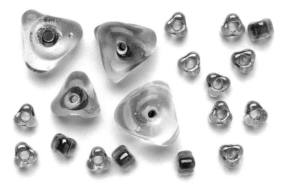

trichroic A gemstone or crystal that displays three different colors, depending on the angle from which the stone is viewed. *See also* dichroic and pleochroic.

trichroism Having the property of displaying three different colors, with each color perceived depending on the viewing angle at which the gemstone or crystal is viewed.

trillings Twinned crystals found in the crystal structure of chrysoberyl and other minerals.

troy ounce A system for measuring the weight of precious metals like gold, silver, and platinum that has continued to be in use since the Middle Ages. A troy ounce equals 31.1 grams or 480 grains, and 12 troy ounces make up the pound. Note that the troy ounce and apothecary ounce are equivalent. The abbreviation of troy ounce is *ozt*.

In the modern metric system, adopted as the international standard in 1958, the avoirdupois ounce (437.5 grains) equals 28.35 grams, and 16 ounces are equal to the pound. The latter system is generally used in the United States, Canada, Europe, and Australia.

tsavorite A light-to-deep radiant green gemstone from the garnet group, a variety of grossularite, composed of calcium aluminum silicate. Trace amounts of vanadium or chromium lend it its green color. Mined in Kenya, it was named after the Tsavo National Park; the Tsavo River runs through it. It has a Mohs scale hardness of 6.5 to 7.5 and the crystal system is cubic. It is also found in Tanzania and Madagascar.

tube beads Beads with a tubular or cylindrical shape, but usually longer than a conventional cylinder bead, as shown in the photo.

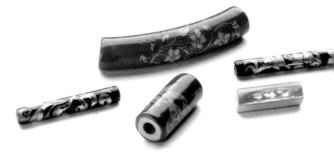

tubular peyote A bead stitch that results in a tube shape. The desired tube shape can also be created with round peyote stitch or flat peyote stitch and then adding a seam up one side to form a tube. The beaded cross shown is one example of using the tubular peyote stitch to create a three-dimensional object. The stitch and resulting object are also called peyote tube. Find stitch diagrams in Part V.

tubular right-angle weave A three-dimensional variation of the right-angle-weave stitch. *See also* right-angle weave. Find stitch diagrams in Part V.

tumbling Also called *tumble polishing, barreling,* or *barrel polishing,* a lapidary technique for polishing and smoothing hard surfaces, like those of minerals and stones, with abrasive grit and a lubricant inside a rubber or plastic barrel that is rotated. A rough rock may take 4 to 5 weeks to polish by tumbling. Glass, metal, and some other materials may also be tumbled.

turquoise A translucent to opaque stone, composed of a hydrous phosphate of copper and aluminum. Its crystal system is triclinic or with grape-shaped aggregates, nodules, or masses, and the Mohs scale of hardness is 5 to 6. Turquoise has a waxy or matte luster. The colors range from nearly white to powder blue, bright sky blue, bluish green, and yellow-green (apple green). It may have a bluish white, black, or golden brown matrix; limonite veins; or be peppered with pyrite flakes. The blue color is thought to come from copper, while the green may come from iron impurities that replace some aluminum or that result from dehydration. Finer grades are valued as gemstones that may be used rough or polished, often as nuggets, in cabochons, or carved into diverse shapes. The somewhat porous stone can fracture unevenly. Turquoise may be found intergrown with malachite or chrysocolla. Iron may substitute for aluminum, making the stone green, and impurities may account for other colors. Most so-called turquoise (a mixture with *chalcosiderite*) found in the United States includes iron.

Turquoise is commonly polished or enhanced; the porous stone can be soaked in an artificial resin to harden it and improve its color. Oil, paraffin, Berliner blue, aniline dyes, and copper salt may also be used to improve the color. The word *turquoise* is thought to derive from the French term *pierre turquin* for "blue stone" or from the word *turquois* for "Turkish." Traders brought the stone, found in Turkish bazaars, to Europe in the 16th century.

The earliest settlers in the Sinai about 8,000 years ago were, according to archaeologists, miners presumably drawn by the abundant copper and turquoise deposits. At least by 3500 B.C., the turquoise veins of Serabit el-Khadim (Khadem) in Sinai had been discovered; Egyptians controlled mining operations.

It was found in China over 3,000 years ago. Turquoise has been popularly used for jewelry and as a paint pigment. It is also found in Afghanistan, Argentina, Australia, Brazil, northern Chile, Israel, Mexico, Tanzania, Turkistan, England, and the United States.

Among the many types of turquoise, independent of geographic location, are *agaphite* or vitreous Persian; *American* or *Mexican* (pale blue to greenish, porous); cobweb matrix; *Edisonite* (mottled blue); *eggshell* (with crackled appearance); and *Johnite* (scaly, vitreous). *Meshed* (or Mashhad) turquoise comes from the city by that name in northern Iran. The stone has also been called *Aztec stone, celestial stone,* and *white buffalo stone* or *albino turquoise* (from Nevada mines). So-called new rock may fade rapidly, while old-rock refers to Iranian high-quality sky-blue turquoise. *Rock turquoise* may have more matrix than turquoise composition and appear brownish or grayish. *Sea form* refers to knobby nuggets that are polished but not shaped. *Nuggets* may also be pebble-size tumbled stones. *Turtle-back* has a cobweblike pattern. *Oriental* may designate genuine turquoise in contrast with simulants.

The stone's color may change when it comes in contact with heat, light, perspiration,

body and other oils, cosmetics, perfumes, or other chemicals. Rings and bracelets should be removed when washing hands. It should be stored loosely, without other jewelry that might scratch it, and cleaned only with a soft cloth. Shown are three cabochons, demonstrating light, dark, and speckled turquoise. *See also* yellow turquoise.

turquoise imitations   The stone turquoise may be confused with the minerals amazonite, chrysocolla (azurlite), lazulite, faustite, smithsonite, hemimorphite, wardite, and variscite (Utah turquoise).

Chalcedony, jasper, marble, howlite, magnesite, prosopite, and serpentine may be dyed to look like turquoise. Odontolite, fossilized bone or tooth, also called *bone turquoise* (vivianite makes it blue), was a turquoise substitute in the south of France. Amazon stone, Eilat stone, gibbsite, calcite and plastic binder, and heated and dyed beryl and quartz rock may simulate turquoise.

Luroc or *lauric* is a synthetic turquoise. *Viennese* turquoise is a false or misleading name for blue-tinted argillaceous earth (clay) or an amorphous mixture of aluminum phosphates, copper oleate, and neolith. *Neolite* and *Reese* turquoise are good imitations with a dark matrix. Powdered turquoise pieces may be baked with a glue, glass, porcelain, or plastic mixture. Chinaware, clay, enamel, faience, glass and frit, limestone and marble, plaster of Paris, and soapstone can also mimic turquoise. *See also* Kingman turquoise, African turquoise, and yellow turquoise.

turquoise treatments   Much turquoise on the market has been stabilized or hardened by use of inorganic mineral salts, such as colloidal silica and sodium silicate (water glass). Oiled and waxed stones may sweat when exposed to sunlight or heat or develop a white surface bloom over time. The ancients typically oiled and waxed their stones. More stable plastics, water glass, and epoxy, when bonded to the stone, enhance its color and luster. Many treatments disguise flaws or fool consumers. Some dyes, such as Prussian blue, may fade or rub off. Fillers may be added. Finer turquoise may be glued to an inferior base. A heat probe can reveal plastic, oil, or wax treatment.

tweezers A tool used in beading to tie and untie knots in stringing thread or cord. It is popular for pearl knotting, although the pearl-knotting tool is specifically designed for that purpose. Several tweezers, made of carbon or stainless steel, are designed for flattening, pulling, and shaping or picking out details of glass beads when they are hot.

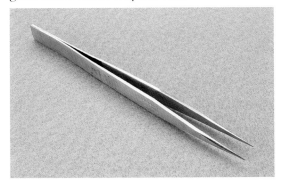

twill stitch A rather uncommon name for flat peyote stitch.

twisted bugle beads A bugle bead with an added twist or turn, giving it a slightly angular appearance and an interesting reflective sur-

face. Shown are black matte and amber silver-lined twisted bugle beads.

twisted wire Jewelry-making wire that has been twisted or turned together to give it an attractive spiraled appearance.

twisted-wire needle A beading aid, made of twisted wire with a hoop or ring (eye) at one end for threading the stringing material. When the wire is passed through a bead, the hoop collapses and the string material is firmly

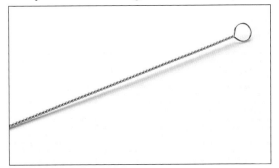

attached. Pearl-knotting cord is usually sold on paper cards with a twisted-wire needle already attached.

twisty A type of stringer (a drawn-out slender glass cane) in which two or more colors are twisted together before applying designs to the surface of glass beads. It resembles a candy cane or a barber pole. *See* stringer and trailing.

two-cut beads Seed beads that have two cuts or facets that add sparkle. *See also* charlotte beads, three-cut beads, and hex beads.

two-drop peyote stitch This technique, also called *gourd stitch* or *peyote stitch,* uses two beads in the place of one to weave the bead fabric. Find stitch diagrams and graphs in Part V.

two-tone beads Also called *inside-color beads,* usually with one color inside and another one outside the bead. They may also have two different finish colors. Some two-tone beads are merely dyed on the inside, but higher-quality ones have colored glass both inside and outside. The color is generally stable over time and does not wear or fade.

The first photo shows the inside color beads with clear glass on the outside. The second photo shows large fire-polish beads that have two different finish colors on the surface. The lavender beads are lavender on the inside and clear glass on the outside.

U

Ultrasuede A trade name for a synthetic suede, made from polyester microfiber and nonfibrous polyurethane, used as a backing for beadwork projects. The stain-resistant fabric can be machine-washed in water or dry-cleaned. It is relatively color-fast and durable.

umbilical pouch The Lakota mother traditionally prepared a beaded pouch before her baby was born. After the baby's birth, the umbilical cord was put inside the pouch. The turtle pouch, symbolizing strength and long life, was favored for the female child, and the lizard pouch, symbolizing speed and the ability to adapt to change—since it even sheds its tail to escape a predator—was preferred for the male child. According to custom, the pouch was kept for the child's lifetime and buried with him or her. The Dakota and Natoka, who like the Lakota are members of the Sioux Confederacy, had a similar practice.

unakite An opaque stone of mottled salmon pink and green, sometimes called *unikite*. It has a Mohs scale hardness of 6 to 7. A mixture of pink feldspar, green epidote, and clear quartz, the stone can be carved and well-polished. It is found in the United States, Brazil, China, and South Africa. Among remnants from glacial drift on the beaches of Lake Superior are pebbles of unakite. *Epidosite* has the same composition as unakite but lacks the quartz. Shown is a simple bracelet strung on 1-mm elastic, using 12-mm round unakite beads accented with size 8 bronze glass beads and unakite chips.

"up-down-up thing" A phrase describing the thread path for beginning each row of brick stitch. The technique prevents the thread from showing on the side edges and helps lock the beads in place so that they sit flat and straight. While my coined phrase may not be in general beading parlance, it's helpful.

uvarovite A transparent to translucent emerald green stone, calcium chromium silicate, member of the garnet group. It is sometimes called *uvaroite* or *uvarolite*. This stone, named after a Russian statesman and amateur mineral collector, Count Sergei Uvarov, rarely occurs in gemstone quality. It has a Mohs scale hardness rating of 7.5 and a vitreous luster. It is found in Finland, Poland, Canada, the Ural Mountains of Russia, and the United States.

Uvarovite may sometimes be confused with emerald and demantoid.

vanadium A silvery gray metal used in alloys, such as that for improving stainless steel. It is soft, ductile, and strong, and resists corrosion from alkalis, certain acids, and saltwater. Vanadium added to corundum serves as a coloring agent, producing the appearance of alexandrite. It is found in the deep blue mineral cavansite (calcium vanadium silicate). Powdered metallic vanadium is a fire hazard and highly toxic.

varietal Indicating or characterizing a variety, such as a variety of a given mineral or stone type or group. *See* variety.

variety In gemstone terminology, a variety is a subset of a mineral group, distinguished by different color, appearance, structure, or other characteristics from other members of the particular mineral group. It may have a slightly altered chemical composition, or certain inclusions may alter its appearance.

vaseline beads A greasy patina distinguishes these Czech trade beads, giving them the sheen of their namesake petroleum product, Vaseline. Their facets are partly molded and partly ground, and their color derives from minute quantities of uranium salts. They are also called *Anna green* and *Anna yellow*.

Original vaseline beads fluoresce under ultraviolet light. (The name vaseline for the beads is lowercase, but the brand name of the product takes an initial capital letter.)

vegetable ivory *See* tagua nut.

Venetian glass beads For centuries, glass beads made in Venice, Italy, have been considered among the highest quality beads on the world market. Among the many fancy and ornate bead types are *lampwork, silver-foiled or gold-foiled, chevrons, millefiori,* and *dichroic* beads. In the last 200 years, manufacturers and individual bead artisans all over the world have been borrowing Venetian, Murano, or similar techniques to create beautiful beads. *See also* Murano glass beads.

vermeil Gold-plated sterling silver. The outer layer or coating of gold is usually electroplated onto the silver base and may appear similar to gold or gold-fill. The thickness of the gold plate will determine the richness of the finished bead. The term is pronounced "vehr-MAY." According the Federal Trade Commission in the United States, to qualify as vermeil, the gold must be at least 10-karat fineness and have a thickness of 100 millionths of an inch or 2.5 microns. Sterling silver covered with another layer of metal other than gold cannot be called vermeil. The older fire-gilding technique, invented in France in the mid-1700s, involved the use of mercury; as a result, some artisans developed blindness. Today most vermeil is produced by a safer electrolytic process. *See also* gold-filled and gold-plated.

Gold-plated bronze or copper are also sometimes referred to as vermeil.

vertebrae Bones from the spines of many types of animals, formed naturally with holes, are used as beads. Although biodegradable, such beads may last longer than other natural materials. Among commonly used vertebrae for beads are those of bovine, fish, and snake species. Shown are fish vertebrae beads from Gambia, Africa. *See also* sea urchin spines.

vertical netting In this beading stitch, beads are added along a vertical plane. The beaded collar shown below and on opposite page was reportedly made by a Lakota artisan. *See also* horizontal netting and circular netting. Find stitch diagrams in Part V.

Viking beads A variety of beads fashioned or worn by the Vikings from roughly A.D. 750 to 1100, when these Scandinavian traders and raiders had the greatest impact on European culture and trade. A sophisticated glass bead-making operation existed in Ribe, Denmark.

Among the beads found in excavations of ancient burial sites and dwellings are colorful lampwork and millefiori beads, shaped from local amber and jet or from imported carnelian, silver, rock crystal, garnet, amethyst, gold, and bronze. Treasure necklaces are strung with beads in a somewhat symmetrical fashion with "treasures," small pendants of gold or other precious metals as well as amulets hung at regular intervals. Beads were also gathered during raids or bought at markets. Viking trading, as well as pillaging, extended into much of Eurasia and the Middle East. Combed, blue glass melon, foiled, millefiori, eye, round, rondelle, tubular, flat, and square beads were created by local Viking flameworkers. The Vikings wore these beads around the neck and also suspended them from brooch pins on dresses and aprons. Males often wore a large so-called *sword bead,* associated with but not attached to a sword.

vintage beads Classic beads, valued for their antique qualities, shapes, colors, materials, and craftsmanship. Generally, vintage beads are more expensive than their modern counterparts because certain molds or styles are no longer available or exist in limited quantities. They are usually identified by their approximate date and country of origin. For example, vintage beads may be sold as "circa 1920 western Germany." In earlier centuries, bead production tended to be more of a cottage industry with individualized glass molds, refined production techniques, and color recipes that were closely guarded family or trade secrets.

vintage buttons European glass bead and button makers of the late 1800s to early 1900s were highly skilled artisans, guarding their molds and their glass "recipes" as trade secrets. Interrupted by political unrest and war, many of their family resources and secrets were literally buried and lost, so the glass buttons that still exist are rare and collectible. Today, modern glassmakers are trying to replicate patterns and molds to satisfy the demand of the current market. The bracelet shown, made by Sylvia Elam, with blue iris charlotte-cut beads, uses the beaded-knitting technique and features a Czech glass button, probably made in the early 1900s, as a clasp or closure for the wristband.

vitrail A fancy bead finish, which some man-ufacturers apply to crystal and glass beads, that has silver and flashes of brilliant colors in greens, pinks, and golds. It provides a rich, warm, and expensive appearance to the beads. It may also be described as mirror, iridescent, or aurora borealis (AB) finish, although there are subtle differences among these various finishes. The French word *vitrail* means "stained-glass window." Shown are bicone-shaped Swarovski crystal beads with a vitrail finish.

vitreous Glassy; having the luster of broken glass or quartz.

vitrified glass To convert into glass or a glassy substance by heat and fusion. Vitrified glass is a surface made shiny or nonporous by fusing it with heat or changing it into glass or a glassy substance.

volcanic glass *See* Apache tears, Pele's tears, and obsidian.

voluta shell The shell from mollusks common to southeast Asia and found on the coasts of Indonesia, Java, Australia, New Zealand, New Caledonia, and Chile, among other places. The Volutidae are a large family of extremely diverse gastropods with 43 genera and about 200 species. They are also called *volutes*. Popular shells with peach or brown bands, such as that of the *Voluta magnifica* or the *Voluta noblis,* are members of the diverse *Voluta* genus. An attractive shell from one species comes in warm creamy shades of

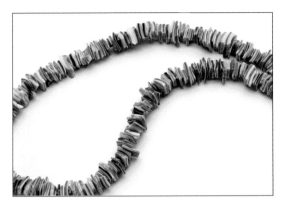

off-white to sand and chocolate. Squared-off pieces of shell like those shown make eye-catching heishi.

W

wampum A string of beads made of quahog (quohog or quahaug, also called suckauhock) shells, a variety of hard-shell clams with beautiful purple and white striations, found along the North Atlantic coast of North America. Probably the most important beads in United States and Canadian history, wampum was once used as legal tender in the original thirteen Colonies. The term *wampum* comes from the Algonquian *wampumpeag,* which means "white strings [of beads]." The Ojibwe term was *waabaabiinyag.* Wampum is also called *peag.* A string of white shell beads made from the channeled whelk (*Busycotpus canaliculatus*) shell was also favored as wampum by Native North Americans or First Peoples. Traders had reportedly confused

wampi (white) and *saki* (black) for centuries. Wampum beads were handmade in a time-consuming process and carefully shaped and drilled, but some breakage is inevitable. The purple beads are twice as expensive and valuable as the white ones.

Prior to European contact, wampum belts were used to record treaties and important agreements between First Nations. Within Native North American cultures, wampum held great significance, involving social and spiritual values. Wampum was also used to honor friendships. It was used in burial, adoption, and marriage ceremonies and during elections. Coastal nations used wampum as a form of barter, especially with inland tribes. A typical string of wampum could be about 6 feet (180 cm) long and contain from 350 to 550 beads.

Since the European colonists had no coinage or legal tender, they adopted wampum as a currency since it was valuable, somewhat rare, handmade, and available.

The Iroquois confederacy–Seneca (People of the Great Hill), Cayuga (People of the Swamp), Onondaga (Keepers of the Fire), Oneida (People of the Standing Stone), Mohawk (People of the Flint), and later Tuscarora—share a sophisticated record-keeping system of beautifully designed wampum belts. Although many original wampum belts have been lost or stolen, the concepts of peace, democracy, and forgiveness have long been ideals and "the backbone of the law" of the Haudenosaunee, "People of the Longhouse," what the Iroquois called themselves. The first remembered use of shell wampum belt was by the Great Peacemaker (Deganawida) and his helper Hiawatha (Ayonwatha) in 1550. The Hiawatha belt represents the first United Nations type of agreement. The original values of the Iroquois Confederacy were copied by the founders of the United States Constitution and indeed by the present-day United Nations itself. Together the Peacemaker and Hiawatha inspired warriors to bury their weapons, symbolically, beneath a sacred tree to bring peace and unity to the original Five Nations. The belt commemorates the founding of the League of the Iroquois under a constitution five centuries ago. It is known as the Hiawatha or Unity Belt, signifying equality and understanding among separate nations and the unity into which they are bound by respect and common beliefs. The Hiawatha Belt comprises a total of 6,574 wampum beads; it has 38 columns and 173 rows with 892 white and 5,682 purple beads. The beads alone are probably worth over $500,000 American dollars in today's currency.

One could say that the Pequot War of 1637 was fought over wampum beads. Dutch and English settlers, realizing how important wampum was, declared war against the Pequot, who controlled the wampum trade as well as the lush Connecticut Valley. The marvelous history and various cultural connections involving wampum are far too complex to detail here.

Shown are genuine white wampum beads with purple striations, graciously lent by Andrew H. Bullock (Wandering Bull). Modern jewelry designers often accent the prized purple or white beads with sterling silver.

warp The set of threads (or yarn) running vertically or lengthwise that are stretched across a bead loom when it is first set up, before weaving begins. Woven through the warp is the *weft:* horizontal thread-bearing beads, or yarn for cloth fabrics. In making fabrics, the original yarns of wool, cotton, and flax had to be stretched. Synthetics commonly used in weaving fabrics today do not need to be. *See also* weft.

waterfall loomed necklace Bead strands of graduated lengths give this design its name. The necklace shown opposite page, top, designed by Rena Charles, consists of loomed beadwork and stringing. The seed beadwork displays delightful details—pen-shell heishi and coral bits for accents and is finished with sterling-silver cones. The beadwork mimics the famous Navajo rug patterns so wildly popular in weaving.

watermelon beads A variety of African trade bead, these chevron beads have the shape and colors of watermelon slices. They are often green with thin stripes or layers of red, light yellow, and white. They are also seen with stripes of brown and blue.

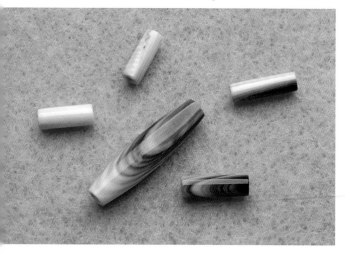

waxed cotton cord *See* cotton cord.

waxed linen Linen is a strong vegetable fiber with two to three times the strength of cotton. This very sturdy material is excellent for stringing heavy beads, as well as basket-making and other weaving projects.

waxing A gemstone treatment that involves the application of wax to enhance color of the stone by filling in and disguising fine surface cracks.

wedding-anniversary metals Metals associated with, serving as symbols of, or honoring wedding anniversaries. For the 6th anniversary the metal is iron; the 8th, bronze; the 9th, copper; the 10th, tin or aluminum; the 11th, steel; the 25th, silver; the 50th, gold; and the 70th, platinum. *See also* wedding-anniversary stones.

wedding-anniversary stones Gemstones traditionally associated with or serving as symbols of wedding anniversaries. For the 15th anniversary, the crystal (leaded glass, typically cut into facets) is the favored symbol, but this is not usually considered a gemstone. Other years and stones are the 17th, turquoise; the 30th, pearl; the 35th, coral or jade; the 40th, ruby; the 45th, sapphire; the 55th, emerald; the 60th and the 75th, diamond; and the 65th, blue sapphire. Since the Middle Ages, wedding anniversary gifts have been a tradition. In her 1922 book on etiquette, Emily Post suggested what was appropriate for the first, 5th, 10th, 20th, 25th, and 50th years of marriage. In her 1957 book, the list was expanded. Later gem and jewelers' associations as well as florists have added to the gift list. *See also* wedding-anniversary metals.

wedding beads In many modern western cultures, pearls may be given to the bride, often by her family, to wear at her wedding since they symbolize purity. Many different traditions exist throughout the world in which beads are considered symbols of love and marriage.

In the early 1800s in the Black Forest region of Germany, the customary bridal crown was embellished with numerous blown-glass and lined beads and mirrors to deflect the evil eye.

Other beads, commonly called wedding beads, are shaped like a pear or lightbulb. These multicolored beads originated in Czechoslovakia and were made for the African trade. They were reportedly used in West Africa and Mali for special occasions, including weddings. In smaller sizes, they are also called drops. In northern India, the groom gives a different type of love beads, called a *mangal sutra* with black beads strung with gold beads and pendants, to his bride. The amount of gold in the strung beads is an indicator of the groom's wealth.

In southern India, the *taali,* a string of beads and anthropomorphic pendants, serves as a wedding gift and good luck charm. The Ndebele in southern Africa make a beaded veil given as a gift to the bride, who wears it on her wedding day. The groom's family makes a plain-canvas bridal apron, called a *jishogolo* (alternate spellings *ijogolo, jocolo,* and *tshogholo*). The apron has a rectangle with five panels or "calves" that allude to the bride's ability to bear children. After the wedding, the wife embroiders the apron with seed beads in a simple design for everyday use or in more elaborate patterns for ceremonial use. Making beaded attire is the domain of Ndebele women, who fashion a wide variety of beaded garments to mark transitions in women's lives.

Maasai men wear a long V-shaped beaded wedding necklace that reaches to the waist, while Maasai women wear a similar necklace beaded on leather, often adorned by straps that hang below the knees and may have cowrie-shell pendants attached.

wedding-cake beads Ornate lampwork beads embellished on the surface with trails or lines, resembling vines, of different colors of glass. Shown are fancy cobalt-colored oval beads. These beads come in a variety of colors. *See also* trail beads.

wedding dowry A gift, typically of money or valuables, given by the bride's family to that of the groom at the time of their children's marriage. Property given to the bride by the groom or his family is called a *wedding dower.* Beads and other jewelry have been customarily given as part of dowries or dowers in cultures throughout the world. Beads may reflect social status or wealth and be passed down in families for generations.

weft The set of horizontal threads, carrying the strung beads, shuttled back and forth across the vertical warp threads. In weaving fabrics, the weft yarn is also called *woof* or *fill. See also* warp.

welding Fusing two or more metals or thermoplastics by melting them and adding a filler material to create a weld puddle at the joint. Heat, such as that from a gas flame, laser, electron beam, ultrasound, or friction, together with pressure produce the weld. A few types of welding are fusion, resistance, arc, gas, energy-beam, solid-state, friction, stir, magnetic-pulsive, explosion, and cold welding. *See also* soldering and brazing.

whipstitch An overcast stitch used to cover the edge of an object with beads, like the brim of the baseball cap shown. Find stitch diagrams in Part V.

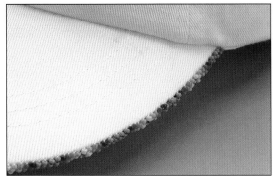

white bronze The term in China, *paktong* or *pakfong,* for nickel silver. Nickel silver or white bronze has no silver content. An alloy of copper, nickel, and often zinc, white bronze is sometimes used in jewelry as imitation silver.

white clamshell Shown are squared-off pieces of clamshell from marine or freshwater bivalve mollusks that have been drilled for use as beads. The white shell of the channeled whelk (*Busycotypus canaliculatus*) was popularly used in North America for heishi and other beads. But many other species of clam were probably used as well. *See* heishi.

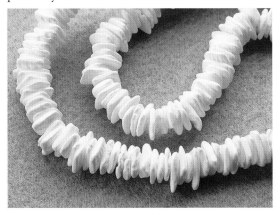

white copper Another name for nickel (*baitung*) in use in China from about 1700 to 1400 B.C.

white gold An alloy of gold and platinum, palladium, nickel, or zinc that is sometimes substituted for platinum. This precious metal is considered even more expensive or rare than gold. Rhodium may be electroplated onto white gold to give it a white surface.

Here are two common formulas for making white gold. For 14-kt white gold, it is 58% gold + 20% copper + 14.5% nickel + 7.5% zinc. For 18-kt white gold, it is 75% gold + 5% copper + 15% nickel + 5% zinc.

white hearts Beads with two layers of glass: a white one at the center, or heart, and a thin outer layer of red, coral, pink, blue, or green. Like green hearts, a similar bead also produced in Venice, but earlier, white hearts are made of wound and drawn glass. Available sizes range from small seed beads to large pony or crow beads. *See also* cornaline d'Aleppo and Hudson Bay beads.

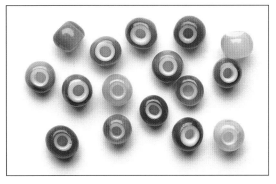

whorl A form that spirals or coils. A whorl spindle, usually made of clay or ceramic in the shape of a bead, is used for weaving thread or yarn from fiber. Whorl beads, however, are wound-glass beads. *See also* spindle whorls.

A whorl is also a turn or coil of a snail shell or seashell.

whorl beads *See* wound-glass beads.

wire Jewelry wire or craft wire is more flexible than conventional wire and comes in smaller sizes or gauges (thickness or diameter of the wire). Wire can also be used for various crafts and may incorporate beading. Shown is an example of wire work created by a woman from the MonkeyBiz bead cooperative in South Africa. *See* jewelry wire and stringing wire.

wire cutters A tool designed to cut wire of different gauges. Stringing wire, or nylon-coated wire cable, requires only lightweight jewelry cutters, while larger-gauge or harder metals call for more heavy-duty cutters.

wire-formed beads Glass beads shaped around a wire that is then withdrawn, leaving the hole for stringing. The wire may have been coated with a kind of sludge or slip that allows easy removal. Some of this substance may remain inside the bead's hole.

wire-strung A method of stringing beads on wire shaped to form a bracelet, bangle, or armband. The technique is used extensively by the Maasai and Samburu (Lokop) of Kenya and northern Tanzania. The Maasai piece shown is from the collection of David Bingell. *See also* wired beadwork and beaded wirework.

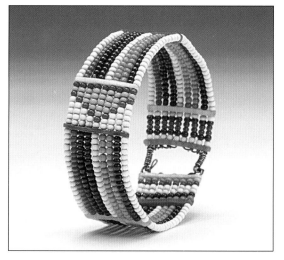

wire-wrapped beads A method of wrapping thin jewelry wire around beads or gemstones to use as jewelry components. With loops attached, they can be used as pendants or *fastened* together to form a chain. Shown are

wire-wrapped beads that terminate the bead fringe on a key ring.

wired beadwork *See* beaded wirework.

wonder beads *See* miracle beads.

wooden beads Wooden beads come from the bark, roots, trunk, or branches of many different trees. The wood may be etched with pyrography (fire writing), carved, and varnished, enhanced with oils, or painted. The advantage of wooden beads is that they are lighter than glass or metal, which can be a factor in jewelry design; they can also have large holes. Some manufacturers call them *Pinocchio beads*, after the wooden puppet of storybook fame. The painted beads shown have intricate designs.

worry beads Similar to prayer beads, these beads offer a type of kinesthetic comfort; some regard them as a material manifestation of a communion with a higher power that can assist in dealing with everyday stressors. They can be a single bead or a set of strung beads.

wound-glass beads These beads are made by twisting or wrapping hot glass around a rod or mandrel. A bead release or separator substance is used to prevent the glass bead from sticking to the mandrel. Wound glass is one of the oldest ways to create a glass bead. Ancient Romans were among the first to make them, and wound-glass beads were made in Iran (Persia) between A.D. 900 and 1300. Common winding techniques are furnace-winding and lamp-winding. In *furnace-winding,* an iron mandrel is dipped into a crucible inside a furnace, and a peak from the molten glass is used to begin to wind the glass around the mandrel. This process also allows the bead to be shaped or decorated. After the bead's final heating, it can be knocked off the mandrel; iron cools faster than glass.

In *lamp-winding,* prepared glass rods or canes are heated over a small lamp and the molten glass is wound around a wire. This technique allows more complex decoration than the furnace-winding technique. Venetian beads were not made by lamp-winding until after 1750.

wraparound jewelry Necklaces, bracelets, rings, and other jewelry made with flexible memory wire that retains its shape when bent and fitted to neck, wrist, arm, or finger. Wraparound jewelry does not require a clasp.

wrapped stitch The technique of stringing beads onto thread and then wrapping them around an object to cover part or all of its

watches so that they can be worn rather than pocketed. They are also worn for special events or fund-raisers, and like armbands, they may denote support of specific causes.

writing beads *See* Krobo beads.

wrought iron Iron with little carbon content (less than 0.05%) that is tough, malleable, and ductile. It can be easily forged. Wrought iron, or "worked iron," is made from the so-called bloom of porous iron mixed with slag and other impurities. Some slag inclusions can give it a fibrous or grainy look. Wrought iron has been shaped into all kinds of objects for centuries. In the Middle Ages, it was smelted in a blast furnace and then processed or refined in a finery force and then a puddling furnace. Modern wrought iron is relatively pure and can be easily welded.

surface. This stitch is also referred to as *coiling.* Zulu beaders commonly use the wrapped stitch for dolls made with fabric glued around a cardboard shape or cone that serves as an anchor or core around which beads are wrapped. Beads strung on needle and thread are wrapped around the object and tacked down from time to time to keep the beads in place. Yarn is often used for the doll's hair. Wrapping fabric and beads around gourds is another method of creating dolls. A Ndebele artist in southern Africa used the wrapped stitch to make the doll shown. *See also* lane stitch.

wristband A band or bracelet that encircles the wrist or lower sleeve around the wrist. It can be made of leather, metal, silicon, ceramic, cloth ribbons, beads, or any number of materials. Wristbands are typically added to

X

X-ACTO knife Also called a *precision, hobby,* or *craft knife,* a cutting tool with a retractable blade that allows razor-sharp precision, used in a great range of crafts. The knife easily cuts leather or fabric backing for beaded projects like belt buckles and hair barrettes. It also cuts leather into fringe, a common element in Native North American crafts. X-ACTO is a brand name.

Y

Y necklace A necklace design that has a long, straight pendant in the middle, forming the letter *Y*. Notice that the clasp is in front, making it easy to fasten. This type of necklace is typically short, between 15 and 17 inches (38 and 43 cm) in length. The necklace bead strand is attached to a rosary finding called a connector link, and the pendant is a beautiful floral lampwork bead, accented with a pink opal glass bead and a rosaline puffy rondelle.

yellow gold Two common formulas for making yellow gold use gold, silver, and copper. For 14-kt yellow gold: 58% gold + 25% silver + 17% copper. For 18-kt yellow gold: 75% gold + 12.5% silver + 12.5% copper.

yellow hearts Venetian wound-glass trade beads made in the 19th century that have yellow in the center. Twisting or wrapping hot glass around a rod or mandrel is one of the oldest ways to make a glass bead. *See also* white hearts.

yellow opal A variety of opals that are honey-yellow, translucent, and that show a play-of-color due to water trapped inside the stone. Its Mohs scale hardness is 5.5 to 6.5. The yellow stone is Mined in Mexico, Peru, and South Africa. The stone is also called *honey opal*. Shown are nuggets of yellow opal. *See also* opal.

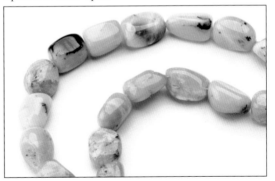

yellow turquoise A so-called turquoise variant that some dispute as being turquoise because of its slightly different chemical composition than standard turquoise—copper with aluminum phosphate. Mined in China, colors range from opaque yellow, green, pink, or cream with a black matrix to lime, pea, or spring green. The stone can take a high polish and has a rich appearance. Some have considered this a yellow jasper, agate, or serpentine. Many turquoise stones on the market have been dyed to alter their appearance. It may be called varietal yellow turquoise. Approach only reputable dealers and consult an appraiser or gemologist to be certain of its value and composition. Shown are yellow turquoise nuggets. *See also* turquoise.

yttrium   A rare-earth metal.

yupana   A counting board used by the ancient Incas. It is also called the Peruvian abacus, although historians have debated that this might have been introduced by the Spanish conquistadores.

Z

Zen beads   A glass bead with a distinctive spiral design, probably Venetian in origin. The term may be used for any bead or set of beads used for meditation. An *eye bead* is sometimes referred to as a Zen bead.

zigzag   A single line or path made with sharp, angular turns in alternating directions that is repeated on the surface of a bead or other object, creating a pattern.

zigzag stitch   Also called a *chevron chain*, a good basic stitch for beading bracelets, anklets, and necklace straps. Shown is a simple bracelet using this bead chain, noted in Horace R. Goodhue's classic book, *Indian Bead-Weaving Patterns*.

zinc   A bluish-white malleable metal. Zinc tarnishes easily and can become brittle or be pulverized when heated. It galvanizes steel to prevent corrosion and rust. It is commonly used in alloys, such as brass or nickel silver. It has been used in making American coins (cents). Zinc oxide has been used as a white paint pigment. In ancient India, zinc was actively mined. Brass has been made with copper and zinc at least since 30 B.C. A typical formula is for about 30% zinc alloyed with copper; red brass is about 15% zinc alloyed with copper.

zipper pull   A beaded embellishment for clothing, purse, or backpack, this is a fun and functional way to add beads for just a touch of color or decoration. It can be clipped anywhere, even onto a key ring. The zipper pull shown uses a beautiful floral lampwork bead as a focal bead. Embellished with a pink opaline 6-mm fire-polish bead and two 4-mm gold pearl beads, it is finished with a lobster claw clasp and a split ring for connecting to a zipper.

zipper stitch A technique that can turn a piece of flat peyote beadwork into a three-dimensional tube by running the needle and thread from one side to the other through the "pop-up" beads.

zircon The transparent to translucent mineral or gemstone, composed of zirconium silicate, may be colorless, yellow, brown, orange, red, violet, blue, or green. Its Mohs scale hardness factor is 6.5 to 7.5. The crystal system is tetragonal, short, and stocky with four-sided prisms with pyramidal ends. Names sometimes used for particular colors of zircon are *hyacinth* (yellow, yellowish red, reddish brown); *jargon* (straw yellow to nearly colorless); and *starlight* (blue). Most commonly found are grayish brown and reddish brown zircons, while colorless varieties are rare. While colorless stones are often brilliant-cut, colored stones are usually emerald-cut. Colorless, heat-treated zircon resembles diamond. It has an

adamantine luster and displays fluorescence. Zircon has a high refractive index (1.95; that of a diamond is 2.4) and strong dispersion but is brittle and its edges may be easily damaged. Zircon is found in Cambodia, Sri Lanka, Thailand, Australia, Brazil, Korea, Madagascar, Mozambique, Myanmar, Nigeria, Tanzania, and Vietnam. Zircons are mined for the metal zirconium.

zirconia Also called *cubic zirconia* or *cubic zirconium,* the white crystalline zirconium dioxide, a popular synthetic gemstone which serves as a diamond imitation. Not to be confused with *zircon* (zirconium silicate), the stone has a monoclinic crystal structure that can be tetragonal or cubic. It is known for its brilliant luminosity and a high index of light refraction. Sometimes jewelers mistakenly refer to this as *zircon,* a term that should be reserved for the naturally occurring mineral zirconium silicate, not the same as cubic zirconia or zirconia.

Cubic zirconia has been made in the laboratory since 1976 and has been often used as a relatively inexpensive diamond substitute. Its crystal system is isometric and monoclinic. Its Mohs scale of hardness is 8.5. Yttrium or calcium oxide may serve as a stabilizer during its creation. Its luster is considered sub-adamantine. Colors may be achieved by the introduction of metal oxides, such as cerium (yellows, oranges, and reds), chromium (green), neodymium (purple), erbium (pink), and titanium (golden brown).

zirconium A metal found in the mineral zircon.

zirconium dioxide *See* zirconia.

zoisite Transparent gemstones, composed of calcium aluminum silicate, that demonstrate strong pleochroism. They are brittle and susceptible to certain acids. The crystal system is orthorhombic, multifaceted prisms, and mostly striated, and the Mohs scale hardness is 6.5 to 7. Species include *tanzanite, thulite,* and *anyolite.*

zone patterns Lines etched or otherwise drawn on the surface of a bead serving as dividing lines between particular areas. These patterns are often seen on dZi beads, which may also have eyes drawn inside particular zones.

Zulu beadwork Beadwork created by the Zulu tribe, prominent in South Africa, Zimbabwe, Mozambique, and Zambia, using almost exclusively glass seed beads, has been a significant part of their cultural expression for over 500 years. The Zulu people have traded with the Egyptians, Arabs, Portuguese, Dutch, and British, often collecting beads, crafted into a variety of objects, such as necklaces, headbands, wristbands, loincloths, hats, capes, and aprons, that have served as tokens of social or marital status, political significance, or personal adornment. Tribal chiefs or kings have been known to wear beaded garments so heavy that they required attendants to assist them in standing up or performing their duties. Distinctive characteristics of Zulu beadwork are the geometric shapes, patterns, and colors used as a code for social communication ("love letters," called *incwadi*) between females and males. Zulu beadwork made for weddings and engagements identifies key participants in the wedding ceremony. A symbolic code is also used by traditional magic practitioners or shamans.

Ancient Zulu beadwork used bones, ostrich eggshells, stones, seeds, and metals. The Zulus formally broke off from other groups in about 1700. Zulu is a Bantu language. Their fine glass beadwork draws on a rich melting pot of ancient sub-Saharan African traditions.

Traders and collectors seek elaborate Zulu beadwork, which may remain in families for generations. Items created for the tourist trade tend to differ from those made for traditional use. *See* ball-and-loop bracelet, made by a Zulu woman.

Shown is a beaded doll created with a firmly stuffed fabric cone, embellished with beads in the Zulu style. Courtesy of Ginger Summit and Jim Widess, *Making Gourd Dolls & Spirit Figures;* photo by Jim Widess.

PART III

Beading Tips and Techniques

This section offers useful information in a Q&A format to take some of the headaches out of beading.

Beading Basics

These questions and answers cover essential information that beginners need to know about the basic materials, tools, and supplies they will need to begin beading.

Q: What are the basics I need to know about beading materials before I begin?

A: Refer to the glossary often to acquire a working knowledge of beadwork techniques and materials. It is often helpful to have some basic information on materials, so a summary is provided here. You will learn with experience what threads, needles, and beads will produce the nicest piece of beadwork. Selecting color combinations is difficult for some, so the easiest way is to look at other people's beadwork, jewelry store displays, and in books or magazines. If you find ones that are aesthetically appealing, you may want to select similar colors. If you have difficulty creating your own color combinations, it is wise to consult a color wheel and learn the rudiments of color matching. You are encouraged to try out different colors that match your personality.

Color numbers are noted for certain seed beads. These refer to standardized colors from certain manufacturers. For example,

Delicas are produced in Japan and are noted for their precise shaping and larger holes. They are often denoted as DB#, referring to a Delica bead. Since they are cut with lasers, they are very consistent in size, which helps make them quite popular with modern beaders. Delica is a trademark of Miyuki Shoji Corp. Antique beads, Treasure beads, and Aiko beads are trademarks of Toho Corp. for cylinder beads that also have a color numbering system. Magnifica is a registered trademark of Mill Hill, Inc. *Cylinder* refers to the shape of the bead. Cylinder bead manufacturers have color numbering systems that are not used interchangeably with other cylinder bead manufacturers.

Seed beads generally come in standardized sizes ranging from size 8 to 15. The larger the size number, the smaller the bead. For example, size 15 is smaller than size 8. Although beads smaller than size 15 exist, they are more difficult to find. Also, not all bead manufacturers have precise cutting techniques, so the sizes do not always match completely. Beginners may need a magnifier to see the difference. A reputable bead dealer will tell you who the manufacturer is and where they were manufactured. Note that seed bead sizes are based on external dimensions, not the size of the hole.

Bead selection can be confusing for beginners. The easiest way to guarantee size consistency is to use the same type of bead for a particular project and not to mix manufacturers. If beads are mixed, the results will be lumpy and uneven. For example, Japanese beads tend to be squarer in shape than beads from the Czech Republic, which tend to be more oval in shape. Both nations produce good quality beads, so the shape is more a matter of personal preference. Czech beads are usually strung on hanks (coiled or looped bundles), and Japanese beads are usually sold in tubes. Japanese beads tend to have larger holes than Czech beads. Colors as well are not standardized among manufacturers.

Bead finishes result in an elaborate selection of gorgeous and exotic beads to select for your projects. However, some finishes are vulnerable to wear, depending on personal body chemistry and contact with preparations like hand lotion and perfumes. If a bead is marked "dyed," the finish might rub off and ruin your beadwork. Metallicized or galvanized beads also have the same tendency. To deal with the problem, there are acrylic products on the market that can be sprayed or painted onto the beadwork. Consult your local bead store personnel to determine whether the color is stable so you can make an informed decision.

Beading needles also come from different countries and manufacturers. Beading needles differ from sewing needles because the size of the eye tends to be smaller since it needs to accommodate the size of the bead hole. The size of beading needles generally coincides with the size of the bead. For instance, a size 10 needle works well with a size 10 bead. However, many people do not know that beading needles are somewhat versatile because the size of the hole is more important than the size of the bead. I usually recommend a size 10 needle for size 10, 11, and 12 beads. I consider it a good generic size because it works well with many beads and projects. If you start working with size 12 or 13 beads, I recommend a size 12 needle. Antique beads tend to have smaller holes than the beads manufactured currently.

Beading thread comes in many sizes, based on the width of the individual piece of thread. It is different from sewing thread in that it is more durable and less likely to have natural components. Synthetics like polyester and nylon have a longer life span than cotton or silk, which biodegrades in 50 years or less. If you want your beadwork to become a family heirloom or be retired someday into a museum, consider the life span of the thread you select.

The most commonly available thread sizes are A, O, B, and D, from small to large. Considering the weight factor of glass beads, you may need to use size D thread for a loomed belt or other heavy piece of beadwork. Size A or O is generally recommended for lightweight and delicate beadwork, such as earrings.

Size B is more often recommended for small but slightly heavier beadwork pieces such as bracelets or necklaces.

Different manufacturers compete to produce a better quality product in a variety of colors as well as black and white. Some beading threads are conditioned with a type of waxy or slippery material to minimize fraying and tangling. Beeswax and other thread conditioners are also on the market to help you prevent those problems.

Another factor to consider when selecting the size of thread to use is how many times a piece of thread needs to pass through a single bead. If you are using a stitch that requires more than two passes of thread, you may have to use a finer thread size. If the only thread you have is too thin to fill the bead hole, you can double your thread and save yourself a trip to the bead store.

The amount of thread to use depends partly on the project. However, as a general rule of thumb, I recommend an arm's length doubled. Even though you may be using only a single thread, you can double the thread back on itself to shorten it to a comfortable length. The length of the thread will be awkward and tangle easily if it is longer than your arm can reach. If you need more thread, it is easy to tie it off and add a new piece of thread. To prevent tangling and fraying, always put the thread on your needle in the same direction as it comes off the spool.

Purchasing beads can be an overwhelming experience. Information on where to purchase beads, beading materials, and supplies can easily be located by looking in your local telephone directory, browsing bead and craft stores, and searching on the Internet for stores and suppliers.

Q: Where do I start when learning how to do beadwork?

A: Fortunate students can have a friend or relative show them how do the basics. Many bead stores have very helpful staff who can show you how to use beading tools and offer friendly advice on how to select materials. Many bead stores also offer classes so you can learn a particular project or technique. Myriad books and magazines on the market present helpful illustrations, photographs, and instructions on beadwork. There are even videotapes on the market that actually show you how to use certain techniques. Additionally, the Internet offers a wealth of information, including many free patterns and resources; animated graphics are available for free on some Web sites. Museums, jewelry stores, and gift shops are also a wonderful way to see beadwork up close in order to examine the beads, color combinations, and construction materials.

Start with a beginner project if you are new to beadwork. Although many of the needle arts provide crossover experience to apply to beadwork, you have to start with the basics. Do not expect to produce your masterpiece with the first project.

Q: How do I know if I am getting my money's worth on jewelry supplies?

A: Beads and other supplies are usually packaged by the manufacturer or wholesaler in standard unit quantities, like a gross, a dozen, 1 kilogram, 1,000, etc. They are usually sold in bulk to wholesalers who in turn break them down into smaller quantities for eventual retail sale. As a general rule, prices are marked up at least 100% to as high as 500% to cover the cost of doing business.

As a general rule, consumers and other buyers get a price break for buying large quantities. Buying a single bead or small quantities is probably the most expensive way to buy beads. Buying a whole strand or a bunch (10 +) usually results in a better price. The number of beads per strand differs based on the bead size. For example, if you want to buy fire-polish beads, usually 25 beads are strung per strand in size 6 mm and larger. Smaller beads like 4 mm and smaller usually come 50 per strand. A huge variety of packaging materials, like plastic tube, boxes, and bags may also contain certain quantities of beads, so if the package does not specify, ask your retail dealer for the quantity. Instead of worrying about counting a whole bag of tiny seed beads, it is good to know that a *hank* of seed beads is roughly equivalent to 1 ounce of the same seed beads loose.

It is worth investing time to learn about pricing and packaging for your favorite beads or supplies so that you can get a competitive price. Precious metals like silver and gold, including wire, sheet metal, findings, and jewelry are often sold by weight, and prices fluctuate with the world commodities market.

Even if prices are clearly marked on items for sale, it is acceptable to inquire with the store owner on whether they sell in wholesale quantities at a discount. Take the time to look at a few catalogs, Web sites, and retail stores to do price comparisons. When you have some idea of the price range, you will be better informed on the going rate or average price for a particular item before you buy it. Of course, if you discover some lovely beads at a yard sale or marked for clearance, you will not usually have the time to do research without missing out on a good buying opportunity.

Ask your beading friends about their experiences to rule out unscrupulous dealers or high-priced stores. Ask store owners about their return policy before buying beads. Many helpful retailers realize that a beginning beader does not always have enough knowledge to make the appropriate purchases, so they will be lenient in allowing returns on merchandise. The smart store owners also realize that they might have a lifelong customer if they treat them honestly and with respect. On the Internet, many Web sites have feedback sections to read and learn about dealers that do not engage in good business practices. Some dealers have tremendously attractive prices, but you need to look carefully to see how much it will cost for shipping and handling, which can substantially add to the price of those beads, especially when being shipped from overseas. If it seems overwhelming to learn so much and to do so many calculations, just focus on one item at a time. Fortunately, with all the competition in the world of beads, the word spreads quickly on where to get the best quality beads at the best prices.

Q: How do I know what a bead is made of?

A: Your local bead store and other beaders are generally the best sources of information on identifying the material a bead is made from. Bead dealers will be happy to tell you what the material is if they were involved in the purchase of the same or similar beads. If the beads came from your grandmother's jewelry box or were bought at a swap meet, you may have to show the beads to several sources. A trained expert like a gemologist or museum curator may provide more information on a bead's age or history. You can compare samples of beads with a known identification source such as photographs from books. You can validate your sources by seeing whether you get consistent opinions from the several different sources.

Q: How can someone tell where beads were manufactured?

A: Japanese beads are most often sold loose or packaged in plastic bead tubes. Beads manufactured in the Czech Republic are usually sold strung in hanks or bunches. Reputable bead dealers, wholesalers, and retail store owners will be happy to tell you where their beads came from. Beads found at yard sales and flea markets or grandma's attic can be more difficult to identify for the novice beader, but if it looks attractive to you and has aesthetic value, it has worth even if the monetary value is unknown. Your beader friends or bead-store owners will usually be helpful and offer their professional opinion on the beads' origins and value.

Q: Which manufacturers make the best seed beads?

A: Beads of many different materials have been manufactured since very early in human history, each having their own qualities and characteristics. When shopping for beads, question what the beads are made of and do some comparison shopping for what price ranges to expect.

Educate yourself about bead finishes and types. Some finishes will wear off with handling or fade when exposed to certain chemicals or even sunlight. Aesthetics are another consideration, since some dyed beads are made in the most beautiful colors. Purples and pinks are colors of sensitive finish, in general, but that does not mean that you should avoid buying beads of these colors. If a bead has a sensitive finish, it can be pretreated with some type of acrylic spray to fix the color. Modern manufacturers are consistently trying to improve their products by coming up with more permanent finishes. An honest dealer, as well as experienced beaders, will be happy to share such information with you, if you ask them.

See the charts on bead sizes to determine the most appropriate size bead for the project. Certain projects, like loomwork and bead weaving, pretty much require consistent sizing of all the beads or the resulting loomwork will be lumpy and uneven. Japanese beads in general are more square-shaped and Czech beads are more oval, which can be a design consideration. However, seed beads are also manufactured in France, Africa, Taiwan, and Italy—some modern and some antique. Older beads are not as consistently sized as the more recently manufactured ones, owing to advances in bead manufacturing technology. Depending on the project, certain irregularities among the beads add character and have a beauty of their own.

Q: What size needle and thread is easiest for beginners?

A: For my beginning students interested in learning how to do beadwork with seed beads, I recommend size 11/0 seed beads, size B thread, and a size 10 needle. These sizes are readily available in most craft and bead stores. If you are not sure of the size of needle, beads, or thread you will need, just try them out to see if they fit.

Q: How long a piece of thread do you need to start a beadwork project?

A: Some projects in books and magazines recommend a certain length of thread. In general, an arm's length doubled is recommended, which is a comfortable measurement to work with. If the thread is longer than your arm's reach, it will be prone to tangling and knots, causing much frustration.

Q: How many beads do I need?

A: If you are doing a particular project from a magazine or book, they usually provide information on how many beads you need. Beads are packaged in many different ways. If they are temporarily strung, they will be sold in certain lengths, such as 16, 18, 36 inches (40, 45, 90 cm), etc. Do not be shy about asking the bead-store owner, or take a portable tape measure to help you calculate the overall length you need for your project. There are usually a standard number of beads per strand for certain sizes of beads. For instance, larger 6-mm fire-polish beads usually come 25 per strand, and smaller 3-mm fire-polish beads come in 50 beads per strand. Seed beads come in tubes or hanks and weigh about 1 ounce (28 grams). Loose beads may be measured by weight. The length of the strand depends on how large the beads are. Your local bead store personnel will help you decide.

Q: How do I figure out what size beading wire I need to string my necklace or bracelet?

A: Beading wire comes in a variety of sizes from many different manufacturers. (Find the chart on stringing wire sizes and recommended bead sizes in Part IV.) You have to consider the size of the hole as well as the size of the bead, because some beads have smaller holes than others. In general, you want the stringing wire to fill the hole because if it allows too much movement inside the hole, it can cause abrasion, especially with beads having rough edges like cut beads, metal, or stone beads. If the wire is too small for the hole, it will also have the tendency to kink or break.

Q: What is the difference between machine-cut or machine-faceted and hand-cut beads?

A: Machine-cut beads are produced with machine technology and are the most consistent or uniform in appearance. Hand-cut beads are subject to human error and may result in beads that are more irregular or have cut marks on the facets. Machine-cut beads will have sharp angles. *See also* Swarovski crystals.

Q: How can you tell if a glass bead is molded?

A: Molded beads may show a seam or edge. Molded beads can be fire-polished to remove the edges, but this process also rounds off the edges.

Q: How do I know what size needle goes with what size thread?

A: The charts in this book offer specific details on sizes of needles, threads, and beads, all made by different manufacturers in different sizes or gauges. The easiest way to learn about sizes is to go to your local bead store and either buy a kit, take a class, or pick a beginner project and ask the staff for assistance. You will quickly learn that for seed beads, there is a generic or popular size that works well with most projects.

Size 11 seed bead is the most popular and works well with a size 10 or 11 needle and size B thread.

For bead-stringing wire, size 0.19 to 0.21 works with a variety of small seed beads as well as large glass beads. Smaller and more delicate beads require smaller wire, while heavy or chunky beads, like turquoise and metal, require heavier-gauge wire. If the gauge is too big, it will not fit inside the hole of the bead; if the gauge is too small, it will be prone to kinking and breaking.

Q: What is the difference between long and short needles?

A: It is mainly a matter of preference as to what length of needle to choose and what feels most comfortable to the user. For certain projects involving stringing, you can string more beads at a time on a long needle than on a short one. For projects done on the loom, the width of the beaded piece will determine whether a long needle is more convenient. For bead embroidery projects, some people prefer short and sharp needles for close-up work with fabric. However, there is no fast rule on needle length other than personal choice.

Q: How do I figure out what kind of stringing material to use?

A: In the marketplace, you'll find a huge variety of thread, string, cord, rope, and metal wire, which can be used to string beads. Deciding which particular stringing type would be best for a particular project depends on a few simple factors. First, consider the size of the bead and its hole. Finding thread designed specifically for beading is a good start, but beading thread comes in many sizes. As a general rule, any stringing material should fill the bead hole and allow minimal movement inside the hole. If a particular beadwork technique requires more than a single pass of thread through the hole of the same bead, a little more space inside the hole is required. If the thread is overcrowded within the bead hole, this could result in stiff beadwork, and the thread may be weakened by being pierced with the needle, especially if a second pass is required. When too much room exists within the bead hole, there is the risk of abrasion, which could also weaken the thread.

Next, consider the weight of the bead. Most stringing materials for beads have a *test weight,* the amount of weight the product can tolerate without breaking. For instance, a 10-pound (4.5-kg) test weight means that a given thread or wire can tolerate at least 10 pounds before breaking. With lightweight beads, such as seed beads, this is not a concern. With heavier beads, like gemstones, the stringing material must be strong enough to tolerate the weight of all the beads without adding strain on the wire and the clasp.

Many beads are sold in strands or hanks with temporary, inexpensive stringing material suitable for shipping and distributing the beads. These temporary materials may be raffia, hemp, nylon fishing wire, or cotton cord; while useful, they are not sturdy or attractive enough for finished bead projects. Certain biodegradable stringing materials, like cotton, linen, and silk, may not be advisable for jewelry that may be subject to environmental stresses such as heat, sunlight, and humidity. Precious-metal wire and synthetic thread are likely to endure over time. Consult with local bead store personnel to receive advice on the best material to use for a particular project.

Most beading thread, designed specifically for certain beadwork projects, can accommodate the desired bead type, weight, and hole size. The preferred and most durable beading threads, like polyester and nylon, are synthetic and lightweight. Thread string can be natural or organic, like cotton, wool, linen, rayon, hemp, or silk. Cotton thread tends to deteriorate more quickly and is not recommended for beadwork unless a specific thread color or type is required to match a particular fabric used in a clothing design. As necessary, cotton thread can be wrapped with a synthetic, like polyester, to make it relatively long-lasting.

Metallic thread consists of fine metal filaments intertwined with a base thread, like cotton or polyester. Thicker materials, often called string or cord, are favored for stringing larger beads. Leather lace, nylon-coated wire cable, and metal chain may be recommended for stringing heavy gemstones or metal beads. *See* stringing thread and stringing wire in Part II. Find the stringing materials chart in Part IV.

Q: What kind of tools do I need to buy?

A: Many tools on the market are specially designed for jewelry-making and beadwork. Depending on the type of beadwork or jewelry that you want to make, an assortment of tools can be helpful. For beading, the basic tools are sharp scissors, needles, and a measuring tape. If you decide to do anything that involves wire for stringing, chain-making, or wrapping, you may need to invest in some pliers for

bending and good cutters. Before you go out and spend your children's college fund, it is prudent to take a class or read a book or magazine, or ask a teacher or friend which tool is most useful for beginners. The tools section shows many different types of jaws for bending, cutting, holding, and manipulating. Probably the most common tools are the needle or round-nose pliers, flat-nose pliers, and some type of cutter that's sturdy enough to cut metal. Keep in mind that some cutting tools are designed to cut thread only, so using them on wire will ruin the jaw's cutting edge. Tools found in a bead store are probably the most appropriate. Although similar tools may be found in a hardware store or toolbox, jewelry tools are more delicate and easier to handle on materials like precious metals. Specialty tools, like a pearl knotting tool or a split-ring opener, have specific functions that are not necessarily useful for all beaders. Try out a tool prior to purchase to make sure that it fits comfortably in your hand. A tool that's too heavy or cumbersome will get in the way. Ask questions and request a demonstration from bead store personnel before buying tools.

Q: What clasp type is the best?

A: Different types of common clasps include the lobster-claw, barrel, spring-ring, S-hook, toggle, hook-and-eye, and safety clasp. (Find definitions and photos for each type in Part II.) Clasps can be made from base metal, precious metal, and a variety of other materials, like glass, bone, cord, and even beads. The kind of material that you choose for the clasp is basically a matter of aesthetics and personal preference. Essential criteria for selecting a clasp are that it functions properly, closes securely, and can bear the weight of the bracelet or necklace. If the clasp is too small or delicate to handle the weight of the beads, it could eventually break. If the beads and other materials are expensive or have sentimental value, it is wise to invest in a good quality clasp, so that the beads are not lost or ruined. Certain clasps are identified as safety clasps, designed with a locking mechanism unlikely to malfunction. A backup chain may sometimes be used for extra security. Magnetic clasps come in different designs, and some have a stronger magnetic hold than others. Although useful for people with arthritis or those who have difficulty with fine motor dexterity, the magnet in such a clasp can have an adverse effect on the magnetic strips in credit cards as well as on heart pacemakers.

Q: How are gemstones measured?

A: In the international market, the carat, gram, grain, and momme are used as units of weight. Find individual listings in Part II.

Q: Can you identify gemstones by color alone?

A: Gemstones occur in many different colors. In most cases, the color alone is not diagnostic because many different gemstones share the same hue. Color is one of the most important characteristics of gems. Color is produced by light, and light consists of an electromagnetic vibration at certain wavelengths. The human eye can perceive only certain wavelengths, but what is visible produces luster, color, fire, luminescence, and "play-of-light" (brilliance)—all terms used to describe the magnificent beauty of natural gemstones. The colors of the spectrum, which produce red, orange, yellow, green, blue, and violet, all mix together to produce white light.

Q: How do gemstones get their names?

A: Many gemstone names can be traced to ancient Greek, Latin, and Asian languages. Nomenclature, or the systematic naming of gemstones, originally had to do with the stone's characteristics, place of origin, or color. *Agate,* for instance, was named after a river in Sicily, and *sapphire* simply means "blue" in Greek. Many mineral names may have come from those mining the particular stones through the centuries. Modern scientific names and descriptions may include the chemical composition, geographic location of the stone, or the discoverer's name. Optical qualities, such as luster, color, fire, or iridescence, may also play a part in the gemstone's description. Since many buyers, traders, sellers, miners, middlemen, and artisans may not agree on a given name or the name may be translated from a foreign tongue, common names for gemstones may vary. Multiple names for a single stone of a given chemical composition, never mind its varieties, may exist.

For instance, ammolite, also known as gem ammonite, calcenite, buffalo stone, and Korite (a trade name), comes from the iridescent fossilized shell of ammonites, composed largely of aragonite. Found principally in Alberta, Canada, and introduced to the market in 1969, ammolite was given official gemstone status by the World Jewellery Confederation in 1981. It is considered rare and valuable.

Unfortunately, some retailers and wholesalers are interested principally in selling their gems at the best price for the highest profit and have invented convenient marketing tactics with somewhat misleading names for certain gemstones. The buyer must beware. An African diamond, for instance, is rock crystal (quartz), not that more expensive stone made of carbon. While many buyers and sellers may understand these terms among themselves, a layman or someone new to beading may not.

All newly discovered minerals are presented to the International Mineralogical Association's Commission on New Mineral Names. This association has a membership of mineral experts from around the world who help sanction and standardize not just new mineral names but gemstone names.

Q: Do laws protect consumers from scams or dishonest sellers who falsely represent given items as precious gemstones, precious metals, or otherwise fail to disclose the value of jewelry for sale?

A: To protect the consumer from false, misleading, or fraudulent business practices, the United States Federal Trade Commission's (FTC) booklet *Guides for the Jewelry, Precious Metals, and Pewter Industries* can assist you in discovery and the regulation of terms used in the United States. A similar commission in Germany regulates the gemstone trade in Europe. Unfortunately, such measures cannot ensure the genuineness of a particular product. The buyer must be cautious when making any pricey gemstone purchases by doing preliminary research, consulting an appraiser, and knowing the dealer's reputation.

You can download the FTC booklet free on the Internet; find the FTC Web sites in the Selected Bibliography in Part V. In the booklet, you'll find detailed information about gold, silver, and other precious metals, gemstones, pearls, and jewelry. The section on consumer protection provides facts about marketing, selling, and advertising of products that may be covered by legislation to protect the individual consumer from dishonest trade tactics.

Whether or not you live in the United States, these guides will be helpful. But to defend yourself from fast talkers, sidewinders, and Web-site scammers, you also might want to check out laws in your country that protect the consumer. The Gemological Institute of America (GIA), International Colored Gemstone Association (ICA), Aussie Sapphire, Jewellers Association of Australia, Canadian Gemological Association, Canadian Jewellers Association, Gemmological Association of Great Britain, World Jewellery Confederation (CIBJO), Department of Gemstones and Jewellery in New Zealand, Gemological Institute of India, Jewelry Information Center, and Cultured Pearl Information Center (check their Web sites) may also provide helpful information to consumers.

Potential Problem Areas

Q: What is the matter if my beading needles break easily?

A: Beading needles are made of very thin metal and are vulnerable to wear and tear. Since they are not very expensive, it is a good idea to keep an adequate supply of needles handy. The tips can get dull with use, and the needles can get bent with pressure. Short beading needles do not bend or break as easily as long beading needles but are not as comfortable to use for some people. Stress can cause more bending and breakage of needles. Starting each new project with a fresh needle can ease the stress. Throw away the bent or dull needle and relax!

Q: What is the easiest way to make thread more manageable?

A: Thread conditioners or beeswax can be of assistance when it is difficult to thread a needle. Another tip is to lick or wet the tip of both the thread and the needle, which works great for many people. Some people use lip gloss that is already on their mouth to help the threading process along. Be careful with this technique, because bead thread can cut the tender membranes of the mouth and lips. Good light is also very important to minimize eyestrain. Stretch the thread before you use it. Doing so will erase the memory of it being wrapped around a spool and decrease the tendency to knot and tangle.

Q: What is the easiest way to thread a needle?

A: The most important thing to have is the right-sized needle for the thread you are using. You need to look for a needle with the largest hole to fit your thread. If you are having trouble threading a size 12 needle, for example, see if a size 10 needle will work better for you. If you view your needle against a white or light background, like a wall or piece of paper, it is easier to see the hole. Cutting your thread at an angle with sharp scissors is also a good suggestion. There is a product called a "big-eye needle," which opens up to a large space for threading. Unfortunately, it is not always effective when using very small beads because such a large needle will not fit inside the hole. (And see the Q&A about visual aids and lighting.)

Q: Do I need any special vision aids to do beadwork?

A: Close-up vision is probably the most important ability to have when seed beading. Obviously, larger beads are easier to see. There are many handicapped, elderly, and visually impaired individuals who thoroughly enjoy beading. The size of the bead and the type of needle can be changed to make it easier. Even special adaptations can be made for the severely visually impaired and even the blind. For people with extreme difficulty in their visual skills, stiff beading wire is easier to feel and thread through the holes of larger beads. If your vision is correctible with glasses, by all means, don't forget to bring your glasses to beading class. Good lighting and good magnification are absolute musts to minimize eyestrain, headaches, and neck aches. Bright but not hot light should be focused on your work area and illuminate the room in general. Special equipment like headgear and magnifier lamps are used by some beaders to ease eyestrain but are not a requirement for everyone.

Visual aids, such as a magnifying lamp or lens, also come in handy for many people. Some prefer a more economical choice of magnifying glasses, which are relatively inexpensive at your local drugstore. Good light is also very important to minimize eyestrain.

Q: Do I need special lighting equipment to do beadwork?

A: Although there are nice lamps on the market, the most important thing is to provide good lighting right on the area that you are beading. Adequate overhead lighting and natural sunlight will minimize eyestrain. Magnifier lamps with lights that fit onto your face can provide good lighting but can also be cumbersome for some beaders.

Q: Is it true that thread has a grain or directionality?

A: Yes, and you should thread the needle in the same direction that the thread comes off the spool. If you do, you will have fewer problems with tangling and knotting.

Q: What happens if my stretchy elastic bracelet gets stretched out?

A: Not all elastic threading material is the same. Some are more resistant to stretching out and losing their elasticity than others. If a bracelet does get stretched out, it may shrink up if dropped in very hot water for a few seconds. Otherwise, restring the bracelet with a different elastic cord. Inquire at your local bead store for the best-quality product.

Q: How do you prevent the thread from tangling while beading?

A: Thread your needle before cutting the thread from the spool. Many twisted threads and cords have a direction. If the needle is threaded from the wrong direction, it can cause undue tangling and knotting. Give your thread a firm tug to stretch out the curls and wrinkles before using it. Also, use beeswax or some type of thread conditioner to minimize tangling. In addition, certain stitches, especially circular ones, have the tendency to twist the thread as you bead. Every few rows, it is helpful to let your needle and thread dangle to let gravity help you unwind your thread before continuing.

Q: What is the problem if my thread keeps snagging and breaking?

A: Abrasion is a sign that there might be a burr or rough spot on the needle. If you find a rough spot, especially on the eye, discard your needle and get a new one. Make sure you have the most generous hole possible to accommodate the thread size and to minimize abrasion. Occasionally, you will find some defective thread due to weathering, but the problem of snagging is more commonly a problem with the needle. If the bead stitch requires multiple passes of the needle through a particular bead, you may be accidentally piercing your thread with the needle. This will destroy the thread fibers and weaken the thread. Occasionally beads with very

small holes will need to be discarded if a smaller needle and thread does not work with them without snagging.

Q: Is there an easy way to apply glue, since I always seem to make a mess?

A: Some jewelry adhesives have a built-in applicator. However, because many of these adhesives are also damaging to human skin tissue, make sure you do not get any glue on your skin or fine furniture. Use a small piece of foil or plastic and apply a small amount of glue to it. Then use a piece of fine wire, a flat-head pin, or a toothpick as an applicator. When you are done, make sure you wipe the glue from the tube tip and clean the lid before closing.

Q: How do I prevent my glue lid from becoming glued shut and ruining the whole tube?

A: When you use the glue for the first time, apply a generous amount of petroleum jelly to the threads of the lid to prevent it from gluing shut.

Q: If I add an extra bead to the pattern, do I have to take it all apart?

A: If you make a mistake and add an extra bead or the wrong color, there is a safe way to break it without having to undo all your work. Place a needle inside the bead you want to break to guard the thread while you pinch it slightly with flat-nose pliers. Clean up the debris because sharp glass can injure sensitive skin or cut your thread.

Q: Why do my bugle-bead projects keep falling apart?

A: Some bugle beads are notorious for having rough edges. Since they are glass beads, the edges can be very sharp and slice right through the thread of your project. Check your beads closely before buying them to prevent such problems. If you do not notice the problem before you buy the beads, you can use a fine sandpaper to smooth off the edges before you start beading. However, that solution can be quite time-consuming. You can also place buffer beads like spacers or seed beads to cover up the rough edges.

Q: If my loom beadwork project looks bumpy and irregular, what am I doing wrong?

A: If your loom is strung properly, your beadwork may look irregular and uneven if the beads you are using are not all the same size. Japanese and Czech seed beads marked the same size are not really the same size and shape. Japanese beads are slightly bigger than Czech beads,

which are more oval in shape. The lesson here is to use the same size and manufacturer of beads on your loom project. Other projects and stitches are more forgiving. Cylinder beads are probably the most precise and consistent in their shape and size. They also have larger holes.

Q: Are there any safety tips for cutting jewelry wire?

A: Yes—be careful to point away from people when cutting wire, because sharp projectiles can be hazardous to others, especially if they hit the eyes. Also, be careful to pick up your scraps: sharp pieces of wire can injure the feet and toes of people and pets.

Q: Is there an easier way to bend memory wire?

A: Memory wire is notorious for being difficult to bend or turn. With the proper tools, round or needle-nose pliers, try bending the tip of the memory wire in the direction opposite to which it curves.

Q: Can I still learn wirework if I have arthritis or weak wrists?

A: Try using the proper jewelry tools, and wrap the wire around the tool instead of turning the tools to bend the wire. Try different gauges of wire, since many finer gauges can be easily bent by hand. There are also wire shapers on the market that make it easier to bend the wire into fancy designs for jewelry and findings.

Q: What can be done to prevent a galvanized finish on certain beads from rubbing off?

A: Try using a clear spray acrylic or fixative on your beads before you use them. Use the lid of an old shoe box and spray in a ventilated area. Shake the beads to get an even coverage and prevent the beads from sticking to each other. Consider alternative beads, like those lined with silver, gold, or copper, as these will also add sparkle to your beadwork. Ask your bead store personnel about beads such as real gold or sterling silver-plated beads, whose finish does not have the tendency of rubbing off. Of course, such beads are more expensive.

Q: Do I need to be aware of any particular allergens in jewelry findings?

A: Some people are allergic to certain metals used in jewelry components. The reactions usually take on the character of contact dermatitis (redness, itching, irritation, broken skin) when the particular metal touches or remains against the skin. Also, a bracelet or ring worn close may cause soaps or hand lotions to be trapped underneath the jewelry and cause skin

irritation. Rarely do hives or infections result, but this of course depends on the severity of the person's allergy. Nickel, a common allergen, is commonly used in metal alloys. Rather than specifying all the potential metal sensitivities, be aware that many metals have other metals added to strengthen the product or influence the color. Plating was initially used to make products cheaper for the consumer. Many products that have direct skin contact, like ear wires, are plated over surgical steel, which is fairly hypoallergenic for the majority of people and used by doctors for medical procedures. Titanium is used as a hypoallergenic metal in implants and in jewelry worn on sensitive or new piercings. Precious metals in their purest form, like platinum or 18-karat gold, generally cause few problems for most people but are more costly. Green staining of the skin can result from copper or nickel and black staining from silver. Although not a true allergy, some people's body chemistry simply interacts with certain metals to cause this temporary discoloration of the skin. The salts present in perspiration can exacerbate the situation by causing corrosion of the metal.

Q: Can I still bead if I am dyslexic?

A: The diagnosis of dyslexia means a lot of different things. While beading does require some visual and motor dexterity, it is possible for most people to learn how to bead and enjoy it. The human brain is versatile and adaptable. In fact, if you have some of the symptoms of dyslexia, beading can be a highly therapeutic activity for the brain. In the section on how to read a bead pattern, you will find more information on people who are right-handed or left-handed. Some people have special talents, which scientists believe are located in different parts of the brain. If you are having difficulty reading a pattern or following a pattern, you might want to consult with a beading teacher to give you some helpful suggestions. A teacher can show you how to master a certain technique and how to hold your beadwork to make it easier. Take notes on what sorts of difficulty you are having, and discuss ways to adapt to make beading more comfortable.

Q: Can I learn how to bead even if I am not creative?

A: Beading is a very creative activity. However, for a beginner it is helpful to have some basic structure and rules. Then, once you gain a little experience and confidence, you will learn that there are many different ways to attach beads together with some type of stringing material. A variety of techniques can be used in order to achieve the same result. If the reader finds it difficult to learn round peyote stitch, for instance, he or she will discover that the same results can be achieved by doing a flat piece of beadwork with flat peyote stitch and seaming both ends together to make a tubular piece of beadwork. Flat peyote stitch looks the same as

brick stitch turned sideways. Loomed beadwork looks the same as square-stitch beadwork.

It is recommended that a beginner start with a basic project and master one technique at a time. Many projects in books, magazines, and kits will clearly identify the skill level for a project. Once you begin to understand how the beads behave with certain techniques, it is much easier to adapt a project for individual results. Even though certain materials are recommended for each project, it is helpful to note that many other materials can also be used. Some materials are not available in a local bead or craft store, although a lot of effort is made by writers of books and magazines to use supplies that are readily available in most large cities. If necessity dictates the substitution of materials, such as larger beads than what is recommended, you might be pleasantly surprised that the results are still satisfactory. Explore different options and observe what happens.

Q: I am a slow beader—does that mean I'm doing something wrong?

A: Beading is a skill that takes practice and patience. You will most likely get faster as you gain more experience. Some people naturally bead faster than others. The most important thing to remember is that you need to acquire the necessary skill level and practice it until you feel that you are ready to try more advanced techniques. There is no race or contest involved. Remember that beading is supposed to be a fun and creative recreational activity.

Mastering Techniques

This section covers general questions relating to beading techniques or methods.

Q: How do I learn how best to combine colors for my bead projects?

A: The first place to start is in a jewelry store, museum gift shop, bead store, or magazines that showcase beadwork and jewelry designs. Examine beadwork that is aesthetically appealing to you and take mental notes on the color combinations. Invest in a color wheel to learn which colors complement each other.

Q: What is a stop bead used for?

A: A stop bead is any bead attached to the end of your thread or stringing wire that prevents the beads from falling off until the string is firmly attached or knotted. Some techniques require that a certain number of beads be strung and then knotted or crimped, leaving your beadwork vulnerable for a while. A crimper bead can be used as a stop bead, or any bead can be knotted or tied on the end. A rubber earring back can also be used as a stop bead. The stop bead is usually removed after the project is completed. Adhesive tape is also used at the end of the wire to prevent your beads from falling off. It is removed when you are ready to finish the project.

Q: What is a crimp bead used for and how is it used?

A: A crimp bead is used with stringing wire to attach a clasp or other finding. It is commonly used with a crimping tool or flat-nose pliers. The tools are used to flatten or "smash" the crimp bead, which is made of soft metal designed to crush easily, thereby securing the wire and clasp.

Q: Which is easier, one-needle couching or two-needle couching?

A: One-needle couching is more efficient, but some people find that the two-needle method helps them to maintain proper tension.

Q: What is the best way to mark fabric with beading patterns?

A: When beading onto fabric or clothing, it is best to use a fabric pencil to mark bead patterns instead of a pencil or pen, which will leave permanent marks on the fabric and smear or discolor it. It would be a shame to do extensive beadwork and then have it ruined by smudged ink. Special fabric markers are designed to be erased when the beadwork is finished.

Some beaders prefer to trace the pattern directly onto tracing paper, card stock, fabric, or leather. Use a colored marker lighter than the background to minimize the marks or visual impression left by the ink or pencil. Fine tracing paper can be beaded on, and then the paper torn off when it is finished.

Another method is to use a tracing wheel, which leaves little pin marks to outline your pattern. However, it is difficult to use that method if there is much detail in the pattern.

If you are transferring a pattern onto fabric, wash the fabric first to preshrink and test it to see what happens (if, for instance, the color runs) when laundered. Borrowing from the sewing arts, transfer patterns can be ironed on and then beaded over; these are called "iron-on transfers." If the fabric is lightweight, it may require some reinforcement, such as fusible interfacing. Dressmaker's carbon paper is also recommended and available in many different colors.

The template method is used in many different crafts and involves taping the template in place and outlining the design with a fabric marker.

If you draw on technical resources, such as computer software, photocopiers, and scanners, you'll be able to create your own or adjust or resize existing patterns for appliqué beadwork.

Q: Is an embroidery hoop advisable for beading onto fabric?

A: It depends on the thickness of the fabric and the weight of the beads. Embroidery hoops are quite helpful for some people who want to bead onto fabric or clothing. Make sure the hoop fits appropriately and is not too large or too small. The function of the hoop is to stabilize the project and prevent the fabric from stretching.

Q: What kind of graph paper do I need to make my own patterns?

A: The type of graph depends on the stitch or technique required by the project that you have selected. In the graph section of this book, you will find three graphs for the popular peyote, brick, and square or loom stitches. Although they may look similar, there are some very important distinctions. Carefully examine the shape of the cells in the graph in order to note the orientation of the bead shape. Oval beads can be oriented horizontally or vertically, depending on the stitch and the thread path. Horizontally oriented bead cells are common to brick stitch; vertically oriented bead cells are more common to peyote stitch. Square stitch is graphed on loom-stitch charts because the alignment of the beads is identical. However, loomwork is done on a bead loom and square stitch is not. Some beaders prefer to use graph paper that has square cells because certain beads, such as Delica or cylinder beads, are more squared off than oval.

You can also download beading graphs from the Internet or buy software.

Q: Can't I use a really long piece of thread, since I don't like to make knots?

A: Excessively long thread is prone to tangling and not really necessary. Do not be afraid of learning how to make knots because, if you run out of thread, it is then a simple matter to attach a new piece of thread. If it is hard for you to learn from a book or magazine, take a class to learn the basics. Knotting is a useful skill that will reward you for many years. Find knotting diagrams in Part V.

Q: What kind of glue do you recommend for knots on beadwork?

A: Many types of glues and adhesives are available on the market, but not every kind is recommended. Heavy-duty or stiff glues are not advisable because they can stiffen the beadwork or plug the bead hole. Liquid acrylic (found in inexpensive nail polish) is a lightweight adhesive that does not interfere with the beadwork since it dries clear and usually will not plug the hole. It has a delicate applicator brush for applying to your knot and it dries quickly. If the hole does get plugged up with nail polish, it can usually be unplugged with a sharp needle. Acrylic sprays are more difficult to control or to apply in a focused area. Read the labels on jewelry adhesives to learn about the product's characteristics. An adhesive that bonds stone to leather will probably work well with cabochons or gemstones; however, such an adhesive is not advisable for more delicate bead projects. White glues that dry clear are often used as fabric stiffeners and help to shape three-dimensional bead objects. Epoxy glue varieties dry overly stiff, which can destroy the flexibility of beadwork fabric and become brittle over time, losing their adhesive quality.

Q: How can I prevent unsightly knots from showing when I add the clasp or finding to my bracelet?

A: When you are beginning your beadwork, start with about a 12-inch (30-cm) tail at the beginning, which can later be used to attach your clasp or other hardware without tying on a new piece of thread. A finding called a *bead tip* is also a very handy way to conceal a knot.

Q: How do I get beads on my hair for braiding?

A: Try using a big-eye needle and large-holed beads, like crow beads for hair embellishment.

Q: Are there standard lengths for necklaces, bracelets, and anklets?

A: The standard length for a bracelet is 7 to 8 inches (18 to 20 cm), including the clasp. The standard length for an anklet is 9 inches (22 cm), and the standard length for a choker is 16 to 18 inches (40 to 46 cm). Of course, it is helpful to carry a fabric tape measure to obtain exact measurements from the person who is going to receive the completed jewelry. The standard lengths always include the length of the clasp. A pendant length is 18 inches (46 cm) for a woman and 20 inches (50 cm) for a man. Jewelry is somewhat personal, so many people have their own preferences for necklace length, depending on their height, weight, and neck length. Longer necklace lengths are described as matinee (20 to 24 inches or 50 to 60 cm), opera (28 to 32 inches or 70 to 80 cm), rope (40 to 45 inches or 102 to 114 cm), and lariat (48 inches or 122 cm, or longer). We've rounded off measurements for metric conversions. Do some test measurements of your own since what's best may vary with the individual.

Using Bead Patterns

Q: Is there an easy way to make your own bead patterns?

A: Use blank graph paper for coloring in your own patterns with colored pencils or felt-tip pens. However, you still have to calculate the overall length and width of the finished product. Different sizes of beads will result in smaller or larger beadwork. There are several software programs that can assist you with designing your own patterns, including some that can actually create a pattern from a scanned image. The drawback to this method is that the software is sensitive to subtle color differences, which can result in an excessive number of bead colors that you will have to buy to create the beaded pattern. For example, a graphed picture of your family pet can require more than ten shades of brown, which are sometimes difficult to discriminate with the naked eye. However, the subtle shading that results will produce a realistic image that will impress your friends and family.

Q: How do you read a bead pattern?

A: Bead patterns are not difficult to read as long as you understand a few things about the various techniques and stitches. Detailed instructions with illustrations are outlined in projects in both of my previous books, *Native American Beadwork: Projects and Techniques from the Southwest* (Sterling, 2003) and *Creative Native American Beading* (Sterling, 2005).

Human brains are most often oriented to be right-hand dominant or left-hand dominant. Visual perception also tends to be right- or left-dominant. Some people are ambidextrous, meaning that they can use either hand equally well. There are, of course, some people who are mixed or cross-dominant. Without getting too technical with neuropsychological explanations, I usually observe my students and advise them to use the hand and direction that feels the most comfortable. Most right-handed persons feel comfortable beading from right to left and from top to bottom. If a pattern dictates that you start at the top or the bottom, right side or left side, it is usually a good idea to follow the author's suggestion. However, no hard and fast rule says you cannot bead from bottom to top or left to right. In fact, I generally recommend to my students that they try beading in the opposite direction from what they are used to in order to exercise their brains. Some students learn that the opposite direction is actually easier for them.

Brick-Stitch Patterns

Unless a pattern specifies exactly where to start, you can generally begin anywhere you choose. The arrow on some patterns that tells you where to start is a convenient tool. Many patterns for brick-stitch earrings suggest that you start at the widest point, which is a sound rule of thumb. The reason for this is that basic brick stitch automatically decreases by one bead with each row. Brick stitch is used in the popular triangle-shaped earring with fringe. Since the stitch automatically decreases in width with each row, your beadwork will look like a triangle. When you finish one triangle and then the bottom half, your beadwork will have

a diamond shape. You will notice that the top half of the pattern is frequently the same as the bottom half. When the first half is completed, you weave your thread to the base or starting row, turn your work upside down, and finish the bottom half. If you started anywhere else on the pattern, you would need to increase the number of beads per row, which involves a little more effort. This book deliberately tries to teach increasing brick stitch, since it makes the stitch a lot more versatile. In addition, increasing allows a beader to produce many different shapes besides diamonds or triangles. Note that round or circular brick stitch differs slightly owing to its three-dimensionality. Most patterns that use this stitch will tell you where to begin for the easiest way to follow the pattern.

Round or Circular Peyote-Stitch Patterns

Round or circular peyote stitch is also a three-dimensional technique. The pattern is flat or two-dimensional, while the beadwork is actually a three-dimensional circle or ring of beads. At the end of each row, you need to "drop down" or "step up" to begin the next row. These terms actually mean the same thing, depending on whether you are working the pattern starting from the top or starting from the bottom. If you turn your work upside down, you will see that it is actually the same. Since you are either stepping up or dropping down at the end of each row, you will notice that the first bead of each row actually shifts by one bead for every row. Some patterns will note this by having a red line drawn through the pattern to mark the shift. However, this is difficult for many beaders to comprehend. I advise my students to look at the beadwork to see that it looks the same as the pattern. The human brain is actually being required to translate a two-dimensional image into a three-dimensional one.

If the pattern image is symmetrical, you could actually start at the top or the bottom and the result would be identical.

Patterns for beaded objects like gourds or pottery are slightly different because the pots are not identical in shape or size. The project calls for increasing the number of beads at strategic points to accommodate the size and curve of the pottery. To attach your beads to the pottery, you start at the neck of the pottery, using background beads. You then add your pattern beads against the solid background beads. Your increases are placed only within the background beads and not in the pattern itself. Find peyote stitch diagrams and a graph in Part V.

Flat Peyote-Stitch Patterns

Since flat peyote stitch is two-dimensional, it is often easier to follow a pattern for it than for either round or circular peyote stitch. If the pattern is only one color, you can start from either the right or the left side. After the flat piece of beadwork is completed, it is then curved into a circular shape and seamed up the side using a technique called a *zipper stitch*. With flat peyote stitch, you bead from right to left and then change directions with each row. You do not need to turn over your

work to begin the next row. Simply continue beading each row, and position your hands to change directions comfortably.

Occasionally you will encounter an odd-count peyote-stitch pattern. Sometimes a pattern dictates the use of an odd number of beads instead of an even number to produce the proper symmetry of design. The illustration for odd-count flat-peyote turnaround is used every other row. If you design your own patterns and do not have a good reason for doing odd-count, use even-count, which is easier for most people to bead. If you are not careful with your thread tension, the edges will not be straight.

Q: What is the difference between peyote stitch and gourd stitch?

A: *Peyote stitch* is a general term referring to several distinct beading techniques. This is a popular stitch that is used to cover three-dimensional objects, but it can also be used for two-dimensional techniques. Its origins appear to be North American, and it has been made popular in Native American beadwork. Often used in ceremonial objects like gourd rattles and peyote fans, peyote stitch has been referred to by several names. Among them are gourd stitch, round peyote, circular peyote, odd-count peyote, even-count peyote, flat peyote, free-form peyote, twill, round flat peyote, two-drop peyote, and three-drop peyote stitch.

What is commonly called peyote stitch may describe a variety of techniques used by different cultures. For instance, the ancient Egyptians used a form of peyote stitch, but so do the peoples of South Africa and the Native Americans. Many individual beaders do not understand the subtle distinctions among these examples.

Some Native American beaders who have assigned a sacred element to a specific beadwork technique, such as peyote stitch, may believe it is inappropriate for the uninitiated to perform that particular stitch. Interestingly, it has become common to identify the same stitch as gourd stitch when used in a secular context, as opposed to a ceremonial context. But this explanation is only about naming and reveals little about the differences in technique. This controversy does not preclude people from using any stitch they choose, calling it anything they choose, and even making ceremonial objects—whether they consider them sacred or not.

It is undeniable that the word *peyote* was taken from the name of a cactus held sacred by many Native North American tribes, used in spiritual ceremonies. That's why some Native Americans consider peyote stitch a sacred activity. The Huichol word *pejuta* means "medicine." Westerners, however, consider it a hallucinogen.

Peyote stitch and gourd stitch are quite similar in appearance. Most ceremonial objects are constructed with what some people refer to as the *authentic peyote stitch*. The beads are offset by two-thirds, and gourd stitch is offset by a half. For beaders familiar with this technique, peyote stitch is beaded by adding one bead every third bead. Gourd stitch is beaded by adding one bead every other bead. Peyote stitch tends to spiral more distinctly than gourd stitch. What is commonly accepted as peyote stitch in many beadwork books and magazines is more appropriately called gourd stitch. Find photos of the so-called authentic peyote stitch in Part II.

Finishing Tips

Find drawings of steps for various finishing techniques in Part V.

Q: What is a crimp bead and how is it used?

A: A crimp bead is used to secure beading wire to a clasp. There are two kinds of crimp beads: *tube-shaped* and *round*. The tube-shaped crimp bead is more often gold-filled or found in sterling silver, while the round ones are more often seen in base metal, silver, gold, and copper. A crimp bead cannot be used with ordinary thread or elastic because it is too abrasive and will break it. It is used with a crimper tool. A crimp bead is made of specially designed soft metal that is meant to collapse with pressure. (*See* crimp pliers in Part II. Find finishing techniques in Part V.)

Q: How do you use a crimper tool and crimp bead?

A: The function of a crimp bead is to secure stringing wire to the clasp and to hold the beads securely in place. A crimp bead is a specially designed bead made of soft metal that easily collapses when flattened with pliers. Flat-nose pliers can be effective but may leave a somewhat unattractive and sharp edge. A specially designed crimper tool is more appropriate and requires two steps. The first step flattens the finished crimp bead into a concave shape, and the second step forms it into a round shape, smaller than the original crimp bead. The finished crimp can be concealed in a bead tip or slid into another bead with a large hole. On the crimper tool, the first shaping area of the closed jaws looks like lips, and the second one looks like a small football or oval shape. (Find uses of the crimper tool in Part V.) The crimper tool's lip-shaped area can flatten, bend, and curve the crimp bead, and the tool's football-shaped area can help you round out the bead. A crimp bead is not recommended for use with stringing cord or monofilament that is not metal, since the friction will break the stringing material.

Q: What is the best way to finish a strung necklace so that it looks professional?

A: Depending on the type of necklace, several acceptable finishing techniques can work nicely.

Knot and Jump Ring If you are stringing with threads or cords, one method is to tie the bead threads in a knot around a metal jump ring and glue it securely. However, that is not always a preferable method, because any time thread is in contact against metal, abrasion can weaken the connection. It is a lot safer to have the strand end(s) covered with an end bead or cone.

Bead Tip Another way to finish off multiple strands of beads on thread or cord is to use a finding called a *bead tip*. There are two types of bead tips. One is somewhat *cup-shaped* and the other is *clamshell-shaped*. Both have a hole in the middle to string your thread ends. (*See* photo under bead tip in Part II.) Gather the threads together and knot them in the center of the cup-shaped bead tip. If you prefer the clamshell-shaped bead tip, you will need to squeeze it shut. The loop on the end of the bead tip is for attaching to a split ring, jump ring, or clasp end.

Crimp Bead If you are using stringing wire, another method is to place a *crimp bead* (also called a *crimper*) on the end of the stringing wire after the beads are in position. Thread the wire through the ring or clasp end and then back through the crimper, going in the opposite direction.

Then use a *crimping tool* or *flat-nose pliers* to flatten the crimp bead. A crimping tool (crimp pliers) takes the extra step of shaping the crimp bead so that it looks very neat and discreet.

End Cap If you are using a leather cord or bulkier stringing material, a finding called an *end cap* or *leather crimp* can be wrapped around the end of the cord and closed shut. A dab of glue adds security.

Ball and Loop When using a cord with no clasp or other hardware, a *bead clasp* (sometimes called a *ball and loop*) can be constructed by wrapping the leather or cord around itself to create the loop. A larger bead can be placed on one end before you wrap the cord around itself. Allow at least 4 inches (10 cm) to make the wrapping. To secure the loop, use either a secure knot or an adhesive applied to the leather end before wrapping the cord.

Care and Preventive Maintenance

This section addresses some basic ways of taking good care of your beadwork in order to prevent having to do repairs.

Q: Is it OK to launder clothing items after they have been beaded?

A: Consider the type of fabric and pre-launder them to prevent shrinkage. Some fabrics hold up well to washing after beading if treated gently. Use a garment bag or pillow case, machine wash in cold water in the delicate cycle, or hand wash. Some beadwork is designed to be removable for laundering. Always consider the fabric and launder accordingly. For instance, silk requires special laundering considerations. The heat from a dryer can also damage some beads. If you turn the item inside out before laundering it, the beads will be protected.

Q: Is it OK to dry-clean clothing with beadwork on it?

A: Dry cleaning is a chemical process that can cause damage to bead dyes and finishes.

Q: How do I know if a particular bead color is permanent and not prone to bleeding or fading?

A: Before you make your beadwork project, ask you local bead-store owner about the permanence of the bead color. Most bead colors are within the glass and will not fade or rub off. However, a few exotic colors are surface-dyed. You can test your beads by putting a few of them on a piece of white paper and spraying with water. If the color bleeds onto the paper, you will know that the color is unstable. You can also test your beads by exposing them to direct sunlight for a few days. If you want to test your beads on fabric, make a small beaded sample and expose it to a washing machine treatment and dryer cycle, as well as to dry cleaning. It is much better to risk a small sample instead of a costly beaded garment.

Q: What are some tips for the care and preservation of beadwork?

A: Although many beaders do not concern themselves with long-term preservation, some basic prevention techniques can help your beadwork to remain in good condition for years to come.

First, consider your materials and plan to have your beadwork outlive you. Use the appropriate threading materials for the bead size. If the thread is a natural product like silk or cotton, it will not last as long as synthetic threads or combination natural and synthetic threads. Natural fibers can biodegrade in as little as 50 years under ideal conditions and in fewer years under harsh conditions. Certain organic materials, such as leather, are biodegradable, and even if the beadwork is intact, it will inevitably deteriorate over time. Synthetic threads have only been around for less than 100 years, so old beadwork was probably made with cotton thread, leather, or other natural fibers. Among Asian cultures, where pearls are a local treasure, it is not uncommon for owners to restring their pearls with silk thread as often as annually. Restringing your grandmother's old pearls is one of the best ways to ensure that your children will see them someday. Avoid exposing such jewelry to abrasion, perfumes, and hair sprays. Use

only jewelry cleaners designed for pearls, since the nacre or coating is sensitive.

If you use thread that does not fit snugly inside the bead hole, abrasion will shorten its life span. Occasionally, you will find that a particular spool of thread seems abnormally subject to fraying or unraveling. Replace it with more appropriate thread. The replacement cost of thread is insignificant compared with the risk of destruction.

Avoid beads with a finish that is prone to fading or rubbing off. Treating beads with an acrylic glaze or fixative may prevent that problem, or you may substitute better quality beads.

Cull or sort out beads that are chipped or broken, since they can easily slice your thread, causing the beadwork to fall apart.

Use prewaxed or treated thread to preserve the life of the thread. Beeswax is a very inexpensive method of preserving your thread and beadwork.

Consider the storage environment or climate. Like many fine things in life, they should not be exposed to temperature extremes of hot, cold, humidity, or dry air. Do not leave your fine beadwork lying on the dashboard of your vehicle to get baked in the sun. Do not wear your fine beadwork in the swimming pool to be exposed to chemicals and water. Do not store your beadwork in a moist bathroom. Do not wear your beadwork when camping, boating, mud wrestling, or skydiving. If in doubt, store your fine beadwork indoors in a safe place where it will not be exposed to dirt, family pets, insects, or other abuse.

Washing any beaded and threaded textile or delicate object can cause damage, so try to keep your beadwork clean. Surface cleaning with a clean damp cloth will probably be the safest way to remove dust and grime. Cleaning agents as well as water alone can cause discoloration as well as fading. Getting water on the backing of beadwork can predispose the article to the growth of molds and other microorganisms.

When ironing a garment with beadwork on it, use care as you would with any delicate fabric. Do not iron the beads directly but turn the fabric inside out and place it over a towel or other cloth for cushioning. Steam ironing is okay as long as the bead finishes are stable. Test a small sample to make sure before risking the whole garment.

Repairs are best done as soon as possible after the damage to avoid losing the beads necessary for the repair. If you did the beadwork, you should possess the knowledge of technique and materials used. It is best to use the same materials if at all possible. If the artist and date of the beadwork are unknown, it is generally best to consult with experienced beaders, bead store owners, or museum curators before attempting the repair. Be extremely cautious in using glues that can actually cause further damage. If you do not have adequate knowledge and skills to repair the beadwork, it is best left alone until the proper repair can be done by an expert. Expert photography is an ideal way to preserve objects that may require an entire makeover in order to restore their original condition.

Very expensive, sentimental, or labor-intensive beadworks should be considered museum pieces if you want to leave them as an inheritance for your grandchildren. Museums, by the way, generally store such items in temperature-controlled and moisture-controlled environments that allow for adequate air flow. Acid-free boxes are good storage containers with some Ph-neutral tissue paper. Nonbuffered tissue paper is recommended for beadwork with leather backing.

It is recommended that strung pieces be stored flat to minimize the weight stress of hanging.

If the items are small, like earrings, it is generally OK to store them hanging in a safe place. Just apply common sense when preserving your precious beadwork for a reasonable time.

Q: Is it safe to use jewelry and metal cleaners on beadwork and gemstones?

A: It's advisable to read the label carefully to determine whether a certain product is recommended for a particular piece of jewelry or beadwork. Consider all materials used, like gemstones, metals, adhesives, fabrics, and even threads. What may be a safe silver cleaner may not be safe for gemstones. What is safe for pearls may not be safe for silk or certain types of threads.

Bead Anecdotes

Here we've included interesting lore as well as a few facts about beads and gemstones.

Q: Is it true that Manhattan was sold for $24 worth of beads?

A: In Martha Lamb's *History of the City of New York,* written in 1877 (250 years after the reported purchase), she claimed that the Dutch bought Manhattan Island for $24 worth of trading beads ("wampum"). Although it makes for an interesting story, no written documentation or evidence suggests there is any truth to that rumor. Reportedly, much trading was going on in the New World, and beads were very well received by the indigenous peoples. Beads were often used as an ice-breaker to initiate trade and friendly relations. Their cultural philosophies relating to land ownership were very different, since native peoples believed that their established communities had rights to live there, although the concept of selling land was entirely foreign to them. While it is possible that wampum beads could have been exchanged, not as payment but as a sort of honorable treaty or agreement, there is no evidence of any written deed or documentation to verify the purchase of Manhattan with beads. More than likely, it was a "deal" that could not be objectively verified. It is also possible that an unscrupulous individual "sold" land that he did not own or else believed himself to be taking advantage of a fool.

In a famous quote from a letter written to President Franklin Pierce in 1854, Chief Seattle said, "How can we buy or sell the sky, the warmth of the land? The idea is strange to us. If we do not own the freshness of the air and the sparkle of the water, how can you buy them?"

Q: Is it true that a war was fought over beads?

A: One could say that the Pequot War of 1637 was fought over beads. At that time in history, the settlements were growing and business interests were developing among the Dutch, the English, and the native population. When the English discovered how important wampum was, they declared war against the Pequot Indians, who controlled the wampum trade as well as the lush Connecticut Valley. Unfortunately, it was only one of many wars waged against the Native Americans for their land and resources. *See* wampum beads in Part II.

Q: Is it true that the U.S. currency was once based on beads?

A: At one time, the wampum bead (which was hand-carved from a seashell) was recognized as legal currency in all thirteen of the original colonies. When the colonists first came to America, there was no legal money or coins. The natives that lived here had been using wampum beads as a way of documenting important events and honoring individuals in ceremonies like weddings and adoptions. They wove belts of wampum beads for these occasions. The colonists adopted as a medium of exchange the wampum beads, which were strung in 6-foot (1.8-meter) lengths. *See* wampum in Part II.

Q: Is peyote stitch allowed for use only by Native Americans?

A: Although some Native Americans believe that this stitch is reserved for ceremonial objects, it does not preclude others from practicing the same form of beadwork. Actually, what is commonly known as *peyote stitch* is more accurately called *gourd stitch*. There are actually two different methods that go by the same name. Many native beaders do not know the difference, which contributes to the confusion on the subject. Both peyote stitch and gourd stitch are practiced throughout the world. For more technical information on the differences between the two stitches, see the question in the technique section that follows.

Q: Is it true that gemstones have been used for healing?

A: At least since the Middle Ages, gemstones have been used for many purposes—psychological, spiritual, and physical—whether as amulets, indications of status or membership, tokens of love, or as gifts and rewards. The term *lithotherapy* refers to the use of stones for healing. What distinguishes magic, sorcery, fantasy, and therapeutic healing may at times be difficult to discern. The field of healing gemstones and crystals has its skeptics and believers. We cannot begin to address or argue for or against the wearing or use of gemstones or crystals to improve one's health. We do know that a lovely necklace or earrings can make the wearer happy, but that's not what's usually meant by healing gemstones or crystals. Gemstones have been used in direct skin contact, much like a copper bracelet that when worn is said to benefit someone suffering from arthritis. A particular gemstone's energetic qualities are thought to be most effective when in physical proximity. The healing, most scientists and medical practitioners would argue, may be attributed to the placebo effect. Whether the result of an energetic, physical, or spiritual change is due to, say, trace elements, the whole stone, or some other cause may be difficult to measure or judge in either quantitative or qualitative terms.

You can make up your own mind. If this complex subject interests you, consult a book dedicated to healing gems and crystals to determine individual gems' properties.

Q: Is it true that beads are addictive?

A: Yes! It is only fair to warn the buyer that well-established evidence shows that beads are addictive to humans. However, it is a fairly nondestructive addiction that can be treated by rationalizing that one needs to acquire more beads for one's health and well-being, one's family, and one's friends. If you are in doubt about whether you suffer from this psychological condition, consult with your local bead store. Most likely they will reassure you that you have come to the right place.

PART IV

Beading
Tables
and
Charts

Bead Shapes

Common Bead Shapes

Horace C. Beck's *Classification and Nomenclature of Beads and Pendants* (1928) became the museum standard for describing the most common bead and pendant shapes found in the ancient world to help determine cultural origin. The book reprinted his 1926 paper that provided a way to classify ancient and tribal beads, such as Egyptian, Etruscan, Anglo-Saxon, Roman, and Syrian beads by form, size, perforation, and materials. Beck distinguished about 56 types among the myriad varieties of bead shapes found in the ancient world. Lois Sherr Dubin created a similar list from her bead collection, shown in *The History of Beads* (1987, 2004).

We have refined these earlier lists to create our own, more contemporary list of common bead shapes found on today's market. See Part I for a discussion of bead anatomy and other common bead shapes.

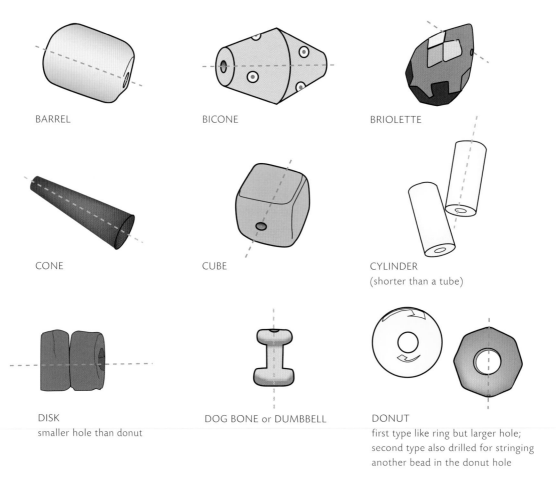

BARREL

BICONE

BRIOLETTE

CONE

CUBE

CYLINDER
(shorter than a tube)

DISK
smaller hole than donut

DOG BONE or DUMBBELL

DONUT
first type like ring but larger hole;
second type also drilled for stringing
another bead in the donut hole

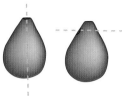

DROP or TEARDROP

DRUM

ELBOW
macaroni shape or curved tube

FLUTED

LOZENGE
threaded two ways

MELON

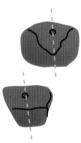

NUGGET
rough-edged, like mineral or
rock; smooth, faceted version

OVAL or ELLIPSOID

PEAR-SHAPED

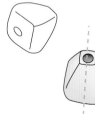

PYRAMID

RECTANGLE

RING or ANNULAR
sometimes called donut but with
larger hole and thinner walls

RONDELLE

ROUND or SPHERE

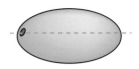

SAUCER or LENTICULAR

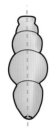

SEGMENTED

SEMICIRCULAR

SPOOL

SQUARE
flatter than a cube

TABULAR

TRIANGULAR

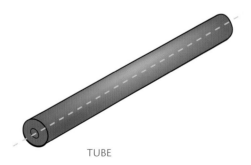

TUBE

Bead Sizes

Bead Size Chart

The circles representing bead sizes are shown at actual size. You can place the desired (round) bead in the circle as a rough check on its size in millimeters. Remember that 1 inch = 2.54 cm = 25.4 mm. Also see separate seed bead chart.

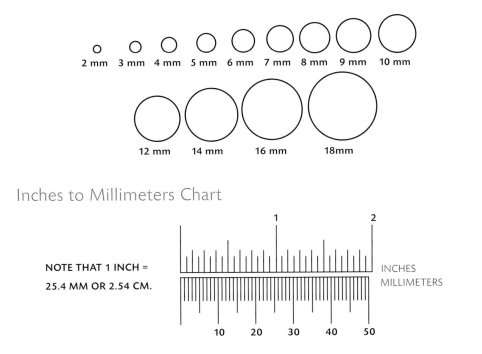

Inches to Millimeters Chart

NOTE THAT 1 INCH =
25.4 MM OR 2.54 CM.

INCHES
MILLIMETERS

Common Seed Bead Sizes

Below find the approximate number of seed beads that will fit on 1 inch of stringing wire, thread, cord, or other material. Note that 1 inch = 2.54 cm or 25.4 mm.

BEAD TYPE	NUMBER OF BEADS PER INCH
6/0 seed beads	9
8/0 seed beads	11
9/0 seed beads	13
10/0 seed beads	15
11/00 seed beads	17

Seed Beads with Thread and Needle Sizes

Popular seed bead sizes range from 5/0 (largest) to 22/0 (smallest). Remember, the smaller the number, the larger the bead, and the larger the number, the smaller the bead. Smaller antique beads are found, but they are rare. Larger modern seed beads are not very popular.

Note that size 5/0 and larger beads require not thread but stringing wire or heavier stringing material, like sinew, waxed linen, leather, or pearl knotting cord. For beads smaller than 15/0, needles and thread are difficult to find.

SEED BEAD SIZE	THREAD SIZE	NEEDLE SIZE
8/0	D or F	big-eye or twisted-wire needle
10/0	B, D, or F	size 10, big-eye, or twisted-wire needle
11/0	A, O, or B	size 10, 11, or 12 needle
12/0	A, O, or OO	size 11 or 12 needle
13/0	A, O, or OO	size 12 or 13 needle
14/0	A, O, or OO	size 12 or 13 needle

Crimp Bead Sizes with Stringing Wire

Round or tube-shaped crimp beads, sometimes called crimpers, are special types of beads used to attach string wire to a clasp. The small crimp beads are made from soft metal designed to collapse or crush easily when pinched with flat-nosed pliers, chain-nose pliers, or crimping pliers. Note that the stringing wire sizes are given in inches (from 0.012 to 0.026 inch), but that beads are commonly measured in millimeters.

ROUND CRIMPERS	TUBE CRIMPERS	STRINGING WIRE SIZE
1.5 mm	1 mm	thin (0.012 to 0.015)
2 mm	2 mm	medium (0.018 to 0.020)
2.5 mm	3 mm	heavy (0.021 to 0.026)
4 mm		heavy (0.021 to 0.026)

Glass Beads

Glass Bead Types

BEAD TYPE	APPEARANCE
Agate	Made to look like the gemstone agate. The glass has white swirled with color.
Charlotte	Beads have a single cut on one side that gives them a bit of sparkle. Most commonly found in Czech size 13, although other sizes are also available.
Color-Lined	Transparent beads with an opaque color lining inside the hole of the bead. The color may be scratched off by the stringing material over time, and certain colors will fade.
Cut	Usually refers to the number of facets in which the bead has been cut to form a hexagon. Charlotte cuts with one facet are also called true cuts.
Gilt-Lined	Inside the bead is a gold-colored lining.
Gold-Lined	Inside the bead is a gold lining.
Inside Color	Transparent beads that have had an opaque color applied inside the bead. Also called color-lined.
Opal	Semitranslucent glass that transmits light but is milky. Good opal glass has a bit of glow.
Opaque	Opaque glass transmits no light. Opaque glass has a dull gloss, although surface treatments are often applied (e.g., matte, rainbow).
Satin	Satin glass has a layered or striated appearance. The exact color depends on the viewing angle.
Silky	Silky beads, like satin, may have a striated, satiny appearance.
Silver-Lined (SL)	Transparent beads lined with silver. The silver lining is much harder to mar than a color lining.
Tortoise Shell	Two or more colors of glass swirled together, like dark amber and black, to produce a bead that has a tortoise-shell appearance. The term may also apply to colors such as blue with black swirls.
Transparent or Translucent	Transparent glass transmits light through the bead—you could read through it. Translucent glass transmits light, but you cannot see through it clearly.
White Heart	White hearts may be any degree of transparency, but they usually have an inner core of white glass.

Glass Bead Finishes

BEAD FINISH	APPEARANCE
Aurora Borealis (AB)	Permanent rainbow finish that can be applied to any color or type of glass bead. The finish is applied to one side of the bead only. The AB finish can be scratched, but should not rub off under normal wear.
Bronze	Bronze beads are coated with gold mixed with other materials, which is then baked on, producing a finish that resembles bronze.
Ceylon	Beads with a transparent/translucent luster. The finish has a pearlized appearance.
Galvanized	Beads plated with zinc in either a shiny or matte finish. The zinc coating tends not to be durable and can rub off during beading. The beads may be coated with an acrylic spray to help stabilize the finish.
Ghost	A finish combining matte and aurora borealis or rainbow.
Glow	A gossamer finish applied to a transparent bead that results in a golden glow over the color.
Gold Luster	Transparent beads that have been coated with a luster gold finish, creating subtle gold highlights on the bead.
Higher Metallic	Beads that are surface-coated with gold and then sprayed with oxidized titanium.
Iris	Iridescent permanent coating applied to a glass bead, giving it a rainbow metallic appearance.
Luster or Lustre	Uniform, shiny finish on the surface of a transparent, translucent, or opaque bead. The coating may be white, colored, or metallic. The beads tend to have a pearlized look.
Marea	One-half gold with a rainbow finish over the gold half.
Matte	Treatment that results in a velvety, nonreflective, frosted appearance.
Metallic	Glass beads with a metal-like surface coating, usually from being heated and then sprayed with oxidized tin. Thicker coatings result in darker finishes. Metallic coatings may rub off or change color.
Mottle	Opaque glass with a marbled gold wash.
Painted/Dyed	Treated with surface colorants that have been applied after the bead is made, usually involving application of pigment and then baking. Dyeing tends to be used with transparent beads. Opaque beads are painted. Strong UV light, as from fluorescent bulbs or sunlight, may cause fading. Some dyes will change color or wash off upon exposure to solvents, such as water or alcohol.

BEAD FINISH	APPEARANCE
Pearl	This term is often used to describe beads with an opaque luster.
Plated	Plain beads coated or electroplated with a metallic finish. For example, silver-plated beads are plated with silver, and gold-plated beads are plated with gold.
Rainbow	Permanent, translucent, iridescent coating. Usually applied over the entire surface of the bead.
Raku	Matte vitreal finish.
Scarabee	Aurora borealis finish applied over the entire surface area of the bead.
Semi-Matte	Matte but with a light polish. Not as shiny as regular opaque.
Supra-Metallic	Baked-on metallic finish with a slightly matte appearance. More durable than sprayed-on metallic coating.
Supra-Pearl	Baked-on pearl finish with a slightly matte appearance.
Vitreal or Vitrail	One-half silver with a rainbow finish over the silver half. Different rainbow coatings are available.

Artist Karen Houben

Gemstones

Here is a sampling of the wide variety of gemstones that have been used throughout the ages in beading. Bone, horn, ivory, pearls, mollusk shells, and coral can also be classified as organic gemstones, so we have included many here. Some gemstones, like turquoise, are named for their color or country of origin. Others, like agate, coral, jade, jasper, quartz, onyx, and serpentine, are also named for color variations, among other characteristics. In parentheses are a few of the varieties of the given stones.

For turquoise alone, here are a few varieties: African, Arizona nuggets, Arizona stabilized, Arizona stabilized black matrix, Arizona stabilized brown matrix, Arizona stabilized light-blue, Arizona stabilized light-blue with matrix, Arizona stabilized with matrix, Chinese blue, Chinese blue-green, Chinese blue-green with matrix, and Chinese green-blue.

Popular Gemstones

abalone

agate (black, blue, blue lace, green, moss, and tree)

amazonite

amber

amethyst

ametrine

aquamarine

Arabic shell

augite (blue and serpentine)

aura, aqua

aventurine (natural and red)

azurite

black stone

bloodstone

bone

canarium shell

cape amethyst

carnelian

cat's-eye chrysoberyl

cebu beauty shell

charoite

chrysocolla

chrysoprase

citrine

clamshell

cockle shell

cocoa shell

conus shell

coral (black, jasper, pink, red [oxblood], salmon-pink, and white)

dendrite

dumorterite

emerald

fire opal, Mexican

fluorite (purple and rainbow)

frogstone

garnet (almandite, pyrope, and rhodolite)

goldstone (blue and brown)

hammer shell

Popular Gemstones (continued)

hematite

horn (buffalo and sheep)

howlite (lapis [dyed], malachite [dyed], turquoise [dyed], and white)

iolite

ivory

jade (jadeite and nephrite)

jasper (apple, coral, fancy, flower, leopard-skin, opaline, picture, poppy, red, yellow, and zebra)

jet

labradorite

lapis lazuli (Nevada and leopard-skin)

lepidolite

lip shell (black, brown, gold, and red)

luana shell

malachite

marcasite

melon shell

moldavite

moon shell

moonstone (rainbow and white)

mosaic shell

mother-of-pearl

mussel shell

nephrite (jade)

obsidian (gold, mahogany, and snowflake)

olive shell

onyx (black, blue, green, and white)

opal (blue-green, multicolor, red-green, white, and yellow)

oyster shell (brown and violet)

pearl (freshwater and saltwater)

pen shell (dark and light)

peridot

pi shell (red and turquoise)

pink shell

pipestone

purple shell

quartz (clear, dark and smoky, frosted, ivory, red, rock crystal, rose, rutilated, smoky, and tourmalated)

quartzite (ivory, red [dyed], white, and yellow)

rhodochrosite

ruby (zoisite and star)

ryolite

sapphire

sapphire, star (black, light-blue, and pink)

sardonyx, striped

seftonite

serpentine (augite, chocolate, dark-green, fishrock, lime-green, pink, strawberry, and watermelon)

soapstone

sodalite

spiny oyster

star diopside, black

sugilite

tanzanite

thulite

tiger iron

tiger's eye (blue, brown, and red)

topaz (blue Swiss and sky-blue American)

tourmaline (green, pink, and watermelon)

turquoise (African, Arizona, Chinese, and more)

unakite

voluta shell

Gemstone Cuts

Common gemstone cuts and shapes include: American, antique, baguette, ball, barrel-shaped, briolette, bud, Ceylon, coat of arms, double brilliant, double rose, drop, emerald, French, free-form, half-brilliant, heart, hexagon, highlight brilliant, jubilee, king, magna, marquise, navette, needle brilliant, net, octagon, olive, oval, pear-shaped, pentagon, petal, rose, rhomb, round, shield, simple rose, square, star, star brilliant, Swiss, trapezoid, triangle, and whirl.

Shown from left to right are the top and bottom of the round, oval, emerald, triangle, heart, marquise, and pear gemstone cuts.

ROUND

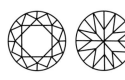

TOP   BOTTOM

OVAL

TOP   BOTTOM

EMERALD

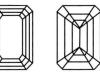

TOP   BOTTOM

TRIANGLE

TOP   BOTTOM

HEART

TOP   BOTTOM

MARQUISE

TOP   BOTTOM

PEAR

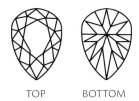

TOP   BOTTOM

Gemstone Treatments

Listed below are common treatments used on gemstones to improve their color, clarity, luster, durability, brilliance, and value. Before buying expensive gemstones, inquire about the treatments given to the stone. Any reputable dealer will provide such information upon request.

Bleaching Chemical agents are used to lighten or remove color from a gemstone.

Coating Some type of finish is applied to the gemstone to enhance its natural appearance.

Diffusion This process is used to deepen the color, but it affects only the stone's outer layer.

Dyeing Color additives or dyes are used on gemstones to alter their natural color.

Enhanced This term refers to some type of treatment that the gemstone has undergone, such as heating or filling.

Filled Surface fractures or flaws are filled with glass, clear epoxy resin, or other substances to improve the gemstone's appearance.

Foiling A gemstone mounted on a solid background is layered with foil to increase its reflectivity and improve its brilliance.

Heated Some form of heating is used to alter a gemstone's color.

Irradiated Some form of irradiation is used to alter a gemstone's color.

Lacquering Some type of lacquer or other substance is applied to the surface.

Laser drilling This technique improves the stone's clarity by using lasers to remove inclusions or flaws.

Oiling and waxing Oil and waxes are used to enhance color by filling in fine surface cracks.

Reconstituted Powdered gemstones are mixed with some type of acrylic material to form a solid block that is cut and polished.

Synthetic or imitation gemstones These stones may have been fashioned in a laboratory. Imitation gemstones are often composed of glass and can make very beautiful beads; however, they should not be sold deceptively as the real thing. Synthetic or man-made gemstones are often much less expensive than genuine gemstones found in the natural world.

Mohs Scale of Hardness

HARDNESS	MINERAL	TRUE OR ABSOLUTE HARDNESS
10	diamond	1,500 to 1,600
9	corundum, ruby, sapphire	400
8.5	cubic zirconia	
8	topaz	200
7 to 7.5	tourmaline	
7	amethyst, aventurine, quartz	100
6.5 to 7	peridot	
6 to 6.5	sugilite	
6	orthoclase feldspar	72
5.5 to 6.5	hematite, opal	
5 to 6	lapis lazuli, turquoise	
5 to 5.5	glass	
5	apatite	48
4.5 to 5	gaspeite	
4	fluorite	21
3.5 to 4	azurite	
3 to 4	coral	
3	calcite	9
2.5 to 4.5	pearl	
2 to 4	chrysocolla	
2 to 2.5	amber	
2	gypsum	2 to 3
1	talc	1

The Mohs Scale of Hardness, developed in 1812 by the German mineralogist Friedrich Mohs, is based on ten standard minerals. Their relative hardness is rated from 1 to 10 in order of increasing hardness: *talc, gypsum, calcite, fluorite, apatite, orthoclase feldspar, quartz, topaz, corundum,* and *diamond.* The typical way of thinking about hardness is that diamond (10) and quartz (7) can scratch glass (5.5). Or, a fingernail would be 2.5, a penny 3.5, glass 5.5, and a metal knife blade about 7.

Today, the sclerometer can measure *absolute hardness,* with a range of about 1 to 1,600. The diamond is 1,500 to 1,600; compare with corundum that has an absolute hardness of 400. The absolute hardness of quartz is 100 and of calcite, 9.

Birthstones by Month

The American National Association of Jewelers, Jewelers of America, adopted in 1912 a list of birthstones assigned to each month of the year. Tanzanite was added for December by the American Gem Trade Association in October 2002. Astrological, mystical (Tibetan), ayurvedic, talismanic, healing, and other traditional or modern birthstones may differ. Some people have speculated that the breastplate of Aaron, described in Exodus 28:15–30, which mentions twelve stones for the Twelve Tribes of Israel, may have been the origin of natal stones, or birthstones, later assigned to the twelve months or zodiac signs.

MONTH	MODERN BIRTHSTONE	TRADITIONAL OR ALTERNATE
January	garnet	rose quartz
February	amethyst	onyx
March	aquamarine	red jasper (bloodstone)
April	diamond	rock crystal (quartz)
May	emerald	chrysoprase
June	pearl or moonstone	alexandrite
July	ruby	jade
August	peridot	aventurine, sardonyx, or sapphire
September	sapphire	lapis lazuli
October	opal	pink tourmaline
November	yellow (golden) topaz or citrine	
December	turquoise, blue topaz, or tanzanite	blue zircon or lapis lazuli

Birthstones by Zodiac Sign

Traditional and modern assignments of gemstones to zodiac signs (astrological sun signs) vary widely. Some also prefer to assign gemstones according to the month, ruling planet, or color most identified with the astrological sign. Some sources assign aquamarine to Aquarius and amethyst to Pisces, for instance, rather than what's listed below. Consult Walter Schumann's *Gemstones of the World,* revised and expanded third edition (Sterling, 2006) for additional sun-sign gemstones as well as planetary and talismanic stones.

ZODIAC SIGN	BIRTHSTONE(S) AND ALTERNATES
Aries (March 21–April 19)	**diamond** (bloodstone, carnelian, jasper)
Taurus (April 20–May 20)	**emerald** (tiger's eye, topaz, tourmaline)
Gemini (May 21–June 20)	**pearl** (aquamarine, citrine, chrysocolla, spinel, tiger's eye)
Cancer (June 21–July 22)	**ruby** (moonstone)
Leo (July 23–August 23)	**peridot** (clear quartz, heliodor, ruby, sunstone)
Virgo (August 24–September 22)	**sapphire** (citrine, peridot)
Libra (September 23–October 23)	**tourmaline and opal** (aventurine, lapis lazuli)
Scorpio (October 24–November 21)	**topaz** (aquamarine, Herkimer diamond, obsidian)
Sagittarius (November 22–December 21)	**turquoise and zircon** (zircon, amethyst, blue quartz, malachite, topaz)
Capricorn (December 22–January 21)	**garnet** (black onyx, black tourmaline, clear quartz, jet)
Aquarius (January 20–February 18)	**amethyst** (chalcedony, garnet, sapphire)
Pisces (February 19–March 20)	**aquamarine** (bloodstone)

Amethyst

Emerald

Turquoise

Metals

Metal and "Metallized" Beads

Note the distinctions between *metal beads*, which are all metal, and metallized beads. *Metallized beads* have a finish over another substance, such as ceramic, glass, or plastic, that is made to look like metal. *Metal finishes* are used primarily on the surface of glass or metal beads or metal findings to enhance their appearance or change their color. For instance, vermeil, which is gold-filled over sterling silver, looks like gold but is much less expensive, since its base is silver.

14 kt gold

Bali beads and findings (sterling and gold-plate over sterling)

gold-filled

large-hole metal beads

liquid silver and narrow tube beads

metal beads with ethnic designs (Bali, Indian, Oriental)

metallized ceramic

metallized glass

metallized plastic

pewter beads

raw and plated metal

sterling silver

vermeil

Metal Finishes for Beads and Jewelry Findings

14 kt gold	niobium
14 kt gold-filled	nylon
antiqued bronze	pewter
antiqued copper	pewter, gold-matte finish
antiqued gold	pewter, silver-matte finish
antiqued silver	rhodium-plated, nickel color
black	silver-plated, bright silver
brass	sterling silver
bright or gilt gold-plated	surgical steel, raw, no plating
bronze	titanium
copper	vermeil, gold-filled over sterling
gold-plated	white metal
nickel	

Karats (Purity) with Millesimal Fineness Equivalents

Karats are commonly used for expressing the quality or purity of gold and platinum, and more rarely for other precious metals. According to this system, 24-karat gold is 99.99% pure gold, 18-karat gold is 75% pure, and 12-karat gold is 50% pure. Anything below 10 karats cannot be classified as gold in the United States. Karats (purity) is also spelled *carats,* but the preferred American and Canadian spelling when referring to purity is karat(s); common abbreviations for karat are k, kt, and ct.

For distinctions between *carat* (*mass or weight*), commonly used for diamonds, and *carat* (*purity*) commonly used for gold, see the definitions in Part II.

Here is the formula for determining purity in karats. One karat is the equivalent of $^1/_{24}$ purity by weight:

$$X = 24\, M_g/M_m$$

X stands for the karat rating of the material.

M_g is the mass of pure gold or platinum found in the material.

M_m is the total mass of the material.

In the *millesimal fineness system,* the purity of precious metals is indicated by parts per thousand of pure precious metal in the alloy. *Millesimal* means one of 1,000 parts or the quotient of a unit that has been divided by 1,000.

KARATS	MILLESIMAL FINENESS
9 karat	375 (cannot be classified as gold or another precious metal in the U.S.)
10 karat	417
12 karat	500
14 karat	585
16 karat	625
18 karat	750
20 karat	833
22 karat	916
24 karat	999

Stringing Materials
Threads, Cords, Filaments, Wires, and More

Threads & Bead Cords

C-Lon thread
Conso thread
DMC Perle cotton
FireLine thread
Gudebrod Silk
Kevlar thread
metallic thread

nylon bead cord
Nymo thread
pearl-knotting cord
Power Pro thread
Silamide
silk bead cord

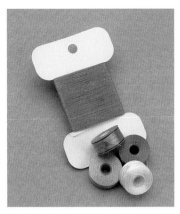

Thicker Cords

artificial sinew
bolo cord
braided leather
cotton cord
European leather cord
hemp
Indian leather cord

leather lace
rubber thong
satin rat-tail cord
suede lace
waxed cotton cord
waxed linen, Irish

Cable Wire & Monofilament

Accu-flex
Acculon tigertail
illusion cord

Soft Flex wire
Soft Touch wire

Other Stringing Materials

cloth-covered elastic
elastic cord
elastic string

gossamer floss
metal chain
organza ribbon

Wire (Craft)

bead craft wire
colored copper wire
French wire bullion

German craft wire
memory wire

Wire (Raw)

copper
fine silver
gold-filled
nickel

red brass
sterling silver
yellow brass

Bead-Stringing Wire

Find the right stringing-wire thickness for the beads you want to use. The wire sizes are given in millimeters for each wire's diameter. Remember that it is not necessarily the overall (outside measurement) bead size that determines the thickness of the wire (thin, medium, or heavy) needed but the size of the hole in the bead. Of course, heavy beads may require thicker or stronger beading wire.

WIRE SIZE	DESCRIPTION	BEAD SIZE
0.012 mm	thin	seed beads size 5 to 15
0.014 mm	thin	seed beads size 5 to 15
0.015 mm	thin	seed beads size 5 to 15
0.018 mm	medium	seed beads 5 to 11 and 2 to 10 mm
0.019 mm	medium	seed beads 5 to 11 and 2 to 10 mm
0.020 mm	medium	seed beads 5 to 11 and 2 to 10 mm
0.021 mm	heavy	seed beads 5 to 8 and 4 mm +
0.024 mm	heavy	gemstones and heavy beads
0.026 mm	heavy	gemstones and heavy beads

Weights and Measures

1 gross (Gr) . . . . 144 pieces = 12 dozen = 72 pairs

$1/2$ gross . . . . 72 pieces = 6 dozen = 36 pairs

1 mass (Ms) . . . . 1,200 pieces = 100 dozen

1 mille (M) . . . . 1,000 pieces

1 inch . . . . 25.4 mm = 2.54 cm

1 ounce (oz) . . . . 28.35 grams

1 pound (lb) . . . . 16 ounces

1 meter . . . . 39.4 inches = 3.3 feet = 1.1 yards

1 millimeter (mm) . . . . $1/25$ inch

1 kilogram (kilo or kg) . . . . 1,000 grams = 2.2 pounds = 35.27 ounces

$1/2$ kilo . . . . 500 grams = 1.1 pound

1 gram (g) . . . . 0.035 ounces

1 centimeter (cm) . . . . 10 mm

PART V

Beading Stitches, Finishing, and Graphs

Beading Stitches

Here are some of the popular beading stitches, or weaves. Note that many stitches can be known by a variety of different names.

Alligator Stitch

This three-dimensional stitch, popular in South America, is also called log-cabin stitch, gecko stitch, and chili (often spelled chile) stitch, alluding to chili peppers.

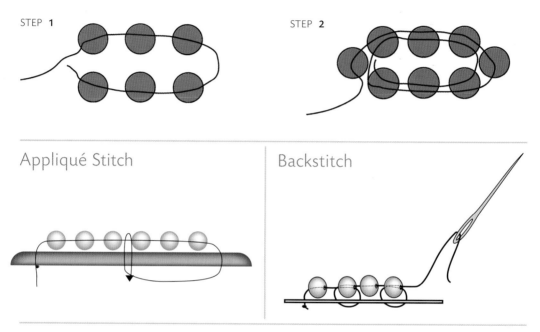

STEP **1**

STEP **2**

Appliqué Stitch

Backstitch

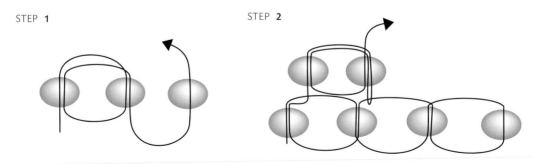

Brick Stitch

Also called stacking stitch, Apache weave, Comanche weave, and Cheyenne weave.

STEP **1**

STEP **2**

Cross-Weave

STEP **1** STEP **2** STEP **3**

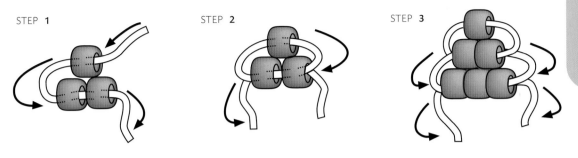

Flat Netting Stitch

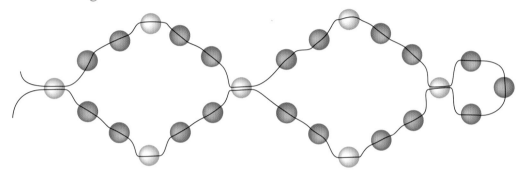

Flat Peyote Stitch

STEP **1**

STEP **2**

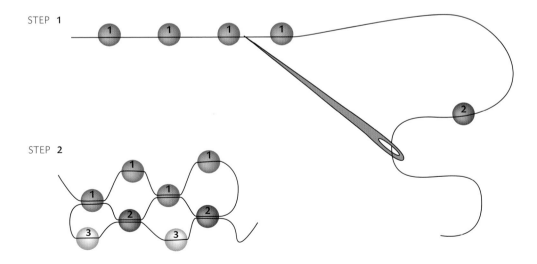

Fretting Stitch

Pick up 3 beads.

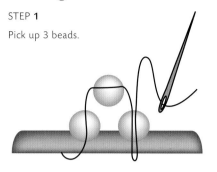

Pick up 2 beads.

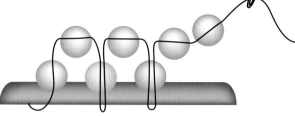

Huichol Lace

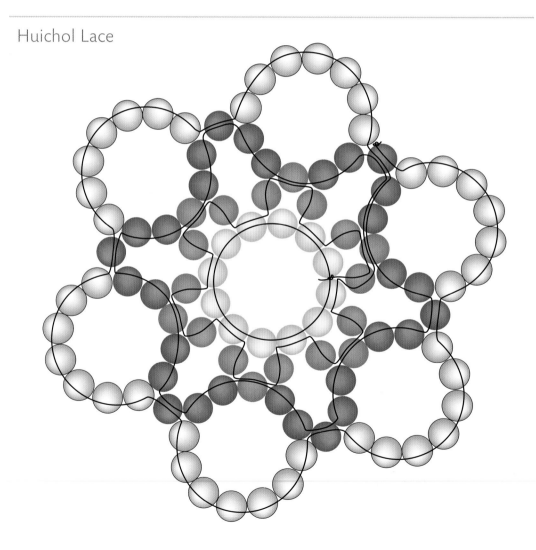

Ladder Stitch

STEP **1**

STEP **2**

STEP **3**

Reinforcing the base

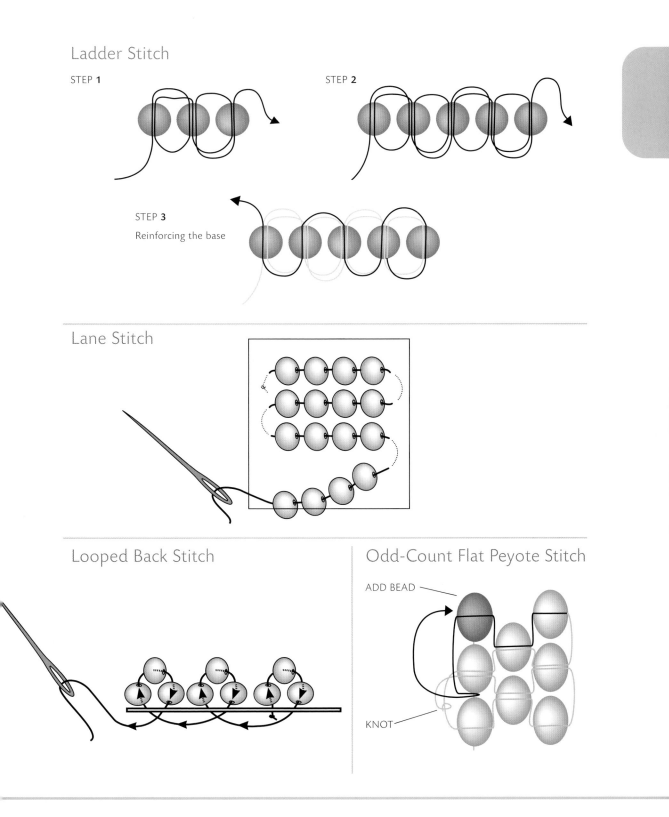

Lane Stitch

Looped Back Stitch

Odd-Count Flat Peyote Stitch

ADD BEAD

KNOT

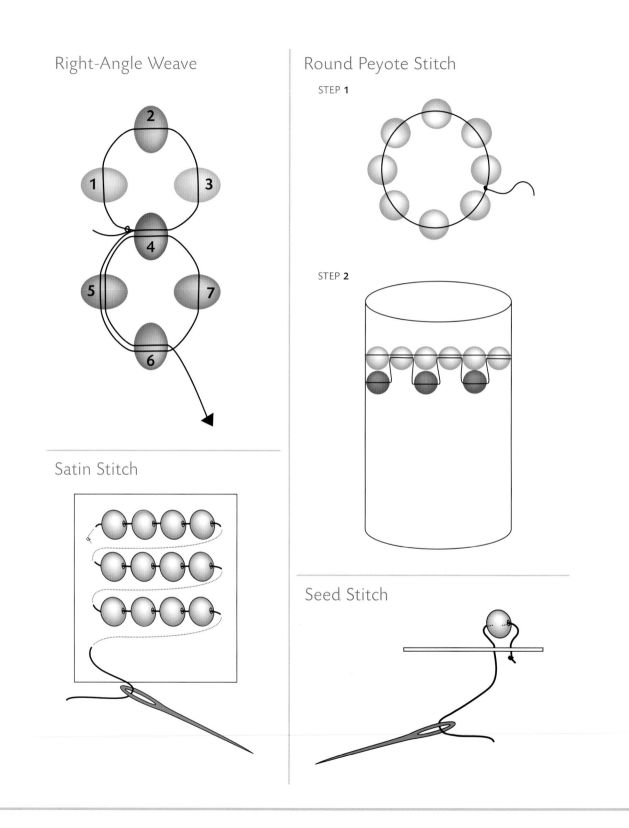

Right-Angle Weave

Round Peyote Stitch

STEP **1**

STEP **2**

Satin Stitch

Seed Stitch

Square Stitch

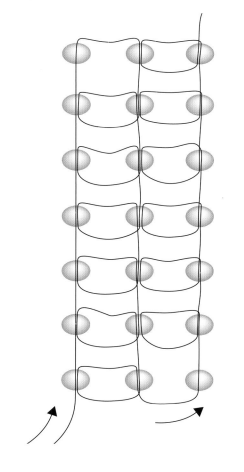

Stacked Seed Stitch

Triangle Turnaround Stitch

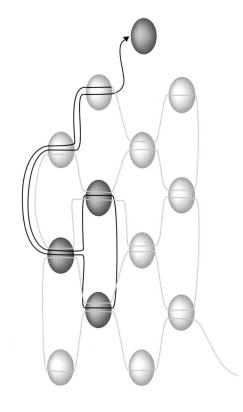

Whipstitch

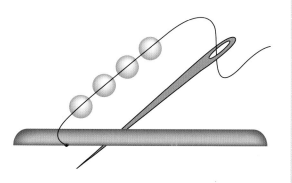

Embellishments and Fringe

Embellishments

Here are five ways to embellish a necklace or bracelet.

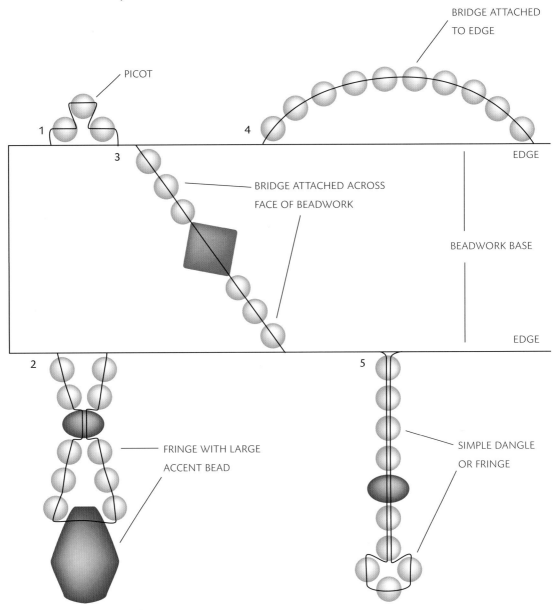

PICOT

BRIDGE ATTACHED TO EDGE

1

4

3

EDGE

BRIDGE ATTACHED ACROSS FACE OF BEADWORK

BEADWORK BASE

2

5

EDGE

FRINGE WITH LARGE ACCENT BEAD

SIMPLE DANGLE OR FRINGE

Branched Fringe

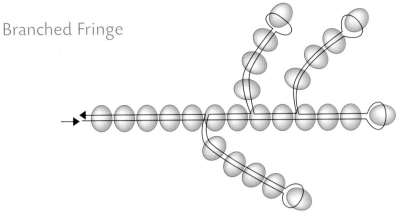

Knotting

Granny Knot

It is not advisable to use this knot when beading since it's really a type of slip knot. Don't confuse it with the square knot, which is more secure. *See* square knot steps on p. 378.

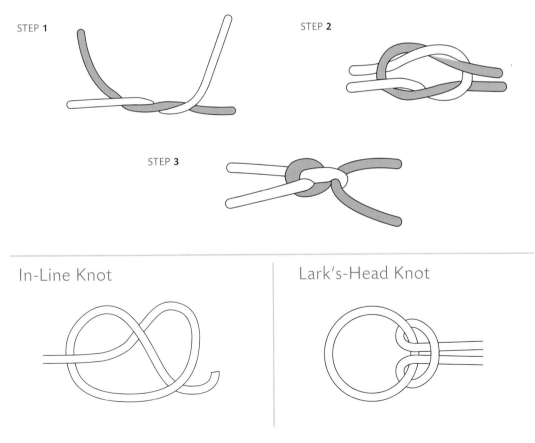

STEP **1**

STEP **2**

STEP **3**

In-Line Knot

Lark's-Head Knot

Square Knot

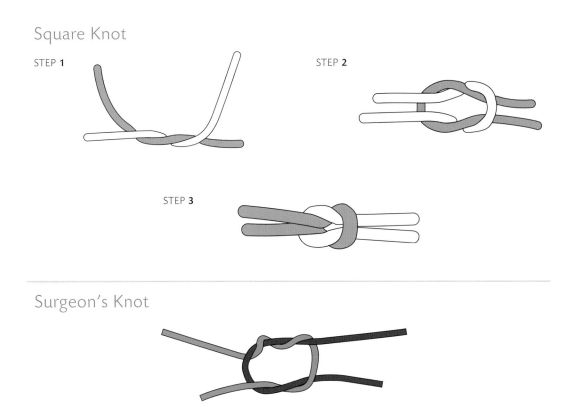

Surgeon's Knot

Finishing

Here are the six most popular ways of finishing a beaded necklace or bracelet.

Knotted-Cord Finishing

Bead-Tip Finishing

STEP **1**

STEP **2**

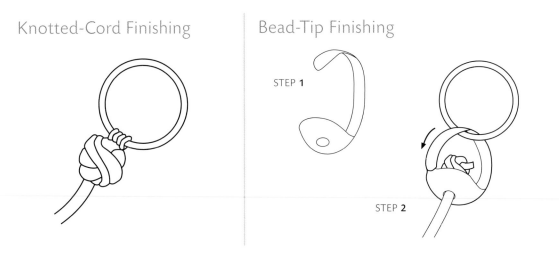

Crimp-Bead Finishing

Crimp Beads

The crimp bead can be tube-shaped and
flattened for a tight fit.

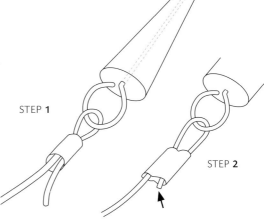

STEP **1**

STEP **2**

A round crimp bead can be tightened with a crimper tool.

Crimper Tool

Use the lips for step 1 and the football for step 2.

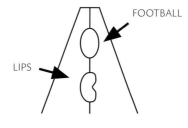

FOOTBALL

LIPS

Eye-Pin Knot with Bead-Cap Finishing

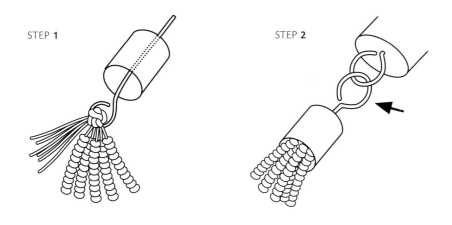

STEP **1**

STEP **2**

Crimp-Ends Finishing

This method works best with cord or leather.

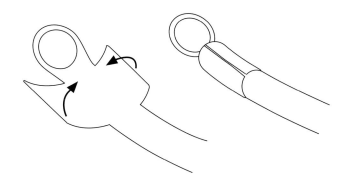

Wrapping-Finishing

This finishing method works best with cord or wire.

STEP **1**

STEP **2**

Beading Graphs

Photocopy and use the desired graph to visualize the work, plan your color scheme, or create designs of your own. The graphs are named for the particular stitch used to create the beaded project.

Brick-Stitch Graph

Brick stitch is also called stacking stitch, Apache weave, Cheyenne weave, or Comanche weave.

Peyote-Stitch Graph

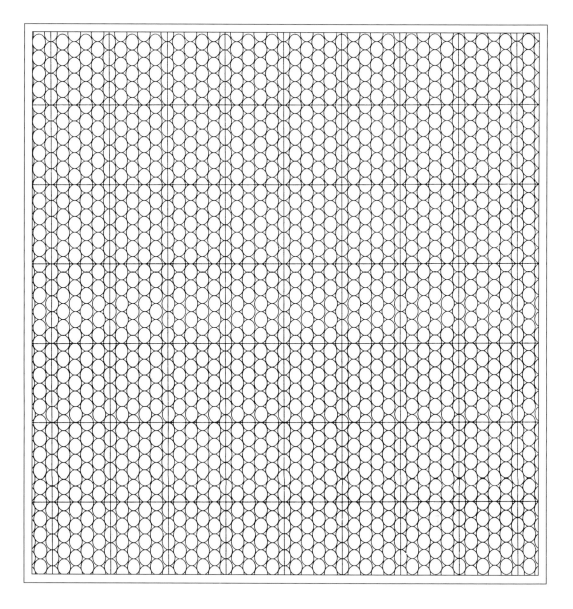

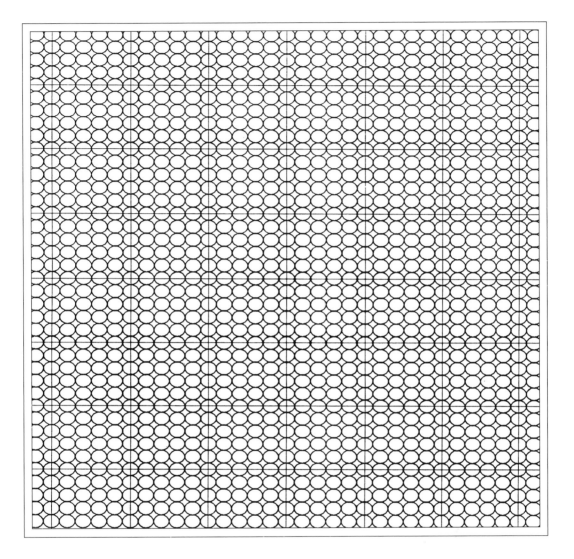

Selected Bibliography

Many specialized books, periodicals, and helpful Internet resources are available on beading. We've used numerous sources in compiling this book. Here are just a few of our favorites on the many historical and cultural uses of beads.

Books and Periodicals

Adams, Kimberly. *The Complete Book of Glass Beadmaking*. Asheville, North Carolina: Lark Books, 2005.

Beck, Horace C. *Classification and Nomenclature of Beads and Pendants.* York, Pennsylvania: Liberty Cap Books, 1928. Reprinted in 1973. Originally published in *Archaeologia,* 77: 1–76.

Benson, Ann. *Beadpoint: Beautiful Bead Stitching on Canvas.* New York: Sterling Publishing Co., 2003.

Benson, Ann. *Beadwork Basics*. Ogden, Utah: Chapelle, Ltd., 1994.

Benson, Ann. *The New Beadweaving: Great Projects with Innovative Materials.* New York: Sterling Publishing Co., 2004.

Benson, Ann, et al. *The Pattern Companion: Beading*. New York: Sterling Publishing Co., 2004.

Blomgren, Paige Gilchrist. *The Weekend Crafter* series. *Beading: From Necklaces to Napkin Rings, 20 Easy and Creative Projects to Make in a Weekend.* Asheville, North Carolina: Lark Books, 1998.

Campbell-Harding, Valerie. *Beaded Tassels, Braids & Fringes*. New York: Sterling Publishing Co., 2001.

Codina, Carles. *The Complete Book of Jewelry Making*: *A Full-Color Introduction to the Jeweler's Art.* Asheville, North Carolina: Lark Books, 2000.

Coles, Janet, and Robert Budwig. *The Book of Beads: A Practical and Inspirational Guide to Beads and Jewelry Making.* New York: Simon and Schuster, 1990.

Constantino, Maria. *The Knot Handbook*. Devon, England: D&S Books, 2000. Republished by Sterling Publishing Co., 2001.

Dean, David. *Beading in the Native American Tradition*. Loveland, Colorado: Interweave Press, 2002.

DeLange, Deon. *Techniques of Beading Earrings*. Ogden, Utah: Eagles View Publishing, 1938.

Dubin, Lois Sherr. *The History of Beads from 30,000 B.C. to the Present*. New York: Harry N. Abrams, 1987.

Eakin, Jamie Cloud. *Simple Techniques for Beautiful Jewelry*. Asheville, North Carolina: Lark Books, 2005.

Elbe, Barbara. *Back to Beadin': Elegant Amulet Purses & Jewelry Using Delica & Seed Beads*. B.E.E. Pub., 1996.

Erikson, Joan M., and Austin, Mary. *The Universal Bead*. New York: W. W. Norton & Co., 1969.

Fitzgerald, Diane. *The Beaded Garden: Creating Flowers with Beads and Thread*. Loveland, Colorado: Interweave Press, 2005.

Francis, Peter, Jr. *Asia's Maritime Bead Trade: 300 B.C. to the Present*. Honolulu: University of Hawaii Press, 2002.

Francis, Peter, Jr. *Beads of the World: A Collector's Guide with Price References*. Atglen, Pennsylvania: Schiffer Publishing, 1994.

Gibson, Bonnie. *Gourds: Southwest Gourd Techniques & Projects from Simple to Sophisticated*. New York: Sterling Publishing Co., 2007.

Gollberg, Joanna. *Making Metal Jewelry: Projects, Techniques, Inspiration*. Asheville, North Carolina: Lark Books, 2003.

Goodhue, Horace R. *Indian Bead-weaving Patterns: Chain-Weaving Designs and Bead Loom Weaving—An Illustrated "How-To" Guide*, revised and expanded edition. Summertown, Tennessee: the Book Publishing Company, 1989.

Grainger, Barbara L. *Dimensional Flowers, Leaves & Vines*. Oregon City, Oregon: Barbara L. Grainger Enterprises, 2000.

Gurley, Elizabeth and Ellen Talbott. *Beaded Adornments: Creating New Looks for Clothes & Accessories*. New York: Sterling Publishing Co., 2005.

Hall, Judy. *Crystal User's Handbook, An Illustrated Guide*. New York: Sterling Publishing Co., 2002.

Hall, Judy. *The Illustrated Guide to Crystals*. New York: Sterling Publishing Co., 2000.

Henry, Peggy Sue. *Beads to Buckskins,* Vol. 2. Hill City, Kansas: Beads to Buckskins Publications, 1991.

Hiney, Mary Jo. *The Beaded Object: Making Gorgeous Flowers and Other Decorative Accents*. New York: Sterling Publishing Co., 2002.

Hunt, W. Ben, and J.F. "Buck" Burshears. *American Indian Beadwork*. New York: Macmillan Publishing Co., 1951.

Jargstorf, Sybille. *Ethnic Jewelry from Africa, Europe & Asia*. Atglen, Pennsylvania: Schiffer Publishing, 2000.

Jargstorf, Sybille. *Glass Beads from Europe*. Atglen, Pennsylvania: Schiffer Publishing, 1995.

Jenkins, Cindy. *Making Glass Beads*. Asheville, North Carolina: Lark Books, 1997.

Karpun, Alexei. *Russian Jewellery Mid-19th Century–20th Century*. Moscow: Beresta, 1994.

Knuth, Bruce G. *Jeweler's Resource: A Reference of Gems, Metals, Formulas & Terminology for Jewelers*, revised edition. Thornton, Colorado: Jewelers Press, 2000.

Konstantinov, Varvara. *My Beaded Garden*. Kostroma, Russia: Jewelry by Varvara, 2003.

Koylova. *Jewellery Arts in the Urals*. Sverdlovsk, 1981.

Lange, Karen E. "Unstrung History." *National Geographic,* April 2007, p. 14.

Lankton, James W. *A Bead Timeline Volume I: Prehistory to 1200 C.E.* Washington, D.C.: The Bead Society of Greater Washington, 2003.

Levy, Stanley. *Bead & Sequin Embroidery Stitches*. East Sussex, UK: Guild of Master Craftsman Publications Ltd, 2004.

Liu, Robert K. *Collectible Beads: A Universal Aesthetic*. San Marcos, California: Ornament, Inc., 1995.

Moiseenko, Elena. *Beadwork and Bugle in Russia 18th–Early 20th Century.* Leningrad, Russia: Khudoznik RSFSR, 1990.

MonkeyBiz. *Positively HIV: HIV + AIDS Education Through Beadwork*. Cape Town, South Africa: Monkey Press, 2003.

Nehring, Nancy. *Embellishing with Beads*. New York: Sterling Publishing Co., 2003.

Picard, John. *Russian Blues: Faceted & Fancy Beads from the West African Trade,* Vol. V. Carmel, California: Picard African Imports, 1989.

Pinkowski, Jennifer. "Humble Brass Was Even Better than Gold to a 16th-Century Tribe in Cuba." *The New York Times,* January 16, 2007, p. F3.

Schumann, Walter. *Gemstones of the World,* 3rd edition, revised and expanded. Translated from the German. New York: Sterling Publishing Co., 2006.

Starr, Sadie. *Beading with Seed Beads, Gem Stones & Cabochons, Vol. #2.* Camp Verde, Arizona: Sadie Starr and Shooting Starr Publications, 1999.

Van der Sleen, W. G. N. *A Handbook on Beads.* Belgium: Publication des Journées Internationales du Verre. Liège, Belgium: Musée du Verre, 1967.

Widess, Jim, and Ginger Summit. *Making Gourd Dolls & Spirit Figures.* New York: Sterling Publishing Co., 2007.

Wilford, John Noble. "Ruins in Northern Syria Bear the Scars of a City's Final Battle." *The New York Times,* January 16, 2007, p. F2. *Obsidian beads and arrowheads.*

Internet Resources

Africa Direct. *African beads and beadwork, artifacts, textiles, baskets, mask, and artwork.* http://www.africadirect.com

American Society of Appraisers. *Appraisals of gemstones, precious metals, and jewelry for authenticity and value.* http:/www.appraisers.org

Anderson's American Indian and Western Shows. Southwest jewelry and turquoise. http://www.americana.net

Answers.com. *Consult for topics, such as the karat, precious metals, and gemstones.* http://www.answers.com

Bead and Button. *Beading magazine.* http://www.beadandbutton.com

The Bead Bugle. *History of beads.* http://beadbugle.com

The Bead Museum. *Global history of beads.* http://www.thebeadmuseum.com

The Bead Site. *The Center for Bead Research is an international institution for the study of beads.* http://www.thebeadsite.com

Bead Style. *Beading magazine.* www.beadstylemag.com

Bead Unique. *Beading magazine.* www.beaduniquemag.com

Bead Wrangler. *Bead and fiber information.* http://www.Beadwrangler.com/index.htm

Beadwork. *Beading magazine.* http://www.interweave.com/bead/beadwork_magazine

Belle Armoire. *Beading magazine.* http://www.bellearmoire.com

The Caning Shop. *Supplies for gourd craft, basketry and caning.* http://www.caningshop.com

The Center for Bead Research, Peter Francis, Jr, director. *The Center for Bead Research is an international institution for the study of beads.* http://www.TheBeadSite.com

Center for Desert Archeology. *Coronado Trail.* http://www.cdarc.org

Collectible Beads. *Rare and collectible beads; Piney Hollow.* http://www.collectible-beads.com

Colored Diamond Encyclopedia. *Photos.* http://www.color-diamond-encyclopedia.com

Corning Museum of Glass. *Resource on glass articles.* http://www.cmog.org

Dzi of Tibet. *Dzi (dZi) beads from Tibet, Nepal, and India.* http://dzioftibet.com

Dzi Crystal. *Photos of dZi beads for identification.* http://dzicrystal.com

Encarta Encyclopedia. *Information about gemstones.* http://uk.encarta.msn.com/encyclopedia_761563821_2/Gemstones.html

Enchanted Learning. *Glossary of gems and jewelry.* http://www.enchantedlearning.com/jewel/glossary/indexj.shtml

Everything2. *Desirable gemstone traits.* http://everything2.com/index.pl?node_id=828322

Federal Trade Commission, United States. *Consumer alerts on buying jewelry.* http://www.ftc.gov/bcp/conline/pubs/alerts/jewelweb.shtm *Defining standards.* http://www.ftc.gov/os/2000/12/jewelfrn.htm *Guides for the Jewelry, Precious Metals, and Pewter Industries.* http://www.ftc.gov/bcp/guides/jewel-gd.htm

Fire Mountain Gems. *Features beads, gems, tools, books and supplies.* http://www.firemountaingems.com/beading_information

The Fur Trapper. *Historical information on trade beads in North America.* http://www.thefurtrapper.com/trade_beads.htm

Gem Hut. *General information about gemstones with photos.*
http://www.gemhut.com/info.htm

Gemstone Therapy. *Healing with gemstones.* http: www.gemstonetherapy.com

Hands Around the World. *Handmade art and jewelry from artists around the globe.*
http://www.hands-around-the-world.com

The Herb Companion. *Botanical beads.* http://www.herbcompanion.com

Hinduism. *Ancient Hindu uses of gemstone therapy.*
http://hinduism.about.com/library/weekly/extra/bl-gemshp.htm

"History of Beads: The Venetian Bead Story." Francis, Peter, Jr. *From the recognized
bead authority.* http://BeadBugle.com/html/history_of_beads_table_of_cont.html

History of the Glass Bead. *History of wound-glass and other glass beads.*
http://www.geocities.com/ladysveva/BeadHistory.html

Indira Ghandi National Centre for the Arts. *Ostrich eggshell beadwork of Botswana.*
http://ignca.nic.in/new_main.htm

International Gem Society. *For professional gemstone information and charts.*
http://www.gemsociety.org/info/

International Trade Commission, United States. *The commission is designed to
protect United States industries against unfair trade practices in the global market.*
http://www.usitc.gov

Italian History and Culture. *Murano glass.*
http://www.boglewood.com/murano/history.html

Jay's of Tucson. *Tools, supplies, beads, gemstones, silver, kits, magazines, and books.*
http://www.jays-of-tucson.com

Jewelry Crafts. *Beading and jewelry-making magazine.*
http://www.jewelrycraftsmag.com

Jewelry Making. *Chemical composition and other information about gems.*
http://jewelrymaking.allinfoabout.com/features/specgravity.html

Joseph Wright Imports. Murano Fine Art Glass. *Glossary of Venetian and Murano
glass.* http://www.josephwright.com

Lapidary Journal. *Beading and lapidary magazine.* http://www.lapidaryjournal.com

Miyuki Delicas. *Japanese producer of seed beads.* http://www.miyuki-beads.co.jp

MonkeyBiz South Africa. *A nonprofit organization showcasing African beaded art.*
http://www.monkeybiz.co.za

National Geographic (magazine). *Ostrich eggshell beads (March 31, 2004) and other topics.* http://news.nationalgeographic.com

NativeTech: Native American Technology and Art. *Indigenous ethno-technology; offers instruction, history, and development of Native American technologies and materials.* http://www.nativetech.org/beadwork/index.php

Nguni Imports: An African Trading Company. *African trading company with beadwork and cultural information.* http://www.nguni.com

Oneida nation. *Historical information on wampum beads.* http://oneida-nation.net/culture/wampum.html

Ornament. *Beading magazine.* http://www.ornamentmagazine.com

Platinum Guild International. *Buying and caring for platinum.* http://www.preciousplatinum.com

Precious Metals. *Gold and precious metals.* http://www.answers.com/topic/karat

Public Broadcasting Service (television). *Lewis and Clark Expedition history, the Pearl, and many other subjects.* http://www.pbs.org

Rings and Things. *Catalog of beads and findings.* http://www.rings-things.com

Shooting Starr Gallery. *Comprehensive beadwork techniques.* http://www.homestead.com/sadiestarr/home.html

Simply Beads. *Beading magazine.* http://www.simplybeadsmagazine.com

Smithsonian Institute. *History of beads.* http://www.smithsonianeducation.org/migrations/beads/essay1.html

Soft Flex Company. *Bead-stringing wire, cords, and threads.* http://www.softflexcompany.com/wire_threads_cords.htm

Step by Step Beads. *Beading magazine.* http://www.stepbystepbeads.com

Tibetan dZi Bead. *Vendor with wonderful photos of dZi beads for identification.* http://www.dzicrystal.com/eng

Turquoise. *Turquoise in the marketplace.* http://www.trashcity.com/turquoise.htm

Unique Property of Diamonds. http://dendritics.com/scales/diamond-properties.asp

Wampum: Treaties, Sacred Records. *Historical information on wampum beads. Wampum belts were used by Native American tribes to symbolize treaties.* http://www.kstrom.net/isk/art/beads/wampum.html

The Wandering Bull, Inc. *Features real wampum beads from quahog shell.*
http://store.wanderingbull.com/gequwa.html

Wayne's Word. *Photos of mescal beads.* http://waynesword.palomar.edu

Wikipedia.com. *Online public encyclopedia has a host of information on metals, minerals, gemstones, jewelry, and bead types.* http://en.wikipedia.org/

World Archaeology. *Photos of bauxite bead production in Ghana, Africa.*
http://worldarchaeology.net/ghana/s_show/index.htm

About the Author

Theresa Flores Geary, Ph.D., taught first by her mother and later by elders from the San Carlos Apache tribe, has been creating beadwork since age fourteen. She has retired from an active career as a clinical psychologist and served, most recently, as a family psychologist for the Pascua Yaqui tribe in Arizona. Besides making jewelry and other beaded objects, Dr. Geary has developed a line of bead kits that she sells to museums, gift shops, and retail stores throughout the country. She also teaches beadwork classes. Dr. Geary is the author of *Creative Native American Beading* and *Native American Beadwork*. Her Web site is www.beadbible.com

Index

finishes and effects (cont.)
textured beads, 286
vitrail (vitreal) finish, 304, 357
finishing tips, 341–343, 378–380
bead-tip ends, 342, 378
crimp-bead ends, 342–343, 379
crimp beads and tools, 341–343
crimp-ends finishing, 380
eye-pin knot with bead-cap finishing, 379
finishing strung necklaces, 342–343
knot and jump ring ends, 342, 378
for necklaces, 342–343, 378–380
wrapping-finishing, 380
fire-polish beads, 123–124
FireLine thread, 279
fishing-net weights, 124
fixatives, 107, 333, 344
flake. See gold flake
flame annealing, 124
flame cutting, 124
flameworked beads, 124
flameworking. See lampworking
flameworking tools, 124–125
flash glass, 125
flash technique, 125
flashback, 125
flat beads, 13
flat-head pin, 125
flat netting stitch, 125, 204, 371
flat-nose pliers, 125–126, 229
flat ovals, 126
flat-pad ear studs, 126
flat peyote stitch, 26, 28, 110, 126–127, 340, 371, 373. See also odd-count flat peyote stitch
flat peyote-stitch patterns, 340
flat, round peyote stitch, 127
flattened beads, 210
flatteners, 127
flexible, defined, 127
flint (flintstone or silex), 127
Flores, Anna, 176
Flores, Joaquin, 78, 261
Flores, Melba, 136, 294
floss, 101, 127
flour beads, 127–128
flower beads, 128
flowers, French beaded, 130
fluorescence, 128
fluorite, 128
flush-eye beads, 128
fluted beads, 351
flutes, 128
flux, 128–129
focal beads, 14, 129
foil beads, 129
foiling, 129, 361

folded beads, 129
fool's gold (pyrite), 238
forging, 129, 183
fossil beads, 129
fossil resin (amber), 24
fossilized wood. See wood, petrified (fossilized)
fossils, 129
foxtail chain, 129–130
fracture treatment, 177. See also oiling
fractures, 130
Francis, Peter, Jr., 11
frankincense, 130
fraud protection, 328–329
free-form peyote stitch, 130
French ambassador beads, 130
French beaded flowers, 130
French hooks, 130
French ivory, 131
French jet, 131
French wire, 131. See also bullion (wire)
freshwater pearls, 131–132, 218. See also specific names
characteristics, 131–132
culturing, 131
types/names, 131–132
fretting stitch, 132, 372
fringe, 132, 376–377
fringe beads, 132–133
fringe earrings, 133
frit, 133, 142
frosted glass, 133
fuel, for lampworking, 134
fuming, 134
funk beads, 134
furnace-glass beads, 68, 134
furnace glass, 9, 142
furnace-winding, 311
fuse, 134
fused glass, 134
fustat beads, 134

gadroon, 135
gadrooned beads, 135
gahu, 135
Gallé beads, 135
galvanized finishes, 135, 356
gangidana bead, 135
garnets, 135–136. See also specific garnet names
as birthstones, 363, 364
characteristics, 135
false or misleading names, 32
gaspeite (Gaspetite), 136
gauge, 136, 167
gauging, 136
gecko stitch, 136. See also alligator stitch
gem chips, 136
gem-setting pliers, 137
gemology, 137
gemstone holders, 138

gemstone points, 138
gemstones, 137–138, 358–364. See also specific gemstones
anniversary stones, 27, 307
associations, 329
bead finishes. See finishes and effects
birthstones, 57, 363–364
caring for. See care and maintenance tips
characteristics, 137
consumer protection, 328
cuts, 138, 360
hardness scale, 197, 362–363
imitation, 158, 217, 361. See also specific imitations
inclusions, 158
knowing composition of beads, 322
naming of, 327–328
organic, 4–5, 214–215, 358
popular, 358–359
precious, 137, 235–236, 328–329
refractive index, 242
relative density, 242
rough, 252
semiprecious, 137, 263–264
silk in, 265
synthetic, 282, 361
treatments, 138, 361
weight measurements, 69, 327, 368
Gemstones of the World, 364
geode slices, 139
geodes, 21, 74, 97, 138–139, 289
geometric shape names, 13
German silver, 139, 207, 208, 266
germanium, 139
ghost beads, 72, 139
ghost finish, 140, 356
Gibson, Bonnie, 51, 62, 63, 78, 102, 134, 148, 149, 224
Gibson, Tricia, 27
gilt, 140
gilt-lined beads, 355
givre beads, 140
glass, 140. See also lampworking
beach, 41
blown, 58–59
borosilicate, 62
cane mass, 68
combing, 87
compatibility, 87
drawn, 104–105, 142, 209
filigree, 123
flame annealing, 124
flame cutting, 124
flameworking tools, 124–125
flash, 125
flash technique, 125

flashing (of color), 125
flux for, 128–129
frit, 133, 142
frosted, 133
furnace glass, 9, 142
fused, 134
fusing, 134
hard, 62, 142, 151
lead crystal (glass), 142, 177, 282
metallized, 365
murrine, 202
pearlized, 220
retorte (twisted), 243
soft, 142, 151, 270
stringer, 278
Thuringian, 9, 290
Tiffany, 290
types, 142
vitrified, 304
glass-bead disease, 140
glass bead game, 140–141
glass beadmaking, 141. See also lampworking
glass beads. See also specific glass bead names; Venetian glass beads
annealing process, 27
color-lined, 85
colors, 140
core-formed, 90
crazing, 93
cut beads, 98
enameling, 112–113
etching processes, 19, 114
feathering, 119
fiber blankets for, 122
finishes, 356–357
folding, 129
ghost finishes, 140
history of, 6, 7, 8–9
mica powders for, 193–194
new technology for, 3
types of, 355
glass cane (rods), 141
glass pearls, 141–142
glover's needles, 142–143
glow finish, 143, 356
glow (phosphorescent) beads, 143, 226
glue. See adhesives
glyptography, 143. See also layer stones
gneiss, 143
gold, 143–144
antiqued, 28
characteristics, 143–144
colors, 143–144
gilt, 140
green, 150
karats (purity), 69, 143, 168, 366
liquid, 180
made of, word for, 33